The Taming of the Samurai

THE
TAMING
OF THE
SAMURAI

*Honorific Individualism
and the Making
of Modern Japan*

Eiko Ikegami

Harvard University Press
Cambridge, Massachusetts
London, England

For my mother, Kiyokō Ikegami

Publication of this book has been supported by a grant from the
Frederick W. Hilles Publications Fund of Yale University.

First Harvard University Press paperback edition, 1997

Library of Congress Cataloging-in-Publication Data
Ikegami, Eiko.
    The taming of the samurai : honorific individualism and the
    making of modern Japan / Eiko Ikegami.
        p.   cm.
    Includes index.
    ISBN 0-674-86808-0 (cloth)
    ISBN 0-674-86809-9 (pbk.)
    1. Samurai—History. 2. Samurai—Conduct of life.
    3. Bushido. 4. Ethics, Japanese. 5. Japan—Civilization—To
    1868. I. Title.
DS827.S3I54   1995
952'.008'622—dc20
94-36784

Acknowledgments

To trace all the strands of my debt to individuals as well as institutions would be impossible, and therefore I have to limit myself here to only a brief mention of some of those. I received a Fulbright fellowship that made it possible for me to finish graduate school at Harvard, after having started in Tsukuba, Japan. After I received my Ph.D., a research grant from the Harry Frank Guggenheim Foundation provided the timely and generous help that enabled me to travel to Japan at critical stages in my research. I was also fortunate to receive a fellowship from the Institute for Advanced Study at Princeton, which permitted me to prepare the first draft of the manuscript in 1991. It was a stimulating experience for me, not only because I was able to concentrate on my writing, but also because the interdisciplinary intellectual community at the Institute helped me to expand the scope of this project. I am particularly grateful to the faculty of the School of Social Science, Clifford Geertz, Albert Hirschman, Joan Scott, and Michael Walzer for their hospitality and generous support. In addition, I gladly acknowledge the various grants I have received since I joined the faculty at Yale University: Social Science Faculty Grants, a Whitney Humanities Center Research Grant, and Sumitomo Grants from the Council of East Asian Studies.

Although I often felt isolated while I was writing this book, struggling to find my own niche in environments totally different from my own cultural upbringing, many people gave me warm support and guidance. Among those, first I want to thank Orlando Patterson of the Department of Sociology at Harvard, who played a central role in supervising my dissertation and was always available for advice and encouragement. He kept an active interest in the development of this project after I finished my dissertation. I am especially indebted to him for our lively discussions regarding the notion of honor in general, as well as Japanese and European individualism and the honor culture of landed elites.

Another crucial part of the intellectual debt I accumulated at Harvard I owe to Professor Alessandro Pizzorno, now at the European University Institute in Florence, who introduced me to a wide perspective on power and discipline. He inspired me through his acute questioning on various aspects of Japan, prompting me to consider in more detail exactly what it was that Japanese experiences could contribute to the content of sociological theories. The third member of my dissertation committee, Ezra Vogel, has been an inspiration to me through his extensive knowledge of modern Japanese society and his ability to communicate across cultural barriers.

Various friends and colleagues have read parts of the manuscript at different stages and have helped me to sharpen my thinking through their generous comments. Among them are David Apter, Martin Collcutt, Deborah Davis, Paul DiMaggio, Michael Donnelley, Tom Eartman, Kai Erikson, Clifford Geertz, John A. Hall, Edward Kamens, Suzanne Keller, Herman Ooms, Charles Perrow, Albert Reiss, David Riesman, Theda Skocpol, Conrad Totman, and Valerio Valerie. I would especially like to thank William Kelly and Henry Smith, whose heroic readings of the entire manuscript provided detailed and informed comments that saved me from making mistakes in a number of places. Another crucial intellectual influence has been Charles Tilly, whose provocative essay "War Making and State Making as Organized Crime" inspired my sociological imagination when I was a graduate student. He later came to be interested in this project, and his encouragement was a great source of moral support.

I would also like to acknowledge the equally important stimulation and inspiration that I received at an earlier age in Japan, during both my undergraduate and my graduate studies. I thank Professors Asai Kiyoshi and Tsutsumi Seiji, who taught me Japanese classical literature, the field in which I majored as an undergraduate at Ochanomizu University in

Tokyo. Completing Ochanomizu's intensive four-year program in Japanese literature helped me to decipher the world of the samurai sociologically, though I was too young to appreciate it fully at the time. Professor Ayabe Tsuneo, then at Tsukuba University, first introduced me to the world of anthropological thinking and provided me with essential encouragement while I was finishing my studies abroad. Professor Sugiyama Haruyasu, in the Faculty of Law at Waseda University, introduced me to the field of Japanese legal history while I was conducting my initial dissertation research in 1986, something that proved to be of great use for the construction of this project.

Many friends have helped me in many ways, including trying to make my use of the English tongue less exotic. In this respect I am particularly fortunate to have received the sustained help of Betsy Fray, whose patient and intelligent copyediting has been essential. My thanks are due Lindsay Waters, Alison Kent, and Christine Thorsteinsson of Harvard University Press for their wise counsel and editorial help.

Finally, I want to express my thanks and appreciation to the two most important individuals in my life. I simply have no words to thank my mother, Kiyoko Ikegami, not only for providing unfailing support and affection, but also for showing me a model of Japanese discipline that combines head and heart in a strict and yet tender way. For my husband, Piet Hut, I have too many words to express my feelings. Briefly, I lovingly acknowledge the intellectual and emotional contributions to this project that only he could have made.

Contents

Illustrations *(Following page 194)*

1. A medieval samurai's compound
2. Victorious troops after the Heiji Rebellion of 1159
3. Kawanakajima Battle, 1561
4. The Tokugawa shogun receiving an audience of daimyo at Edo Castle
5. A fight between *kabuki mono,* 1604
6. Samurai during the final phase of unification, around 1600–1615
7. *Seppuku* after the revenge of the Forty-seven Samurai, 1702
8. Greetings exchanged between Tokugawa samurai, late seventeenth century

Illustrations are reproduced from the collections of Nishimura Hakubutsukan; Seikadō; Tokugawa Reimeikai; Tokyo Kokuritsu Hakubutsukan; and Zenhōji.

The Taming of the Samurai

Major Divisions in Japanese History

Ancient

  (701) Taihō code

HEIAN

  (794) Heian (Kyoto) became the imperial capital city

Medieval

KAMAKURA

  (1185) Minamoto clan defeated the Taira clan
  (1192) Minamoto no Yoritomo became the shogun

MUROMACHI

  (1333) The Kamakura shogunate collapsed
  (1336) Ashikaga Takauji opened the shogunate
  (1467) Ōnin War

THE WARRING STATES (SENGOKU)

Early Modern

UNIFICATION BY ODA NOBUNAGA AND TOYOTOMI HIDEYOSHI

TOKUGAWA

  (1603) Tokugawa Ieyasu established the shogunate
  (1868) Meiji imperial restoration

I

A SOCIOLOGICAL
APPROACH

Introduction

The enigma of Japan, viewed through Western eyes, can be summarized by the question, "How can a nation be so successful in the fields of industrialization and business management, while encouraging its population to overvalue collectivist thinking and the *status quo,* and correspondingly to devalue individualism and bold innovation?" In contrast, the Western model of success places personal initiative at the head of the list of factors held to guarantee high achievement. Must we then conclude that the comparable success stories of the capitalist economies of Japan and the developed nations of the West represent similar functional outcomes derived from deep structural differences? Or can a historical investigation uncover points of increasing divergence from relatively minor initial differences?

In this book, I provide a new angle from which to approach these questions, through an analysis of the cultural development of the Japanese samurai. As I see it, the samurai's cultural transformation holds a key to a more adequate understanding and appreciation of the tensions between individuality and collectivism in modern Japan, as well as in the past several centuries of Japanese history. Western studies of Japan have only recently manifested an awareness of the existence of these tensions, after an initial wave of research that focused on the seemingly alien patterns of Japanese collectivism, distinctive organizational characteristics, and exotic cultural values. The more we tease apart the strands that compose the fabric of contemporary Japanese society, however, the more we find Japanese men and women struggling to maintain their individuality and dignity while occasionally resisting the expectations of the corporate mentality of their culture.

The exploration of this tension takes us to the heart of the so-called enigma of Japan: its paradoxical synthesis of competition and collaboration. We find this duality on all levels of present-day Japanese society: inside each branch and subbranch of Japanese corporations, as well as in the interactions among corporations, and between them and the various institutions of government. On a smaller scale, this tension can be found within the hearts and minds of individual citizens, who are trying to balance traditional familial and corporate expectations of conformity with an increased emphasis on a Western model of individuality. It is misleading to assume, however, that the modern Japanese aspiration for individuality is only a consequence of Westernization. The results of my research indicate that the Japanese have an indigenous cultural resource for the expression of individuality, and that the tensions between individualistic aspirations and normative standards of conformity can be traced through the successive cultural stages of premodern Japan.

An emphasis on the so-called anonymity of the Japanese does not offer a sufficient explanation of their capacity for flexibility and their often bold moves toward social change. With Japan's entrance into a new phase of shared leadership among the advanced industrial nations, it is now obvious that we cannot comprehend its competitive success in the world market strictly in terms of a mental picture of a hive of docile and depersonalized worker bees. It is time that we incorporate a concept of individuality and change into our understanding of Japanese social development. It was my search for an entry point into this type of broader understanding that brought me to the study of the samurai elite culture.

The history of the samurai reveals the presence of a firm sense of self-possession that arose alongside their social existence as landed military lords. By pointing out the presence of such an elitist sense of self-determination in Japan, I do not mean to support a reductionist model of human action, and I do not imply that Japanese individuals are of the same type as, say, American individuals in their way of choice optimization. Rather, I wish to highlight, in my examination of Japanese social developments and of the samurai culture, how the Japanese have attempted, for centuries, to reconcile their sense of individuality with social requirements and responsibilities.

The presence of a so-called collective and harmonious culture in Japan is not the reflection of an intrinsic pattern of values that have persisted since time immemorial, nor does it signify weaker Japanese aspirations for expressing individuality. Rather, it is an ideological product that emerged and developed in a history in which various actors explored different institutional settings for enhancing the trustworthiness of individuals who had otherwise strong centrifugal tendencies. In this sense, Japan's harmonious cultural resource is paradoxically connected with a history of conflicts and struggles. Thus, the study of a collective culture cannot clarify its sources and roots without shedding light on contentious individuals, groups, and movements that unintentionally contributed to the formulation of the "harmonious collective culture." The development and transformation of the samurai culture most clearly exemplify this intriguing dynamic of cultural development. The power and myth of a collective culture usually reach the most effective stage when the origins and genealogies of such a culture are shrouded, and thus taken for granted. It is therefore the task of the historical sociologist to trace and to uncover the historical processes that have given rise to the cultural resources that are now embedded in modern Japanese society.

This book, then, is an investigation of the social processes that developed the cultural resource that enabled the samurai to construct a resilient sense of individuality through an explicit sensitizing of a socially embedded sense self. For this purpose, I have taken a rather unconventional direction. I approach the enigma of present-day Japan through an examination of the process of state-making in the early modern period, through its transition from Japan's medieval feudal society to the construction of a more centrally organized state. I conclude that the cultural development of the concept of samurai honor in Japanese society, as a result of a historical confluence of largely unforeseen events, is a critical ingredient of the social process that created the distinctively modern Japanese cultural mix of competition and collaboration. It is my hope that this approach to a "historization" of Japanese culture will form a counterbalance to the many recent journalistic accounts of Japanese "tradition." Unfortunately, these accounts are full of kaleidoscopic images of random elements of Japanese premodern culture, from Zen and the tea ceremony to the various martial arts of the samurai, which have given us a colorful but overall rather flat image of Japanese tradition without any helpful connection to the present.

I have chosen to concentrate my analysis on the honor culture of the samurai because their notion of honor illuminates most effectively the emerging tensions and mutuality between collectivist and individualist modes of thought. To be sure, honor is a complex, multidimensional concept. According to anthropologists' recent findings with regard to various honor-centered cultures, a strong concern for one's reputation and social dignity lies at the heart of the matter; however, honor at the same time can be profoundly rooted in one's sense of self-esteem and personal dignity. As honor is inevitably a social concept, concerned with the evaluation of individuals within the social groups in which they claim membership, the social and organizational transformations of these groups and the spaces they occupy will predictably affect personal notions of honor. This study of the samurai honor consciousness will illustrate how a set of paradoxical tensions was articulated and transformed in Japanese culture, in relation to the dynamic development of the samurai class itself and its ways of organizing political power. Furthermore, focusing on the samurai honor culture provides a locus of comparison with other societies, in particular those that underwent similar historical experiences of domesticating a violent honor culture.

Clearly, I am not defending the proposition that the samurai class was the sole arbiter of the Japanese honor culture; neither do I consider the samurai's cultural contribution in itself more significant than that of the nonsamurai classes, such as the peasantry, fishermen, hunters, craftsmen, or merchants. At the same time, the importance of samurai contributions to Japanese culture is clear, based upon several centuries of their history as the ruling class. In this respect, samurai culture deserves a thorough examination as a primary component of modern Japanese society.

A number of monographs on Japanese institutional history have appeared in several Western languages in the last three decades. Although many of these works have provided useful and interesting discussions of particular time periods and regions, they have not yet provided a comprehensive picture of the role the warrior class played throughout Japanese history. These monographs, in line with the high standards of current historical scholarship, almost unavoidably tend to obscure the long-term continuity of the process of historical change. As a result, there is very little scholarly literature in English that analyzes the sociocultural development of the samurai class from their ancient origins to their transformation under the Tokugawa regime. Furthermore, their development has not yet been evaluated from a comparative sociological perspective. In a combined attempt to shed light on both areas, I will investigate the social process by which a violent class with an honorific culture emerged, developed, and was subsequently tamed through centuries of state-building.[1]

A study of the samurai's honor consciousness immediately encounters problems of historical imagination. Elitist cultures of honor maintained by exclusive social groups are becoming so rare in the contemporary world that it is rather difficult to reconstruct imaginatively any ancient form of honorific culture. We moderns tend to consider honor simply an empty social category, external to the self; we must take care not to impose this modern notion on the samurai in attempting to study their culture. In addition to this general problem, the study of samurai culture is burdened by prewar distortions in two respects. First, the samurai's symbolic idioms had been heavily exploited for political purposes by prewar militant Japanese nationalists. While promoting a heroic image of the samurai on the one hand, they also heavily accented the samurai's self-sacrifice, stoicism, and loyalty on the other. The net effect of this symbolic reconstruction, which considerably overstressed the virtue of loyalty, lingered in the collective memory of modern Japanese even after 1945. Second, precisely in reaction to this prewar one-sidedness, postwar liberal and leftist Japanese scholars tended to avoid straightforward evaluations of samurai culture, preferring instead to emphasize a comparatively sober image of the samurai, which they situated within the context of political-institutional history. In my opinion, this approach implicitly assumes the legitimacy of projecting modern rational images of personhood onto the early samurai, as if they could be fitted into an economic model of people who were motivated only by the maximization of self-interest. The predictable result of this tendency has been the dismissal of the externally irrational aspects of samurai culture as epiphenomena undeserving of serious historical inquiry.

I wish to distinguish my approach to the samurai from both of these earlier perspectives. Unlike prewar scholarship on the samurai spirit, which tended to take primary epics as well as the samurai's own ideological writings at face value, I have sought to expound a deeper layer of symbolic meanings and mentality expressed in words and deeds alike as recorded in the literature. The most outrageous behavior of the samurai and the corresponding extremist writings of samurai intellectuals are important, not because they represented the average samurai (often they did not), but because the analysis of such materials contains clues to their elusive "ethnomentality" and to hidden power struggles among them. In contrast to the prewar image of the stoic samurai, I have found that a strong emphasis on loyalty in samurai culture became conspicuous only at a relatively late date, with the development and transformation of the vassalage system.

The fact that the samurai's honor culture cannot be reduced to a neatly codified formula does not mean that no social code existed. The *living* form of any honor culture always remains in an indeterminate intermediate position between formula and formlessness. In part, it was socially determined; in part, individually defined. More specifically, though there was always a tacit social agreement on the definition of samurai honor, it could be reinterpreted by a particular individual's will, physical strength, and strategies in the game of honor. One of the reasons earlier studies of the samurai's mentality tended to emphasize their stoicism was that the researchers relied heavily on political and ideological writings generated by the need to discipline the vassal samurai. In essence these documents, which were then analyzed within the context of intellectual history, were codified formulae, or fixed aspects of the samurai's honor consciousness.

Although I also draw upon these materials to clarify the ideological aspects of the honor culture, I believe that an exploration of these writings in isolation would be an inadequate introduction to the *lived* form of the samurai's honor consciousness. By investigating the honor sentiments exhibited in specific episodes I hope to approximate both the living form of the honor culture and the process of its domestication, illustrating the ways in which the individual samurai reacted to constraints imposed by the emerging centralized state.

Fortunately, I have been greatly assisted by the labors of some Japanese scholars who have challenged the legacy of prewar ideology, and I am indebted to many of them. By applying ethnographic methods to the study of the past, they have attempted in a number of ways to present a more lively image of the samurai, having no reluctance to treat the most elusive or volatile aspects of samurai culture. Chiba Tokuji's study of samurai fighting customs and death rituals in comparison with hunters' culture and Ujiie Mikito's examination of the Tokugawa samurai's disciplinary rules and forms of conflict resolution are two such examples. These ethnographic works seem, however, to be less concerned with situating the samurai mentality within the larger scope of Japanese political history. As a sociologist, I am interested not only in the detailed investigation of symbolic meanings but also in the identification of the social forces that conditioned the construction of samurai culture and were in turn influenced by it. It is important to note that the samurai were, after all, the ruling class of Japan, dominating the central stage of their political theater for centuries; their culture was inevitably colored by the political situation of the time. What is needed, therefore, are two complementary viewpoints: the scholar must seek to decode the less accessible aspects of the samurai mentality without hesitating to draw upon a variety of materials ranging from epics to philosophical writings, while locating their symbolic productions within the large-scale political and institutional fields that constituted the backdrop of the samurai's lives and endeavors.

Nowadays, almost all the social scientists who have investigated Japanese society discuss the "traditional" roots of modern Japan. The majority of their references to history seem to have a limited intention, namely, the provision of background information for the understanding of modern Japan. Given this general trend, Robert Bellah's *Tokugawa Religion,* which appeared in the late 1950s, still occupies a unique position in Western scholarship on Japan, as a direct inquiry into the "cultural roots of modern Japan." In this work, Bellah examined the "structure" of the Tokugawa value system through an analysis of the religious and intellectual traditions of the period. Prior to the appearance of *Tokugawa Religion,* with the exception of historians of the premodern periods, Western social scientists did not seriously investigate the Japanese premodern tradition. Thus, the community of Japanese specialists owe much to Bellah's pioneering work.

Although I share many of Bellah's interests and questions concerning Japanese culture, my method differs markedly from his. Owing to a functionalist mode of investigation, he presented the values of Tokugawa society as a static panorama of the past in which the flow of time is arrested. Bellah's work conveys the impression that Tokugawa religious values were all functionally supportive of the social order. In contrast, I focus on the historical genesis and political processes in which the cultural tradition was created. I also find serious tensions within the samurai consciousness, tensions generated by simultaneous aspirations toward conformity and individuality. When Bellah attempted to articulate the meaning of the Japanese cultural tradition, he was perhaps too strongly influenced by Max Weber's famous thesis. Bellah was searching for the functional equivalents of the so-called Protestant work ethic in Japanese culture, overlooking the fact that Weber's thesis is predicated on a Western Christian model of the relationship between society and religion. In Europe, Christianity formed a powerful public institution—the post-Constantinian Church—that not only claimed ultimate possession of universal truth but also wielded sufficient institutional power to compete with secular rulers. In Japan, however, no one religion was strong enough to represent an independent public power to counterbalance the state; the result was a popular tendency to use religious values as a means to achieve social and political ends. Bellah himself later graciously acknowledged this weakness in his study. As he phrased it, his work suffered from a "displacement of ends by means, or the attempt to make means into ends. . . ."[2]

Weber's thesis of Puritan religion, especially Calvinism, as the source of the capitalist ethos itself has been subjected to many scholarly critiques, both theoretical and empirical. Even if we could assume that the thesis is essentially correct in its account of the development of modern capitalist culture in the West, any application of its method to non-Western societies raises some serious questions. Each society has developed its own logic of symbolic resources that could be, within appropriate socioeconomic conditions and timing, utilized for various purposes of social development. Rigid applications of the Weberian hypothesis to different cultures may hamper more accurate observations of the nature of a particular resource's logic in its own terms, and may obscure its historical roots. It is possible to overestimate the significance of a minor element in a non-Western society simply because an analogous cultural item plays a key role in the Weberian model—for example, "rationalization" and "transcendental value"—while simultaneously overlooking cultural idioms that are not emphasized by the Weberian thesis, including the honor culture in Japan. Instead of measuring non-Western societies against an inventory list of specifics supplied by the Weberian model, we should seek to enunciate the development of each society's central cultural themes in its own terms and according to its own historical genesis.

In line with a central awareness of the limitations of the functionalist understanding of the Weberian thesis, my approach to research into the social structures of modern Japan is fundamentally historical. I have chosen to examine a period of several centuries of samurai domination, from the beginning of the samurai era in the late ancient world to the Meiji restoration in 1868. After this period, the samurai as a status group dissolved, although the influence of their mentality continued to course through less visible channels of symbolic idioms. I will allude to these developments occasionally, but I cannot treat them in detail within the boundaries of the present study.

The cultural development of the samurai class was marked by two major cultural themes: control and change. From its inception, the military culture of the samurai included an emphasis on discipline, with the expectation that honorable warriors would control their short-term desires in order to achieve long-term goals. In later Japanese history, the sociopolitical process of the samurai's domestication further rechanneled this tradition of self-discipline to produce a mental disposition conducive to harmonizing each individual's sense of personal identity with accepted social goals and responsibilities. The same process of taming the samurai did, however, permit them to retain an aggressive drive for independence that had originated in the sovereign pride of a landed military elite in the medieval warrior culture. This countertendency toward what I term "honorific individualism" served as a motive for change on both personal and social levels, because a strong sense of individuality has the potential to generate change by risking the violation of conformist norms. I maintain that the production of these two themes as cultural resources can best be understood through an exposition of the *path-dependent* nature of cultural generation and reformulation. The central role of honor, both in collaboration and in competition, is related to the remarkable mode of transformation of Japan, from a medieval feudal society to a more centrally organized state.

I am not asserting that all aspects of Japanese traditional culture should be understood without exception as the cultural dimension of state formation. As samurai honor was an expression of collective elitist discipline, however, we cannot fully appreciate the dynamics of cultural developments without investigating the context of contemporary hegemonic politics. By retracing the main historical path and corresponding social contexts of the samurai's cultural development, my study complements the approaches that others have taken, which emphasize the respective impacts of various religions on samurai discipline.

When I began this work, tracing the roots of the samurai's legacy to Japanese culture first led me to investigate its cultural reformulation as precipitated by the samurai's transformation from a class of semiautonomous warriors into domesticated bureaucrats. I studied a number of examples of seventeenth-century samurai in which the issue of their honor was clearly at stake. My research revealed that the samurai's resistance, reflecting their desire for preserving a modicum of autonomy and individuality, played an important role throughout the larger process of cultural transformation under the Tokugawa shoguns. And the Tokugawa samurai drew heavily upon the symbolic resources of the medieval samurai tradition in order to legitimate their own nonconformist behavior.

Thus, I decided to extend the scope of my inquiries to the very origin of the samurai mentality, as far as it can be traced, in order to identify the origins of the samurai's militaristic and assertive definition of honor. I then charted the substantial changes that took place, first in the transformation of the roaming bands of warriors into more settled military professionals who came to occupy Japan's agricultural land, and later through the period of the Warring States, when much of the country was plunged into civil war. This in turn led me to the study of the organizational transformation of the samurai world, which constituted the process of samurai-led state formation.

In the samurai's practice of honor, the realms of the cultural and the political were inseparably interconnected. The symbolic practices of honor, from the ritual of the warrior's self-willed death to the construction of the honorific ethics of master-follower relationships, were incorporated into the political context of premodern Japan. Why did they construct and transform the practice of honor culture the way they did? This question compels us to examine the dynamics of political-institutional change, because the notion of honor presupposes the existence of institutions with the power to establish honorific values for different forms of action. In other words, the emergence of an elitist honor culture depends on the development of a social group that can enforce internal standards of discipline on individual members. A significant part of the discussion that follows will thus be devoted to the elucidation of the patterns of Japanese state formation from the medieval to the early modern period. Without this conceptual exercise, we cannot understand the origins, practice, and dynamic transformation of the samurai honor culture. Indeed, my methodological disagreement with Bellah's classic work has to do not simply with my understanding of the contents and relative importance of various ideologies but with his failure to provide a sufficient historical account of the origins of the dominant culture.

An important aspect of my work is its sensitivity to the uniqueness of the case of Japan in comparative studies of the transition from medieval feudalism to the early modern world. It is in part a response to the concerns of scholars such as Barrington Moore, Charles Tilly, Perry Anderson, Douglass C. North, Immanuel Wallerstein, and Michael Mann. In the works of these researchers, Japan is sometimes used as a critical test case for a better understanding of the European experience precisely because it underwent an outwardly similar transition during the same time period. As a specialist on Japan, I feel a responsibility to present a more accurate understanding of the comparative meaning of the Japanese experience.

Japanese state formation from the medieval through the early modern period has already been a topic of discussion among specialists in Japanese institutional history. From the standpoint of scholars in the social sciences, however, the theoretical significance of the Japanese experience has not been adequately formulated for the benefit of nonspecialists concerned with the Japanese case in advancing their comparative sociological analyses. Perhaps it is time to open a renewed conversation with scholars in the newer fields of comparative sociological history that have developed over the last two decades. To be sure, the current state of the question does not require me to interpret the Japanese experience in subordination to Western models. Rather, I am taking questions posed by recent sociological works with great seriousness. Following the examples of scholars of European state formation who have drawn upon the cases of Japan, China, and the Ottoman Empire as the standard points of comparison for the construction of explanatory theories of the European experience, I will strategically use comparative models from time to time as reference points in order to articulate the distinctive features of Japanese social development. It is my hope that this analysis of Japanese state formation will contribute to more vigorous intellectual discussions of comparative state formation.

The focus of my analysis is the intricate interconnection of the cultural and political domains during the period of samurai dominance. For this purpose I will illustrate the historical development of the samurai from two complementary perspectives. I may use a telelens, so to speak, to zoom in on specific cases of cultural analysis in some instances. And I may use a wide-angle lens to situate the cultural practice of the samurai in a larger-scale historicopolitical context. Most important, my analysis will connect these snapshots into a coherent picture of the social development of the samurai.

1

Honor, State Formation, and Social Theories

Ancient Japan emerged on the periphery of East Asian civilization. Modeling its law and government on China's, Japan had by the eighth century formed an elaborate system of a centralized state governed by the emperor's court. With the rise of the first samurai-led semicentral government (the emperor's court continued to survive in Kyoto) in the late twelfth century, however, the Japanese pattern of sociopolitical development diverged decisively from the Chinese. From the late twelfth century well into the late nineteenth, the samurai, or landed military class, were the most important and powerful political actors in Japanese society.

No other East Asian society experienced such a long-lasting domination by its warrior class. China, for example, experienced only sporadic feudalization after the establishment of its empire, around 100 B.C., and its centralized state staffed by bureaucrats ruled the empire for two millennia. Although the army had always been an important stimulus for change in China, the Chinese military did not become a hereditary ruling caste comparable to Japan's samurai class. China's central bureaucracy, selected through a set of competitive state-administered examinations, was so institutionalized by the early modern period that even the Manchu (the Qing) military conquest did not substantially change this system.[1] Korea under the Yi dynasty developed the *yang ban,* a hereditary status group privileged to occupy civil and military posts in the bureaucracy. But the *yang ban*'s officeholding was evaluated primarily through Confucian state examinations, and the military examinations were far less important than the civil ones.[2] Thus, in both China and Korea, the Confucian scholar-bureaucrats were usually regarded as superior to the military men. In this sense the rise of the samurai class and the establishment of its rule in medieval Japan were a clear departure from the predominant pattern of East Asian political development. Despite a cultural heritage shared with its neighbors—exemplified by the use of Chinese characters for the written languages, and the common spiritual and intellectual influences of Confucianism and Buddhism—Japan diverged significantly in its sociopolitical structure from its Chinese and Korean counterparts.

The influence of the samurai on Japanese society was pervasive. Even the remarkably swift and thorough program of modern nation-building in Meiji Japan (1868–1914) was carried out primarily by former samurai and those who had learned self-discipline from samurai teachings. The social and cultural dimensions of samurai history are therefore important for understanding not only traditional Japan but the making of contemporary Japan as well.

Several centuries of domination by its military class produced a complex set of social and cultural institutions in preindustrial Japan. An investigation of the transformation of the samurai's honor culture allows us to inspect at closer range the period of several centuries of cultural change connecting the medieval and the early modern (Tokugawa) samurai, while directing us to many important comparative questions. Although both types of samurai were socially very different, honor consistently appeared at the center of their cultural identity as a warrior class.

The Comparative Question of Honor

A culture based on concepts of honor and shame continues to be very much alive in present-day Japan. As the anthropological and historical literature indicates regarding cultures of honor, including those of certain Mediterranean societies, medieval chivalric societies, and the American antebellum South, the culture of honor is often more closely related to open displays of violence than to the maintenance of societal order. A man's honor can be maintained only when he fights to protect it against threats, whether real or imagined. Yet modern Japan is as well known for order and harmony as it is for a keen sense of personal honor.

A historical question that complicates our sociological puzzle is the argument, enunciated in Albert Hirschman's *The Passions and the Interests*,[3] that the rise of modern capitalism in the West served to tame and redirect the volatile search for glory associated with the medieval warrior culture of honor. Observers generally consider that the legacy of honor sentiment and the resultant violence have remained strong in less industrialized societies. Yet here on the rim of Asia is modern Japan, highly industrialized, concerned for order and social harmony, while weaving the threads of its honor legacy into its cultural fabric—a curious anomaly. How do we account for this distinctive cultural configuration?

The identification and articulation of the nature of honor and shame in modern Japanese culture are a complex subject that deserves in-depth research and analysis in its own right. For the purpose of my argument, however, it suffices to note a few comparative characteristics of the modern Japanese honor culture. In modern Japanese, *meiyo,* which is rather formal, is the closest single equivalent of the English term "honor." In colloquial usage the sentiment attached to a concern for one's reputation is expressed by several different words, such as *na* (name), *haji* (shame), *menboku* (face), *chijoku* (dishonor), *iiji* (pride), and *sekentei* (one's appearance in the world), depending on the precise context. A concern for honor can also be expressed by a colloquial saying such as *Mittomonai kara yoshinasai* (Don't do it, you would look bad). The term *na* can even be found in the literature of ancient Japan, and it was frequently used to express the medieval samurai's desire for a good name among his peers. Both *na* and *haji* have been employed consistently to address questions of honor up to the present day. The modern Japanese vocabulary contains more terms to express avoidance of shame than to speak of aspirations toward honor, however.[4] Honor and shame, seeking *na* and avoiding *haji,* are two sides of a single coin in terms of a person's interest in his or her reputation. The sentiment that seeks honor is aggressive and competitive, whereas the desire to avoid shame is conformist. The fact that contemporary Japanese has a larger vocabulary for shame than for honor itself probably reflects the historical results of the taming and refocusing of the society's honor culture.

Since the sixteenth century, external observers of Japanese society have reported on the idiosyncrasies of Japanese behavior and the idioms associated with its culture of honor and shame. The best-known account is Ruth Benedict's, which labels Japanese moral behavior a "shame culture."[5] Although Japanese scholars have questioned her wartime ethnocentrism, methodology, and general approach to culture, many have found her emphasis on honor and shame intriguing and insightful. For example, the Japanese psychiatrist Doi Takeo says of Benedict that "in characterizing Japanese culture as a culture of shame she has pointed out something extremely important."[6] Japanese social scientists now largely agree that a keen sensitivity to shame and a corresponding concern for a good reputation and honor are still important factors in the daily life of the Japanese people.[7] The Japanese are sensitive to issues of shame, as Takie Lebra puts it, "primarily because of their status orientation" and, more specifically, because "they tend to display their status, which makes status easy for others to identify."[8] In particular, an intense concern for one's social appearance, associated with one's status in the eyes of the *seken* (the imagined cultural community in which one's reputation is evaluated), seems to lie at the heart of the modern Japanese sentiment of honor. The concern for honor, however, is not necessarily limited to the external display of status. The most important single aspect of an individual's honor is his or her attunement to situations and ability to meet social expectations, thereby protecting his or her reputation in the *seken*. In the *seken* there are usually no flamboyant displays of aggression; rather, it is filled with subdued, well-mannered, yet strongly competitive strivings on the part of individuals seeking social recognition and honor.

These characteristics of Japanese social relations are observable not only in seemingly "traditional" rural villages but also in urban areas, especially within the culture of the most advanced modern corporations. Collective conformity, avoidance of shame, and the pursuit of honor and prestige through competition all reinforce one another, thereby shaping the remarkable compound of what I would term "honorable collaboration" and "honorable competition" in the organizational culture of Japanese business corporations. This moral resource has been thoroughly exploited, insofar as Japanese business has shown extraordinary growth in the world market. In other words, the culture of honor in modern Japan is closely connected to the functioning of Japanese capitalism.[9]

This connection does not imply that Japanese organizational characteristics are the product of Japanese cultural peculiarities. The origin of the distinctive style of Japanese organization and management must be articulated in its own light. Nor is a conflict-free Japan being suggested. Violence does erupt in modern Japan from time to time. Yet wherever Japanese organizations successfully control internal conflicts we tend to find the culture of honor and shame working to reinforce group conformity while promoting competition among employees to subserve the ends of organizational growth.

Styles of honor culture vary across societies. In the Mediterranean, for example, specialists argue as to whether the primary determinant of honor is economic status or female chastity. Despite such disagreements over criteria for accumulating points of honor in various local societies, scholars of different honor cultures have largely accepted the definition advanced by Julian Pitt-Rivers some decades ago: the notion of honor is "a sentiment, a manifestation of this sentiment in conduct, and the evaluation of this conduct by others, that is to say, reputation. It is both internal to the individual and external to him—a matter of his feelings, his behavior and the treatment that he receives."[10] The common ground is not a fixed moral or economic criterion for social evaluation, but concern with the ability to live up to preexistent expectations; therefore, reputation is clearly the common theme. The multifaceted nature of honor and an interest in reputation as a core sentiment are the essential points of the definition of honor, and I will return to these shortly.

The question of living up to social expectations remains. Fortunately, in articulating the Japanese experience, Mediterranean modes of vindicating honor present a useful basis for comparison. The constant adjustment of the self to social expectations is usually insufficient to define an honorable person in Mediterranean cultures. Although honor is to some extent an attribute of birth, wealth, or virtue, it must also be claimed and verified through occasional action. The massive literature on Mediterranean societies usually portrays the culture of honor in association with conflict and violence. One's honor must be vindicated physically when it is threatened. In his study of the Sicilian Mafia, Anton Blok notes that in Sicilian peasant communities the Mafiosi are deemed "honorable," "respected," "qualified" persons. Only those who have "a reputation for violence" and an ability to "look after their own affairs" command respect.[11] In Algeria, too, Pierre Bourdieu finds that the "complete man must be constantly alert, ready to respond to the slightest challenge"; he is "the guardian of honour."[12] Of course, not all Mediterranean societies place violence at the core of their honor culture. For example, Michael Herzfeld, in a study of specific rural Greek communities, reports that the people of Pefkiot adhere to an extreme avoidance of conflict, preferring covert malice to open aggression.[13] In spite of such variations, the Mediterranean mode of vindication of honor appears to be more conflict-laden than that of modern Japan.[14]

Mediterranean societies certainly do not have a monopoly on violent honor cultures. The honorific culture of the American South before the Civil War is held responsible for legitimating the pervasive violence in the region.[15] For the purposes of my argument, the culture of honor in medieval European warrior societies provides the most interesting information, because it offers a chronological parallel to the samurai's culture of honor. Germanic societies, as Harold Berman notes, lived "by the high value placed upon honor as a means of winning glory in a world dominated by warring gods and by a hostile and arbitrary fate. Honor, for Germanic man, meant 'getting even'; only by getting even could he conquer the forces of darkness that surrounded his life."[16] As the influence of Christianity spread, the Church attempted to reshape this violent warrior culture in the form of Christian chivalry. But the Church was able to change only the surface of the culture. The chivalric ideals of honor and virtue in medieval Europe were inextricably associated with bloody warfare. Indeed, Mervyn James finds that private conflicts among men of honor in early Tudor England "were rapidly translated into the language of the sword."[17]

Although violence is not always a central component of honor cultures, the strong emphasis on violence in the comparative historical literature makes one question the sources of the nonviolent modern Japanese style of honor culture. An ahistorical approach to this question is inadequate, since the emergence of modern Japan is best understood as the outcome of a historically specific convergence of ideas, conditions, and institutional development.

In stark contrast to the modern form of Japanese honor culture, the medieval samurai enunciated and upheld a sharply self-assertive, individualistic culture of honor. In Japan, as in Europe during the same period, the value of honor was originally a function of the attitudes of the self-armed warriors and lords. Honor was important, especially on the battlefield. A reputation for cowardice could prove fatal to a lord's bid for power. As with the tradition of the warrior class in Western culture, the samurai tradition, with its accompaniment of honorific violence and aggression, entered into and became an established part of Japanese culture. The theme of violence was critically important, not because physical activity was the sole criterion of honor, but because strength and a willingness to fight when necessary were the most effective proofs of and vehicles for the honor of the sovereign individual. Honor was a social index of power for landed military lords, and from this orientation there emerged a sense of self-possession in parallel to their feudal landed status and physical ability to defend themselves.

The moment of crisis for the samurai class was the transition from the medieval to the Tokugawa period. The distinctive nature of the samurai's cultural transformation was closely related to the course of early modern state-making in Japan. The vassal samurai serving either daimyo or Tokugawa shogun had to accept very different, much more restrictive conditions in exchange for a secure, largely hereditary, status and income. A Tokugawa samurai was formally considered advanced to full samurai status only when he was incorporated within his lord's house as a *kachū* (literally, "house insider"). The samurai were forced to live in castle towns, usually separated from direct control over their land; and their societal role underwent a major transformation from that of independent, high-spirited mounted warriors to that of sedate bureaucrats. The partial reconciliation of honor and order in the culture of the Tokugawa samurai was an important contribution to the distinctive climate of modern Japanese culture insofar as it generated serious tensions and a mutuality of two modes of aspirations toward honorific individuality and honorific conformity.

Theories of Honor and Power

The preceding comparative examination of a variety of honor-based cultures leads one to conclude that honor is "intimately related to power"[18] as it defines a person's relation to others, and its contentious nature is directly related to this connection. Thus, John Davis defines honor as ultimately "a system of stratification," meaning that it prescribes behavior appropriate to an individual's rank.[19] It is at this strategic juncture of culture and social stratification that changes in social structure can transform the honor culture complex.

Honor as a Cultural Complex

Before discussing the mechanisms that transformed the culture of honor among the samurai, we should briefly examine the meanings of this complex notion, *honor*. The notion of honor operates on a number of different levels simultaneously. For example, honor is a sentiment and an aspiration that all persons in a given culture may share; at the same time, it represents a privilege conferred on the higher orders that often excludes those of lower status. Honor is felt by an individual and must be claimed by an individual; but it is sometimes attributed to collectivities such as a family, an occupational group, a tribe, or a nation. Different emphases and patterns can be found in the honor cultures of various societies, various groups, and various historical periods. Even within one cultural and linguistic area, as Pitt-Rivers observes, honor is "a collection of concepts which are related to one another and applied differentially by different status-groups defined by age, sex, class, occupation, etc."[20]

The complexity of the culture of honor does not end here; honor culture consists not only of concepts and values but also of such symbolic vehicles of meaning and sentiment as rituals (for example, duels), taste (say, dress), etiquette and manners, various folkways, and folk stories. Although the notion itself is apparently universal, some societies have more elaborate and more highly developed sets of honor-related cultural idioms as dominant symbolic social complexes. Japan is one such society. In the following analysis, I use the term "honor" to denote this cultural *complex*.

The Japanese samurai's honor is a cultural complex expressed by various words, forms, and behaviors in different time periods. Because no single Japanese term is broad enough to comprehend a wide variety of meanings across a broad historical spectrum, I will call that cultural complex simply the "culture of honor," and I will explain how the contents of that cultural complex have changed over time.[21] When I refer to a particular aspect of Japanese honor corresponding to a Japanese term, I shall identify that term explicitly.

Transforming a Style of Honor

The multifaceted nature of the concept of honor is an important starting point for my argument. Because an honor culture is a collection of concepts, different combinations of the same ingredients can make up various types of honor cultures across time and space. These sets of symbolic meanings and expressions make up a particular kind of honor, a "style" of culture. A cultural style constitutes a distinct pattern of meaning that provides a frame for the symbolic complex. Although one component of a style can be transmitted independently (as in the case of a folktale passed down for generations that loses its original context), it is more likely that a style of culture will transmit across generations as a complex. Even when a complex style is transmitted more or less accurately, however, the receiver does not necessarily reproduce it precisely in the same manner. Because a style contains various symbolic meanings and devices, its general acceptance still allows for highly individual expressions. One element of the honorific complex might also be replaced by another, or simply softened, while the honorific culture itself remains. Often people incorporate a new social-institutional constraint by adding an element to the cultural complex. I call this process "refocusing." Although a deep concern for reputation persisted down the centuries, the samurai's culture of honor was transformed significantly through this refocusing process.

How was the style of honor changed? What specific mechanisms refocused the cultural complex of Japanese honor? An adequate theoretical discussion begins from the intrinsic duality of honor, which comprehends ideas both external and internal to the self. Unlike Benedict, who considered the Japanese honor culture to be only externally oriented as compared with the internalized "guilt" culture of the West, Japanese and Western scholars alike now largely agree that honor has both an internal and an external dimension.[22] Interestingly, Bernard Williams has recently shown that a similar view of the early Greeks as having no concept of the individual as a source of moral action is equally limited: "By the later fifth century the Greeks had their own distinctions between a shame that merely followed public opinion and a shame that expressed inner personal conviction."[23] The notion of honor not only is expressed as a concern for one's social evaluation but is profoundly connected with one's dignity, self-esteem, and identity. One's honor is the image of oneself in the social mirror, and that image affects one's self-esteem and one's behavior. Because of this very nature, honor mediates between individual aspirations and the judgment of society.

Honor is evaluated not in a world of abstractions but in a concrete community of honor to which honorable people belong. For the samurai, it was this hierarchically structured social world that assessed honor in the first place and then bestowed it on particular individuals. The samurai's community of honor was deeply interwoven with the power structures, but at the same time it existed as a symbolic realm in which the code and cultural idioms of honor were shared. Honor is a symbolic index of the hierarchy of that community, and it also acts as a criterion of inclusion and exclusion from the community of honor. From this mutuality of symbolic and social-structural realms there follows an important understanding: structural changes in this community inevitably affect its style of honor. Because of the linkage of one's collective and personal identity to the idioms of honor, structural changes in a symbolic reference group with which a person identifies affect the individual's sentiments of honor. At the same time, because honor resides in the innermost depths of a person's self-understanding, these structural changes never result in autonomic cultural change, but rather take the form of continuously negotiated revisions.

Honor, Power, and Social Structure

Central to these negotiated transformations is the relationship between power and honor. One of the earliest modern social theorists, Thomas Hobbes, paid special attention to the relationship of power and honor in his political sociology of the state, *Leviathan*. In stating that "reputation of power, is Power,"[24] Hobbes recognized that honor confers power on someone. He was keenly aware of the impact of his contemporary honorific culture, a still vital legacy of the medieval warrior spirit, on the ongoing violent political conflicts and English state formation in the early seventeenth century. Hobbes realized further that "another noxious disease of the mind . . . is to want honour and dignity. All men naturally strive for honour and preferment."[25] Indeed, the human craving for glory poses immense obstacles to peace; he observed: "We find three principal causes of quarrel. First, Competition; Secondly, Diffidence; Thirdly, Glory."[26] All these elements came to the surface in the violent, honor-ridden, Machiavellian politics of the Tudor, Elizabethan, and civil war periods in England. As a result of his observation of human nature's competitive striving for honor, Hobbes incorporated the need for a powerful sovereign in his political theory.

Another insight into the relationship between honor and power derives from the work of Max Weber, who frequently spoke of honor in his historical sociology of culture and social structure. He writes in *The Agrarian Sociology of Ancient Civilization* that "the concept of honor (fides) governed the relationship between patron and client."[27] In the feudal relationship between patron and client, for example, the client, a vassal, tended to become independent, "for the vassal was a self-reliant knight or even prince who equipped himself," yet the patron, his master, retained power over him through various means. The code of honor reflects the nature and dynamics of this power relation.

Weber went on to compare variations in honor ethos across different societies based upon their respective structures of patronage and clientele. In *Economy and Society,* he observes that in the case of the Chinese mandarin bureaucrats—and generally in all kinds of positions depending exclusively upon the ruler's favor—the total dependence of the bureaucrats on the ruler's will did not create an inner guide for "honorable" conduct in relation to the master.[28] In contrast, in the West feudal vassalage combined "seemingly most contradictory elements in its most developed form: on the one hand, strictly personal fealty, on the other contractual stipulation of rights and duties," the system that allowed vassals to hold structural autonomy over their possessions.[29] Only when the dependent possessed independent means was there room for the coexistence of honorific autonomy and honorific heteronomy. Thus, the knight's conduct was molded by "the feudal concept of honor, and this in turn by the notion of vassalic fealty."[30] Weber prefaces his argument with the claim that "the combination of honor and fealty was only known, as we have seen, in Occidental feudalism and Japanese 'vassalic' feudalism."[31]

A cultural idiom that celebrated the warrior's fierce loyalty to his master was one of the characteristics of the Japanese samurai ethos throughout its history. Under the same rubric of honor, however, samurai culture also held in high regard self-assertive actions expressive of moral autonomy. But the complex relationship between the hierarchical structure of vassalage and the nature of the honor culture does not end there. We might inquire, for example, why an act of submission to the patron conferred honor on the client. To answer this particular question, we have to go beyond Weber's formulation. It is easily understandable that, in a patron-client relationship, the client's submission always confers power and honor on the master; indeed, the more reputable and strong the client, the more valuable his submission. But, in a voluntary form of clientele such as vassalage, the client, too, gains honor from his voluntary submission. In exchange for his service, he participates in the higher community of honor to which his master belongs. This form of relationship is markedly different from the dishonorable subjection of such clients as slaves and captured soldiers. In his study of slavery, Orlando

Patterson notes that "a freely established relation of dependence with a more powerful patron can be the basis for expanding one's honorific claims vis-à-vis one's equals."[32] Thus, the instrumental value of honor in the system of vassalage linked otherwise relatively independent social actors and made possible a system of hierarchical alliances.

Of course, the feudatory vassal relationship was bound, not only by benefits of honor, but by concrete socioeconomic ties as well. For example, in the Japanese samurai's system of vassalage, usually called *shujū kankei* (the master-follower relationship) or *go'on to hōkō* (debt and service), the samurai vassal often received new land or confirmation of prevailing rights to land. Both were considered *go'on* (debts to the lord) to be repaid by *hōkō* (service). Vassalage was built upon such foundations of mutual benefit, though it was always a very difficult task for the master to suppress the centrifugal tendencies of vassals who had an independent socioeconomic base.

Two Issues of Trust: *Reliability and Efficacy*

As with any coalition that seeks to form long-lasting exchanges, the samurai's vassalage system, by its very nature, continually manifested a problem that Thomas Hobbes called "a tract of time."[33] Suppose a person promised to be a faithful vassal to a lord at a certain point in time, and agreed to contribute a specific number of soldiers in the future whenever necessary. How could the master trust his vassal to continue to perform his duty faithfully? Or how could the vassal know that his master would reward him appropriately if he were to fight courageously in a battle? Could a person maintain the same intention over a long span of time? In my view, a sociological description of a freely established patron-client relationship should always include two critical questions of trust: one has to do with reliability in the relationship, and the other has to do with efficacy.

Consistency of behavior over a long period of time is the most important criterion of a good vassal. Since vassalage was in essence a military coalition that assumed the vassals' faithful military service in emergency situations, the relationship was built upon trust over the dimension of time. We know, however, that the political facts of life include betrayal and conspiracy, truths that held with particular force in competitive warrior societies. A durable, trustworthy relationship was thus a critical precondition for the samurai system of vassalage. The relationship also relied on the premise that a vassal could supply the requisite armed force in a crisis. To put it simply, if a vassal was too weak and cowardly, or otherwise lacking in ability, he was not a desirable vassal, even though he might have an admirable attitude of loyalty. In particular, in a historical situation of unending power struggles, a lord who wished to survive the competition had to win the trust of the best fighters. Thus, the principles of reliability and efficacy are both important for understanding the master-vassal relationship.

Yet however closely coupled these two principles of trustworthiness in vassalage were, they also had a tendency to become mutually exclusive. The more effective a warrior—for instance, the greater his fighting skills or the more money he had to mobilize a large military force—the more likely it was that he would not prove reliable; that is, he could be sufficiently independent to find a more lucrative source of patronage. This option held particularly true in the Japanese situation because of the general political atmosphere that obtained throughout the medieval period, when various local powers competed with one another for the most desirable vassals. Men of proven military capability could easily change masters.

The fact that vassalage involves the crucial question of trust over "a tract of time" takes us to the core of the samurai honor culture. The culture of honor was both consciously and unconsciously utilized and constructed on an ethical basis in order to reconcile the two contradictory requirements of the vassalage system. In other words, *by supplying an internal principle of predictability for judging the vassal's and the master's actions and intentions, the culture of honor functioned as the ideology of the master-follower relationship.* The behavior of a warrior imbued with a principle of honor would be more predictable and therefore more trustworthy. He would be less likely to barter his reputation and honor for short-term gain than for mere loyalty. At the same time, a man with a keen sense of honor would be more likely to serve his lord effectively in crisis situations. He would not flee from a battlefield in a moment of weakness. Honor was in this sense the achievement of credibility or of a reputation for power. More important, honor was an emotional drive that stimulated warriors to fight bravely, not only for immediate monetary rewards, but also for the sake of a glorious posthumous reputation. This concern for honor provided an internal principle of behavior aimed at a long-term goal. Having achieved this sense, honor thereafter often became an ideological tool in the hands of masters, who manipulated the structure of the master-vassal relationship.

The preceding analysis leads to my central observation, namely, that the history of Japanese vassalage, well into the late nineteenth century, can be considered the result of continuous efforts to reconcile these two qualities, reliability and efficacy. These efforts at reconciliation affected the contents of the cultural complex of honor in order to answer the following questions: When a warlord attempted to impose strict military discipline on troops consisting of free-spirited warriors, how could he succeed? When the Tokugawa shoguns managed to deprive the vassals of their socioeconomic independence (thus establishing the reliability of the relationship by putting the vassals in a "no-exit" situation), how could they maintain the vassals' morale? Tensions inherited from the structure of vassalage thereby led to the development of that structure's cultural and ideological expression, the samurai's cult of honor.

The sociological description of vassalage as a system of long-term exchange relationships allows us to articulate one of the central characteristics of Japanese collective discipline. I maintain that the Japanese historical experience of an organizational system of vassalage trained people to sustain long-term relationships of exchange and obligation outside their kinship structures. This Japanese historical-organizational experience stands in contrast to its Chinese counterpart, in which the persistent power of large-scale lineage systems (clans) and bureaucratic control by the mandarin elite of the central government were the outstanding characteristics.

The fact that a long-term exchange system of vassalage presupposed the uncertainty of the parties involved in exchange relationships actually encouraged the development and sophisticated elaboration of social institutions for constructing trust. Let us consider a counterexample, the case of a small, isolated community in which each member's life is open to continual inspection by others. We can speculate that such a community does not require a refined system for the construction of social trust in order to ensure the stability of long-term exchange relationships. In other situations in which absolute certainty regarding the trustworthiness of others is logistically impossible, we tend to find more complicated social, legal, and organizational institutions, which strive to increase the predictability of human action. Indeed, I found that the Japanese organizational experience of vassalage, which connected socially autonomous armed warriors in a hierarchically structured military alliance, facilitated the development of social-institutional systems of trust. In this setting, their culture of honor took root and flourished.

It is important to emphasize at this point that the Japanese process of state formation from the medieval through the early modern periods represented a continuous revision and reconstitution of this vassalage system. Therefore, although the experience of vassalage itself was limited primarily to the samurai class, being the organizational foundation of successive samurai political regimes, its influence on Japanese society and culture was pervasive. The samurai honor culture reflected and influenced the operational dynamics of this critical institution of vassalage, thereby forming the essence of the Japanese organizational tradition.

The Focal Points of Macro-Structural Interpretation

Although I maintain that the development of the samurai vassalage system and its honor culture were intricately correlated, the honor culture itself was a complex phenomenon that cannot be understood in terms of a single dimension. One must take into account at least four different aspects of samurai life in order to understand fully the dynamic cultural creativity of the samurai class. They include honor as: the ideology of the vassalage system; the sovereign pride of a samurai house; military culture; and the collective identity of the samurai class.

On the basis of the previous discussion of the nature of honor and society, I shall enumerate four foci to structure the discussion of the following historical account of the samurai's social transformation. Together, these four points characterize the social environment that governed the cultural changes in the samurai's honor complex.

The first and most important point concerns the transformation of the samurai's patron-client relationships, namely, vassalage. The development of a political network among the samurai warriors was closely related to the emergence of the ideological dimension of the honor culture that reshaped this relationship. When overlords tried to control their samurai vassals by centralizing power structures and building effective long-term organized military forces, the culture of honor provided a precious moral resource—a desire for posthumous fame—and a passion—for personal glory—that guaranteed that the vassals would conduct themselves as their superiors wished. As the vassalage system was reorganized and control tightened throughout the late medieval period, samurai power consolidated, first locally and then on a wider provincial scale. I will analyze the dynamic changes affecting the samurai's forms of coalition and hierarchy, and then examine the links between those changes and the honor culture.

The second point involves the emergence of the samurai honor culture, which coincided with their rise as a new social class possessing a concrete social base for their power, namely, the *ie,* or house, of the landed military lords. One important feature of the samurai's concept of honor, its power-oriented nature, originated in the "sovereign standing" of the *ie* as the mark of socially autonomous landed elites. During the medieval period, each samurai *ie* held some degree of "statehood," or political autonomy. The *ie* also aggressively defended their sovereign rights and economic interests against competitive equals whenever armed intervention proved necessary. The collectivity of these autonomous landed elites constituted their community of honor, in which their social reputation was measured and evaluated. Thus, my examination of the honor culture proceeds from an analysis of the development and transformation of the structure and political economy of the samurai *ie.*

The third point concerns the military dimension of samurai life: the organization of the troops and the structure of warfare. The samurai constituted a professional warrior class whose honor depended upon their ability to use violence. Physical strength was not the only source of samurai honor, however. Because physical prowess and military skills were effectively expressed only through disciplined conduct, showing that one had control of the situation in a moment of tension was also considered a form of honorable courage. Codes of honor among the samurai thus reflected their distinctive social consciousness of military skills, power, and discipline. The ongoing process of Japanese state formation reorganized the samurai army and produced a decisive new set of controls for samurai violence and its corresponding codes of honor. Changes in battle strategy and technology of warfare also affected the code of honor, which accorded the highest honor to those who deployed their combat skills most effectively. Although these transitions were only one part of the larger process of state formation, military change itself sometimes had an independent impact on the cultural sphere.

The fourth point involves the samurai's relationship as a class to other social forces and groups, which critically influenced their culture of honor because they regarded it as the source of their unique collective identity. The samurai culture of honor symbolically represented what Max Weber called the "status honor" assigned to them collectively. This was a form of collective honor, as he defined it, "connected with any quality shared by a plurality, and, of course, it can be knit to a class situation."[34] The samurai distinguished themselves from the nonsamurai classes as a group of men who were willing to die for honor. The culture of honor also enhanced their military prestige and helped the landed warrior class achieve a position of political and ideological supremacy by excluding those who did not belong to this community of honor. Throughout their history, the samurai could not surrender their culture of honor without compromising the legitimacy of their cultural superiority over other classes. It is for this reason that we must pay particular attention to the politics of class centered on the samurai, in order to understand the formulation, codification, and transformation of their distinctive cultural style.

It is important to consider the samurai culture of honor from a multidimensional perspective. To give a specific example, a mature form of the samurai honor culture was much more than a soldierly expression of heroic sentiments. Let us consider the contrasting case of soldiers of fortune. Hired mercenaries may exemplify behavior consistent with a sense of honor connected to the profession of arms during actual combat, but, unlike the samurai class, they are not likely to generate a style of honor culture with an emphasis on the inner dimension of self-control in peacetime. Moreover, if we consider the samurai notion of honor only as a by-product of military standards and training, it is difficult to comprehend why it remained so important during the two and a half centuries of peace under the Tokugawa shogunate. The fact that the honor culture was the samurai's cultural expression of their collective supremacy as a status group certainly facilitated this development. Only by understanding the complex social constraints emerging from the interactions of the multiple dimensions of honor outlined above can we fully appreciate the internal dynamics of the samurai honor culture.

These four dimensions of samurai life were closely interconnected, and they impacted on one another in the course of Japanese state formation because the changes in them represented the social processes through which the ruling class organized and reorganized its political hierarchies. Although the four foci of my research listed above constitute the basic ingredients of samurai transformation, it is also necessary to pay particular attention to the translation of these organizational and class powers into different governmental structures in successive time periods. These structures in turn affected the organizational and cultural characteristics of the samurai class, the process of which influenced the further development of the state's organization. It is because of this connection that the honor culture of Japan's ruling elite should be considered the cultural dimension of state formation.

The Cultural Dimension of State Formation

The study of comparative state formation, currently one of the liveliest fields in historical sociology, emphasizes variations in early modern state-making in Europe and the subsequent divergent patterns of development in a number of Western societies.[35] Researchers in this field have devised a set of theories to explain the political, economic, and social implications of state-making. The consequences of state formation for cultural development have been explored only recently (an exception being Norbert Elias's classic work *Civilizing Process*[36]) and require further theoretical and empirical elaboration.[37]

To be sure, explicit transitions in the ideologies of nation-states have always attracted scholarly interest. The state's function of moral regulation has recently become one of the central themes of contemporary sociological inquiry. Even Marxist writers, whose historical accounts traditionally focus on material and political power as the chief levers of social change, have adopted cultural analysis through conceptual tools such as the dominant ideology thesis.[38] This has been done partly through incorporation of Antonio Gramsci's emphasis on the importance of cultural hegemony and consensus-building.

My own concentration on the cultural dimension of state formation is not a *prima facie* assertion of the importance of the Japanese state as the direct agent of moral regulation. The Japanese feudal state usually possessed weak infrastructural methods of social control (such as police and the educational system) for direct contact with and regulation of the population. As a result, we must identify the "technologies of power," to use Michel Foucault's expression, in their own terms in order to trace the mechanisms that shape a people's cultural reformulations. Although I do acknowledge that even the premodern state often functioned as a direct agent of moral change, I propose a broader perspective in this book; namely, that the formation of the state has larger, more complex, and often unexpected implications for the cultural sphere. The distinctive character of the state lies in its ability to create and sustain a number of institutions that variously affect people's lives. Although each institution by itself is not necessarily embedded in or intended to serve a particular purpose of moral or ideological regulation, taken together they form an institutional field that deeply affects individuals' decisionmaking. New institutional constraints resulting from state-making transform a society's wider cultural environment in critical and unforeseen ways.

The conventional popular image of the modern state—often narrowly defined as a set of formal organizations or governmental legal systems—as it developed in the West is inadequate for the analysis of premodern polities. In premodern political systems, the lines of distinction between private and public, civil society and public authority, were usually blurred. Rather, the premodern state usually rested on networks of human groups that exhibited some form of statehood on a smaller scale. The medieval samurai's *ie*, with its own territories and armed force, belonged to a continuum of state-like entities. They had their own form of limited statehood in terms of their ability to exercise coercive means and extract revenue from the population living in their territories. These state-like entities depended on abilities to provide protection for the territorial population in exchange for revenue. The power of the central state rested on its functional efficiency in coordinating these virtually autonomous groups and mediating the conflicts that periodically erupted among them.

As Max Weber described it, the formation of a state hinges primarily on the process by which states monopolize the privilege of force majeure. In the early stages of state formation, many parties contend for the right to exercise violence. As a state grows, expands its sphere of influence, and centralizes its institutions, it deprives its constituent subgroups of that right. Private resort to violence is considered "illegitimate" and "criminal," whereas the state's invocation of violence in the form of warfare and legalized executions is "legitimate," as Charles Tilly observes.[39] When a state attempts to monopolize the right to use violence by delegitimating feuds and other forms of private conflict resolution, the concept of honor, originally linked to personal use of violence, is affected.

This model of "state-making as organized crime"—the exchange of protection based on force for revenue—is nowhere more pertinent than in Japan. The history of Japan since the emergence of the samurai class can be summarized as a process during which the samurai collectively legitimated their hegemonic position as those who were able to enforce peaceful behavior on others. They thereby introduced and enforced a new pattern of extracting income from the rest of the population as the landlord class. At the same time, the samurai continually fought among themselves and revised their hierarchies, through which their strongest leaders gained their legitimacy. This process of competition among the samurai bands does not differ fundamentally from the murderous rivalries among contemporary organized crime "families"; however, in the case of the samurai, the strongest individual usually received the title of shogun from the imperial court, and he was automatically legitimated as *de facto* ruler of the country. It was because of this feature of the established mechanism of legitimacy that the cultural reformulation and reconceptualization of samurai violence as "honorific"—that is, the creation and maintenance of the samurai honor culture—became politically important.

A critical aspect of the medieval samurai culture of honor was that it represented the sovereign standing of a socially autonomous landed elite. As a result of their feudal possession of land as well as their military ability to defend their possessions, the samurai class developed the sentiments of honor as a cultural representation of their power and independence. Their basis of independence was translated into a tacit understanding of the individual as the ultimate owner of his body and mind. The samurai's distinctive attitude toward death and self-destruction ultimately stemmed from this understanding of individuality and self-determination. The effective use of violence and the ability to take conflict resolution into their own hands were important, not simply because violence was the sole legitimate expression of honor, but because it was an essential means of maintaining the samurai's sovereign power.

This identification of a sovereign element in medieval samurai culture leads to an important sociological question: Given the high social premium placed upon independence and autonomy in medieval samurai culture, why did feudalism in medieval Japan fail to provide a cultural matrix for a more democratic tradition in Japan? This question may require some clarification. From the perspective of the twentieth century, we take for granted that medieval feudalism in its European form was a period of human oppression on a grand scale; this customary interpretation certainly holds true for the bulk of the population, coercively subordinated to the landed military class. From the viewpoint of the landed elites, however, feudal society provided a certain degree of social autonomy. Since their freedom from monarchical interference was based upon their feudal ownership of land, the local landed elites of Western Europe were always concerned with defending their independence, rights, and interests against the central power.

Interestingly, the political and cultural institutions that developed in late feudal Europe were often identified as building blocks for the construction of democratic institutions. For example, Harold Berman has analyzed the gradual development of medieval feudal law, which protected the vassal's right of recourse to a higher seigniorial court. The early European codes of law arose from the necessity of controlling contested relationships and resolving conflicts among socially autonomous landed elites who could resort to unpredictable violence.[40] Thus, the jurisdictional and administrative immunities obtained by the knights, and their free entrance into vassalage, guaranteed the relative social autonomy of these vassals *vis-à-vis* their superiors.[41] Moreover, it was not only the corpus of civil and criminal law but also the medieval system of representation that had its origins in the military dimension of feudal life.[42] Once again, Max Weber proved insightful in this regard when he pointed out that the rise of self-equipped warriors in the West conferred a certain military autonomy on these individuals, which in turn symbolized and increased their political autonomy.[43] More recently, Brian Downing has argued that many of the characteristics of late medieval European states, such as the existence of decentralized polities with considerable local autonomy, representative assemblies, constitutionalism, and an elitist valuation of freedom and independence, distinguished Western Europe from other parts of the world and predisposed it toward the development of liberal democracy.[44]

Both Europe and Japan experienced the evolution of a feudal system, and their power structures consisted of systems of vassalage in which obedience and protection were exchanged among relatively independent social groups. Around the sixteenth century, both Japan and Europe confronted a phase of major social reorganization, characterized by recurrent civil wars and social upheaval, that eventually resulted in the central government's consolidation of power and internal pacification. This comparative perspective poses an interesting question regarding the Japanese course of social development; the culture and institutions brought into being by the medieval Japanese samurai comprehended the particular set of elements that might have encouraged Japan to take a more liberal democratic direction in its later history.[45]

In the first place, medieval samurai communities placed a high value on the social autonomy of landed elites under a decentralized state, owing to a unique set of power relationships and social institutions that had developed in medieval Japan. Although this culture never developed the type of political legal institutions that characterized medieval Europe, for example, a constitutionalism supported by formal representative assemblies and the principle of rule by law, the Japanese landed military elites and the emerging new forms of horizontal alliance (ikki) did manifest some prototypical features that might have led to the development of democratic institutions. The high degree of village autonomy that marked the late medieval period might have encouraged the construction of more horizontal forms of social relationship, because the Japanese villages had acquired a power base sufficient to withstand complete domination by the feudal lords.[46] Thus, one could rightfully ask why the development of Japanese social and cultural institutions after the early modern period did not move in a democratic direction, but instead placed a high social and cultural valuation on a hierarchical social order. This question compels us to reexamine the Japanese transition from its medieval to its early modern (Tokugawa) polity.

Recent discussions in historical sociology regarding the varieties of political experience in early modern Europe, focusing on the different courses and structures of state formation that took place there, provide us with some comparative theoretical insights. The role of military technology and the impact of fiscal and personal mobilization for warfare received more attention in this context, as exemplified in the theoretical and empirical works of Charles Tilly, Anthony Giddens, Michael Mann, John Brewer, and Samuel Finer. Their studies are suggestive not only because the results of international wars had obvious consequences for each country's geopolitical position in the European pecking order, but also because the military activities of the states decisively shaped the contingent outcomes of government structures, fiscal mechanisms, and power relations among various social units.[47]

For example, John Brewer's analysis of the British state shows that

Britain's military involvements in the late seventeenth and eighteenth centuries, together with the resultant growth of its armed forces, necessitated the formation of a public administration of considerable size devoted to organizing the fiscal and military activities of the state. The result was the emergence of what Brewer calls the "military-fiscal state" in Britain.[48] This conception of the early modern state as a military-fiscal machine that revolutionized the internal organizational structure of society is particularly pertinent to this study, because the early modern Japanese state provides a very different picture. The Japanese early modern state did not produce a machinery of comparable complexity for the task of government administration. The late-medieval Japanese involvement in a long-lasting civil war did, however, produce an equally significant but distinctively different outcome in terms of social-organizational transformation.

I wish to set forth three interconnected propositions in order to gain an understanding of the unique course of Japanese state formation from the medieval to the early modern periods: (1) the fact that early modern state formation in Japan was carried out as a consequence of a vertical military consolidation of power (reconstituted vassalage) among the samurai class, through (2) its clashes with horizontal political alliances; and (3) the forced demilitarization and subordination of the nonsamurai population in the process of state-making together explain the unique nature of the early modern shogunate. An additional factor ensured the collective victory of the landed military class. This was the fact that the forceful vertical consolidation of power around 1600 was carried out in a situation in which the social basis of organized commercial power was relatively weak, for two reasons: the relative underdevelopment of the cities and the relative lack of political organization of the merchant class. The subsequent reformulation of Tokugawa samurai culture into a more hierarchically oriented culture was possible because Japanese state formation in the early modern period took this vertically ordered course of development.

The preceding emphasis on the nature of Japanese state formation does not imply that the transformation of the samurai honor culture represents the automatic outcome of specific social-structural changes. Once institutionalized in a particular form, a culture often persists in this shape even after the social conditions that originally gave rise to it have disappeared. The study of the cultural dimension of state formation actually brings us to the more complex picture of the two tendencies of cultural transformation and cultural persistence, which can only be properly articulated in a detailed examination of historical contexts. They will be presented in the following chapters.

There is a central observation that we can make about this whole dynamic complex, with all its emerging properties of contingency and hysteresis. Overarching the microscopic turbulent patterns of change and resistance is a single relation between social-structural changes on the one hand, and the cultural transformation of the samurai on the other. This all-important relation reveals itself in the dynamic coupling of changing social structures and the imagined communities of honor or the samurai's collective symbolic reference groups.

In general, honor presupposes the existence of a reference community that confers honor on certain individuals within the group. This community of honor has *formal* and *informal* as well as *actual* and *virtual* aspects. Communities of honor can be formal and actual in the ways that they officially and institutionally bestow honor, and the ways they reprimand or punish those who incur shame. In this sense, the community of honor is closely related to the formal power structure of society in that it possesses the actual power to enforce honorific criteria.

The samurai community of honor, however, cannot be reduced to this aspect alone. When a samurai regulates his own behavior based upon considerations of what is deemed "honorable," he has an imagined community, or a symbolic reference group, in his mind that carries his reputation and social dignity. The power of this aspect of the honor community is informal and symbolic insofar as it ultimately resides in each subject; therefore, it exists as virtual, even though it is never less powerful than the formal aspect. In the Japanese honor culture, this imagined aspect of communities of honor has usually been expressed by the term *seken* since the medieval period. Although we can theoretically separate the virtual-symbolic aspect from the actual-power structure of honor communities, in practice the two aspects interact and influence each other. In contrast, the symbolic-virtual dimension of honor cannot be automatically equated with the social-structural dimension of honor.

Earlier in this chapter, I analyzed various aspects of the intrinsic nature and operational dynamics of the notion of honor, which connects individuals to their societies, insofar as it is rooted in each person's sense of self-worth, as well as in societal evaluation of the individual. The use of this intrinsic quality of honor as a telescopic device allows one to focus on the roles of individuals in the dynamic processes of samurai cultural change in the course of their political development.

Culture, Structure, and Human Agency

Sociologists have always been attracted to the intriguing questions posed by the intricacies of relationships between individuals and their societies. Although we moderns cherish the idea of "free will" as the chief component of self-identity, regarding ourselves as the captains of our respective lives, we also experience daily the presence of a confining net of invisible threads, woven into impersonal patterns of constraint. Sociologists have been eager to identify and label the hidden "structures" that affect our daily lives. At the same time, observers who study the micro-practices of social relations in any detail recognize that human beings are more than passive recipients of social constraints producing mechanical responses. Rather, humans are endowed with capacities for setting goals, for acting to achieve those goals, for creativity, and for bringing about considerable changes in their social relations. This capacity of human action, or "agency," to use a favorite term of sociologists, and its relationships with "structures" to which we feel bonded are one of the central issues of contemporary social theory.

This particular theoretical question had been the primary concern of Norbert Elias's work since the 1930s, as he opposed both one-sided social determinism and so-called methodological individualism in search of the source of modern self-discipline and sense of self.[49] But the question of the relationships of individuals to society has received a fresh impetus within the discipline over the last two decades, through such influential conceptual frameworks as Anthony Giddens's theoretical project of "structuration"[50] and Pierre Bourdieu's concept of "habitus" (a preeminent site of cultural practice in which what Bourdieu terms "mental dispositions" and the "world of objects" meet in the construction of temporary sustaining structures). The relation of self to society in the process of social change is an important question for this book, because the detailed study of the actual practices of the samurai honor culture leads us in that direction.

Through a detailed analysis of the practice of the Tokugawa honor culture and the examination of pre-Tokugawa sociopolitical and cultural developments, I came to appreciate the complexity of the world in which the Tokugawa samurai lived. There were two competing mental paradigms, or "structures," that affected the Tokugawa samurai's cultural reformulation. One paradigm emerged from the new institutional field resulting from Tokugawa state formation, and the other from the medieval military "tradition" of the samurai's self-definition. The former type of "structure" tended to confine the vassal samurai within a vertically ordered and tightly controlled system in which they were mostly separated from direct ownership of land in exchange for secure hereditary privileges, earning their income primarily as bureaucrats. Despite the loss of its social base, however, the medieval traditional notion of the self-equipped warrior persisted within the culture, in the form of a sense of military pride. These two structures tended to pull the Tokugawa samurai in different directions. Therefore, it was at the intersections of these two paradigms that the most important sources of dynamic cultural change were located.

The internal contradictions of the Tokugawa samurai's world do not end here. It was not just that these two major structures had significantly different orientations; in addition they were tied to complex sets of symbolic resources subject to divergent interpretations. First of all, the medieval tradition of samuraihood itself was by no means a monochromatic entity that directed the samurai toward a single path. The severe tensions between honorific loyalty and honorific individuality were in effect built into the warrior culture of the medieval vassalage organization. Secondly, the later Tokugawa state system also contained a complex set of symbolic resources. Since the Tokugawa state was built upon the collective victory of the samurai class, the organizational structure of the Tokugawa state, which was founded on the basis of combining the contradictory organizational principles of bureaucracy and vassalage, continuously emitted mixed signals to individual samurai. As a result, not only were there two dissonant structures, but each structure of constraints also imposed its own set of symbols and institutions without regard for the internally contradictory messages. The multiplicity of meanings embedded in these structures, however, provided individual samurai with useful resources for cultural and intellectual creativity. In other words, the process of disciplining the Tokugawa samurai developed in a highly contested cultural terrain, and this complexity of the samurai world in turn empowered the samurai's efforts at cultural reformulation.

The attempt to understand the dynamic changes in Tokugawa honor culture has brought me to the very heart of the question of human agency and social structures. The living form of honor culture always emerges within a concrete temporal dimension, as a set of actions that make a point of honor out of general social formulae or otherwise formless behavior. In the event that a samurai found his honor challenged in a quarrel, it was the individual actor's judgment and strategies that counted most heavily when his honor came under the searching evaluation of his peers. To be sure, unless he followed certain social guidelines and rules, he could not use his behavior to make a point of honor. Such formulae, or objectified rules, amount to "dead" knowledge, however, unless they are practiced and interpreted by concrete actions and words on the part of individuals. In turn, the recurrence of honor in similar social contexts constructs a temporarily stable field of cultural practice. The living significance of an honor culture arises in specific situations and actions that combine to shape inchoate sentiments of honor in a concrete context. From this interpretative perspective, codified honor formulae receive reinforcement and further "structure" from individual practices and reenactments.[51]

The cultural practices of actors and structures cannot be understood strictly in terms of a one-way causal relationship in which the latter sustains the former. How can we understand the capacity of individuals to introduce change if we regard them as dependent on structures? Anthony Giddens proposes to reconceptualize "structure" as a force that simultaneously constrains and empowers the course of human action.[52] Thus, his concept of structuration "expresses the mutual dependence of structure and agency."[53] Structures not only influence the actions of individuals, but they provide the tools and vehicles of actors' practices, which in turn constitute and reconstitute structures. According to Giddens's notion of the inherent duality of structure, a set of "rules and resources . . . are drawn upon by actors in the production of interaction, but are thereby also reconstituted through such interaction."[54] William Sewell, Jr., has elaborated on this point, contending that the dual aspect of structures is the most useful part of Giddens's theory of structuration. Structures as "rules," which Sewell prefers to call "schema," refer to the regulations of social life, "including all the varieties of cultural schemata that anthropologists have uncovered in their research: not only the array of binary oppositions that make up a given society's fundamental tools of thought, but also the various conventions, recipes, scenarios, principles of action, and habits of speech and gesture built up with these fundamental tools."[55]

In contrast, "resources" include the preeminent vehicles of power, which people are able to utilize flexibly to achieve their ends, to make changes, or to dominate others. In my opinion, in the actual practice of culture "schema" and "resource" are overlapping terms rather than clearly distinguishable entities. In spite of this, "duality of structures" is a useful concept because it enables us to articulate the dynamic nature of structures as embracing persistent and regulative patterns as well as elements that can be utilized for change.

My survey of the samurai past provides instances of this dynamic. For example, the more closely I began to examine the cultural idioms of early modern Japan, the more I came to recognize that nonconformist individuals used the medieval traditions of samurai sentiment as the "resource" that empowered their nonconforming motivations. It was interesting and significant to discover, for example, the presence of a military ethic and spirit within the mind of a rational Confucian scholar as the stimulus of his sense of independence.

This study is theoretically concerned with the relationship between the nature and the trajectories of Japanese state formation, and the mechanisms of cultural development of its elite discipline. This focus on the state and the samurai's cultural evolution also has ramifications in the areas of honor, individuality, and sense of selfhood in Japanese society, however. The theme of honor in samurai culture was intimately related to the samurai's vital sense of individuality. After all, why are we moderns attracted to the study of samurai culture? Why do the Japanese continuously create and recreate the image of the samurai in their present-day cultural artifacts? In my opinion, this ongoing interest at the popular level is more than nostalgic admiration for a glorified past; rather, it is the quality of the samurai's passion for independence and individuality, and their painful efforts to reconcile it with their collective identity, that fires the imagination of the modern Japanese.

The notion of honor explicitly links individuals to a larger collective or corporate identity; at the same time, the sentiment of honor incorporates a dimension of self-worth that cannot be totally reduced to the social dimension of the self. But, since the formation of personal identity is possible only through socialization, which amounts to continual revision of one's self-image, changes in the structures of socialization ultimately affect the core of our personal identity: our image of self-worth. In the final analysis, the formation of our self-identity would have been impossible without our accommodation to collective goals and demands. In this sense, *the process of Japanese state formation and self-identity in Japan have been intimately connected.*

Such an intricate and complex set of interconnections among honor, structure, and selfhood can be addressed only through a close analysis of the samurai's mentality in specific historical settings. Let us begin with the social world of the earliest samurai.

II ORIGINS IN VIOLENCE

2 The Coming of the Samurai: Violence and Culture in the Ancient World

Around the ninth or tenth century, while the court aristocrats of the Heian imperial government were enjoying a sophisticated cultural life in Kyoto, certain groups characterized by their might of arms emerged. They were called a variety of names, such as *tsuwamono, mononofu* (terms implying "military" and "arms"), *bushi* (military men), and *saburai* (a term meaning "to serve" for the nobility). The term *samurai* developed from *saburai,* which indicated the men who served at the houses of the nobility.[1]

Originally, the samurai were specialists, or an occupational group who served the ruling class with their military skills.[2] The dominant image one gains of these samurai is of horsemen with bows, arrows, and swords, galloping across the sparsely populated plains of Japan. They were the first social group in Japan with a clear self-identity as military specialists. By the mid-eleventh century, the houses of the samurai were considered hereditary, and a new social status *(mibun)* was established with a distinctive social-organizational basis and culture.

This does not mean that ancient Japan had no military men before the rise of the samurai. Indeed, the military had always played an important role in the history of the ancient state. Some powerful ancient clans were famous for their military prowess, and proud of their own force. The samurai, however, were characterized by their more professional military

47

skills and by a sense of identity as professional warriors, as well as by their unique social-hierarchical organizations. In their mature form, the samurai not only served as hired mercenaries but extended their domination over agricultural land, the most precious economic resource in this predominantly agricultural society, by virtue of their sheer military superiority in competition with other social groups.

The ascendance of the samurai class parallels the course of the Japanese medieval period itself, as the declining imperial power structure associated with the ancient world was undermined. The samurai were landed lords in their own right, but they also encroached upon the estates (shōen) of the old aristocrats through their provision of tax-collection services and protection. Those who managed to win the loyalty of these samurai became their tōryō, or masters. Around the eleventh century, the samurai warriors began the process of building their own hierarchical political organizations, which were distinctively different from the structures and cultural climate of the patron-client relationships at the imperial court in Kyoto.[3]

The Japanese medieval world was characterized by a dual power structure: the new samurai power and the older emperor's court. This basic structure was formally institutionalized when the samurai established a semicentral regime, commonly called the bakufu, or shogunate. Beginning with the Kamakura shogunate in the late twelfth century, medieval Japanese history until the sixteenth century was marked by the gradual expansion of the samurai's power and the corresponding decline of the aristocracy's.

It is significant that the Japanese warrior class emerged and constructed its power base, culture, and sense of identity against the backdrop of the other dominant class, the Kyoto aristocracy, which was weakening politically but was socially and culturally much more prestigious than the samurai. The Japanese aristocrats in the emperor's court did not turn themselves into a class of warrior nobles, nor did the samurai turn into court aristocracy. Until the late nineteenth century, both classes existed side by side, though the court was at best politically marginal from the fifteenth century onward. Officially, the imperial court retained a nominal traditional authority that conferred legitimacy on the holder of the strongest military power at any given time as the acknowledged ruler of the country. The de facto military leader of the country was given an official title by the emperor's court, usually seii tai shogun

(Great General, Conqueror of Barbarians).[4] As this title indicates, the samurai were entitled to govern the country because of their superior military power and their peace-keeping ability.

Japan's was thus an unusual pattern of social and cultural development within East Asia. China and Korea usually placed higher prestige on *bun* (the literati) than *bu* (the military). By contrast, even after they became the rulers of the country, the Japanese samurai did not and could not convert themselves into either court aristocrats or totally civilized social elites like the Confucian upper classes in other East Asian states. Violence for the samurai became the tool through which they could not only extend their sphere of domination but also legitimate their social existence: the samurai were understood by the rest of Japanese society as those who had the power to resolve conflicts and keep the peace.

Through the gradual development of a distinct network of their own political hierarchies (that is, the system of vassalage) headed by samurai chiefs, the samurai as a class eventually gained hegemony over the older aristocracy centering around the emperor's court. The honor culture of the early samurai thus exemplified and embodied their social existence as the emerging military elite of Japan. The term "aristocratic warrior," which often appears in Western literature as a description of the samurai, is from this perspective a partial misnomer. Although an upper-level samurai in the later period could aspire to finance and enjoy a sophisticated "aristocratic" lifestyle, there was a clear sense of status *(mibun)* and cultural differentiation between the aristocracy and the samurai throughout Japanese history.

A cult of honor in Japan emerged only with this development of the samurai class. If one reviews the literature of the period, it is evident that the number of references to honor, usually expressed with the term *na*, or "name," suddenly increases with the emergence of the samurai.[5] This does not mean that there was no sentiment of honor in Japan before the emergence of the samurai; in ancient Japan, *na* was associated with the honor of a clan. The term *na* appears in some poems of the eighth-century *Manyōshū*, the oldest Japanese poetry anthology, as an expression of the writer's pride in being a member of a famous clan.[6] But such examples are sparse. The ancient Japanese sense of honor was no different from the universal mechanism by which honor confers prestige and authority on the powerful. It was neither central to cultural values nor distinctive, as it later was with the samurai.

With the entrance of the samurai class onto the historical stage, the situation changed. The samurai culture of honor added four significant dimensions to Japanese culture. First, the samurai made honor the basis of a unique cultural style and collective identity. The samurai were often called "those men with a sense of shame" *(haji aru mono)*. The definition of a samurai as a member of an honor-driven culture distinguished him from the rest of society—both from the aristocracy and from the peasants who would not have paid with their lives for such a thing as an honorific principle. Honor thus became the samurai's proclaimed *raison d'être*. Second, within the community of warriors, the samurai formulated rules of reciprocity among themselves by using idioms of honor. Honor was important because it governed relationships between patrons and clients; it was a critical component of the samurai's social and political life. Third, with the development of the samurai as a hereditary social category, honor was conceived as an index of the sovereign power of the samurai's house, or *ie*. A strong desire for enhancing the name of one's house was the driving force behind the warrior's competitive behavior. Lastly, the samurai combined honor with military sensibility. Honor was considered the central element in "the way of warriors" *(musha no narai)* and therefore was tightly bound to physical strength and military excellence.

Only with the emergence of the samurai class did the Japanese culture of honor develop into a complex "cultural style" with rich symbolic and normative contents, as well as distinctive idioms for expressing them. A cultural resource becomes a major symbolic style in a society when a dominant group, or at least a significant minority group, nurtures it; a culture becomes institutionalized only with a supportive social base. To be sure, because individual claims of honor ultimately belong to a symbolic domain and the construction of honor is always ideological and cultural, an individual's claim to honor can be separated from that person's social standing. But it is easier and more readily acceptable, for instance, to claim the honor of being independent if one has the material qualifications for such independence. Furthermore, the autonomy of honor is usually restricted because of its collective nature. Honor presupposes a community with the authority to evaluate it and attribute it to the persons who claim it, both within and outside the community. Thus, even though people may make independent claims to honor by inventing their own criteria, the communal acceptance of their assertion remains uncertain. The codes of honor, as well as the structure and capability of the community of honor, are intimately related to one another. In order to arrive at a better understanding of the emergence of the samurai culture of honor, therefore, we shall focus initially on the political and economic aspects of the formation of the samurai class and the structural environment supporting the early characteristics of their culture.

The Emergence of the Samurai

The samurai in his fully developed form was a landed military lord; that is, he was a warrior whose economic base was his control over land and agricultural production. This mature form of the samurai, combining its characteristic economic and military features, assumed a central role in Japanese history only around the late Heian period (the mid-eleventh and twelfth centuries). The origin of the samurai class prior to this period is still a much-debated subject in scholarly discourse. As I will illustrate, I have some doubts about the explanatory power of the conventional picture of the origins and rise of the samurai. The traditional emphasis on economic factors touches upon an important ingredient of the samurai origins, but by itself this seems to be insufficient to explain the emergence of such a distinctive social class. Nor does a newer approach purely from the viewpoint of military history alone appear to be sufficient.

The conventional scholarly interpretation emphasized the samurai's role as landlord, by looking at his emergence primarily within the context of economic development.[7] According to this line of interpretation, the samurai's emergence is tied to the increased stratification of ancient local agricultural communities resulting from agricultural growth and changing patterns of land tenure in the late ancient world.

Prior to the development of the samurai class, during the late seventh and early eighth centuries, Japan had established a centralized state system of government that was closely modeled on the laws *(ritsu-ryō)*[8] and bureaucracy of T'ang China as exemplified by the Taihō ritsu-ryō code (701). Before the development of this state system, the social and political base of Japanese society had been a lineage unit, namely, the provincial clan called the *uji*. To curtail the power of these local wealthy clans, the imperial court imported the Chinese model of government, which replaced clan-based control with a central bureaucracy subject to the emperor. Under this new system, all land officially belonged to the emperor, and every free individual was registered and allotted land by the government. In return, individuals (*kōmin,* or, literally, "public men") were obligated to pay various taxes and to supply corvée service.

Soon, in the mid-eighth century, the state instituted an important policy modification. As a way of increasing tax revenue, the *ritsu-ryō* state enacted a new regulation that allowed individuals to hold newly developed land as their personal property, though it was originally subject to the grain tax. On this legal basis, the court aristocrats and religious institutions had been vigorously expanding their ownership of private land by claiming various exemptions as well as by utilizing the new reclamation code. Meanwhile, the local wealthy clans and farmers also attempted to privatize land by reclamation. Thus, among those local people there emerged reclamation lords *(kaihotsu ryōshu)* or private owners of land who lived in villages *(zaichi ryōshu)*—a class out of which, according to the standard interpretation, the samurai evolved.

Because of their powerful positions in the ancient political structure, the court aristocrats and religious institutions were in a more advantageous position to privatize the land than were the local reclamation lords. These lands privatized by aristocrats and temples were called *shōen,* or estates. The early *shōen* holders then strove hard to gain immunity from government taxation, something that required official government approval. Because local reclamation landownership at this stage was still unstable, and restricted by the framework of the ancient codes, local reclamation landowners sometimes sought the protection of the power-holders in Kyoto by "commending" their own land to them. Thus the actual local owners were able to secure not only their control over land but also immunity from the local government. As a result, by the tenth century a complex layering of land tenure emerged that linked original reclamation lords as the local *shōen* supervisors and the power-holding aristocrats in Kyoto who legally owned the *shōen.* By the eleventh to twelfth centuries, the *shōen* system legally and socially arrived at its mature form by gaining and securing its immunity. The management of the estate was distributed among a number of individuals holding *shiki* (offices or rights),[9] which specified "the share (or amount) of revenue due each rank in the *shōen* hierarchy."[10] Thus vigorous reclamation and the growing privatization of the land produced increasingly stratified social relationships in local communities.

As the land became privatized in the late ancient world, new lands were made arable, and certain peasants became more independent and wealthy in comparison with others in their local villages. The conventional economic explanation of the emergence of the samurai assumed that the samurai primarily evolved from these wealthier farmers, who had become in the meantime *zaichi ryōshu,* that is, landed lords who resided in villages. In particular, since the Heian government originally allowed private ownership only of the newly reclaimed land, the samurai developed out of the class of those who brought the land under cultivation—reclamation landed lords. Unlike the mostly absentee landlords of the Kyoto aristocracy, they developed a close regional network and supervised the farming of the land directly. Because of a combination of declining social control in local areas and some major rebellions and violence in the late Heian period, these reclamation lords armed themselves in order to protect their land and property. Throughout the Heian period, some scholars argue, the total area of agricultural land under reclamation expanded steadily. To be sure, various social groups, including aristocrats and Buddhist priests, contributed to the expansion of arable lands through their initiatives of land reclamation in this period. During the eleventh and twelfth centuries, however, the level of samurai activity in land reclamation became conspicuous. With their active participation in the process of land reclamation, the samurai clearly emerged as a class of landed lords.

Although landlordship was the fundamental social basis of the samurai class in its mature form, a purely economic approach, as articulated above, does not answer some pertinent questions about the early samurai. The accumulation of land on a plot-by-plot basis does not automatically produce a new type of warrior-lord. We may consider the example of the Chinese gentry, who did not become a warrior class. Medieval Japanese society could also conceivably have been dominated by such a nonmilitary landlord class. Why and how did the late ancient Japanese world perform this historic "jump"? Obviously, economic growth was only a necessary, not a sufficient, factor.

One critical factor that must be taken into account is the changing nature of the ancient state's armed forces. Historians are hampered by the paucity of documentary sources for understanding the imperial army's structure, recruitment, and operations prior to the important military reforms undertaken during the reigns of Emperor Tenmu and his wife, Empress Jitō (between 672 and 697). Before their reforms, the power and authority of the emperor's government were built on a contested terrain, with a subtle balance of power among local strong clans possessing their own leaders and ritualistic authority over the local population, and the emperor's court, which upheld its limited power and authority. When the ancient Japanese state attempted to introduce the Chinese model of centralized power in the seventh century, the imperial court also sought to build a strong national army of conscripted soldiers in order to weaken local tribal military power. Tenmu's attempt to outlaw the private possession of military weapons in 685 reflected this intention.

In addition to this domestic concern, the emperors had as their goal the protection of Japan from anticipated foreign invasion. In the seventh century, the northeast corner of the Pacific rim was a site of international conflict. This tension was triggered by the emergence of a strong centralized state in China, which had previously been severely divided. The rise of the Sui dynasty (587–617) and the subsequent emergence of the Tang (618–907) upset the power balance in East Asia, because these Chinese regimes were aggressive in military expansion. The Japanese court not only lost political influence over Korea but also had to fear a potential Chinese invasion of the Japanese homeland. This international threat, as well as the pressing domestic concerns for controlling the power of local clans, accelerated Japan's adaptation of a Chinese-style military organization. The emperor's new model army comprised both infantry and mounted archer units.[11]

Japan's eventual withdrawal from international competition, together with the weakening of the aggressiveness and imperial ambitions of the Tang rulers from the mid-eighth to the ninth centuries, discouraged the further development of a centralized military system. In addition, the emperor's court was not strong enough to overcome the military power of the provincial clans; many local powerful clans still kept their own private armies, which often included skilled mounted warriors. Thus, the rulers of the ancient state before and after the eighth century deliberately enlisted the regional mounted warriors in order to strengthen the military forces at their disposal. It is probable that the prototypical samurai was represented in these armed men gathered under local clans. These ancient private armies cannot be identified with the samurai as a class at this stage, however, because they did not constitute a social category transcending clan boundaries and rivalries.

The complete solution to the puzzle of the samurai emergence is far from obvious, and its details are still much debated among historians. The recent works of William Farris and Karl Friday supply a long-standing need for a detailed investigation of pre-Kamakura military development in Western literature.[12] Both these historians begin by criticizing the work of some earlier English-speaking scholars, which considered the rise of the samurai primarily in economic categories. To challenge this view, they focus equally heavily on the history of warfare and military technology, and they claim that the samurai's appearance can be understood as a contingent result of the ancient Japanese state's military policies and reforms, as well as the sequences of wars and technological innovations.

Although I agree with the military theory of the samurai emergence to the extent that the ascendance of the samurai cannot be understood only in the context of economic history, and that the military developments and policies of the ancient state played a critical role in the samurai's development, I disagree with the scholars' tendency to reduce a complex social phenomenon to a single dimension. The complex issues of changing land tenure systems in Japan, the dynamics of class relationships, the organizational and cultural differences between the eleventh- and twelfth-century samurai on the one hand and ancient warriors on the other are either considered secondary (Farris), or simply not analyzed (Friday). Farris emphasizes the evolutionary continuity of the Japanese soldier from about A.D. 500 to 1300. Indeed, Japan's armies prior to the eighth century contained mounted archers; by the year 800, much of the basic technology of samurai warfare was available to the imperial army. Thus, in Farris's view, the samurai class in the eleventh and twelfth centuries represented little more than an ongoing development of the ancient warriors of Japan, and was "merely one variant of the Asian-style mounted archer predominant in the Middle East and the steppe."[13] This continuity, however, cannot be taken to imply that these earlier ancient soldiers had formed a distinctive social status *(mibun)* and had internalized a group identity as samurai. Social developments within a society always involve a succession of both continuities and discontinuities. The articulation of a thread of continuity should not obscure the measurable changes that the emergence of the samurai as a class brought upon Japanese society. Tracking military developments by themselves provides an insufficient explanation of the political, economic, organizational, and cultural power wielded by the samurai as a class.

What is now required, given the present state of the literature, is a sociological reconceptualization of the question. An important first step toward the untangling of the problem is a more precise articulation of the comparatively distinctive features of the samurai's rise to power. In China and in Europe, professional mounted warriors did not form a differentiated hereditary social category comparable to the samurai class in medieval Japan. One must note important social differences between European knights in the feudal period and the Japanese samurai, because the chronological coincidence of the rise of cavalry as a military force often obscures significant differences between the Japanese and the Western situations. In medieval Europe, as Maurice Keen observes, the French *chevalier* "denotes a man of aristocratic standing and probably of noble ancestry, who is capable, if called upon, of equipping himself with a war horse and the arms of a heavy cavalryman, and who has been through certain rituals that make him what he is—who has been 'dubbed' to knighthood."[14] Thus, the culture of chivalry, which is unique to the West in certain social and religious respects, "cannot be divorced from the martial world of the mounted warrior: it cannot be divorced from aristocracy, because knights commonly were men of high lineage."[15] In Europe, the emergence of the class of feudal knights did not imply a separation from the preexistent social category of aristocracy.

By contrast, the rise of the samurai in medieval Japan entailed not only the emergence of a warrior class on horseback but also a distinct social category of the military clearly differentiated from the aristocracy attached to the emperor's court. The samurai's culture, lifestyle, and economic interests were markedly different from those of the high-born aristocrats of the ancient Japanese state. In Europe, unlike Japan, the identities of nobles and knights overlapped, and as a result the mounted warriors had no reason to challenge the existing feudal framework of the hereditary aristocracy. In China, by contrast, the mounted archers never moved beyond the framework of the Chinese imperial army and, consequently, did not develop into a distinctive class of landed lords. Why, unlike their counterparts in other Asian countries, were the mounted archers of Japan able to escape from the category of hired soldiers? What social, political, and cultural forces equipped them to form a unique social category and eventually compete successfully with the court aristocracy for hegemony? Exploration of these questions will facilitate a better understanding of the distinctive characteristics of the samurai's emergence and their effects on Japanese social developments.

In short, the samurai's assumption of power should be regarded as the emergence of a new social category (status, or *mibun*) which in turn introduced a series of distinctive economic, political, military, organizational, and cultural changes. These features set them apart from the older court aristocracy. Therefore, *a satisfactory approach to the question requires consideration of the "interplay" of a complex set of institutions and social conditions including feedback from the cultural changes themselves, in historical contingency.* In this chapter, I shall focus on the political and social implications of the effective use of violence in ancient Japanese society. In Chapter 3, I will discuss the organizational innovation of samurai vassalage as a factor in the samurai's political advancement. In Chapter 4, I will evaluate the impact of the samurai's honorific cultural practices, especially their distinctive attitude toward death, as catalysts for social change. Since the role of culture in the process of the samurai's emergence has not been effectively assessed in the existing literature, I will devote particular attention to this dimension.

The Nonagricultural Background of the Early Samurai

The question of the rise of the samurai leads to a consideration of the social significance of violence in Heian society. The professional use of violence was endemic to the samurai world view—in sharp contrast with the imperial court culture of the mid-Heian period. The court aristocracy in Kyoto was also in the grip of a cultural obsession with notions of purification and pollution. It was a society that considered blood pollution dangerous and believed that the anger of the slain person's spirit (*goryō*, or "departed spirit") would return to harm the living.[16] Out of this cultural conviction, the Heian court even stopped holding executions between 810 and 1156.[17] This Heian court culture may be understood as the result of an agrarian lifestyle with a set of agricultural values that included not killing any creature that had blood. There was a consequent tendency, during the Heian period, to reserve certain military posts as hereditary positions for members of particular houses of the middle and lower aristocracy. Indeed, when these generals returned from military expeditions, they could not enter the capital city of Kyoto without first undergoing a ritual purification.[18] The dominant court culture of the mid-Heian period thus contrasted sharply with the military culture.

The recently developed social-historical approach to Japanese history has presented a more lively image of the early samurai. For example, Takahashi Masaaki stresses the early samurai's background as hunter-soldiers in the eastern region and seamen-soldiers in the western region.[19] Ōishi Naomasa argues that the regional peculiarity of the ancient eastern territory, the homeland of the mounted warriors, where "the trinity of horses, iron, and shamanism" prevailed, played an important role in the rise of the samurai class.[20] As a result of such recent contributions, it is now generally accepted that many, if not all, early samurai had nonagricultural backgrounds.

This argument for the nonagricultural origins of the early samurai is also supported by the observation that the mature samurai culture in later periods retained many hunter-like customs. Hunting game, for instance, was traditionally an important activity for samurai. The first shogun of the Kamakura shogunate, Minamoto no Yoritomo, was famous for holding frequent large-scale hunting parties. These expeditions not only had a recreational purpose but also provided ceremonial occasions to vindicate his power and to train and test the military skills of his vassals. In a famous ceremonial hunting party in 1193, Yoritomo brought almost all his major vassals to the foot of Mount Fuji. One by one, his selected vassals shot at their horses, which were driven from the mountain to the plain by beaters. When his heir, Yoriie, then twelve years old, killed a deer, Yoritomo conducted a ritual for his son, enshrining the god of the mountain. According to the analysis of Ishii Susumu, "The first game killed in the hunting was the initiation to adulthood for the young samurai and a vindication of his military skill. It could also be considered a blessing from the gods."[21] The game was not simply taken for pleasure; it also had a religious dimension that connected the samurai to their heritage as hunters. Many shogun and daimyo of the Tokugawa period also enjoyed hunting game. Chiba Tokuji, who has extensively studied the ethnohistory of Japanese hunter culture, concludes that the customs and practices of the samurai were quite similar to those of traditional mountain hunters.[22]

Such findings on the nonagricultural background of the early samurai may hold few surprises for students of Western feudalism, in which a mounted warrior class emerged in societies where pastoral and agricultural modes of life had existed side by side and the tradition of a hunting culture had remained vital. But since premodern Japan is conventionally considered predominantly agricultural, and the nonagricultural tradition is consequently regarded as marginal, a social-historical finding of this sort has fresh implications: the emergence of the samurai can no longer be understood simply as the extension of wealth among a particular subset of farmers resulting from changing land tenure patterns. Rather, the development of the samurai class brought some new social and cultural factors into the mainstream of Japanese culture.

If that is the case, where did this nonagricultural, hunter-like culture of the samurai originate? One must consider the special situation of frontier regions—especially the northeastern region, traditionally considered the cradle of the Japanese samurai. In comparison to the center of the ancient state, which was located in Kyoto since 794, the northeastern region was called *azuma* (the east) and was always considered the outside or frontier of civilization because it was the source of political rebellions and hunter countercultures. In the northernmost part of *azuma* lived the unruly eastern hunting tribes called *emishi*, whose skilled mounted archers were an ongoing nuisance to the emperor's government. Unfortunately, written historical sources for the ancient northeastern region are very scarce, and scholars are still undecided about the precise identity of the *emishi*. Some Japanese historians consider the *emishi* to be simply the ancestors of the present-day *Ainu*, who are racially different from the more Mongolian-looking majority of the Japanese population.[23] More recent archeological and historical accounts suggest, however, that the *emishi* cannot be simply equated with *Ainu*, because they were not racially different from the present-day Japanese. If that is the case, then the term *emishi* comprehended various marginal tribal groups dwelling in the northeastern region, including some *Ainu*.[24]

In contrast, the part of *azuma* closer to the center was a more ambivalent frontier. Later often referred to as *Bandō*, or *Kantō*, this region was long considered the cradle of strong samurai bands around the tenth and eleventh centuries and thereafter. *Azuma* in general was famous for its good horses throughout the ancient period, in comparison with the more agricultural society of the southwest regions of Japan. The horses that were bred in the eastern region always fetched high prices from the wealthy aristocrats who lived in the capital.[25] What is more interesting for our purposes is the development of ironmaking technology, which emerged in the northeastern region in the ninth and tenth centuries. Needless to say, the production of iron was critical for weapon manufacture as well as for pasturing horses.[26]

Military conflicts between the native *emishi* population and the troops of the emperor's court increased over the course of the late eighth and ninth centuries. Indeed, after the international crisis of the seventh century and the subsequent weakening of Tang expansionism in the eighth century, ongoing border wars with the *emishi* became the most important military issue for the imperial regime.

The frequent skirmishes between the *emishi* and the troops of the central government resulted in a set of complex interactions between the *emishi*, the non-*emishi* local residents, and the army mobilized by the ancient state. For example, some forms of lucrative illegal private trading developed between the *emishi* and the local population in this region, further increasing interactions between the two groups. Because the ancient state adopted the Chinese conception of an empire—in which the barbarians should bring tributes as a symbol of their subjection to the imperial power—the emperor's court attempted to ban all private trade with "barbarians" in order to protect formal tributary relations. The economic implications of this policy included state monopolies of popular *emishi* products such as horses, leathers, and furs, all of which were sought-after goods in the capital city. It was virtually impossible to regulate all private trading with *emishi*, however. Thus, with increasing military confrontation in the late eighth century, contraband trading with *emishi* appeared to flourish in the northeastern region. As with any other black market activity, it is difficult for scholars to ascertain the precise extent of this private lawbreaking in *azuma*. Various documentary sources that have survived do indicate that local farmers, roaming outlaws, and possibly some officers of the emperor's own troops were involved in smuggling activities.[27]

These military and socioeconomic interactions with the *emishi* generated an ambiguous social and cultural climate in the provinces of *azuma*. The centripetal forces that connected the divergent military and outlaw elements in *azuma* were the forces originally sent by the emperor's court to pacify this violent area. It is commonly acknowledged that the leaders of the early samurai groups derived from the lower and middle aristocracy, whose members were assigned to military tasks on a hereditary basis. Yoshie Akio summarizes a recent consensus: "The core of the early samurai . . . was derived from middle and lower aristocracies who engaged in special military tasks against *emishi* [northeastern tribes] and pirates. Groups of people specializing in hunting and fishing, together with criminals such as murderers, those who were expelled from traditional society, were working under their command." [28]

The origin of the early form of the samurai was apparently related, at least in part, to these violent groups of eastern warriors who had a close affinity with an indigenous nonagricultural people. If the early samurai were originally considered violent outsiders to the agricultural world, how were they eventually able to gain dominance over agricultural communities? It is difficult to answer this question concisely because the available documents are fragmented and ambiguous. Regional and temporal variations also make it difficult to outline a common pattern. One can speculate, however, that not only the strength of the protosamurai but also the social conditions in the local agricultural communities helped to establish a new system of military landed lords.

The Early Samurai in Folklore

The historical material that enables us to catch brief glimpses of the culture of the early samurai is quite limited since these prototypical samurai are mentioned only indirectly in the few available documents. Furthermore, unlike the later periods, when the samurai themselves were able to express their thoughts in writing, the warriors in the late ancient world did not set down many of their thoughts and actions on paper. The social history of the early samurai culture therefore obliges us to borrow heavily from the literary productions of the period, written by nonsamurai writers, in order to piece together an image of the samurai. Contemporary collections of folklore, such as *Konjaku monogatari (Tales of Times Now Past)*, and war literature, such as *Heike monogatari (Tales of Heike)*, are particularly valuable because they provide textured images of the earlier samurai.

For example, *Konjaku monogatari* recounts a story called "A Crusade against the Monkey Gods," which symbolically describes the violent process by which the marginal nature of the early samurai broke through the old enchanted order of a community. [29] *Konjaku monogatari* was written around 1120 in Kyoto, or in Nara. The book consists of thirty-one volumes that include more than a thousand stories. The author or editor is unknown, but is thought to be a person or a group of people related to Minamoto no Takakuni, a Kyoto nobleman formerly thought to be the author. [30] About seven hundred stories are concerned with Buddhism, but there are also lively stories about people from all classes and walks of life, including samurai, artists, thieves, lovers, and aristocrats. The stories were collected from various sources, including oral tradition.

The following is the story of the monkey gods:

Once upon a time, a priest lost his way in the mountains. Walking through a tunnel, he arrived at a mysterious hidden village. By order of the old lord of the village, called *kōri no tono,* the priest was made the guest of a large wealthy house. The man received unexpectedly warm treatment there, to the point of being asked to marry the daughter of the house. So he did, and he became an ordinary secular man with a normal hair style and hat.

When the festival season arrived, however, a secret was disclosed. The house had been ordered to provide a daughter as a human sacrifice to the local gods. It turned out that the family plotted to substitute the daughter's husband. The man agreed to his fate but asked his weeping wife to find a good iron sword for him.

On the festival day, the man was placed naked on a large cooking board and left alone in the shrine. Then huge monkey gods appeared, one after another, and one of them attempted to carve up the man with a cooking knife. The man took his sword, which he had hidden under his legs, and threatened the monkey with it, saying, "If you are a god, this sword cannot hurt you. Shall I cut your belly as a test?" As soon as he had spoken, the monkey started crying and rubbing his hands [a gesture of submission]. The man then swiftly tied up all the monkeys. After setting fire to the shrine, he returned to his house with the monkeys in tow and he himself dressed in samurai clothes, with bow and arrows.

Seeing his samurai bearing and appearance, the members of the house, including his father-in-law, rendered homage to him, rubbing their hands: "From now on, we will respect you, o lord, as our god, and entrust ourselves to you, and follow whatever you order." Then the man entered the residence of the old lord, *kōri no tono* [literally, "county lord"]. The old lord bowed to the floor as a token of submission. The samurai beat each monkey twenty times, after which he released them. He then called the villagers together and ordered them to burn the rest of the shrine buildings. Thereafter, the samurai became the chief of the village, and he governed and controlled the villagers. The village originally did not have any horses, cows, or dogs, but occasionally the man returned to the other side of the mountain and captured those animals to take to the village.[31]

It is the intruder from the outside world (a priest and visitor) who is able to break through the old enchanted village order governed by myths and rituals. Frequent reference to changes in his appearance, from that of a priest to a commoner, from nakedness to the samurai style of dress, complete with bow and arrows, symbolizes this consciousness. The combination of the old lord *kōri no tono* (who has no actual power) and the monkey gods embodies the ancient communal order. "Mediators of conflicts were necessary in villages," Irumada Nobuo concludes in his interpretation of this story; the samurai were the people who were able to adjudicate the various village conflicts accompanied by the breakdown of the ancient village structure. The resolution of such conflicts was impossible within the existing village system if the ancient local system of power relied only on myth. The essence of samuraihood was the warriors' marginality and ambivalence, which allowed them to emerge as mediators, something that resulted from their ability to use violence.[32]

To be sure, the prototypical hero of this folk story, a brave man who prevents a human sacrifice, can be found in many places in the world. It is also common in folklore for an outsider to create a new social order. This story, however, signifies some elements peculiar to the late ancient Japanese situation. *Konjaku monogatari* also contains a story in which a hunter saves a woman from monkey gods. This story describes how the parents of a woman chosen as a human sacrifice are powerless to do anything but weep and deplore their tragic destiny. But the hunter, with the aid of his trained hunting dogs, is brave and rational and never allows himself to be tricked by the myth of the power of the monkey gods. In both cases, the residents of the community are powerless against the enchanted world, and only the outsider with mighty force and cool head is able to free the villagers from its spell. The spirit of the samurai's straightforward, pragmatic behavior, which sometimes dared to violate long-standing taboos, is often praised in the literature of the period. For example, *Konjaku monogatari* includes a story about a particularly vicious evil spirit who could not be subdued even by the power of Buddha himself. The evil spirit is eventually brought down by the force of an arrow, which symbolizes the samurai's military power.[33] Another story in *Konjaku monogatari* tells about a demon who eats human beings alive but is overcome by the fighting spirit of a sword-wielding young samurai.[34]

As more and more arable land became privatized and the practice of distributing public land to free individual peasants came to an end, the local villages became more stratified. The old internal ties among villagers, supported by traditional communal religious rituals, were threatened by privatization, which led to an increasing concentration of wealth in the hands of a relatively small group of rich farmers. The introduction of the *shōen* system also brought local villages into the complex network of new land tenure and ultimately established a link with the Kyoto power-holders. This systemic change tended to weaken the established power of local wealthy clans, which had been lodged in the position of the *kōri no miyatsuko*, or *gun ji*, the "chief of the county." The *kōri*, or *gun*, was a small local administrative unit (*kōri* and *gun* are two pronunciations of a character that signifies "county"); "chiefs of the county" were all appointed by the ancient central state. They were usually not bureaucrats, however, but the leaders of old wealthy clans that dominated local communities.

The ancient *ritsu-ryō* state carried the surface appearance of a highly centralized political system, centered as it was around the emperor's court. The actual power structure, however, took the form of a compromise with older indigenous political forces. Under the surface of the Chinese-style centralized *ritsu-ryō* state, provincial people continued to be primarily governed by the local wealthy clans. The communal, myth-ridden order was the important power basis of these chiefs of local wealthy clans, who held great authority over the people. The movement toward privatization of land thus undermined the power basis not only of the central state but also of older local powers such as the chief of the county who failed to transform themselves into a new type of military landed lords. The character of the *kōri no tono* (county lord) in the monkey god's story may reflect the political impotence of this older type of county leader, whose chief base of authority was constituted by ancient communal beliefs and rituals. In contrast, those local clans who were able to transform themselves into the local power-holders with actual coercive force by absorbing more aggressive military culture might have opened a way to be "samurainized." Because of their confidence in the power of sheer force, the protosamurai were often able to break through and demolish the established local order that depended upon mystical beliefs for its legitimation. Taira no Masakado, a samurai who led the first major rebellion against the imperial court in 935, was said to have styled himself as a new emperor by proclaiming, "This is a time when a man who can win the war becomes the master of the world."[35] It was an eloquent announcement of the beginning of a new era in which bare force and excellence in military skills would change the structure of society.

Political Economy in Local Communities

Reorganization of Local Military Forces

Although strong armed men may have sometimes acted as protectors and mediators within villages, as Japanese folklore suggests, they were not always regarded as such. A number of documents and official chronicles of the Heian period itself blame the contemporary social disorder on violent groups of displaced people. These violent outsiders were seen by both authorities and farmers as "in no way different from barbarians *(iteki)* and [looked] like wild dogs or wolves."[36] Men who always carried weapons and who harmed other people were called "butchers" *(toji,* that is, people who killed animals in order to feed hunting dogs) or simply *irui,* meaning a different order of human being.[37]

The early samurai behaved as "landed lords resembling the bosses of organized crime," retaining the loyalty of "violent mobsters."[38] That the samurai could behave like professional mobsters was no joke to the medieval Japanese. A contemporary illustrated narrative scroll, called "Obusuma Saburō ekotoba," described a particularly brutish samurai named Obusuma Saburō, whose compound always swarmed with rough soldiers practicing their martial arts (see Illustration 1). Obusuma ordered his retainers to decorate the place with human trophies: "Hunt for heads, and hang them on the fence of the horse yard! Keep it up . . . Go after the *shugenja* [mountain monks], or the beggars passing by in front of the gate . . . and chase them down! Shoot them with *kabura* arrows!"[39] The picture illustrating the narrative depicts unfortunate individuals overtaken by Obusuma's retainers. To be sure, the illustration dates from a later period (ca. 1295), and it depicts a fictional local samurai. It is probable, however, that the rare picture from this period reflected an aspect of fierce and wild local samurai life, an inevitable violent aspect of the samurai in their process of growing as a new style of landed force.[40] The culture of honor that emerged from this aggressive class might have remained a "counterculture" in Japanese society if the samurai had remained only "aliens" and "mobsters" in the agricultural community. What were the mechanisms that conferred status and prestige on the local military men?

The structural inadequacy of the military in the ancient Japanese state around the eighth and ninth centuries was the precondition that allowed the local military men to become part of the public office. As we have seen, the ancient *ritsu-ryō* state's army originally was drawn largely from centralized conscription of farmers; although units of mounted archers were present, the military quality of the farmer-soldiers, mobilized as part of their obligation to supply labor to the state, was not high. With the grave social disorders culminating in various uprisings in sparsely populated regions, it became apparent to the central authorities that the conventional military system in local areas was inadequate to meet the new challenges. In battles against mobile enemies, highly trained and skilled mounted warriors were much more effective than farmers primarily drafted as foot soldiers. Since the late eighth century, the state had attempted to reform the organization of local armies. Instead of relying on conscription, they selected more able men from the local areas (called the *kondei* system, 792). With the increasing social disorder in outlying regions caused by the depredations of bandits, however, the incorporation of the local private armed forces into the public force of provincial offices became increasingly necessary. In particular, the local military men's ability to use horses and archery was a very useful resource for the authorities, whose traditional army had a weak cavalry. The importance of cavalry had been recognized in wars against the *emishi* tribe, which had been renowned for its skillful hunter-cavalry. The state's overtures to incorporate the local mounted archers into its local garrisons were made in this context.[41]

Official documents of the late ninth century often refer to the presence of violent and disorderly *tō* (bands). In 861, for example, the government posted martial offices in various provinces because of the disruption caused by "a cunning and violent *tō* of bandits living in the mountains."[42] These predatory brigands often robbed tax-carriers and caused a significant problem for the authorities of the central government. Subsequently, more organized violent gangs appeared in the eastern region, frequently mounting attacks on the local offices of the government. During the late ninth to tenth centuries in eastern regions, there were active packs of marauders known as *shūba no tō* (literally, "bands of hired horses"). These mobile mounted groups sometimes organized themselves in order to conduct a legitimate and lucrative business; for example, they could offer their service as carriers along the major roads. Often, however, they turned to robbery, and worse—they even touched off local uprisings.[43]

These aggressive groups, which absorbed the marginal population, such as unattached migrants and runaway peasants, were often organized by the local wealthy clans as a form of taxpayers' revolt against the taxation of the ancient government. The *tō* might also be headed by descendants of middle and lower Kyoto aristocratic families who had settled in local communities. The core of these violent groups was usually mounted armed men on "fat horses," who were assisting the local delinquents and tyrannizing the villagers.[44] At this point in time, violent groups such as the bands led by men on "fat horses" did not yet fully manifest the characteristics of the samurai as professional warriors, since they included all sorts of marginal people and malcontents. But the contemporary descriptions of these paramilitary groups open the possibility that the samurai bands, with a more professionally specialized armed force and the distinctive identity of their profession in the eleventh century, may have emerged from this breeding ground of violence.

In the early years of the formation of the samurai class, provincial government offices *(kokuga)* played an important role.[45] This connection may appear strange, considering that the interests of each party, the early samurai who tried to expand private control over the land, and the governmental offices that aimed at maximizing tax revenue were in many ways at cross-purposes. In practice, however, these two social forces had managed to build a functional working relationship. In provincial government offices, one important role often assigned to the early samurai was the protection of carriers of tax revenue as they traveled from local offices to Kyoto. Since the public roads were populated by all sorts of thieves and muggers, the local *tsuwamono* (military men) with their intimidating reputation were considered the most suitable for this important job.[46] In addition, samurai were sometimes used as tax-collecting agents on behalf of the provincial office, though they often abused their power and lined their own pockets with public income. Thus, by a number of different paths, the local samurai came to be incorporated into the government's official organization. As a result, not only did the provincial government offices introduce some of the local samurai into formal government forces, but they also appointed certain influential samurai to positions in local government offices, giving them official honor rankings.

In the process of developing into a distinct class, the samurai also started to weave their own network of alliances. Here, the military aristocrats who became "samurainized" in local areas played an important role. Because the power-holders of the Kyoto aristocracy generally looked down on the military as a profession, those aristocrats who supervised military affairs were usually limited to the middle-lower ranks, and often inherited their military rank. Those military aristocrats who settled down in local regions often recruited their own private armed force and thus formed the core of the local samurai bands.

The two major rebellions between 935 and 941 in the remote eastern and southern parts of Japan represented the growing power of the local samurai under such leaders. Taira no Masakado, who organized one of these rebellions, was part of the military aristocracy until he became a leader of the samurai. The rebellion, triggered by pressure from the provincial governors' offices on the local bands of samurai, attempted to take over the provincial offices and to establish regional offices. Although the rebellions of Shōhei and Tenkei were finally suppressed by the emperor's troops, which had already started to incorporate some of the local samurai forces, it became obvious that only the samurai themselves were strong enough to counter the undisciplined military groups emerging in the local areas.

The growth of the samurai class occurred not simply as an extension of the development of an indigenous armed force in local communities; it was also stimulated by the active mediation of the authorities of the ancient state. The incorporation of the samurai into the public power network did not mean that the ancient state was able to keep the samurai in line—quite the opposite. Subsequent developments of the samurai class often created a political situation in which the samurai were able to increase their influence over the local government from inside by utilizing their connections and offices in the *kokuga*.

Political Economy of Violence

The samurai's effective use of military power, and their increased assumption of local public offices, also contributed to the expansion of their economic influence. Let us examine a case history of the *shōen* estate for illustration.[47] This *shōen* was instituted in the early twelfth century in the eastern region by a samurai called Taira no Kagemasa. Kagemasa was famous for his brawn, as demonstrated through his record in combat, but history also shows that he was a shrewd real estate developer. He laid plans to reclaim an extensive tract of land in the region by employing a work force of migrant laborers, and then to donate the land to the Ise Shrine, the imperial ancestral shrine, in order to establish a *shōen*. Kagemasa filed a reclamation application with the provincial government office claiming that the area had belonged to the ancestral lands of his clan. In fact, the area projected for reclamation had not been all a central territory of Kagemasa's clan; rather, it included some areas already populated. The creation of the new *shōen* was clearly part of Kagemasa's plan for territorial expansion. This notwithstanding, the provincial governor did approve his application and gave the land a temporary tax-exempt status. When Kagemasa continued to put pressure on the governor, he finally gained permanent tax-exempt status. On paper, this *shōen*'s owner was the Ise Shrine, which was located far from the *shōen*. Kagemasa was technically only a supervisor of the *shōen*. But by making a small annual payment to the shrine, Kagemasa and his descendants put the *shōen* effectively under their personal control.

It would probably have been impossible for Kagemasa to enclose the large area of land for reclamation without the combination of the actual military force under his command and his political connections to public authority. With his armed force, he could easily mobilize sufficient labor to proceed with the reclamation, and he could quash any local opposition that might have arisen from the villagers whose existing lands were engulfed by this plan. Kagemasa's reputation as the head of a fearsome samurai band thereby helped him to become a major landed lord. In this predominantly agricultural society, arable land was the most highly valued source of wealth. The rise of the samurai's power as military professionals facilitated their aggressive attempts to extend their control over land. The privatization of land through reclamation was the crucial condition that transformed violent military men into institutionalized landed lords, making them an important part of the economic structure.

The samurai's privatization of land through the *shōen* system increased markedly in the course of the eleventh and twelfth centuries. The late twelfth century in particular became what Ishii Susumu has called "the era of the great reclamation in the eastern region."[48] The advancement of samurai power in the agricultural sector inevitably provoked opposition and interference from the established power-holders, however. Local government officials generally attempted to levy taxes on the samurai. Moreover, the fact that the ultimate legal owners of the *shōen* were usually not the local samurai themselves made the samurai vulnerable to government interference. The samurai lords usually held the land through sharing a part of the *shōen* entitlements in the form of *shiki*. In this situation the local samurai sought a new source of protection for their common economic interests. The eventual formation of the first samurai government, the Kamakura shogunate, was possible only with the maturation of the samurai class as a group with these shared political and economic concerns during the twelfth century.

The Early ie *and the Structure of the Samurai Bands*

As samurai landownership expanded, the samurai themselves began to develop a distinctive style of social organization as part of their military leadership. A band of samurai usually united under an *ie* (house), which was a kinship-oriented corporate body that combined both military and economic functions. The core of the *ie* consisted of kinsmen, but it also incorporated nonkinsmen such as retainers *(rōjū)*, servants, and other subordinates, who were usually hereditarily subordinate to the master of the *ie*. The military organization, including strong ties between master and soldiers, was the necessary and sufficient condition of the *ie's* independence. As the warriors collectively protected their lands from enemies, a strong sense of solidarity grew within the *ie*.

Let us look more closely at the actual physical appearance of a group of samurai. The residence of the samurai lord was called the *yakata*, which was usually surrounded by a moat or earthwork. The inside area included the main house for the master's family, cottages for retainers and servants, a stable, and some fields. The fields inside or directly adjoining the *yakata* were under the immediate supervision of the samurai-lord and cultivated by his direct subjects; they were the foundation of the economic samurai's life and usually exempt from taxation. Outside these fields, there were subjected villages cultivated by farmers.[49]

Living with his men, and training them in combat skills in the area surrounding the *yakata*, the samurai-lord attempted to extend his control beyond that central area as far as possible. He provided protection for the villages, adjudicated disputes, and collected taxes. Some of the farmers were also organized as the lord's retainers and fought as members of his band. Thus, the *yakata* was the staging ground for military organization as well as the base of agricultural production.

The development of the *ie* provided a critical step in the development of the samurai culture of honor. A warrior might fight bravely for the sake of his reputation on the battlefield, but with the emergence of the *ie*, he now had a reason beyond his own honorable name for risking his life. The property of the *ie* would be passed on to each samurai's descendants, and the reputation of the samurai house as a whole had to be maintained toward this end.

The *ie* was indeed a cradle of the culture of honor. A contemporary war tale, *The Rise and Decline of the Minamoto and Taira Clans (Genpei seisuiki)*, describes this nascent spirit: "Losing one's good name in bows and arrows means not only shame for oneself in the present moment; it also entails serious shame [for the family as a whole] that decreases the authority of one's ancestral generals." [50] Their awareness of and pride in a continuous bloodline was one thing that distinguished the samurai from the lower classes. The genetic continuity of the *ie* and the protection of its property became a critical concern for its members, and the honor of the *ie* was intimately related to this desire for the perpetuation of the ancestral line.

The precise timing of the establishment of the samurai's hereditary status is not known. Various references in the literature and other documents from the eleventh century and thereafter suggest that samurai constituted a definite social category with a distinctive lifestyle and hereditary family lines.

In sum, there are several viable theories to explain the emergence of the samurai class. They may have originated from within local communities by absorbing quasi-military behavior from nearby violent, non-agricultural populations. As some scholars argued, however, it is also possible that the samurai entered the villages as outsiders. Still a third possibility is that local wealthy clans hired these outsiders and then developed a new style of leadership by absorbing their military technology and lifestyle. The origins of the samurai in ancient Japanese local communities appear to represent diverse historical possibilities and remain obscure. There is also a comparative scarcity of written records of any kind on the local level during the critical period in question. Whatever the eventual outcome of the debate, the important factors that enabled the samurai to dominate the agricultural sector in this period are: their ability to use violence professionally, which separated them from the existing social order; the structural problems of the ancient Japanese state, particularly in the areas of military technology and organization, supplying the precondition that favored the growth of the samurai power; and the existence of social conditions in local communities resulting from changing economic conditions that favored the emergence of a new social force.

Examining the processes through which the samurai emerged as a social status category indicates that the skillful use of violence lay at the core of their identity and differentiated them from the rest of society. Remember the words of the priest-samurai in the monkey-god folk story: "If you are a god, this sword cannot hurt you. Shall I cut your belly as a test?" The story may symbolize an aspect of the social process in which the samurai class broke through a stagnant, myth-ridden power structure by the simple and straightforward belief that stronger power-holders can overcome any resistance. *The samurai revolutionized the structure of local communities, mediated conflicts with the explicit and implicit threat of violence, and finally established a new coercive way of obtaining revenue from an agricultural society.*

The Rise of the Honorific Culture

In the eleventh and twelfth centuries, the samurai emerged as a clearly defined social category that combined two important roles: landed lord and warrior. During this formative period, they could not claim the rich and complex cultural resources of their historical descendants, but they already manifested a set of vivid and distinctive cultural characteristics. Having achieved a certain stability as a class of military landed lords, the samurai were no longer known only as "butchers" and "aliens" to society at large. Their connection to public offices and their settlement within an agricultural society made them more acceptable members of their surrounding culture.

With the political maturity of the samurai class in the late Heian period, the samurai's culture of honor also took a distinctive form. First, the samurai's sense of military pride generated a set of rules that exalted fighting as an expression of honor. Although simple physical strength and martial skills continued to be the basis of their sense of pride, certain rules and idioms served to express that strength. Second, the development of their unique master-follower relationship (vassalage) provided a new dimension within the samurai's culture of honor. The emerging political hierarchies and coalitions of samurai, related to the subsequent formation of the samurai government at Kamakura, constituted a community of honor. In this community, a warrior's honor was publicly evaluated and conferred. During this social process, from the late Heian through the Kamakura periods, we observe the emergence of a sense of pride associated with being a samurai, of a collective samurai identity, manifesting the first signs of a distinctive cultural style.

The following story conveys the earliest and most admirable image of the behavior of honorable warriors found in *Konjaku monogatari*.[51] The narrative concerns two rival samurai, Minamoto no Mitsuru and Taira no Yoshifumi, who fight a duel for the sake of honor. The outline of the story runs as follows:

> The two samurai were competing in military skills. Each of them believed that he was stronger than the other, and finally they agreed to stage a formal battle in a large open field. The appointed day arrived; both samurai had mobilized about five to six hundred men who were fully determined to fight to the last drop of blood. Both troops lined up with their shields. Each side sent a soldier to exchange the declaration of war. A battle usually began with a volley of arrows after the envoys had returned to their troops. Right before the fray, however, Yoshifumi sent another messenger to Mitsuru, saying, "Today's combat will not be interesting if it ends with the shooting of our troops. Our only intention is the testing of our own military skills. Let us not fight in the company of our armies, but let us have a single combat between the two of us shooting with our best skill."
>
> Having accepted this offer at once, Mitsuru stepped out of the line of shields. Yoshifumi ordered his retainers not to assist him and went out to fight. While both troops of retainers stood watching, the two master warriors fought on their horses. The two samurai first spurred their horses while fixing arrows to their bowstrings. Each of them tried to allow the other to shoot first (showing their bravery). They spurred their horses and shot in passing again and again, but each of them was skillful enough to dodge the other's arrows. After a long fight, Yoshifumi said, "Both of us can shoot arrows precisely to their targets. We

know each other's skills. We are not ancestral enemies. It is time to stop." Mitsuru replied, "We have seen each other's skills. Let's stop. It was a good fight." Their retainers, watching the duel and afraid that their masters might be shot at any moment, were pleased when they heard their decision. After the fight, Yoshifumi and Mitsuru got along very well.

In the glorious, wide-open spaces of the Kanto plain, the duel of the two samurai leaders was prompted by a vigorous spirit of honor. The two samurai fought each other in front of their men because their sense of pride would not permit a less honorable course of action. The story suggests the rise of a chivalrous sentiment among the samurai, as well as the existence of some rules encouraging fighting as a way to prove one's honor. The detail concerning the two leaders' attempts to let each other shoot first is an example. The narrative also describes how, for the heralds who delivered official summons to battle, there was a consensus regarding honorable behavior and attitudes. After exchanging the declaration of war, the messengers should each return to their sides without urging their horses, thus showing that they had sufficient confidence to turn their backs to the opponent without moving in unseemly haste. In this collection of stories, the writer displays deep admiration and sympathy for a courageous, simple, straightforward samurai culture. This is one of the earliest literary examples suggesting that the samurai had developed some rules for combat based upon a strong sense of honor.

Of course, to use a collection of folklore as a source of historical inquiry requires caution. There is evidence that these two rival samurai were actual historical figures who lived in the eastern region of Japan around the mid-tenth century. Therefore, since the event presumably took place more than 150 years before *Konjaku monogatari* was written in the beginning of the twelfth century, it is difficult to take this story as a precise reflection of a historical event.

What we should note from this description, however, is its *symbolic* significance to the early twelfth century. As mentioned earlier, *Konjaku monogatari* appeared in the early twelfth century and was edited by an unknown person(s), who was either a priest or an aristocrat in Kyoto. We can only assume that the compiler heard the story just told, which was probably widely shared among his contemporaries, and considered it trustworthy insofar as it presented an ideal image of the honorable warrior. Samurai culture had apparently reached the stage where it could make a favorable impression on the nonsamurai editor of *Konjaku monogatari*. By contrast, earlier in the mid-Heian period, the samurai had not always looked respectable; indeed, court literature often caricatures the samurai as musclemen who were culturally unsophisticated and therefore inferior to the well-bred aristocracy.

In the meantime, some samurai, in particular those who lived in prosperity far from Kyoto, acquired a greater sense of confidence about their own military lifestyle. And their distinctive culture, based upon their identity as military specialists, sometimes made a good impression on the people in the capital city. Even though their manners were simple and unpolished, these samurai with their culture of honor appeared to be men of principle, at least compared with the crafty and underhanded courtier-politicians.

An important asset of the samurai culture was a distinct military achievement-oriented attitude, brought into late ancient Japan through the samurai's military professionalism. In contrast, the ancient Japanese state, centering around the emperor's court, did not fully adopt a meritocratic system of recruiting elites, as had its Chinese model. Instead, the higher governmental positions continued to be occupied by men born into the limited bloodlines of the aristocracy. Conversely, though samurai houses were also largely considered hereditary, the very nature of military professionalism, which required constant demonstration and improvement of military efficacy, prevented the samurai from taking their inherited positions for granted.

In general, *Konjaku monogatari* contains many descriptions of the lively atmosphere of the samurai's *yakata* (residence house), implicitly contrasting it with the bland, passive existence of the aristocracy in Kyoto.[52] The samurai are usually described as uncomplicated, energetic, straightforward men who would risk their lives in order to keep their good name as warriors. For example, as *Konjaku monogatari* recounts, a mighty samurai, Taira no Koremochi, usually called Yogo, when on the verge of defeat by an unexpected attack did not run for the hills as his retainers advised him to do. Yogo said to them, "It would be the shame *(haji)* of my descendants," and sprang to his feet with determination. His unexpected courageous counterattack routed his enemies. Yogo thereafter increased his reputation and was renowned as the strongest samurai in the eastern region.[53]

The leaders of the samurai bands realized that gaining the trust of capable samurai was crucial to their success, and that having a fearsome reputation was important for keeping the confidence of otherwise unruly warriors. Anyone who acquired the stigma of cowardice was at a serious disadvantage in this competition for power. Honor, conversely, was instrumental to success. Yogo's not attempting to escape from the enemy was an instinctively calculated action. If he had fled, he would have been more likely to survive, but he would have surrendered his reputation as the leader of his samurai band. Honorable men needed to be perpetually alert competitors on the field of honor in order not to damage their good names as warriors. This strong drive to keep one's good name was one of the most impressive aspects of the samurai culture in the eyes of non-samurai observers.

The development of certain rules for fighting and the cultivation of a chivalrous spirit should not be overemphasized, however. This idealized image aside, the daily pursuit of honor in the twelfth century may not have been so assiduous as the foregoing stories imply. The war literature of the period also suggests that it was common for the samurai to violate rules of warfare when it suited their purpose.

The following famous episode from *Heike monogatari* provides one such example. Two warriors were engaged in competition for the honor of being the first rider to charge at the Battle of the Uji River, a crucial battle between the Minamoto and Taira clans (riding first was usually considered one of the most daring and honorable actions in battle). The Minamoto troops commanded by Minamoto no Yoshitsune came to the Uji River. The bridges were pulled up and "angry white waves raced downstream." Two warriors of the *genji* troops, Kajiwara Genta Kagesue and Sasaki Shirō Takatsuna, galloped into the river, each resolving to be the first man across. Falling behind, Takatsuna called out to Kagesue:

"This is the biggest river in the west. Your saddle girth looks loose; tighten it up!"

Kagesue must have feared that the girth did indeed require tightening. He stiffened his legs in the stirrups to hold them away from Suru-mumi's belly, tossed the reins over the horse's mane, undid the girth, and tightened it. Meanwhile, Takatsuna galloped past him into the river. . . . [As he arrived at the opposite bank,] Takatsuna stood in his stirrups and announced his name in a mighty voice. "Sasaki Shirō

Takatsuna, the fourth son of Sasaki Saburō Hideyoshi and a ninth-generation descendant of Emperor Uda, is the first man across the Uji River!" [54]

Interestingly, the unknown author of *Heike monogatari* did not criticize Sasaki Shirō's behavior, even though he had cheated his competitor in order to gain the military merit of being the first rider in a charge. Indeed, this kind of violation of the rules of fair fighting was not uncommon among the samurai in the war literature of the period.

Breaking the rules of warfare in order to exalt one's name as a mighty warrior was often tolerated, because people at that time thought of killing and fighting as primal *musha no narai* (customs of the samurai), and exhibitions of one's manliness and superiority on the field were more important than chivalrous decency. Such conduct was further legitimated by the development of samurai vassalage within the public domain. With the maturation of the samurai master-follower relationship, the warrior's self-interest regarding participation in battle—the expectation of economic rewards—was often camouflaged by the moral principles of trust associated with vassalage. The individual warrior took part in battle in order to fulfill his promise to the master that he would contribute his military might whenever called upon to do so. Thus, fighting courageously and achieving military merit became not simply a matter of self-interest but an element in the very foundation of the master-follower relationship.

Furthermore, as the samurai's political power increased, warfare was often conducted as a public cause; that is, the war was ordered by the imperial court, or later, following the establishment of the shogun's authority, directly by the shogun. If the higher authorities had taken responsibility for the war, and if the samurai's military action was seen as a contribution to the public good, the warrior's individual rule-breaking might be more easily tolerated. This understanding of the close connection between military honor and vassalage will bring us to an examination of the structure of samurai vassalage in the next chapter, through which we will further articulate the social-organizational context in which the samurai's distinctive culture emerged.

3 *Vassalage and Honor*

Vassalage: An Organizational Innovation

The emergence of the samurai as the dominant class in Japan was conditioned upon the development of their own hierarchical network of (unequal) reciprocity, or vassalage. Distinctively different from the patron-client relationship in Heian court society, in which a sense of fealty was extremely rare, the samurai master-vassal relationship from the late twelfth century incorporated the formation of strong and durable bonds that gave men the incentive to risk their lives in battle. Such an intense solidarity in patronage relationships was never before found in Japan in comparable forms of alliance. It is important to note, however, that the strength of samurai vassalage lay not simply in its subordination of previously independent vassals, but rather in its successful organization of the samurai into mutually profitable forms of alliance as well as long-term relationships. Only with the organizational innovations of vassalage were the samurai able to transform themselves from the military servants of the Heian ruling elites into a dominant class in their own right.

Before the rise of the Kamakura shogunate, in the late twelfth century, the samurai were involved in three kinds of patron-client relationship. First, some major samurai became the direct clients of the Kyoto aristocracy. In Kyoto, the samurai served as guards for aristocrats and for the imperial court. In return, the samurai tended to use the influence of the aristocracy to increase their own power. Second, many samurai built up connections with *shōen* owners through their work with the management and supervision of *shōen*. Finally, most local samurai had a client relationship—vassalage—with powerful regional samurai that later developed into the large-scale network of reciprocity typical of the samurai class as a whole. It is important to note that samurai vassalage was not yet an exclusive form of client relationship in the late Heian period, because a samurai often had a number of patrons in order to secure his territories. Thus, samurai vassalage and a hierarchical network with older authorities existed side by side. The samurai were caught in this complex web of overlapping clienteles in an ongoing struggle to keep their properties secure.

The Emergence of the Samurai Hierarchy

In the late Heian period, the descendants of the military aristocracies expanded their influence in local areas. They had retained some elements of so-called noble blood, and they often held legitimate military positions in the organization of the ancient Japanese state. Highly respected because of their lineage, and connected to the central government, they were able to form the core of local samurai solidarity. The development of samurai vassalage had been centered around those *tōryō* leaders, who held respected social and political positions in the ancient state, and it brought the samurai onto the central stage of history; by constructing such intraclass coalitions, the samurai turned themselves into serious players for high political stakes.[1]

The Minamoto clan (also known as *Genji*) and the Taira clan (also known as *Heishi* or *Heike*), two houses of military aristocracy that both claimed lineal descent from the imperial family, emerged as the most powerful warrior leaders. Indeed, the eventual sequence of wars in twelfth-century Japan involved leaders from these two great clans. At first, in the mid-twelfth century, the Taira clan gained temporary hegemony, creating a house-governmental office in Kyoto. Because of its relatively small number of dependable vassals and its consequent inability to suppress the power of the Goshirakawa *In* (a retired emperor who, in the position of *In*, yielded actual power in the court government in contrast to the emperor, who by then had become quite powerless in practice), however, the Taira failed to establish a government run by samurai that kept itself out of the *ritsu-ryō* politics of the emperor's court.

The war against the Taira in 1180 was waged by a league of influential samurai families in the eastern provinces, led by Minamoto no Yoritomo, scion of the Minamoto clan. After defeating the troops of the Taira in 1185, Yoritomo established the first government fully under samurai control, the Kamakura shogunate.[2] His success was facilitated by strong pressures from the eastern samurai bands to legitimate their landholdings. Unlike the Taira regime, Yoritomo refused to be drawn into the imperial political order, and he gradually developed independent governmental institutions in Kamakura at a distance of a dozen days from Kyoto.

Yoritomo claimed the highest political authority in the hierarchy of the samurai. To be sure, the continued existence of the imperial court at Kyoto resulted in a dual structure within the medieval Japanese state; therefore, the samurai's connections with *shōen* proprietors, usually Kyoto aristocrats or religious institutions protected by the legal code of the imperial court, also continued even after the formal establishment of the new samurai regime. However, after the war of 1221, in which the Kamakura forces defeated the imperial troops, it was clear that the shogunate was the stronger power.

The Kamakura regime deliberately located their political capital, Kamakura, a considerable distance from the courtly cultural center of Kyoto. The Kamakura samurai cultivated a fierce pride in their military identity and attempted to overcome their feelings of cultural inferiority. The early development of samurai vassalage, their distinctive form of military alliance, was clearly an important step in the extension of their power base and cultural confidence. On the one hand, the Kamakura samurai strongly admired the aristocratic high culture and often sought to learn the characteristic manners of the aristocracy, such as courtly etiquette and the composition of poetry *(waka)*. The artistic refinement of the emperor's court attracted the samurai, who did not have such a cultural resource. On the other hand, the politically astute among the samurai were well aware of the dangerous aspects of emulating this sophisticated courtly lifestyle. Thus, though they appreciated the elaborate artistic products of the court culture, the samurai attempted to construct their pride around military values.

The Kamakura Shogunate and Its Direct Vassals

Those samurai lords who were able to make themselves direct vassals (*gokenin*) of the shogunate gained a critical advantage within their local communities. The Kamakura shogunate began with the formation of personal relationships of trust between the shogun Yoritomo and individual vassals.

The samurai's primary territories, which they or their progenitors had originally brought into cultivation through reclamation, were called *hon-ryō* (literally, "original territories").[3] The shogunate secured and authorized their ownership of these territories and protected a *gokenin*'s rights *vis-à-vis* the provincial government office and the Kyoto *shōen* lords. As the samurai were still struggling to secure their landownership, the authorization of their rights over original territories was the greatest benefit they could gain from the shogun. With the power of the shogunate behind them, the *gokenin* were able to encroach upon the *shōen* system and expand their control considerably. The *gokenin* also gained a critical advantage over those samurai who had not yet become direct vassals of the shogunate.

In addition, as a consequence of several conquests in the process of shogunate state-making, large areas of land once owned by the shogun's enemies were distributed to the vassals. These gifts came in the form of various *shiki*, offices and privileges attached to certain estates or territories. Receiving such a privilege was considered "a new debt," and the land was called *onryō* (land connected to indebtedness). Samurai who had secured the original territories carried a debt (*go'on*) to the shogun as well. In return for both types of debt, vassals owed service duties (*hōkō*), in the form of an obligation to supply armed forces at their own expense whenever the shogunate ordered them to do so. The basic organizational principle of samurai vassalage was simple: an exchange of debt for service, or *go'on* for *hōkō*.

The Kamakura shogunate was established on the basis of an alliance of major samurai lords in the eastern region, and Yoritomo's major vassals in particular had displayed an independent spirit at the beginning of the Kamakura period. This drive for autonomy was not limited to the major *gokenin*, however. Since most of the *gokenin* samurai emerged autogenously, that is, they had acquired their land (*honryō*) by their own reclamation and military force, the relative independence of the samurai *vis-à-vis* the shogun was the prevailing characteristic of the Kamakura shogun-*gokenin* relationship.

Usually, the head of the samurai house, a *sōryō* (a head of the house) entering vassalage, represented both the members of his own *ie* (house) and those of the smaller *ie* subordinate to his own. *Sōryō* were granted extensive autonomous powers (defined by the official code of the Kamakura shogunate) over the members of their *ie*. In turn, they owed the house's military obligation to the shogun as direct vassals. The Kamakura shogunate's collective body of direct vassals ranged from the holder of a small plot of land who was able to supply one or at most a few family members as mounted warriors, to the head of a large samurai clan incorporating hundreds of mounted warriors. These larger bands usually contained warriors from the same lineage as well as warriors from outside the original kinship. The latter formed a vassalage relationship with the head of the band, who was usually the *sōryō* of a large clan. For these rear vassals, the relative autonomy of the *gokenin* led to a general attitude that, in principle, "the master's master (shogun) is not our master."

The shogunate was not able to intervene in the internal affairs of the samurai houses, to deal with such matters as questions of inheritance, an area under the control of the head of the *ie*. The Kamakura shogunate confirmed a samurai's designated heir and succession upon the father's request, but even after this confirmation by the shogunate the father could change his mind and appoint another heir.[4] Each samurai's house was thus effectively an independent organization, allied and united with other houses under the coordination of the shogun. Indeed, the function of the Kamakura government was to control and mediate the "international relations" of these independent social organizations.

Autonomy and Heteronomy in Vassalage

Reflecting their relative socioeconomic independence, the Kamakura *gokenin* often expressed their sentiment of honor in the idiom of defiance. Hatakeyama Shigetada, a famous vassal of the Kamakura shogunate, proudly claimed his pride when it was doubted that he had planned a conspiracy against the shogunate: "I Shigetada, a brave soldier, have been rumored to make my living by robbing people's wealth and treasures through intimidation with my military might. If this reputation about my way of life would have been an empty one, it would be dishonorable *(chijoku)*." Shigetada continued, "However, it is always honorable *(bimoku)* for a samurai [even though it is not true] to have a reputation of organizing a rebellious plot."[5] In the following example, we find Kumagai Naozane, a smaller property-holder who had the reputation of being a brave and stubborn warrior, acting assertively when a matter touched his sensitive warrior pride.

According to *Azuma kagami* (*The Mirror of the East*, the shogunate's chronicle), in the third year of Bunchi (1187) an annual *yabusame* ritual (a game in which mounted warriors shoot arrows on the run at fixed targets) was conducted at the shogunate's official shrine, Tsurugaoka Hachiman. Many samurai were assigned to different tasks during the ritual, and Kumagai Naozane was asked to stand and hold the targets. He was very angry about this assignment: "All the vassals of the shogunate are equal fellows. Those who were assigned to be shooters were mounted, but the men taking care of the targets were on foot. It looked as if there was a hierarchy. I just could not accept such an order."[6]

In the community of the samurai, riding on horseback was an important indicator of status. Only mounted warriors were considered real samurai. The shogun Yoritomo tried to placate Naozane by saying that responsibility for the targets was not inferior to shooting, but Naozane refused the task. Because he rejected the order of the shogun, a part of Naozane's property was confiscated.[7] For this stubborn samurai, the notion of equality among the vassals of the shogun was a part of his sense of honor that he could not compromise. The episode indicates vividly how the indomitable spirit of the samurai's honor was connected to his sense of independence and dignity. The relative socioeconomic independence claimed by followers in the medieval system of vassalage created the basic sentiment of samurai culture, which embraced the individualistic pursuit of a reputation for strength and power.

In spite of all this, it would be misleading to stress only the autonomous dimension of early medieval vassalage, for the dimension of loyalty was apparent as well. A considerable amount of contemporary samurai literature movingly describes the death of loyal samurai who chose to share their master's fate. For example, an old warrior in a desperate battle said, "I have been serving this master until my old age. Now the master is also not young. Since he is facing his last moments of life, why should we not perish together?" He then urged his horse into the mass of enemies.[8] The old warrior and his master are described as being united, not by a calculated exchange of debt and service, but by a close personal bond. "We have vowed to die at the same place" *(shinaba issho de shinan)* is a warrior motto that frequently appears in the war literature, and such manifestations of steadfast loyalty and fellowship constitute the most moving part of that literature.[9] The samurai developed a distinctive mental disposition, style of emotion, and spirit of self-sacrifice based upon the master-vassal relationship and their professional duties in military life.

We cannot fully understand the warrior's willingness to die on the battlefield without considering the development of the samurai's master-follower relationship. There had been, of course, various networks of patronage among the aristocracy centering around the emperor's court. But aristocratic patronage was always characterized by a calculating attitude and never developed emotional and personal ties strong enough to merit the gift of one's life. The strong solidarity of a samurai band consisting of a master and his followers was a very different kind of social bond from what had been previously known to the Japanese. Master and follower were united not only by the exchange of interests—the foundation of their relationship—but by emotional and personal ties as well. Compared with the other contemporary forms of social alliance and patronage, samurai vassalage had a distinctive advantage in its ability to mobilize men's devotion to the point where they were willing to fight to the death.

To be sure, actions of loyalty were not simply natural outgrowths of a warrior culture. There was an aspect of intentional ideological promotion to the shogunate's conduct, evident in certain passages of *Azuma kagami*. For example, when the shogun Yoritomo attacked the Fujiwara clan of Ōshu, Kawada Jirō, a vassal of Fujiwara Yasuhira, betrayed his master and brought the head of Yasuhira to the shogunate's headquarters. Jirō not only failed to receive the reward he expected, but was executed as an "example to others."[10] Kawada Jirō's conduct was considered dishonorable because, as a hereditary vassal to the Fujiwara clan, he should have paid his debt of loyalty. As this example shows, the Kamakura shogunate strove to control the centrifugal tendency of the samurai vassals by introducing an ideology of loyalty. It became the norm in this period that those who owed *on* (debts) to their masters repay them with *hōkō* (service). Those who had received *on* and yet manifested disloyalty to their masters were considered to have deviated from "the way of bows and horses," that is, proper samurai conduct.

Clearly, there is much confusion as to what was considered honorable in the social relationships of the Kamakura vassals, and that is exactly the point I wish to make. Embellishing and protecting one's honor and reputation were vital sentiments in the community of the samurai, and that community was highly institutionalized in the Kamakura period. But the content of the concept of honor was in flux. Honor had not been formulated into a fixed standard of behavior, nor was it defined by legalities. Decisions as to what action could be considered honorable were highly contextual and individualistic. Therefore, under the same banner of honor, the samurai often took the seemingly contradictory actions of absolute loyalty and defiant betrayal.

The question of autonomy and heteronomy among the vassals of the Kamakura shogunate has been a much-debated issue among Japanese historians, and the disputes cannot be separated from the social and intellectual climate of modern Japanese society. A well-known prewar Japanese scholar, Watsuji Tetsurō, once called the samurai master-vassal relationship "absolute subordination" and "the ethic of devotion."[11] This view reflected the nationalistic ethos in the prewar period, which hoped to find the pure model of devotion in the early samurai spirit. Naturally, Watsuji's perspective has been seriously criticized by postwar historians. Besides, when one considers the examples of headstrong *gokenin* like Hatakeyama Shigetada or Kumagai Naozane, it is difficult to accept Watsuji's opinion. In contrast, the postwar historian Ienaga Saburō, in search of an antiauthoritarian tradition in Japanese history, stresses the reciprocal and contractual relationship of medieval vassalage, which resembled that of its European counterpart.[12] Against a view that overemphasizes the heteronomy of the vassals, Ienaga's findings stress the autonomy of the medieval samurai. Although I agree with his view of autonomy, Ienaga's perspective is not without its share of problems. First, although it may have included a sense of reciprocity, the Japanese vassalage system did not develop the abstract concept of a "contract" in the Western sense. Second, an overly autonomous picture of the Kamakura samurai cannot explain the number of documented cases of self-sacrifice and heteronomous behavior on the part of subordinates.

At this point, in order to avoid a conceptual tangle, it may be helpful to assume that there were two ideal types of samurai master-vassal relationship: the first one representing the autonomous aspect characterized by socioeconomic autonomy on the side of followers; the second one stressing the heteronomous dimension of the relationship, wherein the samurai was tightly incorporated into his master's house.[13] These hereditary rear vassals in the second category were obliged to live in a heteronomous relationship with their masters. They also naturally cherished a sense of shared destiny that led to heartfelt devotion strengthened by shared experiences in battle.

In contrast, vassals in the first category, with their own lands, tended to display more autonomous and reciprocal relationships with their masters. The relationships between the Kamakura shoguns and their *gokenin* typically fell into the first category because of their characteristic autonomy and reciprocity. Of course, the actual social relationships between masters and followers assumed a variety of forms along the continuum between these two extremes, and each particular power relationship in vassalage differed to some extent from any other one. Considering the material under review in this chapter, it is natural to conclude that there existed a broad range of master-follower relationships, taking a variety of forms.

The early samurai culture of honor centering around the relationship between masters and vassals thus stood balanced between an honorific aspiration to autonomy and an honorific regard for loyalty. The life of the samurai was constituted by successive moments of tension between autonomy and heteronomy, tensions that reflected broad variations in power relationships between masters and followers, and that could tear apart the very patron-client relationship that had given rise to them. Ideally, this tension could always be resolved in the samurai culture of honor by the requirement that, within any given moment, one should act with all one's mental and physical powers to make a point of honor.

Private Conflict Resolution and Public Jurisdiction

Reflecting the relative social autonomy of the samurai *ie*, local bands of independent samurai during the medieval period resolved their differences mostly by appealing to the principle of self-determinism, namely, *jiriki kyūsai*, or self-redress of grievances. Other social classes, too, more or less accepted the validity of this principle. The use of force was common, and the honor and pride of individuals and groups often erupted into open hostilities. Quarrels and fights (usually called *kenka*) were wars of honor fought on private terrain, and any damage incurred in a quarrel had to be redeemed through acts of revenge. The principle of *jiriki kyūsai* represents a critical characteristic of medieval Japanese society.[14]

To be sure, the samurai's violent quarrels, fights, and conflicts were not always touched off by chance incidents (often called *tōza no kenka*, or accidental quarrels). Many conflicts had deeper economic and political roots in boundary disagreements, irrigation disputes, and the like—cases in which both parties to the conflict used violence to resolve the matter in their favor. A violent conflict of this sort deriving from economic causes was also often simply called *kenka* (quarrel) in medieval Japanese jurisprudence. Indeed, these two kinds of conflict were often indistinguishable. First, an accidental quarrel often originated from previous economic conflicts; and second, material conflicts were often translated into the idiom of honor.

In both types of dispute, the mentality that encouraged private fights was the product of social circumstances in which many groups claimed the right to use force to advance their own purposes.[15] Medieval public authorities did make serious attempts to control the prevailing custom of private retribution. For example, the Kamakura shogunate instituted curbs on the instinctive use of force in an accidental situation.[16] The thirteenth article of the Kamakura shogunate's code of 1232 *(Goseibai shikimoku)* speaks, for example, of "the offense of beating a person." This article opens with a rather positive expression of the concern for honor, when it describes a beating or fight as "caused by the intention of vindicating honor." Yet, the code continues, "it is a serious offense."[17] The Kamakura shogunate and the successor Muromachi shogunate both tried to prohibit violent resolution of personal conflicts by providing alternative forms of arbitration. Indeed, effective adjudication was an integral part of the shogunates' hegemonic foundation.

Accidental quarrels among vassals were obviously a threat to the shogunate's maintenance of the internal order of vassalage, since they might grow into larger conflicts between samurai bands. But what posed an even greater and more persistent danger was disputes over land tenure. The Kamakura authorities were particularly concerned with the prevailing custom of seizing others' territories by force, because such piracy undercut the essential authority and power of the central government.

The shogunate code stated that land and territories should not be taken by violence.[18] The same was true for the code of the subsequent Muromachi shogunate, which repeatedly prohibited private warfare for resolving disputes.[19] If the shogunate could not adjudicate conflicts of interest of this nature, its authority over the samurai would be called into question.

The Kamakura shogunate from its beginning was eager to extend the reasonable system of adjudication to the samurai population at large. The compilation and publication of legal codes and the institutionalization of a court did not imply, however, that the shogun had the police force to deal with boundary incursions, or to recover land already being invaded.[20] Litigations in the Kamakura and Muromachi shogunates could be activated only by outside complaint or accusation generally, and the process remained subject to the initiative and direction of the litigants.[21]

The prevalence of private retribution among the medieval Japanese samurai and the weakness of the public jurisdiction do not imply that the samurai rarely appealed to litigation, however. The medieval samurai made good use of the existing court systems of the Kamakura and Muromachi shogunates whenever possible. Transferring his aggressively individualistic attitude from the battlefield to the court, the medieval samurai could be ferociously litigious. Whether he preferred lawsuits or contests of arms to resolve a conflict depended on the situation of the individual samurai. The shogun's arbitration offered a reasonable solution to those social agents who could resolve the problem by themselves, if they preferred, with violence; in other words, only those who had the ability to defend their own property received assurance of ownership from the judiciary.[22] Thus, the existence of a judicial system not only did not inhibit the spirit of personal responsibility and private retribution; it was built on the foundation of samurai self-determination.

Once a quarrel was brought to their attention, the Kamakura authorities sought to mediate it on the basis of *dōri*, or reasonableness. When he codified the first written samurai law, *Goseibai shikimoku*, in 1232, Hōjō Yasutoki (the Kamakura shogun's "regent") claimed in his letter that the code had "written only what *dōri* dictates."[23] As a jurisprudential term, the word *dōri* appeared most frequently in the literature of the thirteenth century. It was a blend of common sense and established tradition among the samurai. In other words, *dōri* was a principle of consensus that could be accepted by different independent social groups. The Kamakura shogunate stressed that conflicts would be mediated by the principle of *dōri* only after careful investigation. Thus, article 45 of *Goseibai shikimoku* (1232) warned that "punishment without investigation causes deep anger regardless of guilt or innocence. Judgment should be passed swiftly, but on the basis of careful investigation."[24]

Such careful efforts at mediation reflected the realities of the political situation, in which power was decentralized and a number of political groups claimed legitimacy for their use of force. The shogunate mediated these independent social groups' claims as if it were negotiating international conflicts. Both the concept of reasonableness and the principle of self-redress of grievances reflected the relative independence of the samurai's *ie vis-à-vis* the state. In contrast, the concept of *dōri* declined with the expansion of the state even as it restricted the independence of corporate groups. Later, when the Tokugawa state emerged as a pacifier and the ultimate mediator of private conflicts, the Tokugawa-defined law existed in the will of rulers. Against the backdrop of the Japanese historical landscape, characterized by authoritarian power structures and legal culture, I would describe the thirteenth century as the one brief moment in Japanese history when political philosophy put a high value on *dōri*.[25]

Although the notion of *dōri* informed particular acts of medieval adjudication, the concept was never developed into a system of philosophy of law to serve on an intellectual and theoretical level as the basis of the state. Western judicial tradition, by contrast, expanded the moral and philosophical bases of law, stressing the concept of public power as the protector of "justice" during the medieval period. This Western legal concept of justice as rooted in a universal divine or natural order superior to sovereignty, which is central to Western political thought, did not have a parallel development in Japan, where a balance of power maintained by naked force came to the fore more openly. The hierarchical structure of the courts and the legal profession characteristic of Europe never developed in medieval Japan. The relative position of the law and the courts in Japanese conflict resolution appears to be much lower than in the European case.

In short, the high rate of private conflict resolution in medieval Japan reflected a stark social reality—the relatively high degree of social autonomy of the samurai's *ie vis-à-vis* the shogun, and the competitive relationships among the samurai *ie*. The study of the method of resolving conflicts often reveals that the underlying political and emotional dynamics of honor culture operated in the samurai communities.

The *seken*

Concern for one's reputation in everyday social interactions increased with the establishment of the Kamakura shogunate, during which the daily interactions of shogunate vassals became more frequent and complicated. Centered around the shogunate government, a new community was emerging in which information was shared and honor evaluated. How did the samurai culture function in the actual social relations of this community, in peacetime in particular?

Letters (precepts) left by Hōjō Shigetoki (1198–1261) to his family give us a rare insight into the internal operations of this samurai community of honor. Hōjō Shigetoki was an important samurai politician of the period. After the death of the shogun Yoritomo, the Hōjō clan took over the hegemony of the shogunate, including the actual control of the Kamakura government as the shogun's regent, or *shikken*. As a younger brother of Hōjō Yasutoki, the third *shikken*, Shigetoki had assumed important positions in the shogunate. He wanted to transfer the fruits of his wisdom and experience to his sons and family. Two letters, one addressed to his son, Nagatoki, written in mid-life, and another more public set of precepts set down for his family after his retirement are not only the first of this kind of house-precept *(kakun)* composed by a samurai, but also an uncommon primary source of medieval samurai philosophy. The first letter, addressed to his son, was not intended for public consumption, and thus honestly reflected his values and ideas.

From 1230 to 1247 Shigetoki was the high commissioner *(tandai)* in Kyoto, representing the samurai regime to the imperial court, as well as supervising the shogunate's *gokenin* in southwestern Japan. (The *gokenin* in the eastern region, the shogunate's original power base, were more directly tied to the Kamakura shogunate.) Thus, Shigetoki was the effective leader of the southwestern samurai community as well as the shogunate's ambassador to Kyoto. This politically sensitive position trained and honed his political perspectives, sharpening his sense of being a leader of samurai. His experiences prompted an important private letter to his young son, Nagatoki, written in the middle of his career. The letter shows us a frank and candid, often Machiavellian, political philosophy.

As a warrior, Shigetoki shared the belief that military honor was the most important source of reputation; as he wrote to his son, "You should act with imperturbable courage, and you must never be considered a coward; you should constantly train in bow and arrow."[26] His military background comes to the fore here. At the same time, the young samurai should not only not be arrogant, but "on every occasion, try to be charming; when facing others, see to it that they come to think well of you."[27] Shigetoki emphasizes the importance of a humble and polite attitude toward others: "Deliberately take a low posture. Be polite even to persons of no consequence."[28] The father even taught his son some fine points of etiquette, such as how to blow his nose in a well-bred manner so as to avoid public shame. Despite this cautionary camouflage, however, Shigetoki warns his son not to be assimilated into the effete society of the Kyoto courtiers. "[When asked to show your] skill in the polite arts, even if it is something you can do easily, it is best to say that you cannot. . . . You, a warrior, should, [on the contrary,] excel in the skillful handling of public affairs, in possessing sound judgment, and above all, in specializing and excelling in the way of the bow and arrow . . . Never immerse yourself unduly in the pursuit of polite accomplishments!"[29]

The express objective of Shigetoki's letter is to teach his son how to maintain his dignity as a warrior. Its underlying purpose, however, is to inculcate political skills in the young man in order to make him a skillful manipulator of other prideful samurai and underhanded Kyoto aristocrats. Keeping one's honorable reputation was important in this context because it directly affected the outcome of the power game.

Shigetoki's concern for a good reputation in the daily social interactions of the community of honor is obvious when he writes: "Regardless of the benefits it would produce, if any thousands of merits brings you a bad reputation in *seken,* let it go, and stick to your good reputation."[30] To be sure, Shigetoki is not advising his son to be anxious regarding his own reputation, nor does he suggest dispensing with calculation in advancing his self-interest. His intention is the opposite. Controlling and subordinating violent and independent vassals was a genuinely difficult political task, which only the man who grasped the warrior's mindset was able to accomplish. A good reputation in the *seken,* or world of the samurai, was critical for maintaining the confidence of one's warriors. Shigetoki instructed his son, who would become an executive member of the government, that keeping one's reputation was absolutely essential to his future career.

The term *seken* here presupposes the existence of a community that evaluates one's honor and reputation. Shigetoki's usage of *seken* is one of the earliest occurrences of this important word, a key concept in Japanese honor culture. The term was originally Buddhist, implying "the secular world," and was imported to ancient Japan with no particular connection to concepts of honor and shame. In modern Japan, however, the term is predominantly used in relation to one's concern for reputation and refers to sentiments of honor and shame.[31] Indeed, the *seken* is the imagined space of evaluation that extends beyond the limited sphere of one's congenial family members and close associates—that is, *uchi*, or insiders, to whom one can safely expose one's shame. For example, a popular modern expression, *seken tei ga warui* (a bad shape in the *seken*), speaks directly to notions of honor. Avoidance of ridicule in the *seken* has been the popular ethic that has regulated and prescribed Japanese moral behavior both internally and externally. Shigetoki's usage of *seken* in relation to reputation suggests the formation of such an imagined community of shared information (such as the reputation of the samurai) and values (such as the criteria for honor) and, therefore, a certain maturity and institutionalization of the samurai's culture of honor in the Kamakura period.

The term's usage also implies that Shigetoki was situated in just such an informational complex, generated by the rise of a new network of reciprocity—of patron and client relationships—the very change that advanced the development of the medieval state. The samurai's frequent interactions as fellow vassals of the shogunate in the city of Kamakura (as well as in Kyoto, to some degree) were the physical basis of an imagined cultural community in which honor was evaluated.

In teaching political techniques for gaining a good reputation in the *seken*, Shigetoki stresses the importance of congenial personal relationships. For example, he instructs his son in the art of constructing a favorable social climate around him: "Never drink sake, even a single jar, alone. Whenever you have any sake, you should invite all friends of your own status who are able to attend, and have them drink the sake with you. To do so will create an attachment to you."[32]

This advice concerning the importance of personal attachments is of course universal wisdom in the school of political maneuvering. But it was especially necessary within the politics of Kamakura vassalage because the typical master-follower relationship was maintained by the follower's voluntary personal submission to the master. Controlling one's own vassals and extending the hierarchical coalition were the most critical political skills for the heir of any large samurai band. Because the Kamakura vassalage was largely built on the premise of personal trust between master and followers, rather than on any firm legal or organizational foundation, the relatively independent followers were constantly subjecting their masters' trustworthiness to close scrutiny.

In this context, the distinction between two types of followers, those who were incorporated into the house and those who were more independent, became a matter of practical importance for the master. Shigetoki did not forget to impart important wisdom to his son, advising him that the master should treat his men differently according to which type of vassal they were—hereditary or long-term followers versus more independent vassals:

> When men who depend on you for their livelihood and men who only occasionally work for you are together in your presence, you should show more attention towards the latter. For the former, though they sometimes, within your household, grumble against you, are easy to manipulate. But when people outside your control [such as the latter] complain about you, it is only by chance that you may hear about it, and are able to do something [to win them back].[33]

Even within his own house, the capable samurai master should be very careful in order to gain the trust of his subordinates: "You must never show even the young knights in your immediate surroundings what you really think."[34]

Shigetoki's letter reveals the existence of serious tensions within the Kamakura vassalage system, and the consequent delicate attentiveness to behavioral nuances that became necessary for the effective conduct of social relations in the samurai world. Entering the master-follower relationship never automatically guaranteed the vassal's future loyalty to his master. Indeed, continual and deliberate efforts by the master were necessary to keep the trust of the vassals. The samurai always sought to test the capability and trustworthiness of their masters so that they could join themselves only to the men who deserved their loyalty. Only a master who shared the prevailing military ethos and honor could elicit such a strong response from his followers. This tendency constrained masters to use self-control in order to gain a good reputation as a worthy leader of honorable samurai.

Examination of the actual functioning of Kamakura vassalage reveals the social context that affected the nature of the community of honor. The samurai's community in this period consisted of a collection of socially autonomous samurai organized vertically by the system of vassalage. Within this community, the horizontal and vertical dimensions of cultural norms coexisted in inherent tension. Honor was officially bestowed by the authorities; however, the importance of their approval did not mean that the community of honor could be reduced to the hierarchical dimension alone. There also existed a tacit understanding that all members of the samurai class were peers insofar as they were good warriors. A proud individual samurai could claim equal honorific standing within the samurai community regardless of his position in the external political and economic hierarchies. The evaluation of honor in this imagined community of *seken* assumed the presence of the ever-watchful eyes of one's fellow warriors. A competitive attitude that made no allowances for the appearance of weakness in any circumstance was critical to obtaining honorific recognition from one's peers.

In the later Tokugawa period, the world of the samurai was restructured on the basis of a rigid hierarchical principle. In spite of this transition, the notion of samurai as peers—the horizontal dimension of the community of honor—remained strong in the mindset of the Tokugawa samurai. I will analyze this Tokugawa cultural development in closer detail later in this book. We must note here, however, that the important aspect of samurai symbolism, which incorporated tensions between bipolarities such as autonomy and heteronomy, competition and collaboration, as well as between hierarchical loyalty and egalitarian fellowship, was firmly laid down within the social-organizational context of the medieval samurai's world.

4

The Rite of Honorable Death: Warfare and the Samurai Sensibility

Honor as the Catalyst for Change

In the preceding chapters I discussed how the emergence of the samurai class on the main stage of Japanese history was possible only through the warriors' unprecedented use of violence. In this chapter, I shall look at the same social process from a different angle, namely, the samurai's peculiar cultural conjunction of honor, death, and warfare. Of specific importance in this conjunction was a mental disposition that induced a samurai to risk his life for the sake of his reputation, particularly his military honor. This willingness to lose one's life is clear evidence of the emergence of a new norm. The samurai's honorific mentality and unique attitude toward death not only reflected their political economy, which enforced such an attitude, but, along with their professional military skills and technology (including the use of horses, bows, and swords), were a vital force in helping the samurai to achieve political hegemony over the country. Thus, the rise of the ethos of the honorable warrior was as much a catalyst of social change as it was its result.

During the medieval period, the samurai's early culture of honor was construed, not intellectually or abstractly, but as a military mindset and ethos. This "military sentiment" did not imply that honor never developed into an internally held value. On the battlefield, samurai often—though not always—preferred honorable death to the possibility of living in disgrace. That a man's honor was conceived by samurai as something to die for in fact signified the strong internalization of the norm. On this level, honor more than anything else became central to the moral life of the medieval samurai.

The unique samurai mode of battle and death became especially conspicuous after the late twelfth century. In the late Heian period, battlefield casualties were extremely low by modern standards, as the Japanese historian Kōuchi Shōsuke has pointed out, because the defeated warriors simply fled the battle or surrendered to the enemy.[1] The surviving evidence is reminiscent of the ethnographic reports of warfare in other primitive societies in which battling was a ritualistic final stage of conflict resolution. In these instances, even a seemingly large battle with many combatants resulted in only a few casualties. Remaining on the battlefield until he was killed was the last thing on the mind of the ancient Japanese warrior.

The ongoing social, political, and cultural maturation of a professional warrior class in medieval Japan changed this situation. In particular, the newly developed samurai style of patronage (that is, vassalage) nurtured a strong sense of solidarity between a master and his vassals. The organization of the *ie* developed an even stronger sense of shared destiny, expressed by bravery, loyalty, and spirited behavior on the battlefield.

For example, during the Battle of Uji in 1180, which marked the opening of the civil war that eventually led to the establishment of the first shogunate, the samurai of the rebellious group headed by Minamoto no Yorimasa fought courageously in a desperate situation until all had perished. Fujiwara Kanezane, a prominent aristocrat in Kyoto, writing about the battle in his diary, noted with apparent amazement that "the enemy's troops decreased to only about fifty. They were not afraid of death, and did not show any sign of pleading for life."[2] Such sacrificial fighting on the battlefield had rarely been observed before. In this sense, the Uji Battle can rightfully be called the opening of the medieval era, since, as Kōuchi puts it, "medieval battles were characterized by a manner of fighting at the risk of one's life."[3] The emergence of a class of warriors who regarded the battlefield as the place where they would die marked the appearance of a new ethos: the samurai culture of honor.

This culture was not a passive result of social structural change, but an active agent for driving such change. We may consider, as an example, the modification of the prevailing attitude toward "pollution" *(kegare)* in the culture of the imperial court. In royal and aristocratic circles, since the mid-Heian period in particular, contact with death was increasingly regarded as the most dangerous pollution.[4] When the famous poet-aristocrat Fujiwara no Shunzei was terminally ill, he was willing to be quarantined, to spend the last moments of his life in an old, dilapidated temple to avoid contaminating his family. Teika, his son, who visited the temple to see his father, wrote in his diary that he could not stand the "cold air" in the "collapsing temple," and he left the spot at night.[5] The contemporary literature shows that even the emperor's death was treated as a dangerous source of impurity.[6] Thus, social hierarchy evidently did not override the fear of impurity. How could people who subscribed to such a mentality compete with samurai warriors, who were not only unafraid of soiling their hands with enemy blood but also willing to risk their own lives in battle? It became more and more attractive for the aristocracy to leave military affairs to the samurai, partly because of this cultural difference.

Early Medieval Warfare

Samurai warfare was a complex social ritual of death, honor, and calculation. The ideology of honor was embodied, reinforced, and regenerated by the practice of war. This distinctive combination of honor and death was itself closely related to the conduct of medieval warfare in Japan. In order to understand thoroughly the samurai culture of honor in its relation to a peculiar attitude toward death, one must also examine the organization of the military and the style of actual combat.

Throughout the medieval period, the organization of an army was essentially private in nature. When war was declared, mounted warriors accompanied by their private forces took part in the master's battle. These smaller army units were each financed and supplied at the vassals' own expense. Reflecting this private nature of military mobilization, the typical early medieval battle displayed an immature system of strategic command. The mounted men, accompanied by servants, were the major actors on the field.

The samurai hoped to distinguish themselves on the battlefield in order to obtain proper rewards from their masters, as well as to promote their individual and house honor. Medieval battles rewarded individual bravery rather than strategically organized combat, thus encouraging competition in seeking personal honor. Killing a famous warrior or the first rider in a charge was considered an honorable feat, and the successful warrior expected to receive significant rewards. The samurai in this period did not like *uchikomi no ikusa,* or the organized movement of troops, because their honorable behavior and performance could not stand out in a mass of warriors.[7] Minamoto no Yoshitsune, a military genius and younger brother of the first shogun, Yoritomo, and still one of the most popular military heroes in Japan,[8] was actually disliked by his contemporary samurai vassals because his strategic deployment of troops deprived individual samurai of opportunities to show off their military capabilities.[9] The warriors were less concerned with the organizational placement and disposition of masses of troops than with the demonstration of individual military skill and merit. Indeed, the individualistic character of the medieval samurai will come as a refreshing surprise to anyone who subscribes to the conventional stereotype of the Japanese as conformists.

Actual combats on the medieval battlefield were thus colorful rites of violence, death, and honor. A one-on-one battle between mounted warriors opened with a ritualistic "declaration of names," in which the warriors proudly announced their names and often listed the place names of their territories and the honors they and their families had achieved. For example, *Heike monogatari* reports that a proud warrior named Imai Shirō spurred his horse into the troops of the enemy and issued the following challenge defiantly, at the top of his voice, while standing on horseback: "Listen to my voice if you are far away, and come closer to see me if you are nearby. This is the very man, Imai Shirō Kanahira, the nurse brother of the lord Kiso, age thirty-three. Even the lord Kamakura [Yoritomo] knows me; knows that there is such a warrior. Kill me and show him my head!"[10]

In early medieval warfare, mounted warriors were always the major fighters. They wore heavy, colorful armor and weapons. They often sought to fight other famous warriors, because killing a samurai with a great reputation was considered more honorable than defeating an opponent of lesser stature. Their retainers on foot usually were only present to assist their mounted masters and did not play a crucial role in combat. One of these retainers always carried the house flag, in order to distinguish his master's presence. When the master died in battle, it was often the foot retainer's job to proudly announce his master's honorable death.

Warfare was the most intense configuration in which the samurai's quest for glory and honor could be conducted. Battles represented successive moments of tension through which the individual samurai's commitment to honor was tested, and which offered opportunities to win official recognition of that honor. "Lifting one's name *(na)*" was the most important thing on the battlefield, and a samurai hoped to be commended for his performance in the record of his commander, and afterward to be reported to the shogun. This honor-seeking mentality was of course combined with an instrumental intention. Unless "recognized" by one's master, a brave action was useless, as it resulted neither in gaining honor nor in receiving rewards from the master. Thus, the samurai always ensured that their performances were witnessed by their comrades.

To distinguish themselves, warriors wore colorful pieces of armor and distinctive helmets, and they often carried small flags on their backs. After the battle, the victorious commander usually examined the severed heads and listed all the notable individual performances of warriors, including the first rider in the charge and those who had died an honorable death on the battlefield. After recording the warriors' merits, he reported them to the shogun. In the early medieval period, when warfare was still an aggregation of individual warriors' battles, the commander's chief task was to focus the samurai's honor-seeking energy in the best direction. Internal competition among the troops was thus as heated as the fight with the external opposing force.

The structure of medieval Japanese warfare contributed an important factor to the culture of honor. One-on-one combats in medieval battles encouraged the samurai to strive for individual excellence and reputation. Even though the *ie* was a significant unit of fighting and honor, warriors still tended to seek distinction on an individual basis. A contemporary illustrated narrative scroll describes the experience of a young samurai named Takezaki Suenaga, who went to great lengths to have his military performance properly recorded, honored, and rewarded. By acting independently from the troops of his clan force on the battlefield, the man acquired distinctive merit as the first warrior to meet the Mongol army that invaded Japan in 1274. Unfortunately, the note from the local commander that mentioned his brave action was never officially sent to the shogunate. Despite his relatives' opposition, the frustrated Suenaga decided to file a grievance with the Kamakura shogunate. After traveling for two months from Kyūshū to Kamakura, Suenaga fiercely complained and persuasively argued his case in front of a magistrate in the Kamakura shogunate. Finally, the shogunate accepted his argument and generously rewarded this assertive man. The pictorial scroll with its detailed captions was later painted at the request of Suenaga, who wanted to record his brave fights on the battlefield as well as his grievance and eventual victory in Kamakura.[11]

As this case shows, although the basic combat unit was the *ie* supervised by a *sōryō* (a head of the *ie*), samurai often wanted to be distinguished as individuals, and they hoped to be honored and rewarded by the shogun according to their personal merits. The experience of these military professionals raised the individualism of the samurai to the point where honor was no longer confined to the collective.

It is important to note that during this period the samurai were perceived as having a somewhat open social status. It was true that most medieval samurai were samurai because they were born into the houses of the warrior class. But unlike their counterparts in the Tokugawa period, the medieval samurai were not able to rest comfortably with the fact of their hereditary status. Constant struggles and frequent battling over the control of land required the samurai to maintain their reputation of strength, capability, and trustworthiness. In other words, performance rather than family name, achieved rather than ascribed status, was the salient feature in the identity of the medieval samurai. As has been mentioned, in adopting recruits the ancient Japanese state never fully adopted a meritocratic system. Rather, it was those born into the limited bloodlines of the aristocracy, especially the Fujiwara clan, who occupied high governmental positions. Conversely, though samurai houses were largely hereditary, military professionalism, requiring constant demonstration and improvement of military efficacy, prevented the samurai from taking their inherited positions for granted. The centuries-long domination of the warrior class had a significant impact on later individualistic and achievement-oriented aspects of culture in Japan.

Severing enemies' heads was an important custom of samurai warfare (see Illustrations 2 and 3). During the medieval period, a major victory would always end with the piling up of dozens, even hundreds, of chopped-off heads in the commander's quarters. *Azuma kagami* recorded that the insurrection of Wada Yoshimori in 1213 yielded 234 heads of defeated warriors, which were duly displayed along the banks of the Katasegawa River.[12] The origins of this grim tradition are a mystery. To attribute it to the cruel "nature" of professional warriors does not explain much. The symbolic significance of the human head, standing for personal identity, suggests its possible religious implications, such as are commonly observed in the practice of head-hunting in societies that attribute power and fertility to those who possess the heads. Some scholars have pointed out the similarity between the display of defeated enemies' heads and a hunter's ritual that involved offering hunted animals to the mountain gods.[13] But, since samurai literature does not provide much information regarding the mystical implications of human heads in medieval Japan, the religious significance of human heads to the samurai remains unknown.

Whereas cutting off enemies' heads bestowed a significant honor on warriors, those who were defeated and decapitated were dishonored: an exchange of honor and dishonor. Thus, *Heiji monogatari* describes an episode in which the head of a mortally wounded samurai was cut off by his ally in order to avoid dishonor. When Takiguchi Toshitsune was shot in the neck in battle and had almost fallen from his horse's back, his master ordered a vassal, "Don't let Takiguchi's head be taken by the enemy. Bring it to us." Hearing his master's command, Takiguchi voluntarily extended his neck to his fellow samurai, saying, "That eases my mind."[14] But the dishonor of having one's head cut off should not be overly generalized. Being beheaded after brave fighting on the battlefield could still be considered an honorable death. Indeed, masters generously rewarded the sons of such brave soldiers.

The custom of cutting off enemies' heads might have been institutionalized firmly because, as the scope of samurai warfare was expanded, receiving rewards from their masters became the main object of warriors' participation in battle. In this predominantly agricultural society, the redistribution of land from one's master as the result of a victorious war was the surest way to increase one's wealth. The practice of looting and awarding booty to soldiers, so prevalent in Western warfare until well into the early modern period, was only a secondary attraction for the samurai, because the production of portable goods had not yet reached the stage where accumulation of such items in the average village would have been sufficient to tempt looters.[15] The development of cities and the accumulation of capital were relatively premature in Kamakura Japan, and war was fought primarily over arable land. Only by the recognition of his master could the samurai secure and increase his landed wealth.

Nothing was more certain to win such recognition than the evidence of the enemy's head, proving the samurai's competence in combat. Captives also usually had their heads cut off, though a victorious commander might pardon the captured vassals on the condition that they become his vassals. Sometimes a captive's entering the priesthood was a condition for sparing his life. Taking ransom in the form of monetary compensation to save the lives of captives, a common practice in Western warfare, was rare in Japanese culture. Likewise, captives' becoming slaves, also a common practice in many other societies, was out of the question for the proud professional samurai. Thus, a glorious victory resulted in increased wealth and self-esteem, and defeat most likely meant death. A craving for glory and honor through triumph in warfare was wedded to calculated and "rational" interests in the actions of the samurai.

According to custom, the heads of respectable samurai were cleaned and the hair combed before being examined. The cleaning of the decapitated heads sometimes fell to samurai women. A rare eyewitness account, recorded by the daughter of a samurai living in the castle during a battle, yields a description of this repugnant operation. The young girl, later known as Oan, the daughter of the respectable samurai Yamada Kyōreki, experienced the horror of sleeping beside a collection of severed heads in the Ōgaki Castle of Mino during the great Battle of Sekigahara in 1600. Although Oan's experience was written down in a much later period, I cite from it because samurai women's memoirs detailing the practice of wars are so uncommon:

> My mother and I, as well as the wives and daughters of the other retainers, were in the *tenshu* [the highest building in the castle] casting bullets. Severed heads taken by our allies were also gathered up in this area of the castle. We attached a tag to each head in order to identify them properly. Then we repeatedly blackened their teeth. Why did we do that? A long time ago, blackened teeth were admired as the sign of a distinguished man. So, we were asked to apply a generous coat of *ohaguro* [a black dental dye] to any heads with white teeth. [Tooth-dyeing, a popular practice among the ladies of the court in the Heian period, was also affected by male aristocrats and warriors from the late Heian through the Muromachi periods.] Even these severed heads no longer held any terror for me. I used to sleep enveloped by the bloody odor of those old heads.[16]

The castle was under constant attack from the superior forces of Tokugawa Ieyasu. One day, Oan's brother was killed before her eyes. She was too numb to cry during her residence in the besieged castle: "I did not even have a sense of being alive—all I could feel was fear and terror. But then, afterward, it didn't seem like much of anything at all." Oan later narrowly escaped with her family from the doomed fortress. Here it is important to note that, even in the face of imminent defeat, the cosmetic beautification of the heads was regularly carried out. This act of cleaning the heads was in part a sign of respect for fallen warriors. More to the point, it represented a tribute to the victors' honorific pride as men who could defeat heroic enemies. And the tangible proof of one's prowess, in the form of a pile of severed heads, would certainly result in better rewards from one's lord.

Although hundreds of blood-stained heads were the result of calculated actions, it is not difficult to imagine that the fear and excitement stimulated by mortal combat, and the sharp contrast between death and victory, would also shape the minds and souls of the samurai. It was in this context that a residual attachment to one's life in a desperate situation was considered dishonorable.

The Staging of Self-Willed Death

The moment of death became an important occasion for making a point of honor: a man's control, dignity, and concern for posthumous reputation all fused together with particular intensity at this point. From there, an obsession with honorable and "beautiful" death gradually permeated the samurai culture of honor. Nothing is more symbolically suggestive of the rise of the new culture of honor than the tradition of staging self-willed death.

Another unique institution, honorable death by *seppuku* (suicide by disembowelment), made its first appearance in Japan with the coming of age of the samurai class. It is difficult to say when and how this peculiar practice began, as the earliest cases are found only in war literature. An example can be found in *Hōgen monogatari,* the story of the Hōgen Rebellion in 1156, written prior to the appearance of *Heike monogatari.* Here we read how the mighty warrior Minamoto no Tametomo reacted when it became clear that he was about to be defeated: he cut his belly while leaning against a pillar of his house. Later samurai of the Tokugawa period took this as the earliest example of samurai *seppuku.*[17]

Gikei ki also states that the famous general Minamoto no Yoshitsune killed himself by *seppuku* when his residence was attacked. But since *Gikei ki* is known as a product of the much later mid-Muromachi period, this famous example does not have much validity for the period under discussion.

During the war between the Minamoto and the Taira clans, according to *Heike monogatari*, the famous warriors of the Taira (Heike) clan, who mostly came out of the southwestern region and lived in Kyoto for a long time, did not commit *seppuku*.[18] In the last sea battle between the two clans, for example, a famous general of the Taira clan chose to throw himself into the sea with heavy armor, clutching two enemies in his arms and drowning them with him. In the same *Heike monogatari,* however, we find accounts of warriors of the Minamoto clan performing death rituals bearing a closer resemblance to *seppuku*. Minamoto no Yorimasa in the Battle of Uji is one example. He ordered his retainer to cut off his head: "The retainer shed a tear of sorrow at the thought of cutting off his master's head and said, 'It is difficult for me to do this. If you stab yourself first, I will do that [cutting off the head] later.'"[19] Understanding his retainer's hesitation and sorrow, Yorimasa pierced his belly with his sword and then threw his body onto it.

Another example is the suicide of Imai Shirō, a vassal of Kiso Yoshinaka and a warrior of the Minamoto clan, who demonstrated an even more violent way of taking his life. At the last moment Imai shouted, "Look at me, all the warriors of the eastern region; the strongest man in Japan will show you the model of committing suicide."[20] Putting the top of his sword in his mouth, he jumped on the ground from horseback, piercing himself with his own sword.

These two examples are closer to the *seppuku* ritual of the later period. One may speculate from these cases that the custom of *seppuku* began in the northeastern *(azuma)* rather than the southwestern-central region of Japan; however, the precise origin is still not very clear. In those early days the procedure of warrior suicide in battle was most likely not fixed, although there emerged a distinctive sentiment that placed a high value on displaying one's dignity and courage in the last moments of life. The tradition of the *seppuku* ritual originated in the intense and vehement expressions of warrior pride and moral autonomy in desperate straits. The war literature from the Kamakura period onward often describes *seppuku* in battle, emphasizing the self-willed character of the warriors' deaths, but the most telling examples are found in the early fourteenth century, when the decline of the Kamakura shogunate led Japan into a new era of civil wars.[21]

Unlike samurai of the later period, the medieval samurai committed *seppuku* mainly on the battlefield, when it was obvious that they were on the losing side. *Seppuku* in peacetime was less common throughout the medieval period. *Seppuku* as a form of capital punishment was also much more common in the later period, roughly from the time of the Warring States forward.

We can clearly identify a growing tendency in the medieval period to intensify and normatize the mythical status of self-willed death. From this perspective, we can here discern a process of cultural institutionalization. This process is evident in a comparison of the two most famous war epics of the medieval period, *Heike monogatari* and *Taiheiki*. The former was probably originally written in the first half of the thirteenth century, whereas *Taiheiki* assumed its present shape in the late fourteenth century. In comparing these two literary productions, we find that the culture of self-inflicted death had already undergone a transition. In *Heike,* the warriors are presented as brave, strong-willed individuals who often elect to kill themselves. The method of expressing this honorific mentality (that is, the form of the suicide itself), however, is not yet institutionalized in *Heike.* In contrast, *Taiheiki* allows us to identify the ongoing institutionalization and mythification of "glorious" self-willed death in its description of samurai heroes. Suicides in the form of *seppuku* are common in *Taiheiki,* as well as other war epics of the late medieval period. Whereas *Heike* contains accounts of only 6 men's near *seppuku*-style suicide, *Taiheiki* recounts 68 separate instances of *seppuku* involving a total of 2140 men.[22]

Taiheiki aside, there are many contemporary descriptions leading to the conclusion that many aspects of the samurai culture of death became more and more ritualized in the late medieval period. In short, there was a common sentiment observed in the representation of the brave warriors in both *Heike* and *Taiheiki,* but the latter contained a much more highly institutionalized and ritualized expression of that sentiment.

To be sure, I am not asserting that the emotion-laden descriptions taken from war literature, describing the behavior of dying warriors, reflect exactly the historical reality of samurai conduct. It is important to note, however, that episodes of honorable death are the most moving actions recorded in this literature. In particular, both *Heike monogatari* and *Taiheiki,* which appeal directly to the emotions in their praise of the samurai who die honorably, were spread by traveling musical storytellers, and thus popularized widely among the samurai. The descriptions in this literature reached even those who did not read well, helping to construct the samurai's cultural identity. In particular, *Taiheiki* was the most popular samurai "classic" during the Tokugawa period. Even Tokugawa Ieyasu himself (1542–1616, the founder of the Tokugawa shogunate) enjoyed listening to the storytelling (called *Taiheiki yomi,* or *Taiheiki kōshaku)* from *Taiheiki.*[23] We find numerous instances in a variety of genres of Tokugawa literature, including *kabuki* plays, where themes from *Taiheiki* were adapted—a fact that forces us to reconsider the role of these stories in the symbolic construction of the samurai culture. The medieval codification of the samurai's image in this way formulated a cultural repertoire of narrative and poetry that significantly influenced later samurai's imagination and collective identity.

We must note here the particular role of Japanese Buddhism in the samurai's cultural formulation of "honorable violence." Buddhism in Japan did not, as a rule, confront the samurai's professional killing on a moralistic basis, or mount any *institutionalized* opposition to the emergence of violent customs among the samurai. This lack of institutional controls over the samurai's behavior does not imply that the samurai were not religious, or that Buddhism did not have profound implications for their moral life. Because Buddhism generally considered the taking of life to be deeply abhorrent, the samurai were inevitably concerned with the bad karma that would result from the killing required by their role as professional warriors. It was said that Shogun Yoritomo himself burst into tears issuing from deep religious feeling when a priest reproached him for the gravity of his sins, because he was responsible for the loss of many lives.[24] The prevailing sentimental interpretation of the Buddhist concept of the "impermanence of being" *(mujō)* cultivated a sense of the fragility of life in the minds of the bravest warriors from time to time.

The Buddhist teaching regarding nonviolence did not entail any sustained religious opposition to the samurai's occupational and political activities, however. Also, although the samurai themselves generally accepted the Buddhist definition of warriors as hardened sinners, they did not abandon the profession of arms on this account, or modify their practice of honorific violence. Rather, a popularized version of Buddhism promised warriors salvation and protection by the great power of Buddha—a power sufficient to overcome the negativity incurred while carrying out the business of killing. The philosophy of *Tendai-hongaku* (Philosophy of True Awareness), sometimes considered the medieval Buddhist intellectual paradigm, cultivated an ontological understanding of life and death, as represented by its conception of *shōji funi* (oneness of death and life).[25]

This Buddhist ontological philosophy was made accessible to a broader population through the mediation of the so-called new Buddhist sects that emerged during the Kamakura period. For example, teachers of Pure Land sects of Buddhism characteristically preached death as a way to salvation—that is, as an opportunity for "rebirth in the Pure Land" *(ō-jo)*. Thus, the Pure Land devotee was taught to regard death as a desirable gateway to new existence rather than a fearsome enemy. The Zen sects are famous for their versions of the doctrine of oneness of death and life.[26] Furthermore, unlike native Shinto, Japanese Buddhism generally did not consider death itself a source of impurity *(kegare)*. A classic work of Yanagida Kunio, a pioneer Japanese folklorist, provides insight into this issue; Yanagida remarked that "avoiding death-impurity taboos was a serious constraint on the daily life of the Japanese people . . . Buddhism, in particular its popular versions, simply won out in the competition [with Shinto] because of this critical characteristic, namely, not avoiding the matter of death."[27]

Buddhism touched the minds and hearts of the samurai most directly through its accommodation of the anxiety and religious dread arising from their encounters with death in pursuing their occupation. The Buddhist priests' ceremonious conduction of funeral rituals and their prayers for the well-being of the dead were very attractive to the medieval samurai in this regard, and not only to the samurai alone, but to all classes in Japan.[28] We must note at this point that Japanese Buddhism generally did not confront the growing popularity of samurai practices such as *seppuku*. Rather, it facilitated the progress of the samurai's cultural development further in the direction that it had already been taking.

Honor, Death, and Agency

The complex nature of the structures of samurai vassalage, of their culture of honor, their moral autonomy and heteronomy, and their distinctive attitude toward death was thoroughly and brilliantly illustrated in the last phase of the Kamakura regime.

In the late Kamakura period, as the Hōjō clan's monopoly of power over the Kamakura government increased (the main Minamoto family of the shogun had disappeared after the death of the third shogun, Minamoto no Sanetomo, and the shogunal "regents," the Hōjō clan, had acquired power by manipulating the figurehead shogun), the *gokenin* who were excluded from shogunal politics typically kept their distance from the regime. Two defensive wars against Mongol invaders, in 1274 and 1281, also generated increased frustration among the Kamakura vassals, because their military service in these wars, in which no land was conquered, did not gain them very much. Those who were not satisfied with the shogunate's protection and available forms of reward sought new alliances.

In 1333, the Kamakura shogunate collapsed under attacks by the troops of Ashikaga Takauji and Nitta Yoshisada. Both generals had originally been major vassals of the shogunate, but they had allied themselves with the emperor Godaigo, who had raised an army against the shogunate in an attempt to restore imperial power. When the Kyoto headquarters of the Kamakura shogunate fell under an attack by the general Ashikaga Takauji, the following deadly ritual took place among the Kamakura warriors.

When the defeated Kamakura troops led by General Hōjō Nakatoki fled from Kyoto and arrived at a temple in Banba station of Ōmi Province, their number was reduced to about five hundred mounted warriors. *Taiheiki* describes vividly the last moments of Nakatoki and his men. Nakatoki realized the desperate situation of his army: the time to commit honorable suicide had come. Before his *seppuku,* the general made an eloquent speech in front of his loyal men gathered in the yard of the Rengeji Temple: "Knowing the fate of the Hōjō clan shall come soon, you nonetheless steadfastly followed me to this point. Considering the honor of bow and arrow and remembering our close and long relationship, I cannot find words to express my appreciation of your sincerity."[29] Nakatoki continued, "Though I had sincerely hoped that I could reward you with appreciation, the fate of our clan makes us unable to do so. Now I shall commit suicide here, with which I intend to repay my debt of a lifetime . . . I will swiftly submit my head to the Ashikaga, avoiding punishment and gaining merit for your loyalty." [30] After the speech, he cut his abdomen. One of his loyal vassals, Muneaki, immediately responded by saying, "It was I, Muneaki, who wished to commit suicide before you, and serve as a guide in the dark world . . . Just a moment. Let me follow after you to travel the way of death." He withdrew the sword from Nakatoki's body and, cutting open his own stomach, fell down on Nakatoki's knees. Soon, most of Nakatoki's proud and loyal men willingly followed his lead. *Taiheiki*'s description is gruesome: "All in all four hundred thirty-two samurai simultaneously cut their bellies. Their blood smeared their bodies and ran as if it were the stream of the Yellow River. The corpses filled the yard, and the scene was no different from carcasses in a slaughterhouse." [31]

Although the description of *Taiheiki* itself is a literary reproduction, the graveness of the incident is confirmed by a historical document, left in the temple at Banba, which recorded the names of 189 warriors. With the possibility that unknown minor samurai joined the men, the death toll of more than four hundred is not necessarily a literary exaggeration. It is known that at the time of the fall of Kamakura, another mass suicide took place in Kamakura itself. Such self-willed death on the part of samurai certainly proves the presence of an ethos of fealty to one's master.

A closer examination of Nakatoki's speech, however, shows that this ultimate personal sacrifice was made not simply as the result of loyalty and heteronomy. Nakatoki's speech expressed the conviction that a good master was obliged to reward his men's service properly, and he regretted his incapacity to fulfill this reciprocal obligation. The principle of reciprocal obligation between master and followers is fully respected here. The general did not demand the death of his men, but rather asked them to go on living. The deaths of the four hundred men were honorable because they were voluntarily undergone. Personal will is always an important element in assessing the honor of the medieval samurai. Although the action of committing suicide together with the general appears to be the ultimate altruistic sacrifice, it symbolized the autonomy of the samurai at its core sentiment. Therefore, it was necessary for Nakatoki and his men to confirm this principle of autonomy before the mass suicide ritual. Only through the rhetoric of free moral choice could the samurai's action of fealty and submission gain recognition in the literary tradition—at least, the author of *Taiheiki* believed it to be the ideal death for a warrior.

The mass suicide illustrates both the weakness and the strength of the Kamakura vassalage system. On the one hand, as the loyal men's suicide demonstrates, samurai under the Kamakura shogunate maintained a strong sense of honor and loyalty. On the other hand, examination of the names of the soldiers who died in the Rengeji Temple reveals that most were the personal house men of the Hōjō family head *(miuchi bito)*, or were men who had become powerful in the government because of their strong connection to the Hōjō.[32] Ordinary *gokenin* with their autonomous properties tended to act more independently, and most of them dropped away from the retreating troops before the final scene at the temple.

These seemingly contradictory decisions and actions of the Kamakura samurai at the end of the shogunate, whether in the form of loyal martyrdom or proud betrayal, indicate clearly that the core of the samurai culture of honor lay less in a fixed code of conduct than in a conviction of proud moral autonomy: a firm understanding that a warrior is a person who is capable of deciding his own destiny. Actual decisions depended on complicated sets of factors in which the structural relationship between warrior and master played a large role. As I discussed in the previous chapter, the structure and balance of power between master and vassal varied from one case to another. Judgments concerning appropriate behavior within the culture of honor varied likewise.

The Korean scholar Kan Hang, who was taken captive by Hideyoshi's Japanese troops during the invasion of Korea (1597–1600), left an observation about the violence and fearlessness of the samurai. He noted that in some cases when a lord died on the battlefield, his vassals committed suicide at the scene. Kan Hang concluded that these warriors were so stringently incorporated into their lord's household that their entire livelihood depended on his survival. He felt that the samurai's brave fighting was prompted by their concern for reputation: "If someone is considered to be a coward, he cannot find employment anywhere . . . One with facial scars from sword injuries is deemed a brave warrior and is eventually given a great reward." In contrast to the conventional view of the samurai's loyalty, he concluded that such devotion came from self-interest and was "not at all for the master's sake."[33]

On close examination, Kan Hang's observation appears contradictory. He witnessed the vassals who were willing to commit suicide when their lord died, but he also commented that the samurai were calculating about their own gain. How can we interpret his testimony? For one thing, as a Korean Confucian scholar, Kan Hang did not want to admit the existence of internal morality in his enemy. Therefore, he attempted to make sense of their seemingly contradictory behavior from one perspective, that of calculated action. But committing voluntary suicide cannot be explained by self-interest alone.

Despite this bias, Kan Hang's observation is probably accurate concerning the tight incorporation into the master's house of the men who died with their lords on the field. A strong sense of shared fate and personal solidarity between master and vassals was usually possible only in such cases. Toward the sixteenth century, warlords strove diligently to bind their vassals ever more tightly to their houses (a point I shall discuss further in Chapter 6). Thus, the first part of Kan Hang's observation may reflect the tightening of social controls over vassals in this period. At the same time, the continuous warfare among lords enhanced samurai mobility. In many warlords' military organizations, the *watari mono* (moving samurai), who were self-armed and sold their strength to influential lords, played an important role. Of course, *fudai,* those who were more tightly incorporated, serving for generations, could be more reliable, but sheer military competition drove warlords to employ as many capable men as possible. Thus, the emergence of the distinctive custom of dying with one's master on the battlefield was closely related to the nature and structure of vassalage.

To be sure, the preceding analysis of the samurai custom of self-inflicted death does not imply that these warriors always committed suicide when defeated on the battlefield. Even if we confined our analysis to cases of vassal samurai who had been incorporated into their master's house, and had a strong sense of personal bonding, we would find that they did not always choose to die, if only because they were human beings with a normal instinct for self-preservation. What we should note here is the symbolic significance of the institutionalization of a concept of honorable death. During the late medieval period there emerged a cultural admiration of self-inflicted death as a normatively preferable course of action in certain specified circumstances. This ritual suicide was then surrounded by a moral aesthetic, combined with a highly ritualized ceremonial. The result was a cultural mythification of a moral prescription that was not followed in practice by all samurai.

Furthermore, it is important to realize that the samurai's entire life was not dominated by glorified images of military prowess. As a class of landed elites, the samurai had to devote most of their time and attention to property management, which required constant diligence and occasional coercion or manipulation of the peasantry. It is very likely that the many cases of glorified suicide in late medieval Japanese literature did not represent the average practice of contemporary samurai. At the same time, it is also the case that their lifestyle as military men, which forced them to live on the edge of death, resonated to the idealization of death as it was described in the war literature of their culture.

Further discussion of the "real" or "average" samurai's attitude would be pointless in this context, however. As I have indicated in the preceding chapters, the two aspects of samurai violence were the obverse and reverse of the same coin. Because the use of undisguised strong-arm tactics was so critical to the political economy of the landed military lords, the myth of "honorable violence" became crucial to the collective identity of the samurai class. The institutionalization of ritual death then came to symbolize the cultural maturity of this class, which had successfully advocated the honorable status of their violence.

In the first chapter of this book, I outlined the sociological conceptualization of the samurai vassalage system as a relationship between a principal (the master) and an agent (the vassal). Vassalage was originally a hierarchical mechanism for connecting independent individuals in mutually profitable forms of alliance. The ideology of honor supplied an internal principle of predictability and trustworthiness for future interactions in the master-follower relationship. The emerging custom of self-willed death then crystallized the symbolic nature of this relationship. Indeed, through self-inflicted death, the vassal samurai demonstrated his discretionary power over his life—the proof of his sovereign pride as a landed military lord—but he voluntarily placed it at his master's disposition in return for the trust and power that the master committed to him. The main symbolic meaning underlying the concept of "beautiful self-willed death" was the sovereign pride of a military elite; by virtue of their possession of martial skills, the samurai were the owners of their own bodies, and self-inflicted death signified an independent ability to determine their own fates—to control their own deaths and hence, their own lives.[34]

The rise of this custom cannot be understood only within the purview of the samurai master-follower relationship, however. It must be situated within the wider context of class relationships surrounding the samurai. The practice of an honorable exchange of power and trust gave a competitive edge to those practitioners *vis-à-vis* their rivals and subordinates. We have seen how the samurai struggled to overcome their inferior position as hired soldiers. We should also note, however, that in the medieval Japanese villages, the peasantry had developed an increasingly strong voice and power. The samurai feudal lords struggled to control these independent-minded villagers, and they collected tax revenue from them. A master's commitment to his follower in vassalage (the status of local agent of the master) gave the vassal lord an additional power differential over his subjects. In sum, the custom of self-willed death thus simultaneously epitomized his status as the master's agent and an autonomous individual; it also signified the collective superiority of the samurai class.

Honor and Pollution in Cultivating Differences

The hegemonic aspect of the samurai honor culture was perhaps best articulated in comparison with the fate of other status groups whose social and occupational practices were culturally degraded in the process of power struggles. It is intriguing to observe that the rise of the honorable warrior as a hereditary social category virtually coincided with the emergence of the *hinin* (literally, "nonhuman"), groups that gradually acquired the stigma of social outcasts. The *hinin* originally included a variety of occupational groups who encountered pollution in the course of their daily labor.[35] In the later period, however, they themselves were increasingly considered to be bearers of pollution, and were thus set apart as people who fell outside established status categories. In my opinion, the process of the samurai's cultural reformulation—that is, their struggle to redefine "violence as honorable" to the degree of ritualizing *seppuku*—is better understood in the light of the development of Japan's social outcasts in this period.

The ascendance of the samurai and the simultaneous formation of outcast groups have rarely been discussed sociologically as related issues. However, the works of recent Japanese social historians, especially Amino Yoshihiko, who consider the medieval outcasts as members not only of status groups but of occupational groups as well—"professional persons," or *shoku-nin* (literally, "persons with jobs")—permit further discussion of this important issue.[36] Starting from these historical studies, I propose the following sociological interpretation and synthesis.

In the almost simultaneous emergence of the samurai and *hinin* as social groups, the increased intensity of the pollution taboo in the late Heian court society appears to have played an important role. The fear of being *kegare* (impure) was prevalent in the belief systems of the inhabitants of the Japanese archipelago, and was connected to ancient Shinto mythologies. The usual sources of pollution included *shi'e* (death-pollution, also sometimes called *koku fujō*, or "black-impurity"), *san'e* (birth-pollution, also called *shiro fujō*, or "white-impurity"), and *ketsu'e* (blood-pollution, also called *aka fujō*, or "red-impurity").[37] When people came in contact with an impurity they had to be purified through certain rituals, such as *misogi* and *harai*. Although the notion of pollution and the cultural practices surrounding it developed much earlier, and the belief of *kegare* cut across distinctions of social class, it was the Kyoto aristocracy of the peaceful mid-Heian period who developed the most elaborate codifications concerning avoidance of pollution as dangerous. Evidence of a fear-ridden mentality and the observance of complicated codes appears in the documentary sources of the late eighth and ninth centuries, but such evidence is more prevalent in the tenth and eleventh centuries.[38] The people's high level of anxiety was further intensified by the development of the *goryō* (departed spirit) cult in the ninth and tenth centuries. This cult envisioned the world as a dangerous place filled with malevolent departed spirits. The spirits of people who had died under unusual or suspicious circumstances were considered especially dangerous.[39]

The daily life of the aristocracy in the imperial court was thus occupied with a number of taboos that greatly restricted their freedom of action. The most important locus of purity was the person of the emperor; should the ruler be polluted, his person would not only suffer harm, but the very order of the world might be overturned. In such a dire event, the regular course of political and religious activities would be interrupted. Consequently, a courtier who accidentally contracted death-impurity—which could result from something as commonplace as a mongrel dog's dragging part of a corpse into the courtyard—would be forbidden to visit the palace for a certain period.[40] The palace, shrines, and streets of Kyoto needed to be cleaned meticulously before the emperor's procession passed by. But who would volunteer to remove the bodies of dead animals from the street? And what about a servant's accidental death within the confines of the palace? The person who undertook the important task of removing the cause of the impurity for the welfare of others (as it was perceived) would be thereby defiled and endangered. The gods of the Shinto pantheon were not much help as safeguards against the danger of ritual impurity; the sacred space enclosed by Shinto shrines was regarded as a locus of purity on the same level of importance as the emperor.

The emergence of the *hinin* as social groups in the documentary sources coincided with the increased intensity and institutionalization of avoidance of *kegare* at the imperial court. For example, certain duties related to funerals, the disposition of dead animals, and executing criminals were considered polluted because they involved direct contraction of death-impurity. One type of *hinin*, called *kiyome* (purifiers), was organized under the office of *kebiishi*, which handled law enforcement and security matters for the city of Kyoto. The major tasks of *kiyome* included the cleaning of the palace, shrines, and streets for special imperial rituals. The various other occupational groups that were later regarded as outcasts emerged under similar circumstances. Large Shinto shrines also hired groups of *hinin* to maintain the ritual purity of their sacred spaces.[41]

Like the process of the samurai's emergence, the development of the *hinin* as clearly identifiable social groups prior to the tenth century is obscure at best. By the late eleventh century or so, the *hinin* had organized themselves into their own distinctive social groups; the advent of the term *chōri* (heads of *hinin*) represents their underlying social-organizational development. In the twelfth and thirteenth centuries and thereafter, we have reliable information about the activities that the outcast groups performed; these included certain aspects of funeral ceremonies, criminal executions, and removal of dead animals. During the thirteenth and fourteenth centuries, the groups of *hinin* evolved into powerful armed organizations under the leadership of their heads, *chōri*.[42] Indeed, their armed forces were supposedly mobilized as part of the emperor Godaigo's struggle (ca. 1333) to overturn the samurai's hegemony and restore full imperial authority.[43] Many scholars are of the opinion that the early *hinin* were not necessarily simply regarded as shameful, but were rather considered bearers of some unusual power that could overcome the danger of pollution. They were, however, degraded to the status of outcasts in the course of later social development, during the late medieval and early modern periods. The process by which certain frontier military posts came to be occupied by hereditary lower and middle aristocrats, becoming core positions within the samurai organizations, was similar to the path of the *hinin* groups' formation.

Given this cultural preoccupation with ritual impurity and the concomitant development of outcast groups, it is obvious that the samurai, as a military occupational group, courted a certain amount of cultural danger. We must recall here that those violent samurai who extorted revenue from the local peasantry were often pejoratively described as *toji* by farmers. The same term, *toji* (butchers) or *toke* (houses of butchers), was also used as a negative description of some outcast groups, especially *eta,* who handled dead animals and leather.[44] Because of the samurai's involvement in similar activities, their culture always had the potential to be stigmatized as polluted. The identical action of killing, whether human beings or animals, was, however, interpreted variously as either a source of pollution and exclusion (in the case of the outcast) or a source of honor and power (in the case of the samurai). As this demarcation shows, cultural differentiation between purity and impurity is always socially constructed. There is no such thing as "absolute" dirt; "it exists in the eye of the beholder," as Mary Douglas has rightly noted.[45] This shifting interpretation of impurity illustrates the effectiveness of the samurai's cultural reformulation in redefining their activity as honorable rather than as a defilement. Without the formulation of an honorific military culture that cultivated differences in a way that persuaded the rest of the population that their appetite for violence was honorable, the samurai might have remained the cultural inferiors of the aristocracy, and they might have failed to attain their authority over the agricultural population.

Identification of the hegemonic aspects of the samurai's honorific violence does not imply, however, that their culture of honor can be reduced only to the dimension of class politics. Indeed, the most intriguing aspect of their honor culture was its secure anchorage in both the personal and the collective dimensions of social life. Beyond the operation of hegemonic politics, and the warriors' calculating action with a strong demand for being properly rewarded, lay something that cannot be reduced to instrumental and material considerations. This was an implicit espousal of the sense of honor and glory on the one hand, and of self-esteem, dignity, and moral autonomy on the other. In this context, the last moment of life on the battlefield became the most dramatic setting possible for a definitive demonstration of the warrior's sense of honor. The entire existence of the samurai, his pride in feats of arms, his individuality and dignity, crystallized at this supreme moment, and the consummate manifestation of his honor ended in the peculiar ritual of self-willed death. The fact that the samurai regarded the question of death as the central issue of his existence infused his culture with depth and complexity of meaning. Thus, the samurai's attitude toward death was the clearest expression of the conjunction of violence, autonomy, individuality, and dignity contained within and enveloped by the sentiment of honor.

Once an obsession with honorable death became part of the "style" of samurai honor, the resulting cultural code generated its own dynamics. When a cultural practice is firmly institutionalized and woven into the fabric of other social codes, it acquires its own momentum for resisting the very process of social change that transformed the institutional environment in which that cultural practice first emerged. This wedding of violence and honor, this planting of violence within one's sense of dignity, was thus the most forceful part of the samurai culture of honor, the demon that could not be readily tamed. Subsequent political attempts to domesticate the culture of the samurai met with their most serious resistance in this area.

III DISINTEGRATION AND REORGANIZATION

5 Social Reorganization in the Late Medieval Period

The tendency of the samurai to adopt a policy of strategic calculation with respect to their internal coalitions and alliances became more and more pronounced after the collapse of the Kamakura shogunate, which had maintained relatively effective control over the samurai population. Under the weaker Muromachi shogunate (1338–1573), there was no possibility of reconstructing the samurai class as a cohesive social hierarchy under a single authority through the system of vassalage, given the centrifugal tendencies of the *shugo* (the shogunate-appointed, provincial-level governors). The old political ties that had previously served as liaisons among the various social groups were breaking down.

It is important to note that the preceding Kamakura period had by no means had a static social order. The coexistence of two parallel frameworks of central political organization during the Kamakura period, the samurai regime and the imperial court, made the situation quite complex, and the vassals' centrifugal tendencies had always been present. Yet, the two principles of political organization, the shogun-*gokenin* vassalage and the *shōen* landholding system, still provided the basic framework in which each social group was given a place. During the Muromachi period, neither of these principles provided a dependable source of protection, and the samurai were forced to develop a new system of social order.

Reflecting the unstable power structure of the fourteenth century, various new forms of coalition and patronage emerged in the local samurai communities. None of the authorities of the period were strong enough to guarantee protection of the samurai's land rights. At the same time, the influence of the emperor's court and its associated aristocracy declined steadily after the fall of the emperor Godaigo (1338). The loss of the power and prestige of the imperial court meant a further weakening of the political and legal foundations of the *shōen* landholding system.

The conflicts of interest between the legal *shōen* owners (mostly Kyoto aristocrats and religious institutions) and the samurai proprietors continued throughout the late medieval period. As the *shōen*-based land tenure continued to decline, the *shōen* owners' control over their estates was eroded everywhere. Although this appeared to be a victory for the samurai class, it also fundamentally destabilized the system of land tenure. After the disintegration of the *shōen* system, there was no common rule or publicly sanctioned alternative legal framework for land tenure. The resultant instability provided the samurai with a combination of opportunities and hazards.

In addition to these problematic changes in the land tenure system, the complexity of the sociopolitical structure of late medieval Japan posed difficulties for the samurai class. A bird's-eye view of the late medieval Japanese political structure reveals a confusing picture of struggles among various social organizations with highly dissimilar internal structures and principles. Besides the samurai bands, there were such corporations as villages and occupational guilds, as well as armed temples, which had become increasingly aggressive about their rights and privileges. The armed temples were almost as violent as the samurai lords, and they defended rights and privileges of landownership. These different social groups possessed varying degrees of political autonomy and collective property. Thus, not only the samurai bands but Japanese society as a whole underwent an often violent process of dissolution and reorganization.

Each local samurai house competed with its neighbors to acquire exclusive regional landownership during these heated political struggles. Local independent samurai of this type, after the Muromachi period, were often known as *kokujin* (literally, "province men"). *Kokujin* lords usually became vassals of the *shugo* (provincial governor appointed by the shogun), who increasingly privatized his office and its regional possessions. But the *shugo-kokujin* vassalage system was inherently unstable. The samurai lords of the Muromachi period either changed their sources of protection frequently or sought multiple protectors for maximum security. Often, they had to experiment with various new forms of coalition and patronage in order to survive the increasingly violent political competition.

Of particular concern is the eventual reorganization of local samurai into a recognizable and consistent type of coalition and patronage through a centuries-long series of struggles. The study of this process is interesting, because the very changes that increased the autonomy of local samurai houses in the late medieval period eventually produced an ironic result, namely, their submission to the higher authority of the regionally powerful samurai (*sengoku daimyo*, or "warlords"), which restricted in turn their hard-won freedom. The provincial samurai experimented with various types of alliances, including a protodemocratic coalition called *ikki*, but eventually they yielded to pressures to join the hierarchically structured military machine of the *sengoku daimyo*. The Japanese pattern of samurai reorganization resulted not from horizontal consolidation but from a vertical reintegration of the samurai vassals. The eventual pacification of the samurai under the Tokugawa shoguns at the beginning of the seventeenth century was the final result of this process of vertical consolidation. I maintain that this pattern of consolidation is the key for understanding the subsequent social and cultural developments of this class.

Transformations of *ie* and Marginalization of Women

Some Japanese scholars have maintained that ancient Japanese kinship organizations were primarily matriarchal. For example, Takamura Itsue, a pioneer in women's studies in Japan, advanced the influential argument that ancient Japanese marriage was ordinarily matrilocal, and that successions of family names were consequently matrilineal.[1] This perspective, which regards ancient Japan as the golden age of female power, is sometimes questioned by more recent revisionist scholarship. Records of patrimonial practices among ancient elites appear to suggest a more diverse and complex picture of ancient Japanese kinship structures.[2] At any rate, scholars generally agree that, compared with the social position of elite women in later periods, ancient Japanese inheritance systems and

marriage practices generally gave women more room for social and economic autonomy. A corollary to this situation was flexibility of hetero-
sexual liaisons. According to Sekiguchi Hiroko, a woman's sexuality was
not necessarily controlled by her husband or father before the ninth and
tenth centuries; correspondingly, a marriage was not always a permanent
commitment. It lasted only as long as "the positive feeling of two individuals was there." [3]

Even after the tenth century or so, when the Japanese social elite became more patriarchal in character and adopted a more institutionalized
form of marriage, the women in the emperor's court society in Kyoto
played major social roles. Female members of the court had considerable
power to organize and patronize cultural activities. The sophisticated
feminine taste exemplified in Heian literature was not only supported by
the women at court; it represented the general aesthetic mainstream of
the ancient imperial court culture.

In comparison, the early samurai kinship organization incorporated a
patrilineal structure reflecting the male-dominated character of warrior
society. A woman of the samurai class could still inherit property at this
stage, but the fact that she could not participate in military activities,
whether on the battlefield or in the daily browbeating of the peasantry,
placed her in the minor position of managing the samurai household.
Thus, the rise of samurai hegemony signified the extension of a more
straightforwardly male-dominated social system in Japan; it introduced
more patriarchal kinship principles and practices to Japanese elite circles
while openly celebrating masculine values and culture. [4]

This patriarchal tendency of the samurai houses progressively increased in the later medieval period as the result of the internal transformation of the samurai *ie*. Early medieval samurai kinship structures indicate the presence of a transitional pattern in which the marriage custom
moved away from a mixture of matrilineal and patrilineal elements toward *yome tori* marriage, that is, the practice of taking a bride into the
husband's family. [5] The bride's attachment to her family of origin remained strong, however, since she stood to inherit part of her parents'
property. The position of a widow could also be quite powerful; she often
was the general supervisor of the whole *ie*.

During the Kamakura period, the *sōryō* system maintained the continuity of a samurai lineage while functioning simultaneously as a military
and economic organization. [6] Under this system, children, females in-

cluded, usually inherited a portion of their parents' properties. The *sōryō* (house head) typically received the most important part of the territories, took charge of ancestor rituals, and was military commander-in-chief for the whole house. He also usually entered vassalage as a representative of the house. But children other than the *sōryō* usually inherited their own share of land and other properties.

Structurally, the *sōryō* pattern of inheritance intensified existing centrifugal tendencies among non-*sōryō* children, including daughters. In the Kamakura period, the samurai's *ie* was usually conceived of as a large kinship group with a common descent through the male ancestral line. Because of the practice of dividing inheritances, however, a tendency toward fragmentation was always present. New, smaller *ie* were continually created within the larger *ie* by children who were not *sōryō*. Theoretically, these smaller *ie* accepted the general supervision of the *sōryō*. But after several generations of divided inheritance, the kinship ties between the *sōryō* and the heads of the smaller *ie* tended to become weaker and more distant.

During the later Kamakura period, some *ie* attempted to strengthen the *sōryō*'s power and authority as a response to the growing lack of kinship solidarity. In this context, families in the late Kamakura period began to restrict a woman's inheritance to her lifetime *(ichi go bun)*; that is, a married woman could not pass on her inherited property to her children. In this way, women's families of origin were able to avoid the permanent loss of the property inherited by women to their husbands' *ie*. In addition, the Kamakura shogunate generally attempted to support a *sōryō*'s control over his house, since the shogunate was able to control the large samurai bands only through its affiliations with the *sōryō* who became the direct vassals *(gokenin)* of the shogun. Yet non-*sōryō* heirs of independent socioeconomic means often effectively resisted the supervision of the *sōryō*, increasing their personal autonomy. Toward the end of the Kamakura period, nonheir children of the samurai (usually called *shoshi*) began to demonstrate an increasing tendency to place self-interest above loyalty to the larger clan. Here and there, the *sōryō*'s control over the growing complexities of a more extensive lineage showed signs of slippage.

In response to this crisis, during the late medieval period the samurai houses attempted to establish exclusive regional hegemony over the land by erasing the artificial boundaries defined by the *shōen* system. Originally, the direct vassals of the Kamakura shogunate had territories scattered over various areas. The *sōryō,* as well as nonheir male children and women, each possessed the rights to a piece of these possessions, in various forms of *shiki* privileges attached to *shōen.* Indeed, geographical fragmentation of their territories was one factor that enabled the *shoshi* to increase their autonomy. From a military point of view, however, territories owned by different kinsmen and spread all over the proverbial landscape were difficult to protect and weakened the solidarity of the house. After the collapse of the Kamakura regime, when Japan lacked a stable central authority, it became very clear to the more thoughtful *sōryō* that such a fragmented pattern of landholding was too risky for the survival of the *ie* as a whole. Clearly, land that was not effectively guarded invited invasion by neighboring samurai. The decline of the *shōen* system in the late medieval period only intensified this problem.

This political situation provided additional encouragement for the samurai bands to adopt a single-male-heir inheritance system, based mostly on primogeniture, although it was not uncommon for a son other than the eldest to be selected by the parent as heir. The timing of the introduction of single-heir inheritance varied greatly because it largely depended upon the capacity of the samurai's house to support "spin-off" subhouses. By the fifteenth century, however, the practice of single-male-heir inheritance had become a generally accepted institution.[7] Many smaller houses originated by the *shoshi* that had already established their independence from the *sōryō* house started to practice the single-heir system by themselves, and consequently regarded their status as equal to that of the original *sōryō* house.

After the introduction of the single-male-heir system, children other than the heir and female members became more and more dependent on the house. It became common for nonheir male children to be more or less reduced to the position of vassals. The position of women in the samurai's household was also increasingly restricted in this process.[8] All these newer developments in the samurai kinship structure were motivated by the families' desire to protect and to preserve their properties in the highly competitive world of medieval Japan. As a consequence of this transition, however, the samurai houses became even more patriarchal in character. Emphasis upon masculine warrior pride in their honor culture was in a sense the expression of these organizational realities.

It is important to keep in mind that the individualistic character of the medieval samurai rested on two socioeconomic possessions—armed force and land. And the samurai's sense of self-worth, dignity, and honorific aggressiveness was closely connected to these two possessions. The marginalization of women in the course of the samurai *ie*'s internal transformations thus not only reduced the samurai women's social basis of independence but also weakened their cultural resources for claiming autonomy. The sharply hierarchical structure and male-dominated ideology of the samurai houses emerged from this development of the *ie* organizations, which later became the foundation of early modern samurai families.

As a result of all these structural changes, each *ie* became a more hierarchically organized—and consequently more efficient—military organization under the command of a single male head. Thus, the challenge that the samurai class faced at this point of organizational development can be summarized as the need to find a reliable and efficient alliance to bind smaller, independent *ie*.

Seeking New Forms of Coalition

The reorganization of the local samurai population was a difficult task because the new social order had to be established in regions where the organizationally reconstituted, economically strengthened, and increasingly independent samurai *ie* of various sizes were thrown together in uneasy proximity. In comparison with the Kamakura *sōryō* system, which kept a large, complex kinship system loosely interrelated, the new system of single-heir inheritance could no longer rely on common ancestry to provide a sufficiently strong bond to hold the independent multiple *ie* within the larger lineage. The older ties, whether through vassalage or through lineage, appeared less and less trustworthy during the late medieval period. How did the local samurai lords choose to handle this situation?

In the course of the fifteenth and sixteenth centuries, the independent local samurai landlords shared three common interests. First, they wanted to keep their tax revenue secure from interference by increasingly assertive and self-interested villagers. Second, they had to defend their territories against external threats: neighboring samurai lords were constantly vying for territorial supremacy, and trivial quarrels and boundary disputes often triggered major conflicts. Third, they had to preserve internal control over their houses, which were complex organizations consisting of master-follower relationships and family members; policing subordinates and ensuring their loyalty to the house heads was critically important for the samurai lords. If the traditional forms of patron-client relationships as well as lineage no longer provided sufficient stability and security, how could local samurai protect their interests? Some local lords *(kokujin)* sought to construct mutual protection arrangements by sharing rather than fighting over these common interests. These associations of mutual protection, usually called *ikki,* at the same time represented military alliances against threats from the outside.

Ikki literally means "of one intention or in agreement." In the fourteenth century, the term implied the voluntary formation of a party associated for a special purpose. In contrast to the explicitly hierarchical alliance of vassalage, the members of the *ikki* were ordinarily considered to be more or less equal. The formation of *ikki* by local samurai lords was common in Japan from the fourteenth to the sixteenth centuries.[9]

The earliest form of samurai *ikki* was based upon a large lineage group.[10] Soon, however, the independent *kokujin* extended this form of alliance outside the original kinship circles. Using the formal infrastructure of *ikki* alliances, namely, pledges of mutual loyalty, they began to form regional *ikki*. Samurai lords within the same geographical region would form *ikki* regardless of whether kinship connection was involved or not.

The typical process of *ikki* formation reflects the distinctive nature of these new types of coalition. To begin with, a group of like-minded people would gather and work out the purposes and terms of a certain agreement. Their decision would take the form of written rules with members' signatures attached (*rensho kishōmon,* or "a document of oath with signatures"). These signatures were often inscribed in a circular pattern on the documents, to signify the equal status of the members and to avoid quarrels over precedence. Next, a ritual of "one taste of the gods' water" *(ichimi shinsui)* was usually celebrated, in which the document was ceremoniously burned, its ashes mixed with water and then consumed by the signers. This ritual was considered a pact with the gods, which symbolized the mystical *dō shin* (same mind), the solidarity of the contracting parties. As this ritual indicates, the governing spirit of *ikki* alliances was democratic, assuming as it did the equality and independence of each member. *Ikki* rules often stated explicitly that any conflicts among the members should be resolved at a meeting based upon *tabun no gi* (decision by majority).[11]

The formation of horizontal coalitions like *ikki* also became characteristic for other social groups, such as farmers and priests. Villagers (who shared the status of *hyakushō,* or farmers) frequently conducted the ritual of "one taste of the gods' water" and collectively opposed the exploitation of the local overlord. Unlike other periods in Japanese history, when hierarchical structures and ideologies outweighed more egalitarian philosophies and forms of social order, late medieval Japan was characterized by such horizontal forms of associations: not only the local samurai lords but various groups of people formed *ikki,* united by the ritual of "one taste of the gods' water." Through this mystical ritual, they claimed solidarity, or *dō shin* (same mind), and dared to take significant risks on behalf of uncertain causes. This period is rightly known as "the era of *ikki.*"

The Development of Village Autonomy

The development of mutual protection associations within the samurai class cannot be understood apart from its context—the growth of village power confronting the samurai lords on an everyday basis. Since the early medieval period, nonsamurai villagers had often engaged in a form of collective bargaining to protect their own interests. In the late medieval period, the villages' resistance took a more organized form, and their system of self-government developed recognizable institutional patterns. Many villages adopted a more structurally defined self-government. Villagers often formed so-called *sō-son,* exclusive self-governing organizations that protected the collective interests of the village and paid a group tax to the proprietary lord. The most important aspect of these *sō-son* was their retention of a high degree of political independence and a preference for solving their problems by their own devices. As Fujiki Hisashi describes, "Japanese *sō-son* of the late medieval period had their own independent military force primarily consisting of young men *(wakashū)* capable of settling disputes through armed intervention."[12] The young men of the village were expected to be available to serve as a militia in times of emergency, but in addition they had peacetime powers to settle local disputes.

These *sō-son* organizations first appeared in the late thirteenth century near Kyoto and became widespread in the course of the next three centuries. The formation of *sō-son* cannot be documented for every village in this period, and the organizational structures of villages varied greatly by regions. Many scholars agree, however, that the late medieval villages, at least in the Kinai area (regions around Kyoto), achieved increasing economic self-sufficiency and self-governing ability.[13] The samurai lords had to collect taxes from such tough-minded villagers, accustomed to a proud tradition of local self-determination, and therefore the development of self-contained, self-governing villages provided a major stimulus for samurai reorganization.

These self-governing villages arose in the social context of the increased agricultural productivity of the late thirteenth and fourteenth centuries, which contributed to the greater self-sufficiency of small-scale farmers.[14] With the growth of peasant families as production units in the villages, these farmers acquired a share in the management of the village, which had previously been the monopoly of the wealthy members *(otona)*. The *sō-son*-style village strengthened its sense of corporate identity through its inclusion of a more representative cross section of the community at the management level. Although *otona* were usually entrusted with the government of the *sō-son*'s collective properties, the village as a whole took responsibility for the "public" domain, incorporating the interests of a growing number of small, independent peasants.[15]

The independence of these villages was further safeguarded by a "high-exit situation," in which a village could transfer its source of military protection (that is, the local lord). Because there was always a number of greater powers competing for the same given parcel of land, a village could choose one protector over another—for instance, the inhabitants could flee to a competitor's territory, or they could at least invite another lord's intervention. This fluid situation became more noticeably volatile during the Warring States period, in the late fifteenth and sixteenth centuries.

For a particularly instructive example, we can consider a specific *sō-son* called Hineno Estate. Since 1417, its villages had assumed the collective responsibility of paying a fixed tax every year to Kujō, a *shōen* owner and aristocrat residing at the imperial court in Kyoto. At the beginning of the sixteenth century, the village had to contend with no fewer than three competing powers: (1) the traditional, but declining, authority of the *shōen* holder, Kujō; (2) a powerful armed Buddhist temple, Negoro;

and (3) the province governor-lord *(shugo daimyo)*, Hosokawa, who ruled the area. All of them in one way or another tried to squeeze the village for revenue. The power of the traditional *shōen* owners had been gradually slipping away by this time, but Kujō Masamoto (1459–1516), one of the highest ranking aristocrats, was putting up a particularly fierce struggle to regain his rights to the land. Confronted with a crisis over his land tenure, Masamoto decided to live in Hineno and supervise the village directly, a very unusual move for court aristocrats. Hineno Estate is one of the most well documented medieval villages, owing to the survival of an unusual diary kept by Kujō Masamoto, *Tabi hikitsuke (The Travel Note)*.[16]

In 1502, the Negoro Temple decided to invade Hosokawa's territories; the village of Hineno lay in the path of the invading forces. Representatives from Hineno went to the Negoro Temple to negotiate the protection of their village. They finally gained the temple's guarantee of their village's safety by making a large cash contribution. In addition, the temple conceded to the village power to punish any soldiers who were found guilty of misconduct inside its boundaries.[17] Masamoto paid only one-fifth of the sum contributed to the temple; the rest was paid by the village. The incident illuminates the social and economic power that such a village could wield in late medieval Japan. The village was able to pay a high premium for safety as well as the power to punish misbehaving soldiers, suggesting the maintenance of a village force.

Hineno's strategy for surviving the chaotic civil war included making the most of Masamoto's traditional aristocratic authority and avoiding invasion by either Negoro or Hosokawa. The villagers, however, urged Masamoto not to rely on his traditional authority as *shōen* owner, but to take a strong initiative to keep the peace. In his diary, Masamoto expressed his irritation about his lack of sufficient force and economic power in the face of the feisty, independent village representatives. In December 1502, Masamoto found that he did not have sufficient funds to send the customary "end of the year gifts" to Kyoto, and so he asked the village for a contribution. The village representative rejected his request on the grounds that all the available funds should be used to protect the village and stockpile weapons, not to send gifts to Kyoto. Masamoto's qualification as the holder of "public authority" was directly called into question on this occasion. Masamoto himself, depressed by the villagers' response, went to bed that night, completely forgetting the fact that it was a ritual night of *kōshin* when people should not sleep at all.[18]

Not only did each particular village become more independent, but in addition the villages began to group together to form larger networks of resistance. The large-scale *ikki* of farmers grew out of regional alliances formed by these autonomous villages. In the sixteenth century, a Buddhist priest of the Ikkō sect commented on their stubborn spirit of independence: "There are so many *hyakushō* (farmers) all over the country who try not to serve masters. . . ."[19] Like the court aristocrats in Kyoto, they claimed that "farmers were royal descendants *(ōson),*"[20] and did not have a master. Farmers did not like samurai feudal lords, as the priest wrote, because "the people called 'service men *(saburai)*' look down upon the farmers." Note that the old term for the samurai, *saburai,* meaning "those who serve," is used here pejoratively. The proud farmers of this period rejected the samurai's claim to feudal dominion by maintaining that, since the emperor was the sole overlord, farmers were not subjected to the samurai lords. The priest's testimony would seem to suggest that high self-regard and a spirit of independence characterized not only the samurai associations but also the agricultural villages. Because the farmers had such a strong collective spirit, backed by a socio-economic basis for their independence, it was never easy to collect revenue from them. Samurai lords with considerable military force, as well as the traditional *shōen* owners like Kujō, had difficulties in controlling these resistant villagers. In an atmosphere of continual unrest, the villagers understandably assumed that only those who were capable of providing safety and security for their agricultural labors deserved the name of "public power"—the authority to whom they would pay taxes. The movement toward greater village autonomy thus provided a strong motivation for the reorganization of the samurai class.

The Expansion and Limitation of *ikki* Organizations

What complicated the picture of Japanese class relations was the fact that, during the late medieval period, the status boundary between the wealthier farmers and the samurai landlords was not clearly drawn. The more prosperous leaders of the villages increasingly resembled samurai. These powerful farmers usually possessed considerable land acreage and a well-controlled work force. Never having been connected to official public power, they did not have formal samurai status, and they could not levy taxes like the "real" samurai lords. But they often collected rent *(kajishi)* from the peasantry and had considerable influence in their local communities. These powerful samurai-like farmers were usually known as *dogō* or *jizamurai*.[21] They generally functioned as the core members of the *sō-son*, and often resisted the samurai lords who attempted to collect taxes from them.[22]

Given the complexity of late medieval class relations, it is not entirely surprising that the Warring States period witnessed the emergence of some powerful large *ikki* organizations that incorporated people from different social classes. During the fifteenth and sixteenth centuries, these larger *ikki* organizations sometimes included both the *ikki* of *ko-kujin* lords (samurai in the full sense) and those of villagers (*dogō* and lesser farmers) when they tried to set limits to the warring provincial powers. The most famous example of this kind of comprehensive *ikki* is probably the *ikki* of Yamashiro Province. In December 1485, thirty-six *kokujin* lords of the Yamashiro Province and "peasants of all the province" gathered for a meeting during which they attempted to drive out the troops of the two *shugo daimyo*, which had been battling over the region. The *ikki* demanded the immediate evacuation of all the *shugo daimyo* troops from the province, proclaiming the area to be self-governing. Although the leadership of this *ikki* was in the hands of the allied *kokujin* samurai lords, the *so* organizations of the villages throughout the province also played a critical role in sustaining it. Miura Hiro-yuki once called the Yamashiro *ikki* "the people's parliament of the Warring States period."[23] Despite its great reputation in Japanese history, however, the Yamashiro *ikki* was far from an isolated case. It is known, for example, that Iga Province in the mid-sixteenth century was governed by a federation of local *so* villages consisting of *kokujin* and *dogō*. The Iga federation was administered by ten magistrates, but important matters were discussed at meetings of the entire membership of the *ikki*.

If the late medieval *ikki* had developed further along the path toward greater concentration and early modern state formation, Japan might have worked out a different way to consolidate the power of the landlord class in the early modern period. The medieval *ikki* alliances had the potential to generate a more democratic tradition of local self-government in Japan by bringing members of the landlord class together in parliamentary bodies. History did not favor this pattern, however;

the *ikki* failed to become the organizing principle of the landlord class
in the next stage of state formation. As it turned out, the efficacy of a
hierarchically structured vassalage system, reorganized under the warlords *(sengoku daimyo)*, proved to be superior.

How could such a development take place? One should note that the
ikki associations of the samurai lords were in essence military alliances
formed against threats from the outside. Their intrinsically horizontal
structure proved a disadvantage when it came to effective deployment of
armies in the field. As a consequence, some of these associations vested
military leadership in the most powerful member of the association. In
some cases, the members of the association entrusted an outsider, in the
form of an established regional authority, with their collective vassalage.
Such regional leaders of samurai lords then attempted to style themselves
as "masters" of the *kokujin* lords, although they had been originally
allies on an equal basis. Typically, regional concentration of power grew
sequentially through repeated cycles of this process. It was in this context
that the warlords *(sengoku daimyo)* came to power, by reducing the local
independent samurai lords to vassal status. By the sixteenth century,
these *sengoku daimyo* had set themselves up as the "public authority"
(kōgi) of the region, issuing decrees without consultation with or consent
from the central government, thereby tightening local discipline and control over their vassals. Under the aegis of the *sengoku daimyo*, regional
power took a newly concentrated form, the local samurai were hierarchically reorganized, and some new machinery of government was introduced. The impetus in this period was toward regional state formation,
and the local samurai were absorbed into a more vertically layered structure as a result of this pressure.

As a parallel development to the appearance of the *sengoku daimyo*,
the organized resistance of the *ikki* associations also increased during
the sixteenth century. Ultimately, however, even those *ikki* alliances that
held out against the warlords as long as they could were brutally sub-
jugated by the military machines of the warlords and unification rulers.
For example, when Oda Nobunaga's forces fought with the organization
of Ikkō Ikki, Nobunaga's soldiers killed more than twenty thousand men
and women of Ikkō Ikki in one single battle near Isenagashima (1574).
Indeed, Japanese history in the sixteenth century is the record of a process of violent suppression of horizontal forms of social organization by
a strictly hierarchical system of samurai vassalage.

6   A Society Organized for War

The Ōnin War (1467–1477), between the two major vassal-lords of the Muromachi shogunate, decisively weakened the power and authority of the shogunate. Subsequently, the entire country was plunged into more than a hundred years of continuous civil war, lasting until the pacification of Japan under the Tokugawa, around 1600. During this era—usually called the Warring States (Sengoku) period—regional power-holders (warlords, called *sengoku daimyo*) began to establish the independence of their regional polities from the weakening central authority through the reorganization of local samurai hierarchies under their own military forces. There were two typical routes to becoming *sengoku daimyo*. The first was through the office of the *shugo* (province governors). Although they were originally appointed by the shogunate as provincial governors, they gradually privatized the provinces and became daimyo lords. Most *sengoku daimyo* took the second route to power, however, through the action of *gekokujō*, literally, "the lower dominating the upper." That is, vassals or local deputies of the *shugo* would expel their master and take control of the region. They achieved regional hegemony through a combination of military force and political outmaneuvering of their local competitors.[1]

Warfare is one of the chief determinants of major historical change, not simply because it overturns rulers, inflicts devastating casualties on civilians through starvation and disease as well as on the soldiery through direct combat, and redraws political boundaries, but also because it often modifies the internal structure of social groups on the home front. This latter phenomenon is most frequently observed in societies under constant threat of warfare, when each social group is under the continual stress and tension produced by a siege mentality. Domains of the *sengoku daimyo* (warlords) during the sixteenth century were such examples. In the atmosphere of perpetual military combativeness that characterized the Warring States period, only the most efficient commanders could survive. Victory on the battlefield depended on their ability to fill large war chests in order to supply the needs of their military machine.

The *sengoku daimyo* also introduced a number of innovations in order to encourage the economic growth and prosperity of their territories. For example, they initiated improvements in irrigation facilities to increase agricultural production. They also imported and subsidized craftsmen whose skills were necessary to the manufacture of arms and related equipment. The daimyo attempted to control trade and to have a hand in merchants' activities. Developing and exploiting new metal mines in their territories was especially critical to their military and fiscal strength. All these policies were directed toward improving the warlords' abilities to muster both human and material resources for war.

The *sengoku daimyo* and Samurai Reorganization

I have mentioned that the exchange relationship of vassalage incorporated two contradictory desiderata, *reliability* and *efficacy*. The contradiction between these two sought-after qualities in a vassal appeared in its most acute form during the Warring States period. The rivalrous *sengoku daimyo* needed the service of strong men-at-arms. But the stronger they were (that is, the more efficacious), the more potentially dangerous they were to the master (that is, the less reliable). The most reputable warriors were the most likely to be hired away by another daimyo. Or, these heroes could opt to leave their vassalage by finding a more powerful source of protection. They could even construct a secret alliance behind the master's back if they so wished. The outstanding fighters during this period, meanwhile, continued to uphold their social and moral autonomy with a proud sentiment of honor. At the same time, pressures toward compliance and absolute loyalty also increased, because only those daimyo who were able to control their vassals could survive this period of civil war.

In the early stage of *sengoku daimyo* development, the reconstitution of a tightly controlled hierarchy in regional samurai circles was not an easy task for the *sengoku daimyo*. They faced the problem of incorporating different types of samurai warriors into their armies. A number of *kokujin* lords had become accustomed to the horizontal structure of the *ikki* association; even after they became vassals of the *sengoku daimyo*, they retained membership in their *ikki* and held on to a measure of autonomy.

An important strategy employed by some *sengoku daimyo* was the introduction of the *kandaka* system, which assessed the value of a piece of land in terms of a cash unit *(kan)*. This system was an effective means of samurai reorganization. The amount of *kan* levied on each parcel of land supplied the base rate for calculating the level of military duties each vassal owed the *sengoku daimyo*. "Although these changes may appear simple," Nagahara Keiji notes, "it was the registration of all landholdings in terms that allowed the immediate calculation of both the level of dues owed by the peasant cultivators and the level of military service owed by the warrior seigniors that formed the basis of the land-tax system upon which the power of the greatest *daimyo* of the sengoku period was based."[2]

With the help of the *kandaka* system, a *sengoku daimyo* could easily calculate the precise amount of military service owed by each vassal, according to the amount of the *kan*. If a vassal was given any new land, it entailed an immediate increase in his predetermined military obligation in the event of a political emergency. The exchange of *go'on* and *hōkō* (debt and service), then, acquired a clear standard of measurement through the *kandaka* system, which determined the size of each vassal's fief *(chigyo)*. As a result of this standardization, the *daimyo* was able to calculate the exact amount of manpower he could mobilize in wartime.[3]

Unlike the *shugo daimyo* (an earlier form of province-governor daimyo during the Muromachi period), who could only reward their vassals with *shōen*-related offices and rights *(shiki)*, the *sengoku daimyo* were able, through the *kandaka* system, to confer greater rewards on obedient vassals. Given this concrete socioeconomic benefit, the samurai vassals were more easily contained within the organization of the *sen-*

goku daimyo, and their capacity for independence was weakened. Many *sengoku daimyo* also attempted to subsume the wealthier farmers *(dōgo)* within their military organizations. These farmers, who increasingly re-sembled the samurai, were often taken into the new order as lower vas-sals of the *sengoku daimyo.* In wartime, their mobilization would strengthen the daimyo's direct control over his army. Ordinarily, lesser vassals lived in the villages themselves; once reclassified as samurai, how-ever, they were exempted from paying taxes and instead owed military duties to the daimyo. Because these wealthier farmers had a great deal of influence within their local villages, their becoming samurai was also an effective means of policing rebellious villages. Possessing both in-creased concentration of military power on the one hand, and economic incentives on the other, the *sengoku daimyo* thus took over various indig-enous regional social organizations, integrating them into the new sys-tem by depriving them of an independent identity.

In comparison with the *ikki,* the new hierarchical structure of *sengoku daimyo* vassalage had some organizational advantages. First, the recip-rocal obligation based upon the exchange of *go'on* (debt) and *hōkō* (ser-vice) had a concrete socioeconomic basis. Because it was quantified by *kandaka,* each vassal's indebtedness corresponded to his scale of military duties. Second, the internal structure of samurai domination itself had a selective affinity with vassalage. The samurai's house was structured according to a master-follower relationship with its subordinate mem-bers. The samurai's authority over the peasantry also conformed to the model of the master-follower relationship, insofar as he based his entitle-ment to their submission and service on the status difference. Therefore, it was predictable that, in the face of the instability of the *ikki* organiza-tion, a samurai would prefer a hierarchical connection to superior au-thorities, who could both physically secure and theoretically legitimate his "franchisee" position from above.

Military Revolution and Samurai Reorganization

Because the battles of the *sengoku daimyo* were conducted on a larger territorial scale, the nature of combat changed significantly. This change became increasingly apparent during the late sixteenth century. The more powerful daimyo frequently formed or dissolved regional alliances as they struggled for hegemony over larger and larger areas. A warlord could no longer count on winning battles if he continued to rely on traditional war strategies and technologies. The most important changes in the conduct of war during this period included (1) the increased amount of manpower mobilized in battle; (2) a strategic shift away from fights between individual champions, to planned collective movements of armies; (3) the rise of strong fortified castles; (4) the emergence of foot soldiers as a significant strike force, and (5) the introduction of firearms. These changes in the character of military life, and their transformation of warfare itself, were compelling reasons for the vassals to submit to the daimyo's discipline.

Strategic troop movements became the most noteworthy feature of battles during the Warring States period. In contrast with earlier medieval battles, in which skilled archers and individualistic hand-to-hand contests between mounted warriors could decide the outcome of a battle, the *sengoku daimyo*'s troops fought in groups or masses. Indeed, in the sixteenth century, well-known, successful *sengoku daimyo* such as Takeda Shingen and Uesugi Kenshin were also famous for their strategic cleverness and the discipline of their troops. In the new style of combat, the individual mounted warrior had less freedom to maneuver at his own discretion. Unlike the earlier period, in which the infantry was merely an accompaniment to the armed cavalry, the foot soldiers *(ashigaru)* in the sixteenth century became an integral part of the *sengoku daimyo*'s armies. They were often organized under commanders of foot soldiers *(ashigaru daishō)*.

The introduction of muskets also changed the face of battle. It is commonly believed that the Western musket first came to Japan in 1543 through Portuguese traders who arrived at a remote southern island known as Tanegashima.[4] These imported muskets were quickly reproduced by Japanese craftsmen. After the famous Battle of Nagashino in 1575, which conclusively demonstrated the efficacy of muskets on the battlefield, infantrymen equipped with muskets *(teppo ashigaru)* became a critical part of the warlords' armies.[5]

Together with the development of strongly fortified castles, technological advances made warfare extremely expensive. The ability to maintain adequate troop supply lines over a long period of time tested the warlord's ability not only as a commander in the field but also as a quartermaster.

When we review the technological advances in Sengoku Japan and their impact on the battlefield, we immediately recognize the similarity to the radical change in European warfare, in what is often called the early modern European "military revolution." Geoffrey Parker summarizes the European military revolution as follows:

> The military revolution of early modern Europe possessed a number of separate facets. First, the improvements in artillery in the fifteenth century, both qualitative and quantitative, eventually transformed fortress design. Second, the increasing reliance on fire power in battle—whether with archers, field artillery or musketeers—led not only to the eclipse of cavalry by infantry in most armies, but to new tactical arrangements that maximized the opportunities of giving fire. Moreover, these new ways in warfare were accompanied by a dramatic increase in army size.[6]

Although the precise details of technological development and the exact timing of changes differed, radical improvement of fortification, a significant increase in personnel mobilization, the increased importance of the infantry, and the rapid spread of firearms all occurred in late-sixteenth-century Japan as they did in Europe. This parallel development was not entirely coincidental. In the course of the sixteenth century, European civilization was exported in significant doses to the non-Western world, to the degree that it influenced the military technology of this Far Eastern corner of the world. But the Japanese military revolution of the sixteenth century cannot be understood simply as the result of borrowed Western technologies; the timing of the stimulus is also significant. The Western art of war was introduced into a situation in which the *sengoku daimyo* had been fighting each other for regional and then national supremacy for several decades.

The unceasing warfare among the *sengoku daimyo* not only revolutionized the military equipment and political governance of the daimyo domains but also accelerated the structural transformation of the samurai's life. For example, Oda Nobunaga forced his vassals to live in his castle town, an arrangement that ensured the swift mobilization of troops in times of emergency. Many daimyo hired foot soldiers and lesser vassals, placing units of them under the command of higher vassals. At the close of the Warring States period, the warlord Satake Yoshihisa had direct command over three hundred musketeers. He divided them into six units and assigned them to the six commanders who were his higher vassals. Such soldiers, hired directly by the warlord but commanded by the higher vassal, were called *yoriki*, or associate mounted warriors, and their commanders were called *yorioya*, or associate parents. As the term "parent" implies, the *yorioya* were expected to behave like caregivers to the *yoriki*; the latter were still regarded as the direct vassals of the *sengoku daimyo*, not of the *yorioya*. This method of army recruitment, formation, and assignment enabled the warlords to build much more systematically structured armies, in comparison with the older system, which was totally dependent on each vassal's contribution of his personal force.

To be sure, the reconstruction of the *sengoku daimyo*'s military organization was never fully completed. The vassal samurai of the *sengoku daimyo* were never totally reduced to mere hired soldiers. The samurai continued to be armed landlords; in most cases, they still resided in their own fiefs. Of course, the *kandaka* system and the stricter military discipline imposed by the *sengoku daimyo* restricted their freedom. Yet, it was still primarily the individual vassal's responsibility to supply men and material in times of emergency. One consequence of this situation was that there was no unified peacetime system of basic military training for the troops. Victory in battle was still critically dependent on the personal fighting spirit and military skills of each vassal. As a result, individual demonstrations of chauvinistic bravery, such as leading a cavalry charge, continued to be highly honored and rewarded, and the samurai's voracious appetite for fame and glory still fed on the raw material of battlefield heroics.

In order to enforce stricter standards of military discipline on a class of warriors noted for quick tempers, high energy, and a tradition of proud competitiveness, many *sengoku daimyo* introduced stringent military codes of behavior *(gunritsu)*. Obedience of commanders' directives was clearly defined in the codes of many *sengoku daimyo*, and those who violated military codes were subject to harsh punishment.

State-Making and the Law of *kenka ryōseibai*

The samurai vassals of the *sengoku daimyo* retained the tradition of self-redress and private conflict resolution that symbolized their social autonomy as landed military elites, but the warlords' new style of waging war often conflicted with the traditional expressions of samurai autonomy.

The unauthorized use of violence by the samurai not only disrupted solidarity and mutual trust among vassals but also decreased the military
efficiency of the warlord's troops. Thus, the *sengoku daimyo* understandably attempted to impose more rigorous standards of discipline on
their vassals.

The famous law of *kenka ryōseibai* (equally severe punishment of all
parties to a quarrel regardless of the reason behind the conflict) emerged
in this context as the military disciplinary code of the *sengoku daimyo*.[7]
For example, the eighth article of *Imagawa kanamokuroku* (1526)—the
code of the *sengoku daimyo* of the Imagawa family—stated succinctly
that "all parties who are involved in a quarrel, regardless of the reason,
will be subject to the death penalty."[8] *Kōshū Hatto no Shidai* (1547), the
law of the major warlord Takeda Shingen in the Warring States period,
also included this stipulation: "Both parties to a quarrel must be punished regardless of their reasons. However, those who are involved in
quarrels but who keep their patience shall not be punished."[9] Another
warlord, Chōsokabe Motochika, stated in his 100 Articles (1596) that
"all quarrels and verbal disputes are prohibited. . . . Of those who violate this rule, both parties must be punished regardless of who is good
or bad."[10] This was the warlords' attempt to reject the prevailing practice
of *jiriki kyūsai* (the self-redress of grievances) in resolving conflicts. The
restriction of the vassals' social autonomy by the warlords sharply reflected the changing pattern of samurai conflict resolution.

The primary purpose of the Sengoku laws was the establishment of
the daimyo's authority as the ultimate mediator of any quarrels within
the domain. Unlike the codes of the Kamakura and Muromachi shogunates, which only nominally prohibited private recourse to violence, the
law of *kenka ryōseibai* exerted a profound influence on subsequent developments in patterns of conflict resolution among the samurai. By
the beginning of the Tokugawa period, *kenka ryōseibai* had achieved
a kind of common law status. For example, in 1616, the code of the lord
Hachisuka called the law of *kenka ryōseibai* "the great law of the world,"
stating that "those who are involved in a quarrel or dispute should be
punished according to the principle of the great law of the world *(tenka
no gohhato)*. Without prejudice as to right or wrong, both parties will
be executed."[11]

What were the forces that led to this new rule of conflict resolution?
Two historical factors are readily apparent. First, the change was directly

related to the social and political reorganization of the samurai class and the concentration of power in the late medieval period. Second, the change was affected by the more advanced military technology of the sixteenth century, which required more discipline and cohesiveness within units of samurai troops.

As a new network of samurai houses developed in the late medieval period, there was a perceived need to construct some form of coordination among members that would restrict the autonomy of the individual houses. It was not coincidental that an example of the *kenka ryōseibai* appeared in the samurai's *ikki keijō* (the contract documents for forming *ikki*); as early as 1512 *kenka ryōseibai* appeared in a surviving document of an *ikki keijō*.[12] Because the *ikki* came into being as the peace-keeping and mutual defense organizations of the local *kokujin* landlords, the conflicts among the members of the *ikki* were to be settled through the collective will of the *ikki* association. Turning to private retribution as a way of resolving any disputes among *ikki* members would threaten to shatter the solidarity of the organization.

The law of *kenka ryōseibai* was enforced most stringently only with the rise to power of the *sengoku daimyo,* however. The emergence of this law as a widely accepted rule coincided with the incorporation of the local samurai bands (including *ikki*) into one structure under a single powerful *sengoku daimyo*. During this process, the balance of power between master and vassal was still in flux. Most of the *sengoku daimyo* were local samurai, and in this respect they were equal to most of the vassals. In order to establish hegemony as the sole regional authority, the *sengoku daimyo* asserted their monopoly on the position of *kōgi,* the public authority, whereas the vassals were only "private."

The only way to guarantee one's acceptance as the legitimate public authority was to claim the exclusive right to exercise violence. *Jinkaishū* (the *sengoku* law of the Date clan in Mutsu Province; 1536) stipulates that "the crime of injuring someone with a sword should be reported, and should be subject to public punishment *(seibai)*. It is forbidden to strike back personally. . . ." The rise of legislation based on *kenka ryōseibai* can be seen as one aspect of the *sengoku daimyo*'s general policy of undercutting the sociopolitical autonomy of their vassals and securing their position as the official public authority in their respective regions.

It must be emphasized here that the law of *kenka ryōseibai* rejected any discrimination concerning "the judgment of right or wrong." The *sengoku daimyo* intended to maintain their political supremacy; anyone who opposed the daimyo's code should be punished regardless of his reasons for doing so. The new laws marked the end of an era, of a world governed by *dōri* (reasonableness), the principle of local custom and common sense that had been respected by the autonomous samurai population.

Another reason for the widespread acceptance of *kenka ryōseibai* was directly related to innovations in the conduct of war. In essence, *kenka ryōseibai* was a code of military law. It had been a tradition in samurai battles since the Kamakura period that those who led the attacks would be praised and honored most; however, by the sixteenth century it was critical to victory in large-scale combat for the soldiers to charge in unison. Consequently, the individualistic tendencies of some vassals to seek honor and glory for themselves at the expense of strategic movements for the army as a whole became increasingly problematic for their warlords. Private fights and quarrels between competitive fellow warriors during a time of emergency would severely decrease the efficacy of the army. It was at this point that the military rule of *kenka ryōseibai,* prohibiting acts of private violence in the armies, appeared.

For example, the military order of the Tokugawa in 1596 stated, "Quarrels and verbal disputes are strictly prohibited. Those who violate this order will be severely punished regardless of [their] reasons. Their friends and colleagues who aid them in their attempts will be even more severely punished." [13] A similar order of 1600 warns that "if an individual advances in secret, ahead of the other troops *(sente sakikoshi),* and distinguishes himself contrary to orders, he will be executed." [14] If one examines these two Tokugawa codes against the background of the general military change of the time, it is evident that the main goal of the provisions was to facilitate the disciplined strategic movement of troops. Any tendencies toward battlefield exhibitionism on the part of individuals had to be discouraged by means of extremely harsh sanctions.

It would be wrong to conclude, at this point, that the adoption of *kenka ryōseibai* completely obliterated the earlier medieval approval of self-redress of grievances. *Sengoku daimyo* did not always handle quarrels, especially those that occurred in peacetime, in accordance with the principle of *kenka ryōseibai. Kenka ryōseibai* and the principle of self-redress of grievances continued to exist side by side and were inherited as a parallel system by the Tokugawa. A significant proportion of samurai conflicts were settled, as it were, through private means of resolution, including settlements by private mediators *(chūnin)* who could work out solutions agreeable to both parties. The slow pace of change in the samurai's mode of conflict resolution and code of honor was closely related to the transitional nature of state-making during the Warring States period. The consolidation of power in the samurai class, together with the restriction of the autonomous power of the local samurai vassals, was still incomplete at this point in time.

In short, as Katsumata Shizuo states, "The character of loyalty to the daimyo reflected in the sengoku house codes differed significantly from the ideal of loyalty as a self-abnegating service that was inculcated under the later Tokugawa bakuhan political structure." [15] The *sengoku daimyo* did, however, attempt to increase their absolutist authority. Katsumata goes on to point out "the existence of a broadly conceived principle of loyalty to the *kokka* [state]" in the Sengoku law, the logic of loyalty to *kōgi* (public authority) that "transmuted the obligations of loyalty felt by retainers toward the various groups to which they belonged into obligations of loyalty toward the *kokka*. The ultimate goal was the inculcation of absolute loyalty to the daimyo and the establishment of an authoritarian power structure." [16]

Honor and Loyalty in the Warring States Period

For the samurai culture of honor, the introduction of *kenka ryōseibai* created an insoluble problem with regard to the criteria for honorable conduct under provocation. Since the new law used intimidation as its device for prevention of quarrels, it was usually accompanied by the codicil that a party to the quarrel who managed to keep his self-control during the incident would be exempt from punishment. This rule was often criticized by the samurai because it was thought to encourage spineless conformity at the expense of a brave and honorable spirit. A famous vassal of the Takeda clan, Naitō Shuri, offered this indictment:

> In order to prevent quarrels, the rule of *kenka ryōseibai* makes sense to me. However, those who remained patient while being insulted cannot be useful samurai for the lord. If we condone such behavior, the samurai will all become flabby and soft. If the order of the lord encourages patience, it will be safe and orderly for everyone, but the end result will

be a great loss to our lord. If safety is the samurai's only reason for obeying laws, they will stray from the road of manliness. They will all become useless cowards.[17]

Naitō further stated that, if he received shame, he would defy the law and kill his enemies, even though "all the members of our kin would be speared to death by the lord." The ethos of proud and independent warriors refused to submit completely to the orderly rationale of the *sengoku daimyo*.

Shuri's argument clearly cuts to the heart of the problem of samurai discipline. Order had to be achieved, but not at the cost of the samurai's fighting spirit and honor. Those who did not care about preserving honor were useless samurai on the battlefield. How could the lords school their men to be persons who respected rules and order, and at the same time spirited and courageous warriors? The notion of "honor" often mingled with an individual's sense of self-esteem and desire for independence to produce a mixture sufficiently intoxicating to withstand the order and reasoning of higher authorities. In actual practice, the courage and sense of honor of the samurai did not die out even with the imposition of *kenka ryōseibai* during the Warring States period; battles were the best opportunities to recharge their fighting spirit, since their bravery affected their prestige and economic advantage. It was only with the consolidation of power and the achievement of internal pacification that the tension inherent in being both a true samurai and an orderly member of an organization emerged as a serious problem.

The high degree of social mobility and constant warfare understandably encouraged the samurai to adopt a calculating attitude toward their superiors. The breakup of previous contracts and coalitions was one political corollary of the period of continuous warfare. The samurai did not automatically consider betrayal of one's master dishonorable, but they did attach shame to a reputation for cowardice, and they would take extreme measures to avoid the pain of such a reputation. In general, the samurai mindset agreed with the attitude that winning is not the most important thing, but that it is the only thing. This competitive emphasis on one-upmanship was considered a mark of manliness appropriate for the warrior. It can be said that the military dimension of the samurai concept of honor was at its height during this violent period. The general mindset of the samurai of this period was "to serve that master who could use the warrior's ability to its maximum."[18] Ability rather than empty authority, performance rather than inherited position were valued in both vassals and masters. Indeed, it was during this period that the samurai's standards for measuring honor were the most "performance-oriented" rather than "bloodline-oriented." An institutionalized definition of the merit of absolute loyalty to one's master appeared only in the development of the Tokugawa state, in which the structure of samurai master-follower relationships would be permanently altered.

In contrast, the conjunction of self-willed death and military honor that had originated earlier became institutionalized—as well as the subject of increasing mystification—during this period of civil war. In the domain of Uesugi Kenshin, the punishment for the most serious crime involved confiscation of a samurai's swords together with a lifelong prohibition on wearing them. This public infliction of shame was often a more devastating punishment than the death penalty. On one occasion in the late sixteenth century, a man named Nagao Uemonnosuke was subjected to this most serious punishment. His relative petitioned the lord Uesugi Kenshin, on the basis of his father's distinguished military record, to change the punishment to *seppuku*. The lord Kenshin duly returned the man's two swords, and Nagao committed *seppuku*.[19] As with many other war stories of this period, it is difficult to verify the accuracy of this tale. Its resemblance to other stories in which the samurai placed honorable death above living disgrace makes it one of many such narratives in the literature of the period. The ideal of the honorable warrior was deeply engraved in the collective memory of the samurai during this period, and it would be further romanticized by the later Tokugawa samurai as the time when the "real" samurai lived.

The custom of *seppuku* as the honorable manner of death became fully institutionalized in this period. Almost all the defeated samurai generals who chose death over survival committed suicide in this manner. Furthermore, as the case from the Uesugi Domain mentioned above indicates, *seppuku* began to be considered the customary form of legal punishment for samurai during the Warring States period. This symbolizes the institutionalization of the notion that a samurai, even when found guilty of criminal misconduct, should be allowed to decide his own fate. Indeed, the long-lasting stereotype of *seppuku* in Japan—the implicit cultural understanding that remained largely intact until 1945—as a "noble" method of suicide for "the people of excellence" was firmly established during this time of civil war.[20] The military practice of honor was thus codified and glorified in the culture of the samurai during this period, which in turn affected the collective memory of the samurai and the image of their group identity in the subsequent Tokugawa period.

IV

THE PARADOXICAL NATURE OF TOKUGAWA STATE FORMATION

7 *Tokugawa State Formation*

Violence, Pacification, and Legitimacy

At the end of the sixteenth century, the chaotic civil wars among the *sengoku daimyo* finally came to a close when Toyotomi Hideyoshi (1537–1598) achieved a temporary national consolidation of the war-lords. Hideyoshi introduced a number of important institutions of social control that became the basis of subsequent Tokugawa state-making. After his death, the process of political consolidation entered its final stages following the large-scale battle at Sekigahara (1600), which divided the country into two groups of daimyo: Tokugawa Ieyasu and his allies (the Eastern army, with a combined force of 100,000 soldiers), and an opposing league of daimyo led by Hideyoshi's vassal Ishida Mitsunari (the Western army, with 80,000 soldiers). After Tokugawa's decisive victories in the Winter Battle of Osaka (1614), as well as in the Summer Battle of Osaka (1615), during which the son of Hideyoshi died in the fire that destroyed the city's great castle, it became clear that no other warlord could compete with Tokugawa's massive military power. The military superiority of the Tokugawa forces represented a collective victory for the new form of concentrated coercion that Tokugawa and his allies had achieved.

After these decisive military encounters, the Tokugawa regime readily established itself as the "Great Public Authority" *(ō kōgi),* successfully cementing its absolute dominion over the rest of the country. The term *kōgi* (public authority) started to be used by the *sengoku daimyo* to make clear their exclusive rule over a region. The Tokugawa shogunate as the supreme authority for the entire country now stood at the top of a pyramid of lesser regional *kōgi* (the daimyo) by subordinating them. The Tokugawa shogunate itself controlled the largest portion of the land, about a quarter of the taxable landholdings in the Japanese islands. The rest was largely governed by daimyo in various categories (including the daimyo who were the members of Tokugawa's own clan, and the shogunate's direct vassals).[1] The daimyo usually numbered around 260, though the precise figure differed from time to time.[2] Japanese historians have therefore named the resulting Tokugawa state the *bakuhan sei,* which literally means the shogunate *(baku)* and the local daimyo polity *(han)* system *(sei)*.

The Tokugawa pacification was, in many ways, a classic case of state formation through monopolizing the use of violence. It was, in the first place, the result of more than a century of intense and exhausting military struggles that eliminated those daimyo who could not compete on the battlefield. The military origin of the state has an important meaning for the *bakuhan* system, not solely because it produced the Tokugawa hegemony and monopoly of violence, but because it touched upon the *raison d'être* of the system itself.

Because a state exists largely in the minds of its people, the question of the population's acceptance of its authority as legitimate is always a serious issue. Enforcing obedience through coercive force alone, without any voluntary acceptance of the new authority, is too costly for any polity in the long run. Therefore, even when a new regime emerges as the result of an overwhelmingly decisive military victory, a process of legitimating its domination usually follows. In the case of Japan's early modern state formation, the Tokugawa shogunate's armed conquest and the subsequent process of legitimating that conquest were inextricably connected, with the effective monopoly of violence itself the necessary substratum of the regime's legitimacy. Let me explain how this conjunction of power and authority operated.

The Demilitarization of the Nonsamurai Population

The shogunate's forceful pacification was carried out not only at the level of national politics but in every aspect of society. Behind the scenes of drama and glory on the field of battle, which primarily affected the warlords, a far-reaching social reorganization was in operation, a process that ended by depriving a number of social groups of their ability to protect their own interests.

In the process of political unification, armed forces that had been under the control of nonsamurai groups were forcefully demilitarized in the name of "public peace." Toyotomi Hideyoshi's so-called Realm at Peace edicts (*Tenka sōbuji rei,* around 1585–1587) prohibited all violent behavior involving self-redress of grievances, especially battles among the warlords.[3] A similar directive forbidding private conflict resolution was introduced to stop disputes and fights at the village level *(kenka chōji rei)*. This emphasis on public peace was connected to Hideyoshi's radical "sword hunt" measure (promulgated in the Sword Hunt Edict of 1588), which ordered all warlords to confiscate weapons from the villages. Hideyoshi's sword confiscation was linked to another important policy that affected the villages, namely, the so-called Taikō land survey, which meticulously evaluated the productive capacity of each village. These measures of social control that Hideyoshi instituted became the most important building blocks in the construction of the subsequent Tokugawa shogunate's system of domination.

The prohibition of private conflict resolution was strictly enforced with occasional displays of excessive cruelty toward violators. In 1592, a Buddhist priest recorded an entry in his journal about the terrible fate of some villagers who broke the edict of peace when they got into a fight over irrigation water: "The eighty-three farmers of the Sesshū Province who were involved in a fight over water were executed. They were accused because they broke the order prohibiting all *kenka* [quarrels and fighting] on earth. Even a thirteen-year-old youth was executed as a surrogate for his father."[4]

What we should note here is that the fate of the eighty-three farmers was not simply the punishment of lawbreakers but the outworking of the hegemonic political process itself. Although water disputes in medieval Japanese villages often touched off violent controversies, they also symbolized the fact that the villagers had a large say in determining the use of irrigation water—the most important resource for rice paddy agriculture. There had been a customary procedure for resolving such disputes within the context of the self-governing functions of medieval villages. From this perspective, quarrels over water rights were representative of the self-determinism *(jiriki kyūsai)* of the local communities. In this par-

ticular case, a senior member of the village was actively working to resolve the conflict. The authorities executed this village mediator as well
as the disputants, however.[5] The activities of such mediators had been
considered the usual means of private conflict resolution. Thus, the execution of this man signified the authorities' contravention of established
local custom. The incident symbolized the fact that the pacification of
the country entailed the abolition of popular self-determinism. It confirmed the samurai's monopolization of the legitimate use of violence.

This harsh enforcement of the edict was also accompanied by skillful
ideological persuasion. In his declaration of the Sword Hunt Edict,
Hideyoshi maintained that a policy of village disarmament was necessary for "national security and the well-being of the people *(kokudo
anzen banmin kairaku)*." Moreover, Hideyoshi cleverly promised that all
the confiscated weaponry would be used to build a great image of Buddha. In this way, the decree would not only save the farmers from the
present misery caused by quarrels and fighting; it would also contribute
to their good fortune in the next world.

Under the national public power, the rulers argued, all the social
groupings that were presently in conflict in Japan would be relieved of
the stress and burden of self-redress of grievances. This logic of pacification presented by the unification rulers represented, of course, the effective introduction of an ideology intended to legitimate their sovereignty
over the country. The extant social conditions, moreover, made such pacification desirable even if it did set bounds to the independence of social
groups that had previously enjoyed considerable autonomy. The political
instability of the late medieval period gave each social group room to
extend its autonomy and independence. At the same time, the chaos and
uncertainty of civil war had threatened everyone's life and property for
too long. The unifiers of the country persuasively claimed that such self-
defense was no longer necessary. It was perhaps not due merely to rhetor-
ical flattery meant for the authorities that we find a recurrent cliché in
many documents of the Tokugawa period, in the form of an expression
of appreciation for the "peaceful tranquillity of the land" *(tenka taihei)*
under the regime. The phrase at least partly reflected the widely felt relief
from the burden of self-defense. Out of the social experiences of civil
war and unification there emerged an implicit understanding that a sovereignty deserved to be called a public power only when it was able to
provide safety and protection for its subjects.

The implicit cultural message conveyed by the demilitarization of the nonsamurai population was that only men of formal samurai status (that is, those who were vassals of the daimyo or shogun) would protect the nonsamurai population with their shining swords. The logic of this honor-ridden society gave rise to the following premise: only those who bore arms and those who could defend themselves deserved the title of honorable men. The conclusion that followed was that unarmed civilians were incapable of honor. Consequently, the samurai as a status group monopolized the official honor standing. The warrior class's collective monopoly of the use of violence became a cultural mechanism guaranteeing a corresponding monopoly of formal social honor and ensuring the submission of the nonsamurai classes.

This process brought the Tokugawa samurai into a difficult cultural dilemma: they could not formally abandon their militaristic honor culture even though the structure of their daily life changed completely in the peaceful early modern period, because the military dimension of their concept of honor supplied the justification for their domination. The pacification of Japan through the collective monopoly of violence by the samurai class virtually destroyed the medieval tradition of self-determinism, which included various forms of horizontal alliance that might have led Japan in the direction of more democratic institutions, had its early modern state-making taken a different course. The collective honor of the samurai class over other classes could be maintained only on this strict disciplinary foundation. Recall that the process of unification was only made possible by the hierarchical reorganization of the samurai class itself. It was the first unification ruler, Oda Nobunaga, who put the harsh new disciplinary policies into clear formulations. Nobunaga warned his vassals that "loyal men can stay, but traitorous samurai will be ordered to commit suicide, or suffer banishment" (1582).[6] The Tokugawa state was built upon the results of this brutal unification process. Tokugawa state formation facilitated the development of a military-bureaucratic despotism that deeply altered the subsequent course of Japanese social development.

The Logic of the Shogunate's Legitimacy

The ability to keep the peace mattered at the formal level of legitimating the Tokugawa shogunate. In order to build a consensus supporting their domination, Western rulers from the Middle Ages through the early modern period usually attempted to legitimate their position by defining the sovereign's role as the guardian of justice and the defender of the orthodox faith. The Western Church played an important part in conferring legitimacy on a regime's authority in this process. In a similar manner, by 1600, Japan had already developed a well-established political institution to legitimize the samurai regime: the imperial court with its traditional authority gave the *de facto* ruler of the country *de jure* recognition as the overlord of the samurai with the authority to govern the country. Upon closer examination, however, this legitimation of the samurai ruler was not mediated by a notion of justice or other overarching abstractions to justify the overlord's power. The emperor's court itself, though its traditional authority was supported by ancient mythology, had never claimed to represent either moral truth or justice. In the Japanese procedure of legitimating the samurai's rule, the ruler's practical ability to make and keep peace were a critical criterion in determining whether or not he deserved to be the leader of the entire samurai population.

Tokugawa emerged as a peacemaker after centuries of civil war, and his authority was indeed officially predicated on his capacity to enforce peace. This was reflected in the traditional title of *seii tai shogun* (Great General, Conqueror of Barbarians) that Tokugawa Ieyasu received from the emperor. Under the approved leader, an individual Tokugawa samurai's identification with the ruling status group—regardless of his relative position in the military hierarchy—also hinged upon his warrior status. In this way, Japan's early modern social development created a garrison state, which maintained its basic structure during the following two and a half centuries. It is a historical irony that one of the most peaceful eras in Japanese history was obliged to celebrate, at least in theory, the role of military power throughout its existence.

The Institutional Valuation of the Military

The demilitarization of the nonsamurai population also led to the Tokugawa policy sometimes called "rule by status."[7] In the implicit logic of this particular system of status differentiation, all men of samurai status were entitled to bear arms, and they, in theory, collectively protected the remainder of the population, the commoners. "Rule by status" involved the additional distinction that only the samurai were considered fully responsible political agents; therefore, during the Tokugawa period, all government offices were occupied only by men of samurai status. The shogunate stood at the top of the samurai pyramid and, with this qualification, ruled the country. The demilitarization of the nonsamurai population, and the subsequent definition of the samurai as the ruling class, depended on the institutional valuation of the ability to use violence as the source of legitimacy for the samurai's collective domination.

The logical premise undergirding the Tokugawa system of domination continued to assume that the samurai class had a collective monopoly of legitimate use of violence. From this perspective, the alliance between physical violence and military honor continued to be central to the samurai's collective identity. Within the samurai class, however, the *bakuhan* state was based upon the contrasting logic of the *pax Tokugawa*, that is, the domination of the shogunate brought about through a strict limitation of the daimyo's use of military force. Within this second set of structures, the vassal samurai's personal and arbitrary resort to "honor violence" had to be strictly suppressed and controlled. In general, although the daimyo no longer engaged in open warfare, the process involving the transformation of the warrior's competitive and aggressive instincts into a more internally directed and virtue-defined ideal of honor suitable for the organizational lifestyle of the Tokugawa samurai-bureaucrat encountered serious difficulties. These problems stem from the ambivalent logic used to legitimate the Tokugawa system of domination.

The Restructuring of the Samurai Hierarchy

The "Freezing" of the Daimyo Armies

With the sweeping and decisive military victories of the Tokugawa shogun, the student of European early modern history might expect that the shogunate would have dismantled the daimyo's power by building up its own direct fiscal and military machinery, duly extending its direct control over the population of the entire country. The history of Japan, however, did not follow such a path. The Tokugawa shoguns forbade the daimyo to declare war as well as to make independent alliances with other daimyo. Moreover, the daimyo were not allowed to erect new castles or to build large ships. Even a project to repair the stone walls of one's own castle required formal permission from the shogunate.

The shogunate did not demobilize the daimyo armies or incorporate them directly into the national armies under the command of the central government, however. The daimyo were required to retain their own vassals as they always had, and to govern their own subjects in their territories. But the daimyo armies were "frozen" because the Tokugawa overlords did not want the daimyo to use their forces to make war on their own initiative. Indeed, further organizational or technological refinement of the country's military machine came to a halt after the pacification of 1615. The shogunate's isolationist policy, which severely restricted formal diplomatic and mercantile ties with the West, also helped to maintain a domestic political *status quo*.

The Daimyo as Courtier-Vassals

The Tokugawa shogun quickly compelled the daimyo (who had originally held equal status) to accept a hierarchically structured relationship between them, with the shogun as the master and the daimyo as subordinate vassals (see Illustration 4). The daimyo were allowed to govern their territories, but in return they owed the shogun a prescribed amount of military duty, measured in terms of *koku daka* (the productive capacity of a fief measured by a unit of rice output, or *koku*) in the event of an emergency.[8] In theory, the sum of all daimyo military obligations to the shogun amounted to a considerable army; the Tokugawa regime could "field a huge force of 400,000 men," though this capacity was never tested.[9] Each daimyo's *ie* was given a "house ranking" *(ka kaku)* in the shogunate's hierarchy, which roughly corresponded to the amount of *koku daka*.[10] The so-called house daimyo *(fudai)*, who were promoted to the position of daimyo by the Tokugawa, indeed deserved the name of Tokugawa vassals. In contrast, the "outside" daimyo *(tozama)*, such as the lords Uesugi, Mōri, Maeda, and Shimazu, were originally *sengoku daimyo* who had gained their territories through military strength and political shrewdness. Consequently, the assertion on the part of the Tokugawa shogun that he was the master, with the daimyo as his vassals, was a technique to concentrate power in his hands. The governmental positions of the shogunate were occupied by *fudai* and the shogunate's enfeoffed banner men *(hatamoto)*. The *tozama* were largely excluded from the inner sanctum of shogunate politics.

The internal matters of daimyo *ie* were no longer left completely in the hands of the daimyo. Marriages and the disposition of inheritance required official permission from the shogun. The daimyo had to spend alternative periods of residence in Edo and their castle towns *(sankin kōtai)* while leaving their wives in their Edo residence. In the early stages of the shogunate's development, the Tokugawa shoguns willfully confiscated, relocated, and increased or decreased the daimyo's territories, making the daimyo hesitant to challenge the shogun's authority. Moreover, the daimyo were assigned to carry out various large-scale construction projects conducted by the shogunate that placed severe financial burdens on them.

In many ways the daimyo under the Tokugawa system were reduced to the level of sophisticated courtiers at the castle in Edo. The seating arrangement of the daimyo in Edo Castle was used as one of many indices to distinctions in honor that expressed each daimyo house's official ranking at the shogun's court. Life in the Edo Castle was completely regulated by minutely refined ritualistic codes of manners whose details kept the lords preoccupied. There were many symbolic aspects to this etiquette, including ceremonial dress and various decorations that the shogun conferred on the daimyo, which subtly changed the honor ranking of the daimyo's *ie*. Instead of competing on the battlefield, the daimyo courtiers strove to improve their comparative standing in the honor ranking of the shogunate court. They competed for even the most apparently insignificant symbols of honor ranking from the shogun.[11]

Symbiosis

The daimyo did not become refined courtiers to the extent that the French nobility did at the court of Versailles, however. In the case of France, the nobles' feudal power rested on an unstable and shrinking power base. By contrast, the Japanese daimyo were able to retain a strong grip on their vassals, peasantry, and land. The Tokugawa state did not totally deprive the daimyo of their traditional feudal autonomy, but only restricted its exercise as a way of forcing them to acknowledge the shogunate as the ultimate source of authority for the country as a whole. The daimyo could style themselves a minor "public authority" *(kōgi)* as long as they kept within the boundaries of the shogun's "great public authority" *(ō kōgi)*.

The shogunate never established a standard, centralized fiscal system for the entire country, so the daimyo never paid taxes to the shogun; rather, the shogun's central government was financed by the revenue from the vast territories that he directly governed. In addition, the daimyo also retained a judicial system for their own subjects, substantially independent from that of the central government, as well as administrative control over their subordinates. When a particular case infringed on the critical laws and policies of the shogunate, either the shogunate decided the matter directly or the daimyo adjudicated the case in consultation with the shogunate. The daimyo's authority over their subject vassals and peasants actually increased because they were now backed by the higher power of the shogunate. For example, in the event of a violent peasant rebellion, if a single daimyo government proved unable to control the uprising, the shogunate could intervene.[12] A symbiotic relationship between the shogun and the daimyo developed over the collaborative and yet "contested" political terrain of the *bakuhan* state; hence, as Conrad Totman puts it, "Governing activities of *bakufu* [shogunate] and han contributed to each other's survival."[13]

The Daimyo and Their Vassal Relationships

Given this consolidation and reorganization of the power structure at the national level, the daimyo were able to enforce, with more confidence and authority than before, strict control and discipline over their vassals. Consequently, the vassal samurai became socially and economically more and more dependent on their vassalage relationships, without which they would lose even their samurai status. The vassals under a daimyo house became more and more hierarchically organized, and their economic base of independence was severely restricted. Although all the vassal samurai who were under formal vassalage with the daimyo lords shared the same nominal standing as samurai, their actual power, wealth, and prestige differed greatly according to their rankings within the house of the daimyo.

The daimyo authorities also forced vassal samurai to live in the samurai quarters of their castle towns, cut off from direct control over their land. In many cases, the samurai, especially with lower rankings, merely received hereditary stipends, paid in rice. Enfeoffment, considered more prestigious, was often the reward for the upper samurai. Even when they were provided with an actual fief *(chigyō)*, however, their exercise of seigniorial power was significantly restricted because vassals were usually required to live in castle towns. For example, in Kishū han, a vassal who just wanted to visit his own fief had to file a petition with the authorities before leaving the castle town; this procedure was clearly intended to prevent vassals from establishing personal connections with local subjects.[14] In some cases, even though the vassals were nominally enfeoffed, the tax was collected by the daimyo's central bureaucracy and then redistributed to the vassals. In these cases, the vassal had seigniorial power in name only. The manner of paying the samurai varied greatly from *han* to *han*.[15]

In general, the daimyo who had remained in the same domain since the sixteenth century tended to be slower in forcing the samurai to break their old ties with their home villages. In contrast, those daimyo who had moved into a new domain by order of the Tokugawa shogunate found it to their advantage to streamline the samurai hierarchy; and in general, they were quicker to introduce a stipend system. By the middle of the seventeenth century, however, most of the daimyo domains in one way or another had introduced some "early modern" styles of vassal samurai management.

In the preceding centuries of the medieval period, the samurai had duly consolidated their independence by defending their land and property and strengthening the solidarity of their ancestral *ie*. Perpetuating the lineage and prosperity of the *ie* was the most important task for a samurai. Under the Tokugawa system, the vassal samurai did not need to concern themselves with armed defense of their territories. At the same time, the crumbling of their feudal authority weakened their power *vis-à-vis* the daimyo house. The *ie* of the Tokugawa samurai were no longer immune from interference by the daimyo. Every time there was a death in the direct line of inheritance, the new heir needed official permission from the lord to succeed to the headship of the *ie*. Other important family matters, such as marriage, also required the master's formal permission.[16] Compared with the independent nature of the samurai *ie* in medieval Japan, the houses of the Tokugawa samurai vassals were heavily dependent on their masters. In fact, they were almost considered a part of the larger houses of the daimyo or the shogun (if they were direct vassals of the shogunate). The *ie* of each vassal in this newer system carried a basic honor ranking, transferred from generation to generation as if it were a part of the family assets. The *ie* was thus reconstituted as the basic unit of "service" to the state, and the domestic concerns of the individual samurai's *ie* were no longer considered purely private.

At the same time, since each daimyo owed a certain amount of military duty to the shogun according to the size of his domain (measured by rice output, *koku daka*), the daimyo could not easily afford to reduce the number of his vassals. Tokugawa vassalage was a long-term, transgenerational bond between the *ie* of the daimyo and that of the vassal. Once formally employed as a vassal (except in the very lowest positions), a Tokugawa vassal could assume that his *ie* would be in continuous service to the *ie* of the lord for generations to come. As a consequence, although the daimyo in theory possessed absolute authority over the samurai, abusive use of the power to terminate his vassal's *ie* was restricted in practice because such an action would seriously jeopardize the internal solidarity and stability of the daimyo house.

The lives of the Tokugawa samurai were regulated by their incorporation into the strict hierarchy of the samurai organization. The original form of samurai vassalage in the Kamakura period consisted primarily of a personal relationship between master and vassal. The peer relationships among the followers themselves were not strictly regulated. Vassalage was thus conceived of as personal patronage rather than as an impersonal organizational relationship. In contrast, each Tokugawa samurai was placed in a precise position in a clearly stratified organizational hierarchy. The Tokugawa system could properly be called a "regulatory and organizational" type of vassalage. It must be stressed, however, that the transformation of each daimyo's group of vassals into a bureaucratic organization within the Tokugawa state did not undercut the fundamental principle uniting the daimyo lord and his vassals—that is, the military master-follower relationship. Only men of samurai status (meaning those who had entered vassalic relationship with a lord) could hold government offices. In other words, the Tokugawa governmental bureaucracy, which had reached a very sophisticated level by the eighteenth century, was built upon a structural foundation of military organization.

The size of the samurai population is still a disputed question among historical demographers. This is because shogunate population surveys that had been conducted on a national scale since 1721 always excluded the samurai population from the data.[17] Sekiyama Naotarō estimated the samurai population at between 6 and 7 percent of the whole (including women and children of samurai status); other estimates range from 5 to 10 percent. If we assume that roughly one person out of five was an adult male samurai, then at least 1 percent of the whole population was permanently incorporated into central or local government organizations. They all shared the samurai standing, but the actual social and economic positions of these samurai differed sharply according to the ranking they held in the state's hierarchy. The distinctive Japanese form of power consolidation in the early modern period thus inflated the privileged population to a considerable size. As a result, many samurai lacked clear objectives and ambition, making the task of boosting their morale no easy job.

In short, the distinctive nature of Japanese early modern state formation may be attributed to the fact that the consolidation of the country after a long period of civil war was carried out through *a vertical reconstruction of the vassalage system on a national scale.* The formal organization of the state was structured on the logic of hierarchical vassalage, and its mature organizational style in many ways precisely reflected the cultural myth of the samurai master-follower relationship, which had long been institutionalized.

8

An Integrated
Yet Decentralized
State Structure

The mature pattern of Tokugawa society consisted of multiple layers of power structures integrated into the shogunate's hierarchy. Each lower unit of control was allowed to be semiautonomous while owing certain obligations to the higher levels of power. Thus, a person who belonged to a given unit was assigned a certain role in society, and thereby situated within the pyramidal state structure.[1] By assigning each social organization and status group a specific obligation *(yaku)* according to its occupational and status categories, the Tokugawa system was able to construct an idiosyncratic hierarchy consisting of social groups that were internally highly dissimilar. These groups ranged from the shogun to lesser samurai, farmers, townsmen, and outcasts on down to those on the margins of society. If each individual were to fulfill his designated role and feel satisfied with the lifestyle that accorded with his place in society, then—so it was assumed—society as a whole would enjoy peace and prosperity. The resulting structure of Tokugawa social organizations—from the villages to the samurai houses—that emerged during the process of pacification displayed many prototypical characteristics now regarded as distinctive features of Japanese social organizations.

In contrast to the prevalent image of Tokugawa Japan as a "police state," an image that was popularized by the classic work of E. H. Norman, originally published in the 1930s, the actual strength of the regime's control lay in its flexibility. In reality, it gave considerable disciplinary discretion to lower- and middle-range social organizations. It is significant that the Tokugawa shogunate never developed an organized police force at either the national or the local level; characteristically, the commoner section in the city of Edo, with a population of approximately 500,000 to 600,000 in the mid-Tokugawa period,[2] was administered by a corps of about 250 samurai officers *(yoriki/dōshin)* under the two Edo magistracy *(machi-bugyō)* offices. The officers had a range of responsibilities, including maintaining public order, punishing criminals, fire prevention and control, and judging civil suits.[3] The small size of this administrative staff in a large capital city was possible only because the local communities (wards) were given the responsibility of self-policing in cooperation with the authorities. As long as people were fulfilling the duties assigned to their positions in society, and were responsible members of their local disciplinary organizations, the authorities were not concerned with regulating them individually. By being decentralized and flexible, the Tokugawa system made good use of the self-governing capacities of middle-range social organizations, which thereby dealt with unrest from below at an intermediate level. This structural arrangement precluded the possibility of opposition from the bottom levels of society threatening the upper reaches of the hierarchy, namely, the authority of the shogun.

At first glance, compared with the modern nation-state equipped with sophisticated rules and legally prescribed regulations, Tokugawa society looks like a loose collection of organic social groups. Upon closer inspection, however, it is obvious that the system was embedded in the society by carefully devised control strategies. These strategies defused potentially dangerous elements within each social group, and at the same time utilized their self-governing abilities in the service of the state; that is, the traditional disciplinary systems were politicized for the purposes of the newly emerging order of government. Indeed, the Tokugawa period has been described as "the most artificially and politically planned and structured society in Japanese history."[4]

The integration of society through a division of labor was a critical organizing principle of the Tokugawa *bakuhan* state. Local daimyo domains, villages, and other middle-range social organizations were allowed to be semiautonomous, and power was thereby effectively decentralized. The members of each social organization were governed primarily by a chief, who was a member of that organization, not a bureaucrat of the government, and the authorities kept their control over the organization through that chief. In this way, each group was deliberately incorporated into a hierarchical state system with the authority of the central state standing firmly over it. Thus, society was reorganized into an integrated yet decentralized structure framed within a pyramidal power configuration. Social organizations kept their organic autonomy, but that autonomy was confined within the larger framework of social control that the *bakuhan* state provided.

This combination of a decentralized and integrated state structure was visible at the level of national politics in the form of shogunate-daimyo relationships. The configuration of social control penetrated much deeper, however, reaching the very fabric of Japanese social order. Given the stability of the central power structure, Tokugawa social control aimed at reorganizing the population through an interlocking network of various middle-range social organizations—local communities, status groups, and occupational guilds.

The Formation of Early Modern Villages

One of the fundamental features of the *bakuhan* state was its policy toward the agrarian population of Japan. The indirect strategy of social control discussed in the preceding section is best exemplified by the transformation of villages under the Tokugawa regime. The so-called *sō-son* (corporate villages) of the medieval period had been both self-governing and self-armed. They often spawned ferocious peasant rebellions, which posed the most serious threat to the ruling feudal authorities in the late medieval period. The Tokugawa villages preserved much of the legacy of medieval social autonomy, but the exercise of their self-governing abilities was circumscribed and restricted under the new order of the Tokugawa state.

In the course of the sixteenth century, the villages had increased their self-governing capacities and armed forces through the organization of *ikki*. In reaction to village autonomy, Hideyoshi's decisive policies of sword-hunting and cadastral surveys, and subsequent Tokugawa policies along the same line, eliminated the villages' capacity for self-defense and crippled their political autonomy. As a result, by comparison with the medieval *sō-son*, the Tokugawa villages were incorporated much more securely into the state. At the outset of the Tokugawa period, some *dogō* (landed wealthy village leaders) had been moving up in status to become samurai vassals of the daimyo, while others preferred to stay in their villages. Those who entered vassalage with a daimyo were compelled to live in his castle town, thereby losing their main assets—direct control over agricultural production and the personal authority they held over local subjects. *Dogō* who continued to reside in the villages were deprived of their armed forces and denied many of their previous privileges, such as personal control over the villages. As the landed samurai-like wealthy farmers had always formed the core of village-based resistance to feudal military lords, the decline of the *dogō* in the villages secured the daimyo's domination over them.

During the seventeenth century, the ongoing expansion of arable lands through reclamation and refinement of agricultural technology greatly increased the productive capacity of the agricultural sector of the Japanese economy. This agricultural development, together with the decline of the *dogō*'s influence, offered a fresh opportunity to small-scale peasant families who had been subjected to the personal domination of the wealthier farmers. These lesser farm families cultivated their own lands, primarily relying on the labor of the immediate family and relatives. The small-scale farmers were not completely free individuals, but neither were they mere serfs who were totally dependent upon and subjected to a feudal lord.[5] The typical "early modern" village was thus primarily based upon the *ie* of partially independent small-scale farmers *(hon byakushō)*. This early modern pattern of village structure emerged in many areas of Japan in the mid-seventeenth century.[6]

Unlike medieval villages, the villages of Tokugawa Japan were subject to much more intense scrutiny and control from their samurai overlords. The productive capacities and conditions of the villages were exhaustively surveyed, and the inhabitants' names appeared on the lists of a family registration system. The authorities attempted to ferret out all the information that villagers were likely to conceal, in order to maximize their tax revenue. In addition, the shogunate introduced the so-called five-family unit *(gonin-gumi)* in the villages. In this system, a group of five families *(ie)* would be responsible for providing one another with surveillance and mutual assistance—paying taxes, disciplining and prosecuting criminal behavior, and the like.

Although Tokugawa agricultural policies directed at the peasantry were strict, this class did derive some advantages from the regime. For example, the villages themselves, and not the samurai officers, governed the daily lives of their people. The government head *(shōya)* and other executive positions *(mura yakunin)* in the village government were occupied by members of the traditional wealthy elite in the early Tokugawa period. With the upward mobility of the small-scale peasants in the village economy, however, the possibility existed for the villagers to replace their officers. Because the samurai did not live in the villages, in practice the peasants had considerable power over the actual management of their agricultural enterprise. They could experiment with the introduction of commercial agricultural production at their own discretion, something that encouraged the commercialization of the rural economy. The villages continued to maintain some communal properties, and they had their own village codes—even though their self-governing ability was restricted by the legal framework of the new order.[7] Most important, since the Tokugawa villages were collectively responsible for paying taxes, they had, by extension, bargaining power over their samurai authorities in terms of negotiating tax rates and other critical issues. Thus, throughout the Tokugawa period, villages functioned as basic units of social control in collaboration with the authorities, while continuing to be aggressive collective bargaining units against official power.

The Spread of Disciplinary Organizations

This strategy, which amounted to a reconstitution of middle-range social organizations as disciplinary units to maintain the order of the Tokugawa state, was most evident in village restructuring; however, other social groups, such as occupational organizations, guilds, special status groups (including those of priests, outcasts, blind persons, and the like) reorganized themselves along similar lines. These groups were permitted to govern themselves, and they were responsible for their members' discipline and mutual assistance, as well as for fulfilling the group's designated role and duties *(yaku)* to the state.

To illustrate this pattern, I will provide a brief overview of some of these organizations. For example, people of outcast status *(eta, hinin)* were systematically regrouped under several powerful outcast heads. The earlier outcast communities had existed in the medieval period as a distinct category of occupational groups with their own self-governing powers. These groups became increasingly subject to social discrimination toward the late medieval period. With the establishment of the samurai hegemony in the Tokugawa period, the Tokugawa authorities gave them formal recognition as outcasts, casting them into a status below that of commoner.[8]

The most powerful house of outcast families was Danzaemon, which had originally been a member of a leather crafters' group *(eta)* in the Tokugawa Domain. With the shogunate's support, by the late seventeenth century the Danzaemon family had expanded its power over all the outcasts within the shogunate domain, incorporating a number of local outcast communities. In its mature stage, the Tokugawa outcast status group was divided into two major categories, *eta* and *hinin* (the latter being largely beggars during this period). Both *eta* and *hinin* within the Tokugawa Domain and several other provinces were headed by locally powerful families, but these were in turn subject to the ultimate supervision of Danzaemon. As *yaku* (obligations), the *eta-hinin* group under Danzaemon offered two kinds of service to the shogunate: labor for the operation of the penal system (as jail guards and executioners) and the provision of leather crafts. In return, the occupational privileges of the group were protected from outside competition, and the head of the caste was granted a large measure of discretionary power.[9] Danzaemon was even allowed to impose the death penalty on criminals of outcast status.[10]

In a similar manner, the blind, who often supported themselves by special trades such as acupuncture, massage, and music performed on the *koto* and the *shamisen*, were all compelled to join a control unit (regardless of their original status) called *tōdō*. The heads of *tōdō*, the officials known as *kengyō*, exercised a strong paternalistic authority over their members. Under the chief officer, *sō-kengyō*, an executive committee and administrative officers (nonblind) also governed the members of this status group. As with Danzaemon, it was part of the *kengyō's* job to punish criminals within the group. Thus, both organizations, for the outcast and the blind, policed and provided mutual help for the marginal population.

The reorganization of middle-range social groups to serve the state's purposes can be observed in a number of areas of Tokugawa life: regional communities such as villages and town wards; temples and shrines; occupational groups such as craft guilds and other trade groups; and merchant guilds. As a result of this indirect system of control, the political institutions by which the state directly controlled individuals through public institutions of social control were relatively underdeveloped in Tokugawa Japan. Although there were some exceptions after the mid-Tokugawa period, such as the reformatory prisons (named *ninsoku yo-seba*), established for the marginal population, a public medical facility in Edo (Yōjōsho, which remained the only public hospital during the Tokugawa period), and schools for samurai children in both shogunate and local domains, these reforms remained on a small scale. For instance, although the regime had a favorable attitude toward education, Tokugawa schooling did not evolve into a system of universal education that would have incorporated both the samurai and the commoner population. Instead, the *bakuhan* authorities monitored the functioning of the disciplinary social organizations; and if necessary, they imposed sanctions or provided support for the heads of these groups.

This fundamental and characteristic social framework of the Tokugawa state had a major impact on the subsequent orientation of Japanese social relations: it transformed the structures of indigenous social groups, reorganizing them into forms that were more amenable to domination by higher authorities. The heads of such organizations exercised a paternalistic form of authority that was strengthened by the sanctions of the state. At the same time, the internal structures of these organizations were not simply hierarchical and oppressive; they provided genuine mutual assistance and opportunities for participation by group members. Many of the characteristics of modern Japanese social organizations, their organizational culture, and their relationships with state authorities, appear in embryonic form in the Tokugawa pattern of social organizations.

Under the Tokugawa regime's integrated yet decentralized polity, which reorganized previously autonomous social groups in a system of *yaku,* or obligations to the state, nothing in society remained within a genuinely "private" sphere. For example, the criminal conduct of an employee in a merchant house made the employer liable to punishment. Similarly, a disciplinary problem involving vassals might cause their master, a daimyo lord, to incur heavy penalties imposed by the shogun. In the world of the samurai in particular, all the activities that had previously been considered safe from state interference were no longer protected. This shrinking of the private sphere contributed to an idiosyncratic social environment, out of which a distinctive early modern conception of public and private emerged.

The preceding description of the Tokugawa state should not be taken to imply that this system of social control was completely effective in suppressing the discontent of the lower orders. The more closely historians scrutinize the detailed workings of Japanese villages and towns, as well as the interactions between commoners and samurai authorities, the clearer it becomes that the shogunate's and the daimyo's disciplinary power rarely reached below the surface of the people's daily life. By maximizing their privileges of self-government, and taking advantage of the distance between state and local authorities, powerful leaders in the villages or other status or occupational groups were able to wield considerable actual power. In particular, since all the samurai lived in castle towns, villagers had substantial autonomy in terms of the daily administration of their villages.

The integrated yet decentralized system of the Tokugawa state reflected not only the weakness of its social control but also the source of its strength—namely, flexibility. The system allocated a generous amount of room for self-government to middle-range organizations that were better able to respond to local needs. Furthermore, because of this decentralized structure, political opposition from below was usually focused on the immediate local superior; it rarely resulted in direct confrontation with the central government. The shogunate's authority was often utilized as a kind of court of last resort to resolve internal conflicts in a group, or to correct injustices committed by an immediate superior such as the head of the village, a local samurai officer, or the daimyo house. Because of this indirect system of domination, in spite of various rebellions and the weakness of its direct arms of social control, the Tokugawa shogunate was able to avoid becoming the direct target of opposition from below for two and a half centuries.

Threats to the Tokugawa System

Beneath the veneer of this relatively peaceful social order, however, there always remained a potential for dangerous, if covert, competition for political power under the Tokugawa domination. The most critical struggle of this type stemmed from the tension between the established system of domination and subsequent vigorous economic developments.

In order to understand the sociopolitical climate in which the reformulation of samurai culture took place, I will outline a picture of this tension
in which the Tokugawa samurai were caught. Since the primary aim of
this book is the examination of the cultural metamorphosis of the samurai, however, space does not permit a detailed analysis of economic development under the Tokugawa and its sociopolitical consequences.

The Commercialization of the Tokugawa Economy

The Tokugawa state did not change the fundamental system of its initial
control and domination during its tenure. The Tokugawa economy grew
vigorously inside this framework of control, however, and eventually the
social developments concomitant with that growth broke the bounds of
the Tokugawa *bakuhan* rule. The establishment of a decentralized yet
highly integrated political system encouraged economic growth and facilitated the development of a market economy on a national scale. The
subsequent social developments stimulated by these gradual economic
changes encouraged population and commodity mobility. This new
fluidity in turn generated serious problems in many areas for the *bakuhan* system of domination.

The extensive economic development of the sixteenth and seventeenth
centuries, as the result of the reclamation of arable land, caused the accumulation of economic surplus in many villages. The expansion of the
amount of arable land was due in part to vigorous efforts on the part of
the local daimyo, who attempted to extend irrigation construction on a
large scale, and thereby to increase agricultural production. Improvements in agricultural technology in this period also accelerated economic
growth.[11] Moreover, the development of agricultural production continued into the early seventeenth century as the extended period of peace
further encouraged economic expansion. Significant increases in basic
productive forces were reflected in the remarkable population growth of
the early Tokugawa period. Miyamoto Matarō estimates that the population of Tokugawa Japan may have started from 12 million in 1600 to
make a significant increase in the seventeenth century, reaching more
than 31 million by 1720.[12] Thereafter, the population generally remained
around that level.

The increase of arable land reached its limit in the late seventeenth
century. By then, however, the nature of the Tokugawa economy had

undergone a significant change. By the late seventeenth to the early eighteenth century, many Japanese villages were no longer simply self-sufficient, closed agricultural communities. The establishment of a regional daimyo polity and the development of local castle towns encouraged the formation of local market economies into which the villages were tightly incorporated. The commercial production of agricultural commodities first became conspicuous in the relatively advanced area of Kinai (the areas surrounding Kyoto and Osaka), and then spread throughout the whole country. The exchange of commodities was carried out at a national level, and increasing numbers of urban residents began to enjoy the benefits of commercialization.

The pacification of the country provided a social environment conducive to expanding long-distance trade. The shogunate institutionalized a standardized monetary system and invested in a national transportation network, which included major roads with a system of rest stations, and sea lines connecting the major cities. The institutionalization of the alternate residence system for daimyo, between Edo and their local domains, also promoted a steady flow of people and goods between Edo and the provinces. The single most important factor stimulating a market economy, however, was the dependence of the shogunate's and the daimyo's finances on tax revenue paid in rice, which was sold for cash in the market.

Another factor contributing to the growth of long-distance trade was the increase of the urban population in centers of consumption. To give an example, after the establishment of the shogunate, the city of Edo underwent rapid expansion, reaching, by the mid-eighteenth century, a population of nearly one million. By the year 1700, Osaka and Kyoto were also flourishing population centers, as were the local castle towns of the major daimyo domains. The population living in these three large cities in the mid-eighteenth century constituted approximately 5 to 7 percent of the total Japanese population in this period.[13]

By the late seventeenth century, a full-blown national market economy flourished.[14] One more contributing factor was that, during the Tokugawa period, all the samurai and their families lived in cities and depended on the availability of commercial goods there. Commercialization brought a relatively lower price for rice and a higher price for other commodities, a situation that worsened the state of rice-dependent daimyo finances. The increased expense, in particular, caused by *sankin kōtai* (alternate residence in Edo and home area), and of keeping up official bureaus in Edo, increased the financial pressures on the daimyo.

Changing Class Relationships

As we have seen, the seemingly unshakable superstructure of the Tokugawa regime had been built on a highly conflict-ridden political terrain where battles for supremacy had been fought at different social levels. Although the neo-feudal reconstruction of the social order provided a powerful solution to these internal conflicts, the subsequent social and economic development under the Tokugawa system created new kinds of tensions that presented a new challenge to the samurai's collective domination. This threat came from two major sources: the continual unrest of the peasants, and the increasing affluence of the merchants.

Of the two sources of class conflict, the peasantry continued to present the greater threat. Of course, the demilitarization of the villages and the separation of samurai and farmer status kept the villages disarmed and offset the dangerous possibility that local samurai and villagers might form alliances. Yet, because the villages maintained their self-governing functions and paid their taxes collectively, they had the means and the opportunity to form vociferous collective uprisings.

Unlike the conventional image of Japanese peasants in the feudal era, Tokugawa villagers were far from docile and submissive. The Japanese historian Aoki Kōji, who has surveyed a wide range of local documents, found no fewer than 6889 instances of contentious upheaval throughout the Tokugawa period, including 3212 incidents involving peasant *ikki*—actions of complaint addressed to the samurai authorities; 3189 internal village conflicts; and 488 urban disturbances of some sort.[15] Although most of these contentious movements were relatively nonconfrontational—such as filing petitions repeatedly—they were sometimes organized into large-scale shows of force that continuously threatened the foundations of the samurai domination throughout the Tokugawa period.

In general, the frequency, intensity, and scale of peasant collective actions increased over time toward the late Tokugawa period. The commercial economy apparently influenced Tokugawa peasant unrest. Commercial agriculture spread into the rural areas, displacing self-sufficient farming, creating social stratification within villages, and contributing to the emergence of a class of poor farm laborers. All these elements destabilized the village power structure and increased intravillage conflicts, thus indirectly threatening the samurai administration, which relied on the villages' capacities for self-discipline. The expanding commercial economy also brought about the deterioration of the economic base of the rice-dependent daimyo and shogun. Their attempts to increase the taxes on grain, and to extract more revenue from commercial agriculture (such as the silk and cotton industries of rural areas), often triggered large-scale protests. During the second half of the Tokugawa period in particular, it was not uncommon for many villages to form an alliance and field powerful demonstrations of several thousand angry peasants.[16]

In sum, the threat from the villages brought problems as well as opportunities for the samurai class: problems, because their economic base continued to depend upon tax revenue from agricultural production; opportunities, because putting down peasant rebellions offered the only realistic possibility of demonstrating the samurai's coercive force, since there was no formal warfare among the daimyo. For the daimyo, this need for the samurai to act as a peace-keeping force against peasant rebellion in times of emergency was another reason, though not the only one, that the reduction of the vassal samurai was difficult.[17]

Compared with the peasantry, the Tokugawa merchants were less of a political threat as a class; nonetheless, their increasing economic superiority to the samurai class became obvious. The commercialization of the Tokugawa economy was highly favorable to the merchant class, which engaged in trading various commodities. Both the daimyo and the shogunate were slow to shift their source of revenue in a direction suited to an age of commercial economy; thus, their finances continued to depend primarily upon the grain tax revenue, and the merchants enjoyed comparatively low taxes. The price of rice generally decreased in the eighteenth century compared with the soaring prices of commercial commodities. This development further eroded the rice-dependent economic base of the samurai. After the mid-Tokugawa period, the daimyo continually borrowed cash from major merchants in order to meet immediate expenses, putting up the next year's tax revenue as collateral. Individual samurai did the same. Given their largely fixed stipend from the lord, and their increasingly sophisticated urban lifestyle, many vassal samurai were caught in worsening financial straits, and were prone to carry large debts.

The far-reaching socioeconomic changes experienced during the Tokugawa shogunate's long tenure did not produce fundamental alterations in its political structure. The state continued to avoid the direct supervision of individual subjects, and it maintained its basic integrated yet decentralized structure. It continued its dependency on the self-governing capabilities of villages, town wards, and various other professional and status groups. The samurai remained the sole political officeholders, and the commoners continued to be shut out from the political process.

To understand the connection between this phenomenon of hierarchical decentralization and the central argument of my book, it is particularly important to note that, in order to keep this integrated yet highly decentralized social system functional, solidarity among the samurai vassals themselves became increasingly important. Because the state had no effective agents of external enforcement other than the presence of the samurai, popular internalization of obedience and habituation to the men of the samurai status was of the essence. Under this circumstance, civil order depended to a great extent on the voluntary acceptance of the authority and the *status* supremacy of the samurai.

As an integrated part of this pattern of domination, the samurai maintained their official monopoly on social honor. For the samurai class to maintain its political-cultural hegemony was not an easy task, however, caught as it was between a vigorously assertive peasantry and increasingly wealthy merchants. As they confronted both serious financial constraints and challenges from the peasantry, the samurai were politically required to maintain their sense of warrior pride. This they had to do in spite of the fact that their daily reality had little to do with the glory of battlefield heroics but increasingly resembled the lives of colorless bureaucrats. Surrounded by a prosperous urban consumerism and an attractive culture of townsmen, the life of the ordinary Tokugawa samurai was ridden with many cultural contradictions politically fixed in a changing society. It was in these uncongenial circumstances that the refocusing of the samurai's collective identity took place.

9

The Tokugawa Neo-Feudal State: A Comparative Evaluation

We have thus far examined the major characteristics of the Japanese early modern state on its own terms. Let us now observe Tokugawa Japan from a comparative standpoint, in order to ascertain more clearly the distinctive characteristics of Japan's early modern state formation.

To arrive at a comparative assessment of Tokugawa society, it may be useful to reexamine certain historical notions, such as "feudalism," that are frequently used to describe Tokugawa Japan. Concepts such as "feudalism" and "absolutism" may have some comparative utility if they are intentionally used as ideal historical types.[1] In particular, such an exercise may be helpful for those who are not specialists on Japan but who are well informed concerning the history of Western social development. Like any other notion of an ideal type that is originally derived from actual historical experience, however, these particular concepts have often been used to convey different meanings. Thus, we must begin with an examination of the various usages of these notions.

Feudalism

Feudalism as a generic term is loosely used to describe the social, political, and military structures that were typical of medieval Europe. Scholars have tended to emphasize different aspects of social life as characteristically feudal, however. Traditionally, in British and German medieval historiography, "feudalism" refers to military and judicial functions embodied in the *feudum* (the fief) as the system of military organization. This definition focuses on the legal aspects of feudalism—knightly contractual services and exchanges of protection and fidelity. This is the narrow definition of feudalism, often criticized as reducing a more complex underlying social reality to a single issue.[2]

A broader political definition of feudalism, focusing on larger configurations of political structures, usually emphasizes such characteristics as fragmentation of political power; the placement of public power in private hands; and a military system of vassalage. To summarize the essence of their functions, Joseph Strayer looks at feudalism as "a method of government, and a way of securing the forces necessary to preserve that method of government."[3] These three political characteristics are almost entirely applicable to the political structure of medieval Japan. But in the case of Tokugawa Japan we must note some important deviations with respect to the first and second points, because early modern Japan achieved a high degree of political concentration with the establishment of the shogunate as a strong public authority in the name of *kōgi*. The military system of vassalage was also transformed. Within the peaceful Tokugawa society, the master-vassal association was characterized not by a contractual-reciprocal relationship (although Japanese medieval vassalage did include an element of contractual relationship insofar as it was conceived as the exchange of *go'on* and *hōkō*) but by the vassal's total dependence upon and loyalty to the master.

The economics-oriented Marxist interpretation holds that feudalism is essentially a mechanism for transferring agricultural surplus to the lordly class. Thus, the institution of lordship is specific to feudalism, and it is "within the lordship," to borrow the words of R. H. Hilton, "that the two main classes of feudal society meet for the transfer of the surplus and its conversion into landowner income."[4] This focus on the economic foundation of feudalism is, however, no longer the monopoly of purely Marxist interpretations. From an economic perspective, both medieval Europe and Tokugawa Japan were unquestionably feudal societies. There were two main classes in the Japanese mode of production, samurai lords and peasants. The mechanism of vassalage can be regarded as the samurai's political technique for extracting economic surplus from the peasants.

It is the very technique of surplus transfer that is visibly different in Japanese feudalism, however, particularly in Tokugawa feudalism. The economic component of feudalism, as indispensable as it may be to an understanding of the substructures of Tokugawa feudalism and of the similarity between the European and the Japanese experiences, cannot encompass the differences between the political structures and the important implications of those structures in both East and West.

A synthetic definition that perceives feudalism as a social system rather than a solely economic or political system was most notably advanced by Marc Bloch in the form of a combination of Marxist-economic and liberal-political definitions. Bloch considered the following to be characteristic of feudalism: "a subject peasantry; widespread use of the service tenement (i.e., the fief) instead of salary supremacy of a class of specialized warriors; ties of obedience and protection which bind man to man within the warrior class assume the distinctive form called vassalage; fragmentation of authority—leading inevitably to disorder; and, in the midst of all of this, survival of other forms of association, family and State."[5] Tokugawa Japan deviates from the last two features of this definition—fragmentation of authority and survival of other forms of association. "Survival" seems too weak a term for the renewed importance of the *ie* and the politically restructured villages and other social organizations. Furthermore, the formation of the more integrated Tokugawa state is not a mere survival. It was obvious in Tokugawa Japan not only that "other forms of association" had significant positions in society but that social organizations such as *ie*, villages, and occupational groups were intentionally reorganized to serve the ends of the Tokugawa state.

This examination of various definitions of feudalism reveals that Tokugawa society can be regarded as a version of feudalism from almost every angle, but that it still differs from the ideal types generated by the European medieval experience—particularly in its political structure. In order to put Tokugawa Japan into a comparative perspective, identifying its difference from Western feudalism according to the dimension of static structure is not enough. The comparative nature of the Tokugawa state should be understood in the context of its dynamic genesis, the nature of the historical transition from the medieval to the early modern Tokugawa state.

The Genesis of the Tokugawa State

Absolutist states in Europe are usually perceived as products of social discontinuity from the feudal medieval past. One of the attractions of Perry Anderson's widely read book *Lineages of the Absolutist State* is his emphasis on the social continuity underlying the early modern states of Europe. In *Lineages,* Anderson presents his basic hypothesis that absolutism was essentially feudal because it was "*a redeployed and recharged apparatus of feudal domination,* designed to clamp the peasant masses back into their traditional social position."[6] Whether his model of the absolutist state better articulates the nature of European early modern state formation is a much debated question that has not yet been resolved. Unlike Anderson, who stresses a strong connection between feudalism and the absolutist state, some scholars (including Immanuel Wallerstein) pay more attention to the connection between the rise of mercantile capitalism and the absolutist state.[7] The rising bourgeoisie pressed the state to institute policies favoring economic nationalism, and thus demanded a strong government.

The applicability of these two models seems to be different within each European country. Some European states evidently had a strong bourgeoisie, while others experienced close relationships between the landed aristocracy and the monarchy. It may be more useful to consider these two schools of interpretation as two distinct patterns of absolutist genesis, rather than to regard either of them as one model applicable to all cases.

The genesis of the Tokugawa regime does not much resemble the mercantile model. In the early sixteenth century, trade and commercial activities were on the rise in Japan, but in spite of that fact, the merchants never developed a strong power base as a class. Consequently, the power structure of the Tokugawa state does not reflect the influence of the merchant class. Furthermore, the shogunate's policy of isolating the country and restricting international trade at the beginning of the seventeenth century struck a serious blow at the first generation of mercantile associations, whose business was increasing in the late sixteenth century. Thus, in the formative process of Tokugawa state-making, merchant capital did not play a significant role. Tokugawa state formation can best be understood as a redeployment of feudalism, confronting the serious crisis of feudal domination in the late medieval period, rather than as an accommodation to mercantilistic development.

On the basis of the preceding analysis, I propose that the distinctive trajectory of Tokugawa state formation can be understood as follows. The Tokugawa state was a redeployed political apparatus that emerged out of the late medieval turmoil of class struggle. Both medieval and Tokugawa Japan were ruled by the samurai class, and thus there was an apparent continuity. Toward the end of the Japanese medieval period, the villages became stronger and more independent, and the farmers often formed *ikki* associations against samurai lords. Because of the villagers' feisty and independent attitudes, ensuring a steady flow of tax revenue from the agricultural communities became a critical concern for the samurai lords. By suppressing the villagers on the one hand, and competing with one another for territory on the other, the samurai class reorganized itself and reconstituted its social hierarchy. This reorganization of the samurai contributed to the formation of the Tokugawa *baku-han* state, which not only reconstituted the national hierarchy of the military houses but also reconfigured the entire country's variety of social organizations, securing the domination of the military landlord class over all others.

Absolutism

If Tokugawa Japan can be regarded as a reorganized form of feudal domination, which Anderson considers the chief characteristic of the European absolutist state, why not call Tokugawa Japan simply "absolutist"?[8] Let me examine this proposition.

The concept of "absolutism" is more elusive than "feudalism," owing in part to the greater differences among the various structures of the early modern states in Europe. Most scholars would agree, however, that absolutism as a historical concept has two important characteristics, which Michael Mann describes as follows:

1. *The monarch is the sole human source of law,* although as he is subject to the law of God, some residual right of rebellion exists if he transgresses "natural law. . . ."
2. *The monarch governs with the aid of a permanent, professional, dependent bureaucracy and army.* The officers, civil and military, have no significant autonomous power or social status except for that conferred by their office.[9]

If we transfer Mann's first criterion to Tokugawa Japan, we could consider it a genuinely absolutist regime, perhaps to an even greater extent than the corresponding European states. The Tokugawa rulers established their absolute authority, and all the Tokugawa laws *(hō)* issued solely from the shogun's authority. There was no representative body of any sort to curb his power. Furthermore, Japan lacked an equivalent of the European concept of natural law, or of the law of God, to which the European absolutist monarch was theoretically subject. Although the term *hō* (law) frequently appeared in the documents of the shogunate, the Tokugawa codes were either administrative ordinances or authoritarian decrees and edicts—in either case simply written commands. From this perspective, the Japanese shogun's authority was even more absolute than that of early modern European monarchs.

With respect to the second characteristic, Tokugawa Japan certainly diverged significantly from the European pattern of the absolutist state. As I demonstrated earlier, the shogunate never attempted to do away entirely with the daimyo's influence over the local land and population; moreover, it never introduced direct institutions of government, such as a national bureaucracy, a standing army, national police, or a national taxation system, to enforce direct supervision of the citizenry and their possessions. My reluctance to label Tokugawa society "absolutist" is also partly due to the state's lack of a fully developed centralized organizational political apparatus (a public treasury, a separate judiciary, a national bureaucracy, police, and a national standing army) as it is found in a modern Western state. The absence of permanent and direct state political apparatuses alone could not preclude the use of the absolutist label, however. It is well known that not all European early modern states had such elements, but some scholars still define them as quasi-absolutist states.

The fundamental difficulty that I have with categorizing the Tokugawa state as absolutist is that such a definition obscures the distinctive characteristics of Japan's early modern social change. Defining Tokugawa Japan as absolutist would be to imply that Europe and Japan reached similar conclusions when they confronted the crisis of the feudal mode of social and political institutions. Indeed, the specific Japanese responses to the crisis of late medieval feudalism, the characteristics and combinations of its social and political reorganization, cannot be understood by analogies to Western absolutism. Japan's reorganization of social, political, and military institutions, such as a stipend-supported hereditary ruling class separated from landownership, indirect control based on semiautonomous daimyo domains and villages, and strict status distinctions that differentiated samurai, farmers, and merchants, has no real Western counterpart. In particular, the transformation of the samurai class from feudal military landlords to paid bureaucrats whose direct influence over land was strictly limited represents a distinctive self-transformation of a ruling class.

In Europe, the national bureaucracy under absolutist regimes developed as an arm of the monarchy, which attempted to bring the functions of the government within a centralized structure. Bureaucracy was by its nature a completely different type of organization from the aristocracy, who based their rights and privileges on an accident of birth. During the early modern period, the king or emperor's immediate bureaucracy emerged in the face of opposition from a still-powerful noble class. Of course, it is important to note that these fledgling European bureaucracies did not assume a rational meritocratic shape from the outset. In French law, as Hans Rosenberg explains, the *officiers* were the numerous patrimonial officials who combined public authority with rights of private ownership. Although the appointment of *officiers* had to be approved by the crown, once the position was obtained, the income it generated in the forms of fees and perquisites was almost like the income from a landed estate. Acquiring such an office was also a springboard for acquisition of noble status. In contrast, the *commissaires* appeared later as a small body of "new bureaucrats," and as salaried subordinates to the monarch.[10] In reality, these two categories overlapped, but technically they were legally distinct.

The important point to be made here is that the Tokugawa samurai bureaucrat was different from either the *officiers* or the *commissaires*. The samurai cannot be accurately compared to the *commissaire,* because his samurai status, a prerequisite for officeholding, was commonly acquired by birth. But his offices were not considered private assets, and there was no institutionalized sale of offices in Japan. Aristocratic patrimonial elements continued, since the *ie* of the samurai included property, honor, and the income attached to it. Because the Tokugawa samurai's *ie* was no longer socially autonomous, insofar as inheritance required the permission of the lord, the privileges attached to the *ie* were not completely personal property. Moreover, the governmental post itself was usually not inherited, although the assumption of a particular government post was not entirely meritocratic, either. Each office was usually linked to the appropriate range of honor status of each *ie;* therefore, a son of a lower-status samurai *ie* had a limited opportunity for promotion.

The Tokugawa samurai bureaucracy was functionally similar to the Western early modern bureaucracy; that is, the regime increased job specialization, followed regulations and precedents, and introduced objective and impersonal patterns of management. Tokugawa "professionalization" had an apparent limit, however. The fundamental premise of Tokugawa "bureaucracy" lies in the logic of vassalage, which was very different from that of the West. The Tokugawa samurai were thought of as persons who combined the roles of the aristocracy, the military, and the bureaucracy, three functions that were increasingly divided among distinctively different social groups in early modern Europe. Yet, the samurai were different from the European aristocracy in that they totally lost their socioeconomic base of independence. Therefore, in order to underscore the distinctive experience of Japanese early modern state formation, my sociological view reinterprets the genesis of the European and Japanese states in the following way: *Medieval Europe and Japan arrived at different solutions, the absolutist state and the Tokugawa neo-feudal state, respectively, in response to the crises of feudalism in the late medieval period. The Japanese solution offered Japan a critical environment for the unique cultural development of the Tokugawa samurai.*

The Tokugawa state was an organizational mechanism that collectively secured the common interests of the military landlord class; that is, it was a neo-feudal state. The distinctive characteristic of the Tokugawa state organization, as I have articulated it in the previous chapters, was its manner of achieving centralization and pacification while preserving the semiautonomous nature of various social groups. This achievement in turn was the result of responding and adapting to the social challenges that the samurai class, by the late medieval period, had been confronting for centuries. The Japanese solution to the late medieval crisis of feudalism, which regrouped various social organizations into a decentralized yet integrated pyramidal power structure, offered Japan a special environment for the subsequent development of distinctive styles of social and cultural institutions. In this sense, the strength of the Tokugawa regime cannot be understood only in terms of its authoritarian "absoluteness." The preserving of social organizations' (including villages') self-governing abilities yielded some degree of autonomy to group members while relieving them of the burden of self-defense.

This unique form of feudal redeployment in Tokugawa Japan was the final result of compromise between the central and daimyo powers and the various social organizations that had been empowered in the previous periods. John Hall recently wrote in opposing an overtly authoritarian picture of the Tokugawa system presented earlier by such writers as E. H. Norman: "Seventeenth-century social theory did not subscribe to concepts of individual rights or political representation; yet the *bakufu* [shogunate], *han* [daimyo domain], and *mura* [village] governments did provide for dispute resolution and arbitration. . . . [For example] the *ie* system of family organization offered a mechanism that protected the individual from arbitrary demands from outside the system."[11] At the same time, we should note that this flexible, decentralized aspect of the state system was the source of the successful Tokugawa domination. For two and a half centuries before the fall of the Tokugawa regime, the complex, multilayered structure of the Japanese state was thus able to absorb various levels of contention (such as rebellious peasant movements) in the middle level of the political system before they became critically threatening to the system at large.[12]

Interestingly enough, Anderson's model of absolutism, namely, recharged feudalism essential to survival, may apply more to Tokugawa Japan than to the European cases. If Anderson had accurately fitted his model to the parameters of Tokugawa state formation, his speculation that feudalism was the common gateway to industrialization in Europe and Japan could have been modified.[13] In both Europe and Japan, it was not simply the medieval forms of feudalism—as Anderson has argued— but the historical experiences of redeploying and reshaping them that played an important role in the formation of their respective trajectories of industrialization.

This redeployment of the feudal system of domination was so successful that the Tokugawa military landlord class was able to retain its exclusive ruling position until well into the second half of the nineteenth century. However, the success of the new political strategy was possible only with the faithful collaboration of the samurai, who functioned as middlemen between the state and the villages by enabling the machinery of the

Tokugawa state to extract taxes from the resistant peasant population. Maintaining the solidity of the samurai's standing, while effectively transforming them from warriors into bureaucrats, became increasingly necessary in this context.

To be sure, the nature and content of the "crisis" that the Japanese and European landlord classes confronted during the late medieval period were not the same in the East and the West. Some important factors differentiate the Japanese from the European experience of early modern state-making. The comparative critical difference between the two situations can be articulated as follows: different relationships existed between the organized power of the landed elite and two competitive forms of organized power. The first relationship was between the state and an organized religious power; and the second was between the state and organized capital power. In both instances, the Japanese landlord class, which was involved in the task of early modern state-making, experienced less interference from these two competitors than did its European counterparts.

Religion and the State

The great difference in the relationships between religious power and secular feudal power in Europe and Japan respectively must be acknowledged. Although the concept of feudalism is a sociopolitical term, the actual European development of feudalism and the subsequent early modern state formation were inseparably influenced by the religious power of the medieval Church. Japanese feudalism developed without a supportive religious power comparable to the institutional strength of Christianity. This structural difference does not mean that Japanese medieval people were not deeply religious: I am here referring to the institutional relationships and balance of power between a religion and a state. Buddhism, the dominant religion of Japan, never developed a powerful *single institutional* center equivalent to the Catholic Church, which claimed a monopoly of orthodox faith. In terms of ideological content, Japanese religious institutions usually did not generate a power of normative monopoly, thereby claiming superiority to the sovereign's political jurisdiction. Unlike the medieval Church, which asserted the existence of universal standards of truth and justice that were greater than the secular sovereignty of any one European country, the medieval Japanese

Buddhist temples did not establish normative and transcendental values to which the secular authority should, in theory, be subject.

Joseph Strayer has argued that, in contrast to the Japanese situation, the role of the state in Europe was first clearly defined through its functional differentiation from the Church, during the period of what was called the Gregorian Reformation and the Investiture Controversy (1075–1122). During this process, which is sometimes called the "Papal Revolution," the Roman Catholic Church gained both autonomy and considerable control over secular forces by asserting its supremacy over the laity. This authority included the claim that justice should always be defined by the Church in its capacity as the guardian of ultimate truth. Unexpectedly, the Church's institutional victory required a corresponding redefinition of the state's role, since the Church could not perform all political functions. It then became the duty of secular rulers to dispense justice to the people. In short, "The Gregorian concept of the Church almost demanded the invention of the concept of the State." [14]

Christianity also provided many conceptual and organizational techniques that proved to be useful in the construction of state organizations and secular law codes. But the important point here is the configuration of the Church and secular rulers, which required the assumption that justice existed prior to secular laws as the embodiment of the transcendental truth that was, in theory, monopolized by the Church. Harold Berman, who investigated the origin of the Western legal tradition, extended Strayer's thesis by stating, "The revolution in law was closely connected with the revolution *in the church* and the revolution *of the church,* which in turn were closely connected with the revolution in agriculture and commerce, the rise of cities and kingdoms as autonomous territorial polities, the rise of the universities and of scholastic thought, and other major transformations which accompanied the birth of the West . . . during the next eight centuries and more." [15]

The impact of the Papal Revolution on the rise of the West remains the subject of scholarly debate. For the sake of comparative analysis, however, we must acknowledge the intimate connection between the Church and the origins of the modern European state. In ancient Japan, by contrast, Buddhism had always been "protected" by the "patronage" of the emperor's court and its aristocracy, and the major temples prayed for the peace of the country and the personal well-being of their patrons. There was only a weak ideological impulse in Japanese Buddhism to place religious values above secular political ones. This phenomenon is often explained by the mystic nature of Buddhist religious thought. But it is difficult to attribute the distinctive Japanese relationship between secular and sacred powers to the inherent nature of Buddhist doctrine alone. If we look at the historical experience of Buddhist kingship in Southeast Asia, we see that Buddhism played an institutionally and ideologically much stronger role in supporting and legitimating the sovereignty.[16]

Medieval Japanese society represented the highest level of political empowerment of religious institutions in the history of Japan. Through their ownership of *shōen,* Buddhist temples and some Shinto shrines legitimated their political power and fielded strong private armed forces to protect their socioeconomic interests. The "feudalization" of religious power was obvious in these instances, and great temples such as the Enryakuji wielded significant economic and political power. In an effort to improve its governmental effectiveness, the Muromachi shogunate patronized a group of five Zen temples, Gozan, from which it recruited talented priest-intellectuals to serve in the shogunate's administration and diplomatic corps. Despite these forms of empowerment, however, religious institutions in Japan never evolved into a single independent "public power" with sufficient institutional autonomy to stand apart from or oppose the secular authority. The characteristic theme of European feudalism, namely, the potential for conflict and simultaneous symbiosis of two public powers, sacred and secular, never emerged in Japanese feudal development. Even the limited political empowerment that can be observed in the medieval armed temples in Japan was forcefully ended by the emergence of the *sengoku daimyo* and the subsequent demilitarization policies of the unification rulers.

This general subordination of the sacred to the secular affected Japan's early modern state formation at its foundations. Furthermore, the formation of the Tokugawa state was a turning point in the course of Japanese history insofar as it represented the final triumph of secular power over religious competitors. The Buddhist temples were completely disarmed and subjected to secular control in the process of Tokugawa state formation. In fact, the largest and most violent *ikki* at the end of the Warring States period was connected to the powerful Ikkō sect, a Pure Land sect of Buddhism. This form of political resistance was brutally crushed in the late sixteenth century by Japan's unification rulers. The Buddhist temples were protected, but they were subjected to careful surveillance under the Tokugawa regime. Each sect of Buddhism and Shinto was granted a semiautonomous disciplinary power over its local temples and priests, similar to that of many other Tokugawa social organizations, but the religious groups were strictly supervised by a "magistrate of temples and shrines" *(jisha bugyō)*. Under the Tokugawa *danka* system (a kind of parish organization), everyone had to register his or her name on an official list *(shūmon aratame)* at one of the local Buddhist temples. The expansion of the *danka* system was encouraged by the Tokugawa regime in order to suppress Christianity.

By receiving indirect and direct state protection, together with a secure income from the customary contributions of the *danka*, the Japanese Buddhist temples were forced to abandon their characteristic medieval social aggressiveness. The authorities generally disciplined sects that placed religious values on a higher plane than civil obedience to "the master of the country." The most well known case of this kind was the continuous rigorous persecution of the Fujufuse branch of the Nichiren sect.

Therefore, when the *de facto* rulers of Japan attempted to legitimate their regime, they could never expect to have their power endorsed and legitimated by the higher authority of a religious institution. Of course, on the one hand this meant that the Japanese feudal power had fewer constraints from the clergy. But on the other hand, the absence of a concentrated transcendental religious power meant that the Tokugawa shoguns had no reliable form of legitimation other than formal recognition from the emperor's court. The drawback was that the imperial authority in Japan then did not have a spiritual authority comparable to that of the Christian Church; the emperor simply lacked moral influence over the population at large. (In many ways, the prewar image of the absolutist "god-emperor," or the paternalistic head of the family state, was the creation of post-Tokugawa Japan.)

Tokugawa subscription to Neo-Confucian ideology, which inculcated values supportive of a hierarchical social order, arose in this situation. Confucianism itself did not have very deep social and institutional roots in the Japanese population prior to the advent of the Tokugawa shogunate, however. Thus, after establishing national hegemony by means of naked force, the Tokugawa shogunate had to maintain its authority by relying on various secular political rituals and symbolic representations to signify the new social order and hierarchy.

In order to understand the unique development of Japan's warrior culture, we must consider this relationship of Japanese feudalism with religious institutions. In Europe, the Church attempted, though not always very successfully, to transform the violence of pre-Christian warrior cultures into an ideal of Christian knighthood. In this sense, the medieval European warrior culture was a product of the interaction of secular and religious institutional powers. In Japan, neither the medieval nor the Tokugawa samurai had this forceful experience. There was no *organized* intervention by a religious-ideological power representing transcendental values that institutionally challenged samurai practices in any fundamental fashion. Even though they had the desire, the religious traditions of Japan did not have a sufficient institutional basis in most situations to enforce their values on the samurai population in general. Rather, religious authorities tended to accommodate the spiritual needs of the samurai as they inevitably confronted violent and painful death in the course of their occupational functioning. Therefore, the samurai culture of honor developed and transformed itself in general, as a set of immanent ideological and cultural characteristics of a social group intensifying and solidifying its collective identity and cohesion.[17] It was natural that the cultural development of the samurai class was influenced largely by those dynamic changes within the political structures that affected the samurai class itself. This is the primary reason that I have concentrated my attention on the relationship between state-making and the samurai's culture of honor, rather than considering the subject solely from the perspective of intellectual history.

Capital and the State

Although medieval Japan had much in common with Europe, it diverged radically from the European pattern with respect to the organized power of capital, typically represented by the autonomous political power of urban population centers. Since cities grow up chiefly as repositories of concentrated capital, their relation with states as repositories of concentrated coercive means in the process of state formation could create differing social developments, as Charles Tilly discussed in relation to European countries.[18] In contrast to the European experience, with few exceptions—such as the city of Sakai for a brief period in the sixteenth century—the medieval Japanese city did not achieve an impressive degree of autonomy and self-government. In fact, the development of urban centers during the medieval period was quite limited in Japan. Prior to the close of the Warring States period, the ancient imperial capital of Kyoto was the only large city in Japan with a population in excess of 100,000 at one point; 100 major castle cities were not yet in existence before the late sixteenth century. There was no city truly comparable to city-states or merchant cities in the European medieval period, such as Genoa and Venice as well as the towns of the Netherlands. Although commercial activities were on the rise in medieval Japan, Japan entered the seventeenth century with a comparatively less developed commercial network than the most advanced regions of Europe.[19] The merchants of late medieval Japan thus did not form an impressive political base as an organized class that could compete effectively with the power of the military lords. Rather, it was the coalitions formed between rebellious villagers and part of the samurai population in *ikki* alliances that posed the greatest threat to the dominance of the samurai class.

In contrast, the capital accumulated in the large urban centers of Europe during the period of early modern state-making was sufficient to provide a power base for an emerging social class to develop independent political strength. Furthermore, after the European monarchies achieved pacification within their domains, they continued to wage international wars and compete with each other in the world market. In the process of continuing to build up a strong "military-fiscal machine"—the most costly venture to which they were committed—the rulers of the European states provided a number of lucrative opportunities for merchants to expand their income and other resources. This, in turn, resulted in the expansion of the power of merchants in the political sphere.

With the growth of the *sengoku daimyo* in the late sixteenth century, urban construction underwent a boom in their castle towns. After the pacification of Japan, the cities rapidly expanded during the first half of the Tokugawa period under the framework of the decentralized yet integrated Tokugawa state system. The local castle towns in the daimyo domains where the samurai were forced to reside became centers of local politics and economic growth. In addition to Kyoto—a traditional political center—the two major cities of Edo and Osaka developed as national political (Edo) and economic (Osaka) centers. In particular, the city of Edo underwent remarkable expansion. It claimed a population of only a few thousand citizens in 1590 when Tokugawa Ieyasu first became the lord of the region, but it rapidly developed into a national political center in the seventeenth century. By 1700 its population approached a million inhabitants. Miyamoto Matarō maintains that by the eighteenth century more than 15 percent of all Japanese lived in major cities and towns of some kind.[20]

With the development of cities and the increasing economic edge of the merchant class, a student of European history would expect the influence of the merchant class on the political process to undergo commensurate expansion. Nevertheless, no European absolutist state was more successful than the Tokugawa in blocking increased bourgeois influence on the government. How was this resistance possible? Three points of explanation stand out. First, the Tokugawa state had emerged as a garrison state when the commercial impulse was relatively weak, at least by European standards; the Japanese cities had not developed a high level of independence, and the merchants had not become powerful enough to penetrate the circle of ruling elites. The remarkable expansion of a commercial economy came only after the establishment of the Tokugawa state.

During the last few decades of the Warring States period, when changes in military technology had enlarged the scale of battle, and the outcome of the competition among warlords depended upon their supplies, some merchants had increased their political importance by supplying the warlords with weapons and other resources. The expansion of international trade during the sixteenth century also gave these merchants significant opportunities to increase their wealth and political power. But—and this brings us to the second point—with pacification under the Tokugawa, and the subsequent virtual withdrawal of Japan from international trade, this generation of merchants lost any opportunity for further growth as political merchants. Once the war had ended, the shogunate and the daimyo continued to favor the older system, which defined the provision of arms as the responsibility and obligation of every samurai vassal according to the stipend or fief he had received from the lord. Thus, the lords' direct military expenditures remained comparatively small. Without the opportunity to engage in the lucrative business of war, the merchants were unable to break into the Tokugawa system of domination.

The Japanese experience was different from European instances in which cities were able to establish their autonomy during a period when the central authority of the state was still relatively weak. Thus, Japan's early modern state formation was carried out through the initiatives of the military class, whose efforts in turn were subject to minimal interference by an organized commercial class. The fact that the commercialization of the Tokugawa economy got under way only after Japanese state formation took a decisively military turn had a great deal to do with the subsequent cultural development of Tokugawa society.

Finally, Tokugawa Japan imposed a policy of strict status demarcation that excluded the merchants from the political process. In the same manner that the status distinction was enforced on the farmers, the merchants were confined to their designated function in society. The shogunate did not approve of the ambiguity of both dealing in goods and being a samurai. In early modern Europe, the pervasive institution of the sale of offices enabled successful merchants to purchase status, privileges, and the actual income attached to the office. The purchasing of estates also often enabled merchants to enter the upper layers of society. In Japan, by contrast, the sons of Tokugawa merchants had little opportunity to cross their status boundary through education or the purchase of offices and estates. Their inferior status was reinforced by such symbolic signals as dress codes and enforced humility in the presence of samurai officers. The tax burden on merchants was less than on farmers, however.[21] Thus, if they accepted the symbolic framework of domination, the merchants were much freer than the farmers to accumulate wealth.

To be sure, Tokugawa merchants and townsmen were by no means simply an oppressed group. Merchant houses were constantly lending money to the samurai, and they controlled their finances. They also supported a rich cultural tradition; from *kabuki* theaters to popular literature and *ukiyoe* wood-block printings, most of the aesthetically impressive artifacts of Tokugawa Japan were the fruits of townsmen (commoner) culture. Without the patronage, consumption, and participation of these early modern citizens, what we now consider the most attractive aspects of Tokugawa culture would never have flourished. In the later Tokugawa period, the culture of these townsmen was very attractive to the samurai who were also urban residents, to the point that samurai and commoners often participated in common cultural activities. Wealthy merchants also learned some "high" culture of the samurai, and they often participated in sophisticated cultural activities. Thus, in the private sphere of cultural socializing status boundaries became less important. It must be noted here that the samurai's participation in the townsmen's culture was strictly limited to their "private," or off-duty, life, which was officially rated inferior to their "public" life. In addition, the extension of urban culture did not result in the townsmen's political empowerment. As a result, despite its attractiveness and potential for innovation, the culture of the early modern Japanese cities never generated an alternative cultural paradigm for a new elite's discipline in the public sphere.

Individual samurai, furthermore, had no right to engage in commercial activity under Tokugawa rule. The samurai were therefore unable to strengthen their relative economic position by taking advantage of the expanding commercial economy. This remained the case even though, in the late Tokugawa period, many daimyo aggressively promoted the production of commodities in their domains as a response to their weakened rice-dependent finances, in order to increase their own revenue. State involvement in economic policies did not mean, however, that an individual samurai could also be a merchant working for his own profit. The implementation of a strict status system thus prevented the development of an entrenched class with both economic and political hegemony.

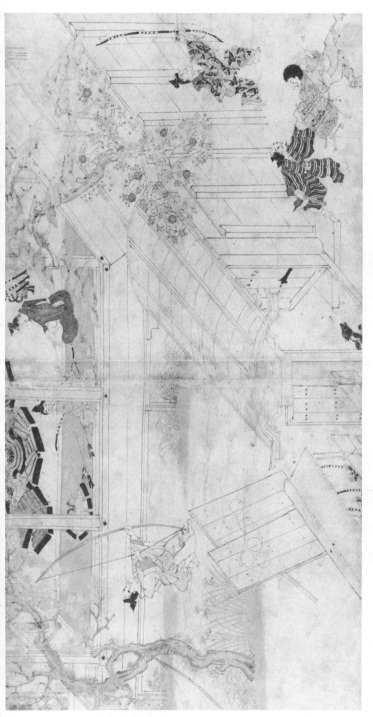

1. A medieval samurai's compound. The captions for this pictorial scroll mention the orders given by Obusuma, the master of the local samurai compound, to his retainers: "Hunt for heads and hang them on the fence of the horse yard! Keep it up . . . Go after the *shu-genja* [mountain monks], or the beggars passing by in front of the gate . . . and chase them down! Shoot them with arrows!" On the left, a retainer is training his martial skills in the yard while others tend to armor and bows spread throughout the room behind him. On the right, an unfortunate individual is overtaken by Obusuma's retainers. *Obusuma Saburō ekotoba* (ca. 1295)

2. Victorious troops marching in the main street of Kyoto with the head of Fujiwara no Shin-zei after the Heiji Rebellion of 1159. *Heiji monogatari emaki* (ca. 13th century)

3. Kawanakajima Battle, 1561. Moments after one samurai manages to sever and win for himself an opponent's head, another enemy samurai uses the occasion to return the favor. *Kawanakajima kassen byōbu*

4. The Tokugawa shogun receiving an audience of daimyo in Edo Castle. The Tokugawa shogunate prescribed many detailed ritualistic rules of behavior in Edo Castle designed to enhance the "shining authority" of the Tokugawa shogun. *Tokugawa seiseiroku*

5. A fight between *kabuki mono* (deviant men) during a Toyokuni festival of 1604. The young man on the left is portrayed with his torso half-naked and an extraordinarily long sword with a red sheath slung at his waist. The following words are inscribed on the red sheath: "I am a man twenty-three years old! I have lived too long! I will never restrain myself!" These are clearly the words of a frustrated would-be hero in the era of unification. *Toyokuni saireizu: Tokugawa reimeikai bon*

6. A group of samurai dashing violently through a narrow street in Kyoto. During the final phase of the era of unification, around 1600–1615, the city of Kyoto was filled with disorderly, violent samurai who attempted to use their last chance for upward mobility. *Rakuchū rakugaizu: Funaki byōbu*

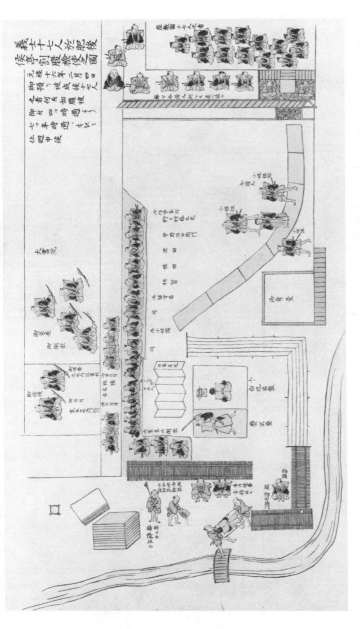

7. *Seppuku* after the revenge of the Forty-seven Samurai. This illustration shows part of the Forty-six Samurai's *seppuku* at the mansion of Lord Hosokawa. One by one, the accused men were led from the waiting area to the ceremonial execution place. After each decapitation, the body was carried away on its futon, and the two tatami mats were replaced with fresh ones. Around this time (1702), *seppuku* had become more and more ritualized, turning into a customary punishment reserved for the samurai class. *Akō gijin sansho*

8. Polite greetings exchanged between Tokugawa samurai. This picture illustrates a street greeting on a New Year's day in the late seventeenth century. A lower samurai assumes a humble, kneeling posture while the higher-ranking samurai returns the greeting from a standing position. *Shiki fūzoku zu maki*

V

HONOR AND
VIOLENCE IN
TRANSFORMATION

10   *Honor or Order:*
The State and Samurai
Self-Determinism

During the medieval period, when the samurai culture of honor was taking shape, violence and honor became inextricable components of the warrior's sense of dignity. In the warrior society, the samurai's ability to use force to solve their problems symbolized their sovereign autonomy, while government intervention to restrict outbreaks of honor violence reflected the presence of a hidden balance of power between the state and the vassal samurai. Through a close examination of the samurai's private use of violence, including personal quarrels, fights, and acts of revenge, we can observe the ways in which the "objective" social constraints on the practice of honor—that is, legal depositions, bureaucratic procedures, and above all the pacification of the country itself—were understood by the samurai.

Samurai Quarrels

Let me begin by sketching a prototype of samurai quarrels and fights (usually called *kenka*). Although the ways of adjudicating *kenka* changed greatly over the course of time, the basic emotions engendering violent conflict—one could call it a "mental schema" of samurai quarrels—seem to have been remarkably similar and persistent throughout the periods.

The following testimony of a samurai reveals that quarrels and fights played a major role in the samurai's life: "Quarrels arise from anger generating extraordinary courage, even to the point of risking death. Fights on the battlefield, on the contrary, are not based upon personal anger; we fight with enemies only on the strength of the moral principle of loyalty. Thus battles cannot stimulate more courage than quarrels."[1] The anger felt in quarrels was a deep and heartfelt emotional response, an indignation over the fact that one's sense of honor and dignity had been challenged. In contrast, participation in warfare initiated by a samurai's master was seen as a duty, without the same impulsive emotional component. The samurai fought wars not only out of sheer moral conviction; loyalty was, at least partly, an ideological legitimation of fighting. In reality, warfare provided the best occasions for a samurai to reap rewards (such as material benefits) through a demonstration of honor. The point of the testimony cited above is that, in contrast to this instrumental aspect of warfare, a private quarrel often aroused a strong emotional response in the day-to-day life of the samurai.

One emotional ingredient necessary to touch off a quarrel was extreme sensitivity to insult. The samurai cultivated a hypersensitivity to challenges to their honor. As a consequence, they learned to react swiftly and instinctively within the confines of the code of honor. Recall the case of Kumagai Naozane, who became outraged when he was told to go on foot to hold a target on a ceremonial occasion rather than to have a more honorable assignment. Such an insult (as he perceived it) should not be shrugged off, even though the shogun was responsible for the unintended offense. Hypersensitivity to perceived slurs was an essential quality in an independent man of honor. Misjudgment in the handling of such an offense could seriously damage his reputation. Honor was a fragile possession, secured only by constant attention to and mastery of the successive incidents of tension in daily life.

An example of the intensity of the violence that could be unleashed in *kenka* can be found in the literature of the twelfth century, particularly in *Konjaku monogatari,* which relates a story about a samurai who was ordered by his master's brother to commit a murder. The man carried out the killing, but only when the master's grievance became his own personal affair. This case is one of the oldest and most detailed descriptions of a samurai fighting violently for the sake of his conception of honor. The story goes as follows:

Once the famous mighty samurai Yorinobu visited the house of Yori-mitsu, his elder brother, to attend a party. During the party, Yorinobu took aside one of his brother's retainers, Taira no Sadamichi, and or-dered him to kill a man who lived in Suruga because the man was rude. Sadamichi thought that it was outrageous for Yorinobu to make ar-rangements for murder during a social gathering, and he decided to disobey the order. After all, he reasoned, Yorinobu was not his direct master; his brother Yorimitsu was.

A few months later, on a trip to the eastern region, Sadamichi unex-pectedly met the man who was the target of Yorinobu's order. After they spoke for a while in a friendly way, the man asked Sadamichi about Yorinobu's order. Sadamichi replied that he would not carry out the order because he was a retainer not for Yorinobu but for his brother. The man was pleased, but, tempted to add some boastful words, he said, "Even if you had tried to kill me, with my military skill, you could not kill me very easily." Sadamichi took this as an insult and im-mediately decided to kill him. After they left each other on the street, Sadamichi and his retainers followed the man and attacked him. The man was killed by an arrow, and Sadamichi cut off his head and brought it to Yorinobu.[2]

What is significant about this story is that initially Sadamichi did not want to kill the man simply because his master's brother ordered the murder. When the man sneered at his military competence, however, he changed his mind instantly. Although the offender's words were nothing more than a thoughtless outburst of pride, Sadamichi took them to heart as a slur on his own martial skills. The matter suddenly became a threat to his sense of honor, making vindication necessary.

This concern for honor persisted as a motivation for samurai fights throughout later Japanese history despite radical changes in the samu-rai's societal role; it continued to be a social requirement for the samurai to display such an extreme sensitivity to insult. The Tokugawa master fiction writer Ihara Saikaku (1642–1693) wrote a vivid description of a typical samurai quarrel. The narrative opens on a stormy day, when two samurai pass each other on a bridge:

As they passed in the middle of the bridge, Jitsuemon's umbrella col-lided with Tahei's. Tahei pushed him away, exclaiming, "What an in-solent man you are!" After these offensive words, Jitsuemon was in no

position to apologize for the accident. "What right do you have to insult me?" he countered. Tahei recognized him, and replied, "What do
you mean, insult you? . . . It's you who should apologize to me, but
instead you hurl abuse. I'm not going to put up with that!"[3]

This exchange touched off a deadly fight that issued in a protracted
episode of revenge. Saikaku's story was based on a famous historical
event, the Mido no Mae Vendetta, which occurred in 1687, eight months
before the publication of *Buke giri monogatari*.[4] The details in the preceding citation are, of course, Saikaku's literary invention. Other historical documents have preserved a similar account of this nonfictional
rainy-day encounter, however. Clearly, Saikaku's imaginative reconstruction of this scene, based upon a well-known contemporary event,
blended his commanding skills as a fiction writer with his knowledge of
samurai culture. The conviction that triggered Jitsuemon's reaction was
the strong belief that a samurai should not appear weak or soft in any
situation, and should always be on the lookout for the slightest affront
to his honor. The samurai who perceived such a challenge should exact
retribution on the spot. The difference between the medieval and the
Tokugawa attitudes was that this adversarial approach to quarrels was
no longer automatically approved of in the Tokugawa period.

A quarrel provided an important means for vindicating one's position
as a samurai because it was considered a kind of "mini-battle." Showing
one's back when challenged on the street was as shameful as doing so on
the battlefield. As we have seen, the reality of warfare had produced cultural attitudes among the samurai that approved of self-control and courage at the moment of decision as an important test of a warrior's mettle.
Similarly, a quarrel necessitated on-the-spot reactions in defense of one's
honor. The samurai's behavior at such a critical moment was considered
a valid indication of his future performance in battle.

Extreme sensitivity to "insult and challenge" to masculine honor, and
the notion that a man should not exhibit weakness in any situation, can
be observed not only in the history of samurai culture but also in the
practices of many other cultures in the world today in which "honor" is
a central component of a man's self-esteem. In the streets of the Chicago
Chicano community, for example, where an honor-bound subculture
predominates, Ruth Horowitz reports that the culture "emphasizes manhood and defines violations of interpersonal etiquette in an adversarial

manner"; and that "any action that challenges a person's right to defer-
ential treatment in public" will be interpreted as an insult to that person's
honor, since "honor demands that a man be able physically to back his
claim to dominance and independence." A challenge to one's honor,
however trivial, will place him in a position where he may be derided as
weak. "Sensitivity to insult is particularly keen in the public situation,
where judgments can be made readily by others."[5] In such a situation,
honor compels an individual to take an unequivocal stand, to enforce
his claim immediately, "no matter how small the incident may seem."[6]
Pierre Bourdieu's ethnographic study of Algeria reveals the presence of
a similar sentiment. In the honor-conscious culture of the Kabyles, the
challenge itself bestows honor on its recipient; it is "a high point in the
life of the man who receives it."[7] The basic emotional tone expressed in
the honor contests of these cultures bears a striking resemblance to that
of the samurai in different periods. A short reaction time and an appropriate response to a challenge to one's honor are prerequisites to being
esteemed as an honorable man.

The contemporary subcultures mentioned above are instances in
which the culture of honor thrives in opposition to modern laws, and to
interventions by the state's official police force. When local communities
introduce more effective external agents of conflict mediation and control, private conflict resolutions are usually restricted in scope and frequency. The internal rules of the honor game inevitably change in such
situations. Despite the persistent honorific mentality, the samurai's ways
of resolving and adjudicating conflict underwent a similar course of development in response to a change in the sociopolitical context of the
samurai.

Three Stages of Development

One can distinguish three stages in Japanese social development in regard to managing the private use of violence as a means of conflict resolution among the samurai. The first stage characterized the medieval period (roughly the twelfth to fourteenth centuries), when the principle of
jiriki kyūsai, or self-redress of grievances predominated; the second stage
occurred in the late medieval or Warring States period (around the fifteenth and sixteenth centuries), when the famous law of *kenka ryōseibai*—equally severe punishment of all parties to a quarrel regardless

of the reason behind the conflict—emerged; and the third stage occupied the Tokugawa period, when the pacification of the country complicated the samurai's private recourse to violence as a way of settling quarrels.

A spontaneous fight between individuals could, in the medieval period, quickly escalate into a conflict between two social organizations.[8] If a member of a particular *ie* was killed, even if he was only a peripheral or junior member of that *ie*, the incident became at once a matter of honor for the whole *ie*, and could set off a chain reaction of private retribution. Revenge was considered not a legal right but a behavioral norm because the honor of the *ie* was the representation of the power of the *ie*.

The introduction of *kenka ryōseibai*, during the Warring States period, was a major turning point in Japanese legal and cultural history, as it symbolized the decline of the samurai's self-determination, the rise of the absolute power of the warlords, and the end of the principle of *dōri* (reasonableness). It also facilitated a new stage of development in the samurai honor culture during the Tokugawa period. To be sure, during the Warring States period, *kenka ryōseibai* did not totally replace the older tradition of *jiriki kyūsai* (self-redress of grievances), since the vassal samurai of this period still kept some degree of social autonomy. Thus, the traditions of self-determination and the authoritarian *kenka ryōseibai* coexisted in the contested terrain during the Warring States period.

The internal pacification of Japan was a process that effectively demilitarized the nonsamurai population by depriving them of the right of private conflict resolution. The prohibitions imposed on the nonsamurai social groups represented not only the results of internal political pacification but also the process by which the samurai as a status group came to acquire a collective monopoly on the legitimate use of violence. This monopoly in turn conferred an official monopoly of honor on the samurai class by excluding the nonsamurai population from honorable status. In this honor-ridden society, the ability to defend oneself by force of arms was closely connected to one's honor status. The authorities in this period did need to impose social and political controls on the impulsive resort to violence by the samurai. They sought to bring about this end without sacrificing the samurai's collective honor, however. Because of this consideration, the curbing of honor-based violence among the samurai became a politically sensitive issue for the Tokugawa rulers.

Individual samurai intuitively followed the rules of the game dictated by their culture in order to vindicate their honor. In these moments of risk and crisis, the samurai spirit of honor received its fullest expression, and successful individuals came away with a glowing sense of their own importance. Nevertheless, a violent fight—a moment when powerful institutional constraints and individual personal judgment were fully engaged—often had serious consequences. For example, a simple spontaneous fight often escalated into a chain reaction of ruthless revenge; and it could invite intervention from a superior authority. Therefore, in the samurai's mind, a quarrel required his on-the-spot evaluation of social, legal, and symbolic constraints.

In this chapter, I will analyze the third stage of the management of private use of violence: Tokugawa ways of dealing with quarrels, fights, and revenge among the samurai. The Tokugawa regime was moving steadily toward the establishment of a long-lasting peace under an internally cohesive central authority. The conflicts at the national level of the daimyo houses were clearly described and disallowed in the *Buke shohhato* (The Law for Military Houses—the Tokugawa shogunate's most important legal code directed at the samurai): "The governors of provinces and other lords are forbidden to engage in private disputes."[9] The code, however, did not establish equally clear standards for dealing with the *kenka* (quarrels) of ordinary samurai vassals. In addition, even though *kenka ryōseibai* had acquired the status of a kind of customary law by that time, it was not formally inscribed in the shogunate's official code. The result of this omission was that there was no fixed legal formula for handling the samurai's personal conflicts. The process of civilizing the samurai's *kenka* moved forward only by means of a trial-and-error process involving a variety of specific cases.

Violence, Eros, and Honor: The Cultural Climate around 1600

Around the end of the sixteenth and the beginning of the seventeenth century there were three dimensions of radical social structural change that brought about the internal pacification of Japan: the ending of the civil wars among the daimyo and the establishment of a stable central authority; the separation of samurai from landownership and their forced move to the social and political restrictions of the castle town, which limited their autonomy; and the demilitarization of the nonsamurai population and the strict status distinctions between soldier and farmer.

When I visualize the mental climate of the samurai around the time of

Japan's forcible unification, a climate characterized by the foreclosure of opportunities for upward social mobility through military heroism, I am always reminded of an impressive painted screen that depicts the historic festival that took place at the Toyokuni Shrine in mid-August of 1604. On 14 and 15 August 1604, two hot and humid summer days, the excitement of the citizens of Kyoto was reaching its peak. These two days represented the climax of a week-long festival, celebrated on an unprecedented scale at the Toyokuni Shrine in commemoration of the seventh anniversary of the death of the ruler Toyotomi Hideyoshi. The titular deity of the Toyokuni Shrine was the deified form of Hideyoshi, "Hōkoku Daimyōjin," and the 1604 festival was financed and organized by the Toyotomi family. In 1600, Tokugawa Ieyasu had claimed victory over his opponents in the Battle of Sekigahara, which firmly established his military hegemony over the country. Although Toyotomi Hideyori, the son of Hideyoshi, still lived within the mighty castle of Osaka, the ascendancy of the Tokugawa clan was further cemented by Ieyasu's installation as shogun in 1603. The gorgeous pageants at the festival the following year included a massive parade of horseback riders and beautiful dancers. This display apparently represented a political protest on the part of the Toyotomi family against the growing consolidation of Tokugawa power. More than a thousand dancers, gorgeously costumed, representing the five townships of Kyoto, danced in the city's streets, in the emperor's residence, and in the shrine itself. The magnitude of this festival is documented by a number of contemporary records, as well as by local artists' dynamic and colorful pictures.

Particularly eye-catching is the lower quadrant of one especially colorful, large painting of this 1604 festival that captures both the motions and the emotions of a mass of excited people. One detail of the illustration vividly depicts groups of angry men who are clearly about to precipitate a violent fight (see Illustration 5). On the basis of their clothes and hair styles, they are apparently *kabuki mono* (deviant persons).[10] The young man on the left is portrayed with his torso half-naked and an extraordinarily long sword with a red sheath slung at his waist. We can make out the following words on this red sheath: "I am a man twenty-three years old! I have lived too long! I will never restrain myself!" These youthful, defiant words, as well as the explosive physical energy that surges through the lines and colors of this masterpiece, express the frustration of an entire generation of would-be heroes. With the advent of lasting peace under the Tokugawa regime, the time had passed when men from the lower classes could gain an honorable status through martial prowess. The young man in the picture might indeed have lived too long, or, to put it more precisely, he was born too late. The era of the "lower beat the upper" *(gekokujō)* in the Warring States period had long since passed.

The young man in the illustration is a representative of a new social phenomenon in early modern Japan. Around 1600, when Japan's unification rulers were about to put an end to more than a century of civil war, groups of strange individuals known as *kabuki mono* appeared on the streets of the larger cities. *Kabuki* literally means "crooked," or "deviant and licentious," and *mono* signifies "a person." The term *kabuki* was popular around 1600; one could say that it caught and summarized the mood of the postunification period. Those groups of people who deliberately violated the prescribed rules of behavior were called *kabuki mono*. These *kabuki mono* were characterized by bizarre and faddish dress as well as by aggressive and unruly behavior. The term *kabuki* as a type of theatrical production grew out of this usage. Some *kabuki mono* wore imported velvet collars, short kimonos with lead weights in the hems, wide belts, and so forth.[11] Some favored nonconformist hair styles such as *ōbitai* (with the head shaved above the forehead and temples) and *ōnadetsuke* and *ōsurisake* (long hair hanging loose rather than secured in the customary topknot).[12] Their showy red scabbards and distinctive large sword guards were also considered signs of deviance by the general population. Their preference for odd fashions symbolized their frustration and protest, and also represented their group solidarity. Their passions erupted most flagrantly in numerous street quarrels.

On the basis of various contemporary documents that recorded the punishments meted out to the *kabuki mono*, we know that these deviants were mostly either masterless samurai *(rōnin)*, servants who worked for samurai, or lesser members of the samurai class who could not find a suitable place within the new social order of the unification rulers. After the pacification of Japan, these *kabuki mono* had few opportunities for access to the higher levels of society. The frustrated would-be samurai had no alternative outlets for their aggressive ideals and energies except these private battles pitched on city streets. The *kabuki mono* formed gangs that drew members from scattered locations, and they disturbed the peace by their frequent involvement in street brawls. Most of the members were young adults and adolescents who had pledged themselves to one another in a blood ritual of brotherhood and had promised mutual assistance, even at the risk of their lives.[13]

We cannot know the psychology of the *kabuki mono* in detail because there is no evidence that they wrote about themselves. We can speculate on the basis of circumstantial evidence, however. The young man's comment as recorded in the 1604 picture—"I have lived too long!" *(ikisugi taruya)*—is hardly exceptional. We know from several other pictures and an actual sword sheath surviving from this period that the *kabuki mono* appeared to like this phrase, and they inscribed it on their belongings as a written symbol of their lifestyle.[14] Their frustration derived from the fact that the new social order imposed a strict status line between the nonsamurai and the honorable status of samurai, and they were on the verge of exclusion from the official circle of honor. Even though they were employed as foot soldiers or household servants by samurai masters, they commonly demonstrated a stronger sense of loyalty to their peers in the group. Given the apparent finality of the political situation, they might well have reasoned that they had nothing to lose by risking their lives in honor-based street quarrels or acts of revenge on their superiors. Tokugawa and daimyo authorities repeatedly announced various ordinances against the *kabuki mono* during the early and mid-seventeenth century after meeting with their resistance.

Although the *kabuki mono* themselves represented only a minority of the urban population, their actions and way of life tell us something about the social rip tides in the cultural undercurrents during this time. Because many frustrated samurai clung to older notions of the legitimacy of violence and honorific sentiments, the process of their taming in the early Tokugawa period proved to be difficult.

With this general cultural climate at the beginning of the seventeenth century, the new system of social controls had not yet effected a sufficient degree of stability to create a general mood of confidence and security. Many reminders of violence-ridden practices from the previous periods contributed to a social climate of uncertainty or confusion (see Illustration 6).

An examination of the historical records of samurai quarrels and fights during the early seventeenth century indicates that both the principle of self-redress inherited from the past and the comparatively recent rule of *kenka ryōseibai* influenced attitudes as well as behavior. At the same time, however, the effect of the Tokugawa pacification on samurai conflict resolution was rapidly apparent at the national level. The daimyo exhibited considerable fear of the unification rulers—first, of the Hideyoshi, and then, of the Tokugawa shogun. Not only did they limit their own use of force for resolving conflicts with other daimyo, but they also took special care to restrain their vassals from involving themselves in private quarrels with the vassals of other allied daimyo. For example, when Lord Maeda Toshitsune of Kaga han was ordered to assist with the construction of the Sunpu Castle of the Tokugawa clan in 1612, he promulgated a code consisting of seventeen articles for his vassals in which he prohibited any conflicts with other allied forces out of concern that the aggressive behavior of his vassals might elicit reprisals from the shogunate.[15] The code proclaims:

> Regarding quarrels and fights, those who fight with other masters' samurai, even with good reason to do so, will be executed. In verbal quarrels, let others talk slanderously if they must. In these matters, forbearance is the best policy in all situations. Should you lose face, it will not be accounted as your shame . . . Since this [the castle] is an important project for the *kōgi* [public authority, that is, the Tokugawa shogunate], those who are patient will receive credit for a good attitude.

During the Warring States period, the rule of *kenka ryōseibai* was intended primarily to promote internal discipline and facilitate the strategic movements of the warlords' armies. But under the Tokugawa regime, it was partially redirected toward preventing dissension within the framework of the Tokugawa state. One should note, in the example above, that Lord Maeda had to give a moral guarantee by emphasizing the importance of patience to his samurai, assuring them that this behavior would not bring them dishonor. The need to include this assurance within a proclamation reflects how thoroughly institutionalized the aggressive aspects of the code of honor had become in the samurai culture of this period.

The legacy of the Warring States period was a persistent presence within each daimyo's domain during the first half of the seventeenth century. The self-assertive aspect of the culture of honor derived from the medieval tradition that the internal affairs of a samurai's *ie* rested in the hands of the head of the house.

The strength of this tradition was reflected in an incident that occurred in 1611, also in the Kaga han. During this time the *kabuki mono* took over the streets of the larger cities. One day, Lord Maeda Toshinaga heard that his *koshō* (page) Osada Ushinosuke had hired a violent *kabuki mono* called Testujinosuke as a house servant. The lord gave Ushinosuke a direct order to turn over this dangerous man to the authorities. But Ushinosuke claimed that he did not have such a person in his employ. Continuing to speak to Lord Maeda in a proud manner, he said, "Even if I do employ such a person in my household, it is against the way of the samurai to arrest him and deliver him to you." In other words, following the medieval tradition, Ushinosuke believed in the independence of a samurai's *ie*, and his subsequent right to deal with all the men in his house as he saw best. His house should be a place of sanctuary, safe from public prosecution. In defiance of his lord's order, Ushinosuke secretly gave Testujinosuke some travel money and helped him to escape from Kaga territory. As punishment for his disobedience, Ushinosuke was ordered to commit *seppuku;* Tetsujinosuke was also arrested and put to death.[16] Thus, this case ended in the total defeat of the independent spirit of the samurai. But in his very defiance, Ushinosuke proved that the older medieval tradition of the autonomy of the samurai house was still alive in the minds of the early Tokugawa samurai.

The solidarity of the *kabuki mono,* which was symbolically displayed by their common adoption of deviant clothing, had more than a cultural dimension; it posed a real threat to the Tokugawa political order. During the early seventeenth century, both the shogunate and the daimyo houses frequently issued ordinances to prohibit young men from joining the *kabuki mono,* as well as the hiring of *kabuki mono* as servants or retainers in the samurai households. These ordinances represented an official response to a series of violent crimes connected to these social deviants. One such surprising incident is recorded in the *Chronicle of the Tokugawa Clan (Tokugawa jikki).* In the seventeenth year of Keichō (1612), a chief of military men for the shogunate (ōban gashira) named Shibayama Gonzaemon killed his servant, who turned out to belong to the *kabuki mono.* In one sense, the slaying was a "normal" event, considering the feudal prerogatives of masters over their in-house servants. Immediately following the servant's death, however, another servant in Shibayama's household rushed to the scene and killed Shibayama on the spot. This shocking murder of a high official of the shogunate was apparently an act of retaliation for the killing of the servant's *kabuki mono* friend. Ten days later, a suspect was finally arrested and confessed to being involved with the *kabuki mono*. He stated that the members of the group were mostly boys and young adults, united by a blood vow of brotherhood, who had pledged mutual assistance at the risk of their lives, even to the point of rebelling against their masters or parents. Following the suspect's confession, more than seventy *kabuki mono* were arrested in the city of Edo. The group was headed by a young man named Ōtori Ichibyōe, who was arrested, tortured, and later executed.[17]

The fact that the *kabuki mono* youth took revenge for the sake of his peer against his master illustrates that during this early stage loyalty and obedience to one's master had not yet been established as the absolute ethical value. Intimate committed relationships between two individual samurai were sometimes considered more important than the social obligations of hierarchical relationships. This sentiment was most acutely represented by the positive moral value attached to male-male love relationships among the samurai during this period. This attitude toward homosexual love produced a number of collections of short stories as well as some aesthetic and ethical guidebooks for the proper conduct of male love, such as *Shinyūki (The Book for Soul Mates; 1643).*[18] The romanticized male-male relationship in these books typically involved a boy (called *wakashu,* whose "beauty flowers when his forelock is unshaven"; that is, a boy prior to his coming-of-age ritual, which involved the assumption of an adult male's hair style) and an older lover, called *nenja,* who protected the boy. These guidebooks to samurai homosexuality usually commended exclusive relationships and praised lovers who sacrificed their lives for the sake of their beloved.

Violent fights over the favors of beautiful young boys were not only a normal part of samurai life during this time; they were often considered acceptable expressions of honorific sentiments. Even though not all samurai were involved in homosexual affairs, the life of male-dominated samurai communities fostered cultural attitudes that idealized relationships of trust between individual warriors and expressed them in the idioms and sentiments of intense male love. The way in which contemporary popular literature about the samurai romanticized the beauty of young boys resembles medieval knights' devotion to their noble ladies. The samurai's behavior in quarrels over male-male love, however, was so violent, competitive, and conflict-ridden—as is evident in literature of the period and various historical records—that one is reminded of reports from ethnographers regarding Mediterranean societies' acceptance of honorific violence centered on female chastity.[19] We cannot fully understand some of the incidents of honorific violence among the samurai without taking the prevailing sentiments and erotic aesthetic of male-male love into consideration. To suppress the samurai's private use of violence—whatever the reason behind its eruption—proved to be a difficult undertaking during this early phase of Tokugawa rule.

The official policy of the daimyo regarding the use of personal violence for conflict resolution among vassals had not yet been firmly established in the early seventeenth century. When a fight was only a matter of honor between reputable samurai, the case was sometimes considered their private affair. Unless they disrupted the state's internal order, impulsive fights that had to do with honor occasionally went unpunished by the authorities. One particularly clear example of official forbearance was a bloody quarrel between two young samurai, which occurred in 1630, again in Lord Maeda's domain (Kaga han). This quarrel took place fifteen years after the last great Japanese conflict, the Osaka Summer Battle.

In the Six Month of the seventh year of Kan'ei (1630), according to Kaga han shiryō, Maeda Higo, a noble young samurai (a grandson of Lord Maeda Toshiie), went to a river accompanied by a group of young comrades. After enjoying a pleasant swim, he and his companions were crossing a bridge to return home. From the opposite side of the bridge, two other young samurai, Murase and Sakabe, came walking toward them. In the middle of the bridge, Kaga han shiryō describes, "the sword sheaths carried by Higo and Sakabe bumped each other. At once, Higo slapped Sakabe's shoulder with his fan and Sakabe drew out his sword with a shout." The accidental contact of their swords was taken as a challenge and immediately precipitated a deadly fight. Higo's friends came up to help him, and both Murase and Sakabe were killed in the river. Soon the tragic report reached their families, and the incident instantly escalated into a family feud. Murase's father, Murase Kuemon, rushed to the site with a long sword in hand to avenge his son's death. Kuemon killed two of Higo's retainers and injured another before finally being killed himself. Sakabe's father, Sakabe Jirobei, also came rushing up with a spear to seek revenge, but "the press of the curious crowd hampered his way." It is not clear if this detail was true or not; it may be the excuse of Sakabe's father, who failed to get involved in the fight. In any event, feeling ashamed of his failure to exact revenge, Jirobei voluntarily went to a temple to enter the priesthood, leaving the city. The episode was reported to Lord Maeda, but nobody in either party was punished. The document does record that Higo was obliged to live the rest of his life in constant fear of revenge.[20]

The full narrative conveys the feeling that at this point in time, the samurai of the early Tokugawa period did not much resemble the self-controlled and stoic samurai of later centuries. These Tokugawa samurai still cultivated a warrior mentality and its accompanying belief that fatal quarrels were a matter of honor. Indeed, the course of the quarrel in the foregoing example was not so different from that of a medieval *kenka*. Despite the fact that *kenka ryōseibai* was generally acclaimed as "the great law of the world" at this stage, it was not always put into practice consistently. The cultural mores that considered samurai quarrels affairs of honor, as a kind of duel outside the realm of public jurisdiction, were difficult to modify. Furthermore, this case also demonstrates that samurai quarrels tended to expand into family conflicts, and that sometimes the state chose not to intervene but to leave the conflicting parties to resolve the matter through feuding and private retaliation. Sorting through chronologically arranged collections of daimyo documents, such as *Kaga han shiryō* of Kaga han, or *Kasei jiki* of Aizu han, one can easily find a number of similar examples of instinctively aggressive behavior in samurai quarrels in the entries of the early Tokugawa period.

It should be added that this incident in Kaga han occurred prior to a famous reform measure known as *Kaisaku hō*. This complicated land reform policy, implemented between 1651 and 1656, was a critical turning point in the development of the Kaga han as an early modern polity that excluded the samurai from having direct control over the land.[21] The pace of the vassals' incorporation into the local daimyo's political structure differed from place to place; one can safely state that in the first half of the seventeenth century the samurai still maintained some structural and cultural autonomy.

Kenka as an Index of Preparedness

The definition of samurai honor in terms of violence was generally considered more important than maintaining social order, not only by the

individual samurai (who were the subjects of the daimyo's incorporation), but also by the authorities themselves, who had been socialized
in the traditional ideology and had not entirely freed themselves. The
following case is from the Okayama Domain and occurred in 1647, at a
time when the memory of the last great civil war in Osaka (1615) was
no longer fresh: "It was a holiday, and every samurai came to the castle.
Ogiwara Matarokuro was criticizing his colleague Ikoma Genba. They
had been on bad terms for a long time. Genba, who came to the castle
late, heard of Matarokuro's slander but suppressed his anger. Nothing
happened in the castle."[22]

The incident was essentially trivial, but somehow it became an official
case. Matarokuro was ordered to commit *seppuku* on the grounds of
his slanderous misconduct. Genba's attitude was praised as a model of
peaceful forbearance in the castle when the lord was present. Still, surprisingly, his sentence was quite severe. The authorities confiscated his
land and position *(kaieki),* and their sentence explained why: "Some action should have been taken [on Genba's side]. His behavior was too
soft and safety-oriented. His attitude is unsatisfactory for a samurai who
serves a young lord. Because of that, though we pity him, his property
should be confiscated . . . This decision does not imply that, in a similar
situation, all samurai must fight each other until one kills another. This
is something that the law cannot prescribe."

The nature of this moral dilemma is obvious. If a man retaliates in
answer to an insult, he will be executed in the name of law and order. If
he keeps quiet, he might survive, but he will be dishonored in the samurai
community. At the same time, since the Tokugawa system did not allow
commoners to hold governmental positions, the samurai's military status
was also their symbol of social dominance. Thus, both the state and the
samurai never abandoned the principle that lay at the base of their military culture. The problem for the samurai was that, although he was
fully incorporated into the state's political structure and had no economic basis for independence, he was required on moral grounds to demonstrate his ability to deviate from the organization's laws when they
touched his personal honor. Moreover, the sentence "This is something
that the law cannot prescribe" also reflects the authorities' confusion
and ambivalence about the issue.

The collective honor of the samurai class was in fact the symbolic
architectural foundation of the Tokugawa *bakuhan* state. The samurai

were politically defined as men worthy to be the rulers of Japan because they were warriors; it was therefore difficult for the authorities to reject this aggressive tradition of honor in its totality. They hesitated to formulate explicit rules forbidding the samurai to fight back under any circumstances. As a result, the process of taming honor-bound violence developed slowly, lagging behind the speed of other social and political changes within the Tokugawa system.

Adding to the complications were the contradictions inherent in a situation that compelled the samurai to take private quarrels even more seriously than before. They had by this time lost their usual opportunities to vindicate or publicize their military honor on the battlefield. After the fall of Osaka Castle in 1615, there were no more wars among the daimyo. Occasions for open demonstration of one's claim to honor through military prowess were scarce in the seventeenth century. Nonetheless, the prevailing contemporary samurai ideology still enjoined maintaining a perpetually competitive attitude. If such an attitude were dropped, a contemporary samurai noted, "though you may wear two swords . . . you will be like a farmer or a townsman who is camouflaged in the skin of the samurai."[23] Therefore, a quarrel actually provided a rare chance to flaunt one's aggressiveness, courage, and physical strength.

The quarrel was also considered an accurate index of a man's preparedness during this period: his conduct under stress would reveal the quality of his mental and physical discipline. The samurai always had to be ready for a sudden crisis situation. Failure to rise to such an occasion received the humiliating label of *fukaku* (unpreparedness or negligence). *Fukaku* is a difficult concept to translate. Strictly speaking, it is not so much a specific act of cowardice as a want of preparedness to meet the challenges that a samurai would face. The warrior ideal of this period criticized a lack of proper attitude as much as improper behavior. Thus, the Tokugawa authorities often condemned both dimensions of a samurai's behavior: the act itself and the spirit behind it. Being labeled *fukaku* could have serious consequences. Therefore, even though the immediate cause of a quarrel might be trivial, the quarrel itself was an occasion (and actually almost only an occasion in this peaceful time) that revealed the samurai's quality of preparedness as a warrior.

The result was an ironic situation for the samurai. The Tokugawa shogunate had achieved a monopoly of the legitimate uses of violence, and the samurai were thereby increasingly deprived of the social and political basis of their autonomy and independence. In spite of the transition, or perhaps because of it, a capacity for decisive action in tense situations became all the more important as a surrogate for displays of manly courage on the battlefield.

Winds of Change: Honor and the Tokugawa State System

The alliance between samurai honor and physical strength was apparently unquestioned in the Aizu Domain, from which we draw the following episode from 1642. Upon closer examination, however, this intricate case also indicates the presence of a subtle change in the samurai community, a self-controlled quality in the samurai themselves that prevented the characters in this story from giving uninhibited expression to their craving for honor and glory.

In the nineteenth year of Kan'ei, a small fight between a samurai of Aizu han and a few men from Yonezawa han had serious consequences. *Kasei jikki,* the chronicle of the Aizu han, covers this incident in full detail. The person representing the Aizu han was Uchida Sanjūrō, who was on his way from Edo to Aizu after a year of service at his lord's Edo office. Sanjūrō was traveling with four colleagues, but he happened to arrive first at the Ashino station, where overnight lodging and other travel facilities were available. At the inn, he was standing in the *en* (an open corridor that was also used as a veranda) of the suite belonging to the party of Hirabayashi Kuranosuke, a *karō* ("house elder," a senior executive) to Lord Uesugi Danjō of the Yonezawa han. The document describes the incident as follows.

> A retainer of Kuranosuke told Sanjūrō to leave the premises and insulted him. Sanjūrō answered this challenge with a "proper" response *(aisatsu).* The man attacked Sanjūrō, and a fight ensued in which other retainers of Hirabayashi joined in. Sanjūrō succeeded in injuring one man on the forehead with his sword before being wrestled to the ground. As the Yonezawa samurai were about to bind Sanjūrō with rope (a serious disgrace for a samurai), the mediator, a manager of the station, arrived on the scene and stopped them from doing so.[24]

An insult, challenge, and violence—it was a classic set of opening moves for a samurai quarrel. This set in motion a long chain of complications revolving around the complex issue of honor. Sanjūrō apparently recognized that he had been deeply shamed by almost being tied up. He had also wounded the other *han*'s samurai, which could have serious diplomatic consequences. He immediately decided to clear his name by committing *seppuku*. He sent a messenger to Edo to ask for an officer to verify his *seppuku*. The messenger met Sanjūrō's four colleagues, who were approaching the station from the road.

Hearing the report of the incident from the messenger, Sanjūrō's four associates first wondered (according to their report to the authorities later) if his behavior at the critical moment was sufficiently honorable for a stalwart samurai of the Aizu han. As they proceeded to the scene of the incident, they even discussed how to handle the matter, concluding that "if Sanjūrō had behaved like a coward, we ought to accuse him and let him cut his belly immediately."

As soon as the four men arrived, the station manager attempted to reassure them: "[Sanjūrō] fought very well. He was overwhelmed by many opponents, which could have been the fate of even a hero like Hankai [a legendary hero]. Although he was beaten with a stick, he also gouged the enemy's forehead. Therefore, there is no fault of *fukaku* (negligence)." In spite of the station manager's exoneration, Sanjūrō was considered *fukaku* (negligent) anyway. Soon his supervisor also arrived at the station, and Sanjūrō was ordered to commit *seppuku;* doing so, he died.[25]

Subsequent developments took a strange turn, however. After the incident, rumor spread within the community of the Aizu samurai that the behavior of the four men on the road was not desirable for samurai. The implicit criticism seems to be that they did not immediately attempt to take revenge on the Yonezawa samurai. Hearing the prevailing rumors, the authorities reopened the investigation and called in the four men for explanation.

Sanjūrō's four colleagues reported their conversation at the station. They had been aware from the beginning that Sanjūrō's enemies should not be allowed to live if Sanjūrō had to die. There was a serious problem, however: those who had hurt Sanjūrō were not full-status samurai but *matamono,* or retainers, of a senior samurai. An insult given by these lower-status men should be returned to their master—that is, Hirabayashi Kuranosuke, a *karō,* or elder, of Yonezawa han. One of the four colleagues, Saburōuemon, had thoughtfully opposed this plan, pointing out that if this incident were to expand into a wider conflict with another *han*'s superior official, it would not be good for their lord.[26] The precarious situation was created by the fact that the quarrel had broken out in a public space (the station) with the samurai of another independent *han*.

After the investigation, the authorities were quite indecisive, as in the previous case of Okayama han. If they did not punish the four samurai, from then on, regardless of what happened to their colleagues on such trips, the samurai of Aizu han would not take any action. It would be disgraceful to have such samurai as their vassals. But, if the authorities acted punitively, thereafter the samurai would have to behave aggressively in such situations, which could cause many problems for the lord. The authorities hit upon a clever solution. The four samurai in the station were not punished for their reaction, but their incoherent and misleading way of reporting the incident, according to *Kasei jikki,* was condemned. The sentences of the four samurai were very severe. Saburōuemon was ordered to commit *seppuku,* and the others were discharged from their positions. This severe punishment reflected the public opinion of the Aizu samurai community toward the four men's conduct.

Beneath the surface of a seemingly unchanging concept of honor as a militant virtue, however, a subtle transmutation of the ethos was at work. To begin with, there was an obvious transference of the locus of honor. In the old days, the primary bearer of the standard of honor was the individual samurai and his house. The honor of the larger polity was not necessarily the chief concern of the individual vassals. In this story, however, the honor of the local polity, the Aizu, was the central focus for all the characters. Of course, the different participants held divergent opinions about the best policy for upholding the honor of the Aizu. The majority of the Aizu samurai community appeared to be worried about gaining a reputation for being weak and preoccupied with personal safety. In contrast, Saburōuemon and the three other samurai expressed concern that hasty action might cause diplomatic friction with Yonezawa han, which would put their lord in the difficult situation of having to save face. Indeed, if the shogunate had to interfere in such a dispute between two daimyo, consequences for the lord could be disastrous. Thus, Saburōuemon's perspective implied that the honor of the Aizu was preserved through avoiding a political crisis that might jeopardize the integrity of the Aizu as a local state. From the Aizu samurai community's point of view, however, the honor of the collective resided essentially in its military strength, and the individual samurai's behavior in public provided a critical part of its general reputation as a power to be feared. In effect, the Aizu was still regarding itself as a garrison state. On both sides, the individual samurai's behavior was evaluated in conjunction with the honor of the Aizu han as a whole.

This conclusion was not derived simply from fear of surveillance by the Tokugawa. The transition of the seat of honor from the individual to the local polity was accelerated by the fact that all the daimyo were forced to take up alternate residence in Edo and in their hometown. For the daimyo and their vassals, this cyclic pattern of relocation helped to shape a new imagined cultural community—the *seken*—in which the reputation for good or ill of each daimyo house was evaluated. The increased ease and security of long-distance trade and travel, which was encouraged by pacification, also made individual samurai conscious of the presence of societies beyond the borders of their local daimyo polity. The nature of the Tokugawa state—the decentralized yet integrated hierarchical state system—was the laboratory for all these modifications. Furthermore, new Tokugawa patterns of labor and residence also produced a long-term community of samurai who were structurally vulnerable to mutual evaluation. All the Tokugawa samurai were compelled to live in the samurai sections of the castle towns when they were not assigned to the daimyo's Edo office or to any other special posts. The daimyo usually provided houses or residential lots for his vassals adjoining the castle, and this collective habitation formed a dense information-gathering space in which people could constantly observe and gossip about their neighbors and colleagues. Maintaining a good reputation in this claustrophobic local society assumed greater importance for the samurai as a way to preserve their honor.

In addition to protecting his own honor, each samurai was required to consider the honor of the lord. Even more to the point, each vassal's honor depended not simply on the lord's personal honor but also on the collective honor of the local state. Multiple layers of *seken*, with a different standard of honor, emerged in this context, causing the individual samurai to question the criterion of honor. The parameters of honorable action were multiplied, increasing the complexities of decisions exponentially. But no legal standard for evaluating either crisis situations themselves or one's conduct within them was ever handed down by the authorities.

The Frustration of the Tokugawa Samurai

The early to mid-seventeenth century was thus a period of frustration for many samurai. With the increase of governmental restrictions on private violence, combined with progressively tighter political and economic incorporation into the daimyo's system, they lost a permissible expressive form for their violence-ridden culture of honor. A new value and form had not yet appeared. The frustration felt by many samurai found several outlets. One noteworthy phenomenon of the period was violence turning inward upon itself; in other words, instead of directing his aggressive impulses against external opponents, the samurai released them on himself. The sudden rise in the incidence of *junshi,* or suicide by *seppuku* following one's master's death, in the first half of the seventeenth century was a sign of this reflexive aggression.

The act of *junshi* itself was not new to the seventeenth century; there were occasional instances of it in the medieval period. But these incidents of suicide usually took place after a battle in which the samurai had lost his master. Very few examples of self-destruction on the occasion of a master's death by illness were recorded before the pacification of the country. In contrast, in the early seventeenth century, the practice of *junshi* acquired a new popularity. When Lord Tokugawa Tadakichi (the fourth son of Ieyasu) died in 1607, it was reported that five of his men chose death. On another occasion, when the famous daimyo warlord Date Masamune died in 1636, fifteen samurai committed *seppuku.* In this particular case, six of them were rear vassals whose masters decided to follow the lord even to death. By then, *junshi* had become almost fashionable. Indeed, for those samurai who had received special favors from their deceased master, committing suicide was considered normal behavior. In 1634, when Lord Satake Yoshinobu was dying, an executive samurai of the lord's Edo residence admonished his vassals that the lord did not desire them to die after him even though "it is the fashion in contemporary society to cut one's belly after the death of the master. They consider such an action a meritorious deed."[27] Despite Yoshinobu's wish, however, two samurai committed suicide after his death. Thus, in the first half of the seventeenth century, every time a major daimyo died, there would be some samurai who committed suicide.

The motivation behind the action of *junshi* varied. Since those who committed *junshi* were often honored and their heirs rewarded handsomely, adding one's name to the list of loyalty suicides was sometimes a calculated action. It was also an external demonstration of one's skill in martial arts, turned against the self. From this perspective, the popularity of *junshi* in the early seventeenth century can be considered a form of protest by samurai who were otherwise compelled to stifle their customary expressions of aggressive self-display.

Junshi was sometimes related to the homosexual association of the master and vassal.[28] Indeed, male-male love was often an additional emotional force in the solidarity and functioning of samurai armies from the medieval period. It was partly in this atmosphere of acceptance of homosexual relationships that the daimyo customarily employed many pages in their castles. These pages were mostly young boys who were typically attired in elegant kimonos. The relationships between the master and these boys were not always sexual, but if they were, contemporaries simply regarded such liaisons as a normal part of the warrior's lifestyle. When these boys grew into adulthood, they often became trustworthy political associates of the lord, rising rapidly through the ranks. Quite often, these former lovers of the lord willingly committed suicide after their master's death. In such a case, the act of *junshi* represented the wedding of death and Eros, wrapped in the official ideology of samurai loyalty. Obviously, such an intimate expression of personal loyalty was situated at the opposite extreme from the ongoing organizational transformation of the samurai society that reduced a personal and intimate relationship of vassalage to a more impersonal hierarchical one.

The custom of *junshi* and the mentality behind it posed an obvious problem for the Tokugawa authorities, who attempted to construct a more orderly form of government. But the practice of *junshi* continued to rise in frequency. In 1657, when the lord Nabeshima Katsushige died, twenty-six of his samurai committed suicide.[29] The passion for *junshi* was reaching its peak. In 1663, the Tokugawa shogunate finally issued a formal declaration prohibiting *junshi,* saying that the master should command or persuade his vassals not to act in this way after his death. Five years after this prohibition, when a vassal named Sugiura Uemon committed suicide following the death of Lord Okudaira Tadamasa, the shogunate severely punished all the heirs, both the master's and the vassal's. The shogunate reduced the size of Okudaira's fief by relocating the Okudaira house from Utsunomiya (110 thousand *koku*) to remote Yamagata (90 thousand *koku*). Two sons of Sugiura Uemon's were executed.[30] Not surprisingly, enthusiasm for *junshi* waned considerably after this decisive action. Finally, in 1683, the article regarding the prohibition of *junshi* was incorporated into the code of *Buke shohhato* (The Law for Military Houses), the shogunate's most fundamental law for the samurai class.

Restricting the samurai's propensity for violence was an extremely difficult problem for the shogunate and daimyo authorities, because it touched an exquisitely sensitive cultural nerve, the samurai's sentiment of honor. From the late seventeenth century through the beginning of the eighteenth century, however, official responses to the samurai's use of violence showed some modification.

First, the political authorities enunciated a more detailed set of principles for preventing the outbreak of conflicts. These rules tended to emphasize the importance of good order and peacefulness over the vindication of samurai honor. Second, once a conflict did occur, a system of adjudication was instituted that took causes and provocation into account to some degree. Needless to say, this evaluative practice moved in the reverse direction from the principle of *kenka ryōseibai,* which usually ended in someone's immediate *seppuku* regardless of the reasons for the original quarrel. These changes were still not firmly institutionalized during this period, however, and the traditional cultural fusion of the samurai's honor with violent behavior continued to be influential.

Given the increasing pressure to comply with orders coming down from higher authorities, the samurai's dilemma in conflict resolution was intensified. On the one hand, the samurai were more strictly controlled and incorporated into the state system; on the other, they were required to demonstrate their moral autonomy when it touched upon the matter of their honor. In the structural and ideological foundation of the Tokugawa system of domination, the samurai were cast as the sole political actors as a result of their inherited status as warriors. The implicit ideological assumption behind this distinction was that the samurai were considered to be autonomous and independent individuals because they were able to defend themselves. With this merger of military and political status, quarrels were still the decisive test of the samurai's moral autonomy and social honor.

The fact that human life in all of its dimensions was always at stake at the moment of samurai conflict clearly increased the significance and depth of these dramaturgical events. Clifford Geertz drew his distinction between "deep" and "shallow play" from his observations of Balinese cockfighting, in which betting is the factor that determines the depth of play involved in a village. For the Balinese, there must be a wager involved if the cockfight is to be a "deep" and meaningful activity. If we transfer Geertz's distinction to the honor games of traditional samurai culture, we see that it was essentially the warrior's life and self-esteem that were being "wagered." A street-corner incident or quarrel would call into question his social identity, that is, whether he really deserved the title of "samurai." That is why seemingly trivial yet outwardly dangerous games of honor represented a form of "deep play" in Geertz's sense. The samurai *kenka* was a meaningful and dramatic interaction for its participants, as distinct from "shallow play," or a comparatively trivial or boring activity.[31] The intensity of the game of honor in the samurai culture was a by-product of the high value that the participants ascribed to their imagined symbolic community of honor. Out of the deep complex of meanings involved in quarrels over honor, a variety of institutional developments and personal attempts at reinterpretation of the samurai's collective identity arose in Tokugawa Japan.

Above all, we find that this early modern culture of the samurai was not simply "out there" as a formless abstraction, and that individual samurai were not detached observers of cultural phenomena. They were active participants in a succession of honor-sensitive events through which they fashioned and reformulated cultural meanings. Their perceptions themselves, in turn, were filtered through highly institutionalized samurai cultural codes that had been, by then, active for centuries. Not only the ordinary vassal samurai but also the daimyo and the executive samurai in the Tokugawa system were caught in the meshes of this cultural preoccupation with honor.

Although the social actors of the Tokugawa period struggled as best they could to make sense of the shifting sociopolitical environments caused by Tokugawa hegemony, their responses and cultural adaptations failed to keep pace with political changes themselves. There is an apparent limit to an individual's cognitive ability to comprehend the social-institutional matrix in which he or she is situated. Because a full consideration of all the meanings and technicalities of social environments that surround the self is difficult for an individual, a person is consequently not always able to choose the behavioral option that is best suited to his or her interests.

Because it had been solidly entrenched until the beginning of the Tokugawa period, the cultural code of samurai honor was a persistent symbolic lens that filtered the samurai's perceptions and mental construction of his world. The understanding of individual Tokugawa samurai was clearly transmitted by and through *a priori* cultural codes, in which the samurai class had been immersed for many generations. Although the formation of the Tokugawa state radically altered the objective reality of the samurai's life, the samurai as individuals continued to socialize according to the standards of the older, institutionalized cultural world, using the idioms of honor as the means of communicating with, and evaluating, one another.

It must be emphasized that the structural incorporation of the samurai class into the new state system did not automatically produce "domesticated samurai." The creation of a new content for the samurai honor code was not so much the result of conscious planning by the Tokugawa as the by-product of events, contested by the samurai, negotiated between the state and the samurai, and repeatedly renegotiated. The successive daily points of tension at which the samurai felt that their sense of honor was being tested—and there were many such points of tension in the lives of men who carried two swords with them at all times, who were exposed to the unrelenting scrutiny of colleagues in a closed, competitive, hierarchical world—produced crucial pressures during the gradual change in the honor culture. Only by reacting to numerous samurai conflicts did the authorities gradually develop a new outline for a solution.

11 The Vendetta of the Forty-seven Samurai

The emotional dilemma resulting from the cultural contradiction of the Tokugawa samurai is perhaps best exemplified by the vendetta *(kataki-uchi)* of the famous forty-seven samurai. No samurai story is more widely known in Japan than this story of revenge (commonly known as *Chūshingura,* or *The Treasury of Loyal Retainers*). From the time of the incident itself (1701–1703) and throughout the Tokugawa period, despite the shogunate's strict suppression, numerous theatrical productions and fictional versions of the story were produced, with the motif of revenge running like a thread through all of them.[1] Although the event itself is well known, I would like to reexamine the act of revenge itself within the historical context, because the details of the account reveal subtle nuances in the mental landscape of the Tokugawa samurai. It was an incident that at once reflected and affected cultural metamorphosis: it not only indicated the ways in which the honor culture of the samurai was changing; it inspired the future course of that culture.

Historical Outline

On Third Month 14, 1701, Lord Asano Naganori made a surprise attack on Kira Yoshinaka, wounding him in the shogun's castle at Edo. The fourteenth of Third Month (21 April in the Western solar calendar) was the day that the shogun received the imperial delegation in the castle, and thus it was an important ceremonial occasion for the shogunate. As a daimyo, Lord Asano was the person of rank designated to receive this delegation. Kira, who held the position of *kōke*, was responsible for the smooth functioning of official ceremonies for the shogunate government. Kira's wounds were superficial; however, Tsunayoshi, the fifth Tokugawa shogun, was outraged by a major breach of the legal code as well as of court etiquette in his own castle on this high occasion. Lord Asano was ordered to commit *seppuku* the very same day. Asano's fief in Akō was confiscated, and his house was officially discontinued. The vassals of Lord Asano, as a result of this punishment, all became masterless samurai, or *rōnin*.

The motivation behind young Lord Asano's sudden fit of rage was unknown. The records, both of the investigator of the shogunate *(met-suke)*, Okado Denpachirō,[2] and of a witness, Kajikawa Yoriteru, state that Asano had claimed that "'a personal grudge' *(watakushi no ikon)* against Kira made him lose his temper."[3] Immediately following the incident, contemporary public opinion was not particularly sympathetic toward Lord Asano.[4] The simple fact that he failed to kill Lord Kira on the spot, even though he had the nerve to pick a fight at such a time and place, made him look less than manly. In other words, the popular mind did not consider the attack on Kira itself disgraceful, but Asano's failure to "follow through" showed *fukaku*, shameful incompetence as a warrior.

Some contemporaries also regarded the shogunate's reaction to this event as improper, because they classified Lord Asano's attack as *kenka*. If the incident was a personal *kenka* between two samurai, the shogunate's response should be based upon the principle of *kenka ryōseibai*.[5] Why did Kira get off without punishment? In what had become by now the traditional interpretation of *kenka*, the fact that one samurai was ordered to kill himself while the other was let off seemed unfair. The hasty execution of the daimyo lord's sentence on the same day, without careful investigation of the facts of the matter, received additional criticism, even from observers within the shogunate. The expectation that the former vassals of Lord Asano might retaliate in some way increased.

In the meantime, Ōishi Kuranosuke Yoshio, the former senior elder of the Asano house, had begun to lobby to recover Lord Asano's good name. Some people hoped that the shogunate would allow Asano Daigaku, a younger brother of the deceased lord, to succeed as titular head of the house.[6] But all efforts in this direction were in vain. On Twelfth Month 15, 1702, the fifteenth year of Genroku, a group of Lord Asano's former vassals burst into the mansion of Lord Kira in Honjo ward, Edo, and killed him. The leader of the revenge group was Ōishi Yoshio. This well-organized outlaw behavior surprised the people of the peaceful Genroku era, but at the same time it drew enthusiastic praise as an act of retribution for the death of their lord. The shogunate's treatment of these samurai became a controversial issue; two months later, however, forty-six of them were ordered to commit honorable *seppuku*. (This revenge group was commonly known as the Forty-seven Samurai through fiction and theatrical productions, but only forty-six men were sentenced to *seppuku* by the shogunate because one was not arrested, having left the spot after the act of revenge to report the incident to their hometown. Therefore, some contemporary versions of this incident referred to the group as the Forty-six Samurai.)

The Akō masterless samurai immediately became the heroes of the time. Within a month, Nakamuraza, a *kabuki* theater in Edo, performed a production entitled *Akebono soga no youchi*, which apparently derived its theme from this vendetta. The shogunate immediately prohibited the *kabuki* performance. Commoners in the audience loudly applauded the manly action depicted on stage, detecting its implicit criticism of the authorities. But the impact on the samurai community was even more profound. From 1702 through the remaining one and a half centuries of the Tokugawa period, the intellectuals of the samurai class proceeded to debate the meaning of the forty-seven samurai's action. A significant number of probing philosophical essays on the subject were written during this period.

Why were the serious intellectuals of this time so obsessed with the meaning of the samurai revenge? Why did the incident become so telling for the Tokugawa samurai? Tahara Tsuguo, a Japanese intellectual historian, summarizes the situation in precise terms:

The reason [for the preoccupation] was that the forty-six samurai were sentenced to death, even though it was by *seppuku* [honorable death] not by [dishonorable] decapitation. People in the Tokugawa period regarded their action as befitting the way that vassals-samurai should live. . . . If the shogunate's decision had been considered a simple miscarriage of justice, it would have posed a less serious ethical problem for the samurai. But the critical question arose because of the shogunate's point of view. The logic of this decision was to order the death of the forty-six samurai because they broke the "public law" by forming a conspiracy and killing a high official of the shogunate. This official reaction was so obvious and appropriate; that was why the case presented a serious problem.[7]

In other words, the supporters of the order of the Tokugawa *bakuhan* state consisted of the shogunate and the *han;* they had to come up with a morally coherent and logically consistent explanation of an absurdly tragic situation. The action of the Akō samurai was based upon the moral principles of the samurai way of life; in spite of that, the men had to be sentenced to death.

The case of the forty-seven samurai clearly highlighted a number of serious questions concerning the culture of the samurai. Note the critical historical timing of this incident: 1702. Throughout the seventeenth century, as we have seen, the violence of the samurai was progressively restricted, but approval of a spirit of vengeance and a warrior version of the honor culture survived. With the turn of the eighteenth century, however, recollections of the wars were not only fading from the collective memory of Tokugawa Japan but also becoming a piece of history. The social and political containment of the samurai, their exclusion from land as a source of economic independence, and their reorganization into the bureaucratic hierarchy of the Tokugawa state had been completed in most of the domains. The shogunate's supremacy within the country as a whole appeared to be unshakable, and the daimyo had consolidated their symbiotic relationships with the shogunate. Inside the framework of the state, the shogunate and the daimyo encouraged the proliferation of a variety of court rituals leading to an increased concern for matters of etiquette that visually symbolized the new order of society.

Added to this renewed interest in formality and ceremonial matters was the booming commercial growth of the Tokugawa economy, noticeable since the late seventeenth century. The samurai were able to enjoy the benefits of urban commercialism, and some adopted a sophisticated urban lifestyle. This springtime of Japanese culture was later remembered as the prosperous "Genroku Taihei" ("the Peaceful Era of Genroku"); but it was also the time when the samurai's warrior spirit was clearly fading. This social and cultural climate provided the stage for both the actors and the audience of this unusual vendetta.

Although this revenge was often viewed as the highest expression of the traditional samurai ethic, it was in reality a new style of retaliation. There was no comparable historical vendetta in which a group of many vassals fought on behalf of their lord. Kinship had played the most important role in samurai feuds since the medieval period. There were specific instances in which retainers and house servants joined those who were plotting a revenge. Generally, however, these loyal retainers helped to carry out the plot, which was officially headed by the victim's son or other relative. In the case of the forty-seven samurai, no relative of Lord Asano prosecuted the revenge, and the project was entirely planned and carried out by Asano's vassals. The solidarity of the forty-seven samurai was made possible only by the maturation of the Tokugawa form of daimyo polities. In this form, the vassals of daimyo houses felt a sense of shared destiny with the organization of the *han* polity, or *o-ie*. *Ie* means house, and *o* is an honorific prefix. The master's house was often called *o-ie* as a sign of respect. The word meant not only "the household of the master" in a narrow sense; it also denoted the organization of the daimyo house, including the vassals who belonged to it permanently.

The Honor Consciousness of the Avengers

Unlike most other cases of samurai conflict, in which we must deduce the contents of the men's consciousness primarily from their actions rather than their comments, this famous act of retaliation left an exceptionally rich deposit of primary materials and contemporary discussion. In particular, Horibe Yasubei Taketsune, a radical member of the group who had been stationed in Asano's Edo office, left a fairly comprehensive record of the group's two years of discussion and argument. The record consists of Horibe's memos and chronologically ordered correspondence files, in particular the letters between Ōishi Kuranosuke Yoshio, who then lived in Kyoto, and three radical members who resided in Edo.[8] The examination of their letters, together with other contemporary sources, provides some rare insiders' perspectives on the incident and their honor consciousness.

Ichibun *versus* o-ie

The action of the avengers had been in the planning stages for nearly two years, but the members of the group were not united on the direction of their action. The letters exchanged between Ōishi and the radical members indicate that there were two contending factions within this group. The more conservative position was represented by Ōishi Yoshio, who was more concerned about the honor of Asano's *ie* than about personal loyalty to the deceased lord. Ōishi patiently sought legitimate ways to restore the honorable name of the house of the Asano. For him, and for many others, the continuity of the *o-ie* was the most important precondition for maintaining the honor of the Asano vassals.[9] He thought that if the shogunate would only permit the younger brother to inherit the Asano title in such a manner that he could save face, then the vassals should suppress their personal anger for the sake of the master's *o-ie*.[10]

In contrast, the radical members of the group expressed "personal" and emotional unity with the deceased lord more strongly, and clamored for immediate drastic action. As an example of their mindset, Horibe wrote that the members hoped only "to ease the angry mind of the late master."[11] The continuity of the *o-ie* was a less important issue, because, in the first place, "if the deceased lord had been thinking of the importance of the house descended from his ancestors, he would not have allowed himself to be carried away by anger."[12] At first, the radicals proposed to go down fighting in Akō Castle as an act of protest against the shogunate's confiscation. Their second proposal was to take immediate revenge on Kira.

In their letter to Ōishi, Horibe and two other radical members expressed their frustration with his cautious attitude, saying that "because we [the members residing in Edo city] have to look at Kōzuke [that is, Lord Kira] alive here, it is extremely frustrating. . . . We only hope to give vent to our indignation as soon as possible."[13] The minds of vassals, Horibe claimed in this long letter, "should not waver from an attitude of resentment concerning the treatment of our late master, and there is no other path [other than killing Kira] to fulfillment of our martial duty."[14]

The sentiment expressed here was that of warriors, willing to die at their master's side, in a battle whose outcome was a foregone conclusion. Once a quarrel started, it should be sustained until one party was killed and their warrior spirit was satisfied. The *kenka* initiated by their master had been aborted, resulting only in his death. This sentiment against leaving the quarrel unfinished was expressed again and again by the radicals in the group, in order to light a fire under the more cautious members. In their opinion, Ōishi's plan looked only "half-baked" *(namanie)* in postponing the decisive action.

Several members of the group tended to emphasize their personal loyalty to the deceased lord. Although the feelings of those who had been private attendants of the lord were probably sincere, it is doubtful that everybody in the group felt a strong personal attachment to him. In fact, even members of the revenge group were obliged to admit that the behavior of the young lord in Edo Castle had been thoughtless and impulsive.[15] It could not have been very easy to stimulate strong feelings of loyalty when the behavior of the lord had not been praiseworthy. Then what could have energized the members of the revenge group who carried out this difficult project of retribution?

What provided the emotional explosive charge was their sense of personal honor. For one thing, this sentiment was deeply rooted in their sense of pride and dignity. From the beginning, the radical members repeatedly demanded that their sense of pride *(ichibun)* be satisfied. Against Ōishi they insisted on the necessity of immediate radical action. "If we continue in this way . . . we will expose our living shame."[16] Their frustration was evident when they said, "Seeing that our master's enemy is still alive, where shall we show our face *(menboku)?* Please uphold the pride *(ichibun)* of the samurai of the house. . . ."[17] *Ichibun* (literally, "one part") is the core of a person's pride, without which his honor is a hollow shell. If Asano's samurai had allowed Kira to remain alive, it would have brought shame not only on the memory of the deceased lord but also on his living vassals. It was the matter of *ichibun* that they had to defend for the sake of their manhood. Although the radical group realized that their act of revenge would violate the laws of the shogunate, they felt that, as vassals of a daimyo house, they had no direct obligation to the shogun. The more important goal was to vindicate their personal honor as samurai.

By contrast, Ōishi believed that the locus of loyalty should be the "house *(ie)* of Asano," and protecting the honor of the organization (the house) should be the vassals' priority. After it became clear that the recovery of the Asano family's good name was not possible through petitions and similar peaceful means, Ōishi and the radical members jointly agreed upon revenge. With no means of recovering the house of the Asano, the only way to retrieve what honor was left was to kill Lord Kira. Ōdaka Gengo, one of the more reflective members of the group, wrote about this situation to his mother:

> We had been patient until now . . . because we were hoping that, if Daigaku were allowed to succeed to the lordship, and Kira were to receive some sort of punishment, Daigaku would have a better appearance in the *seken*. If so, the *ie* of Asano would stand even though our lord had been [killed] in this way. . . . [But since this hope appears to be in vain] . . . if we only watch to see how things turn out, that would be the way a coward would act, and not the attitude that a real samurai should take . . . We will stand up for the way of the samurai and take revenge on the enemy of our master. . . .[18]

At this point, then, no difference remained between the conservative and the radical members; they agreed that an act of revenge was the only way in which they could vindicate their honor as Asano's samurai.

The initial difference between Ōishi and the radical members appears to suggest that there were two conceptions of loyalty—personal and organizational—among the samurai of this period. Horibe's notion of loyalty was personal and emotional, as exemplified in his claim that the most important obligation was for the vassals to prolong the personal anger of their deceased lord. Their individual sense of pride as samurai, the aggressive, instinctual, warlike heroism, was apparently a derivative of the medieval tradition of the ideal samurai. Although Horibe also believed that the honor of the Asano house was important, he saw it as being vindicated only through the vassals' forcible manifestation of honor. Ōishi disagreed with the radical concept. He could not completely deny the moral legitimacy of warrior honor and the place of heartfelt personal loyalty to the dead man, but he felt that such sentiments should be limited to the higher value of the *o-ie*.

Hitomae *and* seken

Whereas the term *ichibun* refers to a samurai's individualistic feeling of pride inherent in his sense of dignity, the frequently occurring terms *hitomae* and *seken* have to do with a concern for his reputation. *Hitomae* (literally, "person-front") denotes the honorable status that allowed a man to face his peers. In other words, it was his social appearance in the *seken*, the imagined community of honor, in which his honor was implicitly reflected and informally evaluated.

The radical group put pressure on Ōishi by saying that "here [in Edo], daimyo, *shōmyō* (lesser lords), and banner men," in other words, all the members of the samurai community (thus, the *seken*), in Edo were gossiping that "the house of Asano, with its long-standing honorable reputation, ought to have some vassals with principle who would not allow the master's enemy to survive."[19] They criticized Ōishi's attempts to lobby for his goals: "All the people of Edo are gossiping that Daigaku could not face up to others *(hitomae)* if he would be content to allow his brother to commit *seppuku* [and would not do anything to Kira] even if the shogunate granted him a million *koku* of fief."[20] Although they talked about personal loyalty to the deceased lord—and their feelings were not hypocritical—at the heart of the matter lay the question of their own honor, their own personal sense of pride as well as the *seken*'s good opinion of them. In this respect, the radical members' sense of *ichibun* was intimately connected to a concern for their reputation in the *seken*.

Ōishi did not overlook the weakness of their argument. In his reply to the letter from the three radicals, Ōishi criticized their concern for their reputation in the *seken* as too preoccupied with externals. "If you would let go of your private *(watakushi)* worry, and look at the essence of the matter, the criticism of the *seken* would not bother you."[21] Ōishi maintained that they should not lose their heads over a self-centered misconception of loyalty. For Ōishi, their deceased lord's real wish would have been the continuation of the *ie*, which could be granted only with the shogunate's permission. The radical group's claim was therefore unreasonable, and effectively disloyal to the dead master, because it endangered the chances of ever recovering the honor of the *ie* (house) of the Asano.

This does not mean that Ōishi was concerned only with the mere titular continuity of the *ie*. Like other group members, he was deeply involved in maintaining a sense of honor, yet in a different way. Ōishi was keenly aware of the necessity of recovering the full honor status of the Asano house *(hitomae)* in the community of honor. He wrote in his letter that he wanted to restore a setting in which Asano Daigaku could "have good *hitomae*," in order to face his colleagues with honor.[22] It would be shameful, for example, if Daigaku had to serve patiently as a courtier in the Edo Castle while Lord Kira stayed on as his colleague. Ōishi hoped that the shogunate would impose some kind of penalty on Kira to help Daigaku save face *(menboku)*.

The term *hitomae* ("person-front") suggests full and equal status within an honor community, plus the underlying continuity of ethos from the medieval samurai's culture of honor, namely, approval of competition for honor based upon the assumption that samurai should be sovereign individuals. To be sure, Ōishi and the radical members had different ideas about the kinds of actions or situations that would restore *hitomae*. But both sides took for granted the importance of having good *hitomae* in the *seken*. Therefore, both factions agreed at the end of their discussions that killing Kira was the only way to recover their *hitomae*. It is important to note that their frame of reference for judging their honor status *(hitomae)* is collective; that is, the whole samurai community from the daimyo down to the lesser vassals, the fellow samurai who shared their samurai status. They intended to vindicate their claim to membership in this reference group before all the others who belonged to it.[23]

That appeal to the collective reference group made a decisive difference to those who supported the official ideology of the Tokugawa shogunate. For them, the samurai's honor was nonexistent without the state's seal of approval. From the official point of view, the samurai's honor was inseparable from a respect for the law and hierarchical order that made up the Tokugawa state. This difference of opinion about the relative merits of individual achievement versus group approval was the source of the political controversies that initially divided the forty-seven samurai.

The discussion among the forty-seven samurai reveals that it is misleading to assume that this cultural field of honor held the same meaning, or usage, for every social actor who moved in it. In general, it is a common feature of a shared public symbolism that it gives each actor interpretive freedom within a certain range of discourse. Beyond that point, however, a particularly rich set of diverse meanings was embedded in the symbolic repertory of the honor culture. The samurai culture of honor was essentially a cultural complex consisting of a set of logically and emotionally interrelated yet distinctive kinds of symbols. It had multifaceted meanings, which themselves were set within sentiments of honor. At the heart of this multifaceted cultural complex lay an acute concern for reputation, which in turn became deeply internalized in each individual's self-understanding and sense of dignity. The samurai culture of honor thus embraced a wide range of emotions and concepts.

This rich and colorful tapestry of symbols woven into the samurai culture of honor was the basic resource for those who wanted to make their own personal reinterpretations of the tradition. For example, lower samurai could appeal to the honor tradition as an instrument for asserting their share in the superior class status of the samurai. Even though the Tokugawa samurai's world was highly stratified, its humbler members could argue that all those samurai who claimed the title should be granted respect as warriors. The diversity of the contents of the culture of honor was an additional valuable resource for individual actors, who could bend honor-related idioms to their own purposes.

Intellectual Debates on Moral Righteousness

The proper disposition of these samurai avengers became a political problem because it revealed the shogunate's standards of judgment concerning the way of the samurai. Some records of the period indicate that, even within the government, there were those who praised the deed of the group as most honorable and attempted to save their lives.[24] Although Kira's murder challenged the shogunate's authority, it was a very honorable course of action from the perspective of classic samurai ethics. Indeed, loyalty to one's master had been a major component of the shogunate's official ideology. In spite of that, however, after two months of consideration, the shogunate ordered the forty-six samurai to commit *seppuku*. The sentence announced that the decisive will of the shogunate was the upholding of law and order.

The reason behind the shogunate's decision was explained by a Confucian scholar of the time, Ogyū Sorai, as follows: Although the action of the samurai might have been predicated on their moral principle, the rightness of their action was limited to themselves alone. "If a private principle predominates over a public principle, how can the law of the world stand?"[25] As Sorai's opinion indicates, around this period a distinctive dichotomy between the public sphere (*kō*, or *ōyake*) and the private (*shi*, or *watakushi*) was introduced into the cultural code of Tokugawa society. In the case of the forty-seven samurai, the debate circled around the issue of the relative value of two loci of morality: the shogunate and the house of Lord Asano. For scholars living at the time, such as

Ogyū Sorai, the latter belonged to the domain of the "private," which should be subordinate to the claims of the "public." Having constructed a chain of obedience linking the various levels of the pyramidal state system, the shogunate was trying to superimpose a "great public authority" on the regional daimyo authorities. Therefore, although Ogyū Sorai conceded that revenge was legitimate within the sphere of ethics held by the individual Asano samurai, he subordinated their private values to the logic of "the great public authority," the shogunate.[26]

Despite such a firm official stand, many Tokugawa people, samurai and commoners alike, revered the forty-seven samurai as cultural heroes, and their personal possessions, including their swords and clothes, were treated as popular "relics."[27] Aside from sentiment on the popular level, serious intellectual discussion continued throughout the Tokugawa period. One of the earliest writings about the forty-seven samurai was by a Confucian scholar employed by the shogunate, Hayashi Nobuatsu. He tried to give due honor to the avengers' spirit of loyalty while affirming the shogunate's decision as lawful and just. Hayashi was sympathetic to the forty-seven samurai, to the point of writing a poem in the Chinese manner about their heroic nobility. But "from the perspective of law," he said, the strict punishment was necessary. For Hayashi, the two value systems, the state's and the samurai's, were equally important.[28] By contrast, another Confucian scholar named Muro Kyūsō praised the forty-seven samurai without reservation as men of true principle. Kyūsō composed a sentimental biography of them entitled *Akō gijinroku (The History of the Men of Moral Principle in Akō).*[29]

At the other end of the spectrum of opinion, Satō Naokata took a hard-line law and order position. Writing in 1705, he argued that the forty-seven men were hardly the men of *gi,* or moral principle, that they had been made out to be. Satō claimed that Kira's murder was not a legitimate act of revenge, because it was not Kira who hurt Asano. Asano had been executed because he violated the law on a very important occasion and thus neglected his public duty. The forty-seven samurai also broke the public law. In every respect, Satō thought, in the logic of the state's good order, both Lord Asano and his vassals deserved punishment.[30] Many Confucian scholars other than Satō Naokata had criticized the propriety of Lord Asano's initial action because he broke the law by attempting to murder his colleague and abandoned his assigned duty of receiving the imperial delegation owing to his personal anger. Some commentators also questioned the unthinking character of the forty-seven samurai's loyalty to the deceased lord; without examining the integrity of the master's conduct, how could they deserve the name of "men of moral principle"?

The view persisted that a vassal's denial of primary loyalty to his immediate master would erode the foundations of the feudal state. The local "particularism" that emphasized vassals' loyalty to the daimyo lord rather than to the shogunate remained a strong force in Tokugawa society. For an ordinary vassal who served under a daimyo, the authority represented by the daimyo was itself "public," and the shogunate's authority was felt to be comparatively distant. As long as the Tokugawa regime took the form of a decentralized yet hierarchically integrated state system as the basis of its domination, the samurai's primary attachment to the regional daimyo house could not be questioned. Thus, opposition to the shogunate's treatment of the forty-seven samurai came principally from several groups within the ruling elite, including some authorities in the daimyo houses, Confucian scholars, and some officials of the shogunate.

The opposition was usually based on the argument that denial of the samurai's loyalty to their immediate lord (even though it contradicted the order of the shogunate) would jeopardize the basic structure of the Tokugawa system. In other words, this view granted some autonomy to the moral sphere at the local level of government and considered it part of the public sphere. The shogunate's decision to order the forty-six samurai to commit honorable *seppuku* was a small but symbolic statement that the shogunate took such a popular sentiment into consideration. Thus, despite the shogunate's efforts to defend its decision, and despite voices such as Ogyū Sorai's and Satō Naokata's, one should not assume that the order of the shogunate completely replaced that of regional polities.

The debates among scholars, which were carried on intermittently until the end of the Tokugawa period, often involved the dissection of minute details of the case. But these rigorous academic efforts helped to refine and articulate a new direction for the samurai ethos. It is interesting to note that one of the main points of disputation centered around the question of whether or not the forty-seven samurai deserved the name of "the men of *gi*," or moral principle. The form and content of *gi* were defined very differently by the various debaters, but the importance of *gi* was almost taken for granted.

Interestingly enough, the forty-seven samurai themselves did not use the term *gi* very often in their letters. For the radical members of the group in particular it was neither moral virtue nor justice that most deeply concerned them. It was the action itself, as the pure expression of their emotion, that would vindicate their honor. It must be noted that, in the medieval tradition of samurai honor, an abstract virtue was always less important than the concrete enactment of the warriors' military spirit, specifically by the effective use of violence. The debate among the Tokugawa intellectuals regarding the nature of the samurai's *gi* reflects the changing cultural climate of this period; it was part of an ongoing process that I call "moralization" of honor. It was at about this time, partly as a result of the increasing influence of Confucianism, that the samurai started to codify their culture of honor as a character virtue.

An Emerging Multiplex Set of Symbolic Reference Groups

The revenge of the forty-seven samurai created a sensation within the samurai community because it sharply illuminated the potential for contradiction among the various levels of concern for honor and propriety that existed within the community. The incident touched upon the most sensitive and quite possibly the most vulnerable part of the ideological foundation of the Tokugawa state; that is, the logic underlying its multilayered power structure. From the viewpoint of the Tokugawa shogunate, the three levels of loyalty ought to have formed a neatly structured hierarchy. The collective submission of the nonsamurai population to the samurai as a class; the vassal samurai to the authority of the local daimyo; and the daimyo to the Tokugawa shogun—these were the organizational layers that formed the pyramidal structure of the Tokugawa regime.

The samurai class was able to maintain its domination over other classes through its construction of this integrated state system. The daimyo, for their part, were able to reinforce their authority over their vassal samurai with the help of the power concentrated in the shogun's hands. At the same time, the shogun's power was itself based upon the assumption that the daimyo would mobilize their loyal vassals to participate on the shogun's side in any military emergency. In this way, a symbiotic relationship among the different levels of power was established on potentially contested political terrain. By organizing the power of its professional warrior class along these lines, the Tokugawa state established absolute control over the country. In this respect, the early modern Japanese state had compensated for the weakness of the feudal vassalage system, which operated on the assumption that "the master's master is not the master."

This particular structural system possessed an inherent internal dissonance, however. The shogunate claimed to be the supreme authority in Japan, superordinate over all local polities. At the same time, it never discredited or contradicted the local samurai's primary loyalty to their regional daimyo. As we have seen in the context of the disagreements among the various schools of samurai intellectuals who were attracted to neo-Confucianism, there was no ideological consensus concerning conflicts of interest between the Tokugawa shogunate (*ō-kōgi*, the great public authority) and a local daimyo polity (*kōgi*, the public authority on a smaller scale). Put slightly differently, the structure of the Tokugawa state inevitably created overlapping levels of loyalty in the public domain; the potential for friction or outright conflict between the different levels in turn presented the individual samurai who had to live within this complex institutional field with genuine social and personal problems.

In addition to this potential for contradiction between the different loci of organizational loyalty, the structure of the Tokugawa state engendered another psychosocial problem for the samurai. Although it was the organizational "system" of the Japanese state that empowered the samurai class, the system's optimal operation depended upon the ideology of vassalage, which always presupposed a "personal" relationship between master and followers. Indeed, a vassal's personal loyalty to his immediate master had served historically as the source of emotional energy for building a sense of solidarity in the armed forces of medieval Japan.

The collective status of samuraihood provided another important symbolic point of reference that members of the "Forty-seven" had to take seriously. The correspondence between Ōishi and the more radical members of the group indicates not only that the two subgroups within the conspiracy had different opinions about the proper course of action, but also that their opinions were shaped by different symbolic reference points. Horibe and the radical members who resided in Edo were more vulnerable to a concern for reputation; living within the dense information space of the capital city, they were very likely to believe that all samurai at whatever status level who were living in Edo were noticing them and talking about them. In contrast, the cautious attitude of Ōishi might have reflected not only a personal style of thinking things through carefully but also his physical location. Unlike the radical members who lived in Edo, Ōishi did not live within the swirl of rumor and gossip that characterized Edo but was stationed outside it, in the castle town of Akō; he later lived in Kyoto.

A detailed examination of the case of the forty-seven samurai shows that the Tokugawa samurai inhabited a complex and contradictory social world. Indeed, the decentralized yet integrated structure of the Tokugawa state created a multiplex set of symbolic reference groups that imposed different loci, standards of morality, and expressions of honor and loyalty upon their members.

Public Men versus Warriors

In spite of this complexity, however, the analysis of the classical Japanese revenge story reveals that the instinctual, violent expressions of the samurai's sense of honor, a strong tradition in the samurai culture since the medieval period, were no longer unconditionally praised in Tokugawa Japan. The judgment of the shogunate, to condemn the avengers to an "honorable" death, sent the samurai community a message that the shogunate placed the values of law and order above those that had governed the medieval lives of the samurai.

A new rationale had been introduced for suppressing the samurai's individualistic and ungoverned displays of warrior pride through impulsive actions in tense situations. Quarrels could be considered a form of behavior appropriate only on a lower level of morality, because they pertained to the individual level. Although it might still be thought admirable for a samurai to vindicate his honor, such justice was only "private," and the private sphere was assigned a lower moral status than the public one. On the basis of this argument, the private use of violence for conflict resolution was seriously compromised. The dignity of the samurai was to be maintained, not by physical strength alone, but by his devotion to the public welfare. In other words, the samurai should always be a "public man." Clearly, not all samurai behaved according to this principle. However, this ideological reconstruction gave weight and momentum to the further suppression and rechanneling of samurai violence and honor sentiments.

The assumption that a samurai should be a public man in self-control was made not only by the authorities but by the commoners as well. Ihara Saikaku (d. 1693), a great fiction writer in the late seventeenth century—and a commoner—shows an awareness of the new attitude among commoners toward the samurai:

> The desirable attitude and mindset of the samurai nowadays are very different from those of old. In the old days, the most important thing for the samurai was courage and unconcern for one's life. They involved themselves in unnecessary *kenka* by magnifying small provocations such as "sheath hits." They believed that a samurai's achievement lay in exalting his name through killing or wounding others on the spot and leaving the scene triumphantly. But nowadays such behavior is not at all the real way of the samurai.[31]

Here, Saikaku intended to tell his contemporaries that open displays of violence should not be considered the way of the samurai in Tokugawa society. Of course, his very criticism indicates that traditional practices were still normative in late-seventeenth-century Japan, when the Tokugawa samurai were experiencing a social transition of enormous proportions. Even so, there was an emerging counterdiscourse that emphasized the public duty of the samurai. Saikaku wrote that a samurai should not throw his life away by precipitating a private quarrel, because "the master provides the samurai with an appropriate stipend in order that he should be useful to the lord some day. To throw oneself away for a private grudge means disregarding such a debt to one's master, and pits human badness against the principle of heaven. Even though the samurai might gain a great reputation, he cannot exalt his name through such conduct."

Saikaku also claimed in the preface of his book that "the human mind is the same in everyone. Given a long sword, the person is a samurai; with an *eboshi* hat, a Shinto priest; with a black robe, a Buddhist monk." Every station played a distinctive role in society, and with this division of labor, every station was equally important. In the same way, the samurai's special vocation in his house *(kagyō)* was the military, which should be connected not to an individualistic definition of honor but to a spirit of public obligation.

Because of the ruling functions assigned to the samurai's role in society, Saikaku required a higher moral standard of the samurai, saying that "giving up one's life for the sake of private affairs such as quarrels and fights is not the true way of the samurai. Devoting one's life to *giri* [duty, obligation, or responsibility] is the way of the samurai." However, as the forty-seven samurai, and especially their radical members, indicated, the bureaucrat had a more adventurous counterpart, in the ideal of the samurai that lived on the spiritual legacy of the medieval warrior. Indeed, in spite of his moralistic comment here, in which he promoted a new model of the samurai as a public man, Saikaku himself wrote many samurai stories for entertainment in which the protagonists were individuals who instinctively sacrificed their lives for the sake of honor.

"In the early modern state system of Japan," Mizubayashi Takeshi points out, the samurai ideal, which combined "vehement action with an intensely emotional ethos and an aggressive fighting spirit," coexisted with its opposite extreme, the rationally organized bureaucracy that produced "an emerging large corps of passive bureaucrats created by the Tokugawa state."[32] Although the development of the Tokugawa bureaucracy became more conspicuous at the beginning of the eighteenth century, however, a second model, that of the samurai-bureaucrat, was apparently the favored model by the middle of the Tokugawa era. As we have seen in examples of criticism of Lord Asano—that he was derelict in his public duty—state officials were now placing a higher value on devotion to public duties. The traditional heroism of the individualistic samurai was now valued only on the level of personal morality, *watakushi*. The built-in contradiction and opposition of these two types of character ideals were obvious. But the real complexity of the cultural dilemma of the samurai lies in the fact that even the most dutiful samurai-bureaucrats, or neo-Confucian intellectuals, often had a latent fascination with the medieval tradition of passionate intensity in the samurai's way of life. And this reservoir of intense feelings, deeply related to the samurai's use of violence, was the wellspring of the pride and self-esteem that sustained them in their sober bureaucratic devotion.

12 Proceduralization of Honor

Social Control: The "Bonsai Approach"

Inculcating the virtue of patience as a way of keeping the number of private conflicts to a manageable level was one means that the Tokugawa authorities employed to control the more volatile aspects of samurai culture. But patience, as we have seen, strained the samurai's integrity as men of honor, which could ultimately jeopardize the moral and political basis of their dominant position in society. Moreover, from the authorities' perspective, suppression of the samurai's sense of honor was a delicate business, insofar as the samurai's traditional self-image as fighters had been the fundamental support of their *esprit de corps*. Thus, a complete rejection of the medieval ideals of warrior culture could demoralize the samurai and cripple the efficacy of their service. Conversely, if the authorities were to attempt to toughen the moral sinew of the samurai by appealing to their pride in warlike behavior, they would be encouraging the aggressive, contentious, and undisciplined tendencies of the samurai. Beyond that, the authorities themselves, whose own sense of honor had deep roots in the samurai culture, had no certain definition of the degree of patience required of an honorable samurai.

Facing serious cultural dissonance, the Tokugawa authorities hit upon one ingenious solution: to support the tradition of honor while simultaneously attempting to transmute and convert that spirit of honor into other forms or directions that would better serve the purposes of the

241

state. The authorities commonly employed two disciplinary strategies. First, they would attempt to tame the violent elements of honor by confining their exercise within the cage of bureaucratic procedure. Second, they would allow the Tokugawa practitioners of honor to reinterpret the old tradition in more moralistic terms. As we will see, some "outlets" for honor violence were retained in order to show that the authorities sanctioned the martial spirit of the samurai. In the course of these developments, some components of the culture of honor, particularly the more violent elements, were transmuted, stifled, or redirected.

The new patterns of proceduralization eventually reduced the samurai's honor culture by shrinking it to fit within the confines of a bureaucratic and procedural code. This "bonsai approach" understandably took several generations to reach full maturity. The samurai were also vulnerable to arbitrary discipline imposed from above; after all, they were trapped in the economic toils of the Tokugawa system, separated from their original land tenure and forced to live in castle towns, like the bonsai in a pot.

In Tokugawa Japan, generally, taming the samurai's violence through the narrowing aperture of the law and refocusing the samurai's cultural identity through the lens of morality were always twin aspects of the same process. Tokugawa law was never considered a separate entity from the government and bureaucracy. The famous legal aphorism in Tokugawa Japan *hi ri hō ken ten* (the unreasonableness, the reasonableness, the legal codes, the power, and heaven) conveyed the prevailing philosophy of power. This aphorism means, according to Ise Teijō (1717–1784), a famous scholar of the time, "that the unreasonableness cannot defeat the reasonableness, the reasonableness cannot defeat the legal codes, the legal codes cannot defeat those in power, and those in power cannot beat heaven."[1] To be sure, "heaven" here does not mean, in the Western sense, a universal divine Justice superior to the sovereign; rather, it implies the rule of nature—for example, the time of sunrise—which even the king with his supreme human power cannot move by his order.[2] The point of this aphorism here lies in the law's being considered a higher power than reason. The source of law was defined not as an abstract concept of reason, justice or natural law, but as power itself. The Tokugawa rulers assumed the right to define the law as they saw fit, and those who were governed had to bow to authority with unconditional submission.

Despite the relative underdevelopment of the Tokugawa legal system

compared with those in the West, however, the principle of rule by law—
that is, rule that depended neither on the whim of the authority nor on
uncontrolled private practices of retribution—came to be more important together with an overall increase in bureaucratization and political integration. One can document extensive development of the Tokugawa bureaucracy in the late seventeenth century; and, by the beginning
of the eighteenth century, the structure of its system of government had
finally reached a mature stage. This development was carried a step further by the eighth shogun, Yoshimune, under whose reign (1716–1745)
the legal and judicial system underwent considerable expansion. Although the Tokugawa bureaucrats were still samurai thoroughly steeped
in their military ethos, they tended to seek a more rational approach to
conflict resolution. For example, the reasons for quarrels were taken into
account more seriously according to the prescribed rule, and attempts
were made to avoid arbitrary decisions by the Tokugawa bureaucrats in
charge of jurisdiction.

Although the careful operation of Tokugawa "rule-by-bureaucracy"
superficially resembled the earlier Kamakura tradition—which insisted
on careful investigation of the reasons behind the conflicts—the fundamental assumption was very different. It was during the Kamakura period, when the samurai class formed a central regime based upon alliances among the relatively autonomous samurai houses, that *dōri*
(reasonableness) became the primary principle of conflict resolution. In
contrast, the advent of this "pseudorationalizing" of Tokugawa rule occurred only after the forceful institutionalization of *kenka ryōseibai* in
the Warring States period, the military rule that replaced the older medieval pattern of conflict resolution based on *dōri*.

The Partitioning of Honor

The process of taming and reconstituting a violent culture of honor involved a partitioning of its cultural practices, a strategy that drew lines
of demarcation between what was considered good and bad. Not all the
old customs and values were retained. But certain selected practices of
the honor culture were preserved, sometimes being reinterpreted according to new standards of discipline, sometimes put on display to show
that the Tokugawa state still supported the traditional heritage of the
samurai.

Under the law of the Tokugawa shogunate, private retribution by samurai was prohibited in principle. In the *kenka* situation, the samurai were
required by their culture to prove their manhood by a swift, decisive
reaction, which might result in killing the opponent on the spot. But
successful defense of one's honor did not mean exemption from punishment by the authorities. The historical records indicate that there were a
few concessions officially made by the shogunate's law (and generally at
the daimyo's level too) to the samurai tradition of violent private retribution. These included: *burei-uchi* (literally, "disrespect-killing"), the samurai's killing of a commoner in reprisal for disrespectful behavior on the
commoner's part; the killing of an unfaithful wife and her lover, usually
called *megataki-uchi* (wife revenge);[3] and registered revenge, in which
official permission was obtained to take revenge. They were considered
legitimate outlets for violence connected with honor. In these three instances, the Tokugawa laws did not punish samurai even when they committed murder. These provisions symbolically reflect the presence of a
critical political conjunction of honor, violence, and the samurai's status
in Tokugawa society.

Burei-uchi was the term used to describe the situation in which a samurai injured or killed a commoner because of abusive language or demeanor that was regarded as an insult to the honor of the samurai. In
such a case, the samurai was exempted from any official accusation. Apparently, this was originally related to the samurai's feudal prerogative,
an integral part of his seigniorial power.[4] In general, a master's disciplinary prerogatives over his servants and retainers were widely upheld in
Tokugawa criminal procedure. *Burei-uchi* was, however, not limited to a
samurai's own servants or subjects, but could be applied to any commoner.[5] The political implication of *burei-uchi* is obvious. It permitted
a collective defense of the honor of the samurai class, by giving individual
samurai the right to defend their honor and, consequently, a legal means
to demonstrate their collective superiority to commoners. Therefore, it
was applicable even to the lowest-ranking samurai, such as a foot soldier.

As the peaceful Tokugawa era wore on and its system of domination
became more sophisticated, however, recourse to *burei-uchi* was often
regarded as crude and ill-bred. The code was no longer automatically
applied to all samurai-commoner physical conflicts. For example, in
order to have the case considered *burei-uchi,* the samurai had to prove
that the commoner had been genuinely rude to him. This usually re-

quired eyewitness testimony. There also emerged a corollary assumption that the samurai need not kill the commoner in such a case; he should be satisfied with merely injuring him. The Japanese legal historian Hiramatsu Yoshirō has noted that there emerged "the custom that the samurai's abusive use of *burei-uchi* privilege should be restricted."[6] Thus, though *burei-uchi* remained on the books as a legitimation of the samurai's superior status, its actual application quickly became fairly restrained.

The second exemption, *megataki-uchi,* was the provision commonly described by the popular saying that the offended husband had a right to cut his wife and her lover into "four pieces" when they were caught *in flagrante.* The right of a samurai husband to kill an adulterous wife's lover had been traditionally accepted as a custom of the samurai community during the Kamakura period. In medieval samurai society, the handling of such a scandalous situation was considered an internal matter for the *ie.*[7] The rise of "wife-revenge" was apparently related to the establishment of a more rigid marriage system in Japanese elite circles in general, as well as the emergence of the highly patriarchal samurai *ie.* No similar practices of condoning the killing of one's wife's lover can be found in ancient Japan prior to the tenth century.[8]

Interestingly, during the Kamakura period, there was as yet no implication that the husband should also kill the adulterous wife as punishment for her sexual misconduct. Important here is the fact that a samurai's wife at this stage was still an independent actor, with her independence based upon her right to inherit property. In comparison, during the Warring States period, a different rule emerged—in the actual practice of the samurai community as well as in the legal codes of the *sengoku daimyo*—implying that the samurai husband had the right to punish on the spot both his adulterous wife and her lover.[9] This move was apparently related to the internal transformation of the samurai *ie* during the late medieval period, during which the women of the samurai lost much of their previous social and economic autonomy. Thus, the Tokugawa shogunate simply continued the established custom of the previous period.

Comparative studies indicate that, when a culture of honor is marked by masculine aggressiveness in an environment of competitive family honor, the sexual behavior of the women in a family is often considered an index of the family's honor. A man's honor is threatened if the sexual purity of his women (wife, sister, lover, or daughter) is compromised in any way. Anthropologists of the Mediterranean basin have frequently reported cases in which the theme of female virtue was predominant in the vocabulary of honor and led to violence.[10] In Greece, John Davis notes, "a man is honorable when he meets certain exacting standards of manliness and is untainted by successful attacks on himself or his women."[11] Japan's warrior society, too, had an aggressive male-dominated culture in which the competition for honor among the *ie* was critical. A man's ability to protect his own women from other men was certainly important for maintaining his honor. Defending women's chastity was not the primary theme of vengeance in the samurai society in comparison with the degree of importance and intensity reported in Mediterranean cultures, however. The theme of women's virtue and virginity was relatively subdued and secondary in the scheme of the Tokugawa samurai culture of honor.

The right to kill an adulterous wife together with her lover was granted to commoner husbands in Tokugawa Japan as well. Unless they were carried away by outrage, however, commoners resolved the problem without taking such extreme measures. Commoner husbands sometimes simply divorced unfaithful wives, or settled the matter by accepting reparative payments from the lover. In the samurai's case, too, taking the extreme measure that custom and law permitted regarding the adulterous wife and her lover was not a legal obligation. It was only a well-established privilege that exempted the samurai husband from criminal prosecution.

The samurai husband who was involved in an act of retaliation never recovered his honor completely. This was especially true as the Tokugawa samurai became more and more deeply concerned with their reputation within the *seken*. An action as sensational as killing an erring wife and her lover would make the samurai's marital problem known to the community; it would expose the shame of the house to the world at large. The husband might even be accused of *fukaku* (negligence); he would have serious trouble in the samurai community, and he would lose face among his colleagues. The need to retaliate was seen as proof of the husband's previous stupidity, and was almost considered "an additional shame."[12] It was natural for a samurai to want to avoid a public display of his private failure. Because of the way the situation was viewed by others, samurai tended to conceal incidents of a wife's infidelity. If the husband did commit murder, he would report it to the authorities, if possible, as a natural or accidental death.[13] Thus, although the samurai husband was allowed to kill an adulterous wife as part of his right to supervise his household as its head, use of this permission was, in practice, much restricted.

If, in the later Tokugawa period at least, these exemptions— disrespect-killing and wife-revenge—were not often claimed, why did these privileges remain important in the Tokugawa judicial system? These two outlets for violence were retained because they conveyed significant symbolic messages of the valuation of the samurai's cultural and social tradition: the samurai's status superiority to other classes (in the case of disrespect-killing) and the disciplinary prerogative within the samurai household (in the case of wife-revenge). Since these privileges were used infrequently, their major impact was largely symbolic: to induce in samurai, samurai women, and commoners a conscious awareness of the full implications of the Tokugawa power hierarchy.

The situation was very different in cases of so-called registered revenge, the third exemption from prosecution for personal retribution. In these instances, murder was not only allowed but also encouraged and praised by the Tokugawa authorities as a flower of the true samurai spirit. The Tokugawa introduction of registered revenge was probably the most successful innovation, in terms of the regime's intention to enclose samurai vengefulness within the framework of the Tokugawa order, while at the same time supporting the samurai's defense of their honor.

Revenge, or *katakiuchi*, in the Tokugawa period was officially granted only when one's lineal forbear (for example, parent, older brother, uncle) had been murdered and the killer had escaped from the state's punishment by fleeing from the scene of the crime. Private retribution was not allowed if the criminal had been apprehended and was being served with justice by the authorities. Most of these officially granted revenges were carried out by sons of murdered parents (especially fathers). If the murder victim had no children, other family members could become avengers. In some cases when there was no male heir who could appropriately take the avenger's role, the victim's wife or daughter could be an official avenger. In other words, revenge was granted as a way of defending one's family honor.

In the early Tokugawa period, continuing the legacy of medieval Japanese culture, samurai revenge still tended to involve a number of family members. For example, in the case of the famous Jôrurizaka Revenge (1672), both the avenger and the target organized dozens of their own family members, rear vassals, and other assistants as participants in fights.[14] Loyalty to one's *ie,* and the honor violence caused by such intense attachment to it, posed a potential danger to the order of the Tokugawa state. The registered revenge system, institutionalized by at least the mid-Tokugawa period, provided an intelligent form of control over this area of honor violence.[15] The Tokugawa avenger could not defend the honor of the house on the basis of his own arbitrary decision; he needed official permission to take revenge. It was a disciplinary mechanism that transformed traditional free-floating vengeance from a private affair between two autonomous samurai *ie* to a state-sanctioned practice for vindicating a family's honor.

To carry out a legal revenge, the Tokugawa avenger first had to apply for permission from the authorities. In the case of a samurai who was a vassal in the service of a daimyo, this first step usually took the form of petitioning one's master for leave to seek revenge. When the petition was granted, the daimyo had a letter sent to the shogunate to put the avenger's name on the official list.[16] The town magistrate of the Tokugawa shogunate then registered the samurai's name on the list of official avengers, and a copy of the entry was returned to the potential avenger, giving him permission to attack his enemy wherever the culprit might be found. The names of any helpers (called *sukedachi,* usually the avenger's relatives) were also required to be registered. In some instances, an avenger registered his name and his helpers' names directly on the list at the shogunate magistrate office. This registration at the shogunate office was an important procedure for avengers, because their targets often hid themselves in the general population of large cities such as Edo and Osaka, which were governed by the shogunate. Enemies also had the option of moving to another lord's domain, which would make the business of revenge difficult without the shogunate's support. Without the shogunate's country-wide authority, the avenger would have encountered problems in proving to the local authorities that his action constituted a formal revenge and not just a random killing.

The precise process leading to the development of such legal procedures is still unclear, but by at least the late seventeenth century the system of revenge registration had been well established on a national scale. In 1701, when Akabori Mizunosuke murdered Ishii Uemon, a vassal of Lord Inaba and the father of Ishii Genzō and Ishii Hanzō, he left town immediately. The brothers thereupon registered their names as avengers at the shogunate magistrate's office. During his escape, Akabori found employment at the house of Lord Itakura and changed his name. Having procured this information, the Ishii brothers went to the castle town of the Itakura family and waited for an opportunity to kill their foe while working as servants for one of Itakura's vassals. When they finally succeeded in killing Akabori near the castle gate, the brothers placed a letter addressed to Lord Itakura beside the body. The letter explained that Akabori had murdered their father; it went on to claim that they "had received permission from the Edo public office granting [them] the right to conduct a vendetta anywhere." [17] Lord Itakura did not attempt to punish the Ishii brothers who had killed his vassal.

Soon after fulfilling their vendetta, the brothers sent an official report to the Edo magistrate's office that read as follows: "On Eleven Month 17th, the eleventh year of Genroku [1698], we had registered our names as avengers for our father with the former town magistrate, Lord Kawaguchi Settsu. We wish to report here that we have achieved our aim." The brothers movingly concluded the report to the shogunate: "Under the shining authority of the shogunate, we were able to sweep away our long years of anger. We are profoundly appreciative of this favor and would like to express our deep gratitude." [18] Indeed, only with the backing of the shogunate's authority would the brothers have been able to achieve their goal without being prosecuted as murderers by Lord Itakura.

Although such successful vendettas were always officially praised, the Tokugawa authorities did not intend to permit the medieval type of endless family feuds among its vassals. The shogunate did not allow second-round revenges; the official revenge was considered a kind of a duel that closed the matter for all the parties concerned without regard to the result—even in instances in which the avenger was killed by his opponent. But in a situation such as that of the Ishii brothers, the official vendetta was in a sense fulfilling the function of public justice. Because the Tokugawa state was marked by a decentralized system of control, there was no effective national police force or bureau of criminal investigation. Thus, registered revenge was not simply a lawless form of behavior given free rein in the private sphere. The action of vengeance was carried out in a

controlled political arena from which the state had deliberately with-
drawn, and private retribution served as a permissible social outlet for
the culture of honor.

Registered revenge offered both context and occasion for demonstrating the spirit of an honorable samurai, as a vindication not only of individual and family honor, but also of the honor of the local state. When
an officially licensed avenger had successfully killed his opponent, he
would be honored and rewarded by his immediate master as an exemplary samurai. If a samurai could not manage a successful outcome to
his affair, however, he might find himself unable to return to his previous
position and status. Before an avenger left on his mission, therefore, the
authorities would often exhort him, and any helpers, as follows:

> If you achieve your great aim, it will not only fulfill your filial duty but
> also entitle you to receive special benefits from the lord. If your behavior
> proves cowardly, however, it will not only bring shame upon you, but
> also disgrace the superior's good name. Therefore, you should muster
> courage, control and steel yourself, manfully achieve your goal, and
> return successful.[19]

As this admonition indicates, revenge was officially "commanded" by
the lord. Because vendettas were usually carried out by hunting down a
fugitive murderer outside the domain, avengers often spent years on the
killer's trail, an ordeal that called for resourcefulness, determination, and
self-discipline. In some cases, the hunt went on for decades; the avengers
and their assistants might have to cross the boundaries of many daimyo
domains. Given all the hardships and sufferings the revenge party had to
endure, the dramatic details of a vendetta were often on everyone's lips,
and they were even turned into theatrical productions such as *kabuki*
plays, puppet theaters, and *kōdan* story-telling.[20]

Thus, the custom of registered revenge preserved an important symbolic outlet for the spirit of vengeance while remaining confined within
the procedures dictated by the Tokugawa state. By officially mandating
and even glorifying selected attempts at revenge, the Tokugawa authorities were also able to present themselves as the official guardians of the
samurai's honorable spirit while controlling and normalizing its violent
content.

In Western European history, the duel evolved as a highly entrenched form of the dramaturgical display of honor. In Italy, Spain, France, Germany, and England, the duel flourished as a social institution, though its form and significance underwent considerable transformation from the medieval to the early modern period, surviving in modified form well into the nineteenth century. European cultures drew a distinction between formal judicial and private duels, but both closely represented the idioms of honor.[21] In Japan, by contrast, a duel existed (usually called *hatashiai*), but it was less formalized. One can speculate that, because the rules of the Japanese *kenka* preferred an immediate and decisive defense of one's honor, preferably at the scene of the "crime," they provided less room for the development of the ritualistic formal duel. Cases of formalized fighting were not totally unheard of, but they were comparatively less pronounced or publicized in Japan. A public duel, presided over by the sovereign, whose presence was central in European cases, rarely occurred in Japan. Ordinarily, Tokugawa registered revenges were prosecuted by avengers wherever and whenever they encountered their foes. On occasion, a daimyo lord or a magistrate might sponsor a public duel between the avenger and his opponent. In these instances, the combat between the two participants could be staged in the presence of officials and the general public. Reliable historical accounts do not include many such instances of *kataki-uchi* transformed into public gladiatorial spectacles, however.

The less-ritualized *kataki-uchi* form of duel, however, did not diminish the important effect of registered revenge on Tokugawa culture at large. What we should not overlook here is the meaning encoded within the *whole procedure* of the registered revenge; this procedure, as a whole, explicated and dramatized the political ideology that provided the critical underpinning of the hegemony of the Tokugawa regime. In essence, the Tokugawa samurai could defend the honor of their ancestral houses only with the permission and support of the state. The structures and procedures of registered revenge symbolized this new reality of the samurai world.

The institutionalized valuation of Tokugawa registered revenge promoted, and helped to construct, the ongoing creation of a new language of samurai ethics to provide internal support for the Tokugawa system of domination. In this new moralistic revision of the way of the samurai, revenge was reinterpreted as the moral exercise of *kō*, or filial piety. According to this model, successful avengers were paragons of the samurai spirit, and not simply because of their physical prowess and courageous spirit; in the newer interpretation, these licensed agents of justice deserved honor because they achieved the virtue of *kō* by overcoming logistical and economic difficulties.

Kō (filial piety) and *chū* (loyalty) were both considered important virtues in Confucianism. In China, however, filial piety was always the first priority in the approved Confucian moral order. *Chū,* loyal devotion to the sovereign, was also an important Confucian virtue, but the Chinese valuation of *chū,* as opposed to the Japanese, did not override the obligation of filial piety. Of course, an individual's loyalty to the sovereign could bring honor and fortune to his family; therefore, *chū* was an important precondition for the promotion of *kō.* When the two principles came into conflict, however, Chinese Confucian thought usually placed children's obligations to their fathers above other duties.[22]

The Tokugawa version of neo-Confucianism clearly reversed the order of *chū* and *kō.* It was often said by Japanese writers of this period that "the samurai of this country" should always consider loyalty to one's master more important than obligations to a parent.[23] The Japanese version also articulated the conviction that the only way of promoting one's *ie* was by devotion to public duty. As we have seen with reference to the punishment of the Akō's masterless samurai, according to the logic of the *bakuhan* state, *chū* was essentially a public value, whereas *kō* was relegated to the inferior status of a private value. The procedure of registration encoded the meaning that fulfillment of filial piety was made possible only through the protection and endorsement of the state, both in the person of one's immediate master and through the shogunate. The individualistic and autonomous use of violence was considered "private" and "illegal," while, as in the case of proceduralized revenge, officially prescribed usage of individual force was permitted and positively encouraged. Thus, the samurai's (nominal) self-armed warrior spirit was able to assert its value only through the logic of the state.

The peculiarly Japanese inversion of the hierarchy of loyalty—placing *chū* first and making *kō* secondary—is usually described as the result of the particular development of Tokugawa neo-Confucian ideology. This ideology, however, did not simply spring fully formed from the minds of Tokugawa Confucian scholars. The political reality of the incorporation of the samurai houses into the *bakuhan* state system anticipated the intellectual development, thereby prompting samurai intellectuals to try to make philosophical sense of their social reality.

The Transformation of Ritual Suicide: *Fan seppuku*

Another example of the strategies for confining honor violence can be found in changes in the practice of *seppuku* suicide. A purely reflexive form of violence, *seppuku* was a manifestation of honor-violence directed toward the self. *Seppuku* acquired a new symbolic overlay in this period, however, insofar as it came to signify the official honorable status of the samurai.

Originally, *seppuku* developed as a form of suicide for a warrior confronted with defeat in battle. Thus, it was above all a death ritual characterized by an instinctual explosion of the warrior's aggressive energy and military ardor. During the perpetual fighting of the Warring States period, *seppuku* became a more institutionalized feature of the culture of the samurai. The records of this interregnum frequently include self-dramatizing displays of heroism in the actual performance of *seppuku*. Samurai would sometimes cut open their lower abdomen and literally eviscerate themselves before losing consciousness.

It was only during the Tokugawa period that *seppuku* became a firmly institutionalized and ritualistic form of death penalty, reserved exclusively for the samurai class. *Seppuku* was thus no longer simply an external manifestation of individual pride; it played an important symbolic role in the Tokugawa system of punishment. Many Tokugawa collections of judicial precedents clearly indicate that *seppuku* was reserved for the samurai alone. For lesser samurai, other forms of execution might be imposed. But for the upper banner men and the daimyo, *seppuku* was the only form of capital punishment.[24] The imposition of any form of the death penalty other than *seppuku* was considered dishonorable for a samurai, because it denied the accused man's status of honor.

In general, honor was the most important ethical consideration of the Tokugawa penal system. The application of the law was intended to differ according to the social status of the accused. It was a customary procedure of criminal law in this period that a samurai of superior status receive his sentence without formal investigation by the court; the samurai attached deep shame to accusation and prosecution in public space.

This procedural option was, as Hiramatsu Yoshirō has explained, "not a preference for informality but a method that would show respect for the honor of the suspect; it was applicable only to the upper samurai such as the daimyo and the banner men."[25] If an investigation did take place, it was conducted without the suspect's direct involvement. For example, in a case concerning direct vassals of the shogunate, the shogunate official first investigated matters without questioning the suspect. Next, a formal letter of inquiry in a sealed envelope was sent to the suspect, who could defend himself by sending back a "letter of response." But when the subject of a criminal investigation realized that his deed was known to the authorities and that he could deny the accusation only with difficulty, he would often choose to commit suicide before his case was officially brought to court. In this situation, the suspect's death was often treated as if it were the result of natural causes, and no further punishment was imposed on the surviving members of his family.[26]

Within this new penal environment, the action of *seppuku* became a public rather than a private matter in the Tokugawa period. *Seppuku* as capital punishment was usually performed in ritual fashion, in front of officials who were designated to examine the conduct of the suicide. On these occasions, the act of *seppuku* not only signified the honor of the accused individual but embodied the authority of the state as well. As a result of this symbolic dimension, there emerged a keen concern for the proper ritual form of *seppuku*.

Although the chances that the samurai would ever need to act on the proper procedure might be minuscule, the knowledge was regarded as an essential component of their "etiquette." More to the point, a samurai bureaucrat might encounter a situation in which he would have to officially supervise a *seppuku* ceremony. The accused samurai, especially if he were of higher status, was usually first detained at a different samurai house awaiting final sentencing. The house that was serving as the place of detention for the accused samurai was supposed to prepare the proper setting for *seppuku*, in the event that the authorities ordered the defendant to kill himself. This expectation came about because the symbolic meaning of *seppuku* had become so important politically.

It was in this context that the Tokugawa experts on traditional manners and etiquette *(kojitsuka)* first enunciated the claim that there was a set of "proper" manners for *seppuku*. Even the guidebooks to good manners written for the samurai sometimes discussed the formal etiquette of *seppuku*. One of the most authoritative experts on formal manners during the Tokugawa period, Ise Teijō, gave a list of instructions for the correct preparation of the *seppuku* ritual: the proper manner of taking a bath, as purification before the *seppuku;* the most appropriate hair style; the correct manner of dressing (mostly white), and so on. Teijō goes on to prescribe that the victim's death seat for *seppuku* should be two tatami mats covered by a white sheet. When the man places himself on this death seat, he should first be served with a small ceremonial tray holding two sake cups and a plate holding a collation. The manner of serving this food to him, as well as his consumption of it, involved some very complicated points of etiquette. After this food ritual, a ceremonial sword, wrapped with white paper around the middle (as a handle), was placed on a wooden tray in front of him. The *kaishaku* (the headsman who decapitated the victim) stood behind the man. Ise Teijō maintains that the remaining details of etiquette can be taught only by oral tradition.[27]

Around the mid-Tokugawa period, as *seppuku* became more securely institutionalized as the punishment of choice for the samurai class, its actual procedure became in practice not so much suicide as a form of decapitation. The *kaishaku* of the Tokugawa period was an executioner who stood behind the accused man and cut off his head with a sword. It is true that a medieval Japanese committing *seppuku* was also usually beheaded by a *kaishaku,* but the *coup de grâce* was delivered only after the man had actually cut open his abdomen. The custom of having a *kaishaku* present for the suicide arose because the self-inflicted wound might not be immediately fatal. Thus, the samurai's self-control and courage were expressed through the extent of the incision he could make before the *kaishaku* severed his neck. But the custom of allowing the *seppuku* to proceed to the point of actual self-stabbing gradually faded away in the peaceful Tokugawa society. Usually, the moment that the accused man began to extend his hand toward the sword, the *kaishaku* beheaded him. Furthermore, in some instances the sword provided for the samurai was not the genuine article; a wooden imitation might be placed on the tray in front of the accused man. In fact, the ceremonial object might not even be a dummy weapon; sometimes the symbolic item presented on the wooden tray was just a fan. In these cases, the *seppuku* was called *ōgibara,* from the words *ōgi* (fan) and *hara* (belly).

In the old-fashioned way of committing *seppuku,* the warrior often exhibited extreme or revolting forms of self-inflicted violence in the last moments of his life as a manifestation of courage and aggressive energy. The violent enactment of *seppuku,* particularly instances in which the dying man pulled out his own viscera through the wound in his abdomen, were sometimes called "belly of mortification" *(munen bara),* because the action was regarded as a symbolic expression of the warrior's anger. The Tokugawa code of etiquette, however, frowned on this kind of extreme display as inappropriate to its more orderly way of life. For one thing, the Tokugawa samurai ordered to end his life by *seppuku* was not killing himself to keep his honorable name clear of the shame of suffering defeat in battle; it was not an enemy but most likely his master who was commanding his death. Expressing anger against the authorities through an act of "belly of mortification" not only was a breach of a newer standard of good manners, but might result in the infliction of additional punishment on his family. Accepting one's death sentence quietly, with self-control, was highly praised as behavior befitting an honorable samurai.

The account of the Forty-seven Samurai again offers an enlightening case in point (see Illustration 7). After their revenge on Lord Kira, the avengers were taken into custody and placed under house arrest at four different daimyo houses. Their *seppuku* ceremonies were conducted in these four houses. The record of the house of Lord Mōri, where ten of the avengers were held, provides a detailed account of the actual procedure.[28] The appointed place for the *seppuku* ritual was a yard in front of the hall of Ōshoin, a part of Mōri's Edo office. The vassals of Lord Mōri originally prepared ten sets of fans wrapped in white paper, but the shogunate officials advised them to supply real, short swords. The ten condemned men were provided with new white formal kimonos and new undergarments. Two tatami mats covered by a white cotton futon were placed in the yard as the seat for the death ritual. The yard was enclosed by white screens and hangings, and Lord Mōri's vassals were stationed as guards. One by one, the accused men were led from the waiting area to the ceremonial place of execution. There were five *kaishaku* on this occasion who acted in turn as headsmen for the ten samurai.

The ritual was bloody, but it proceeded efficiently and quietly. After each decapitation, the body was carried away with the futon, and the two tatami mats were replaced with fresh ones. Ten coffins had already been prepared and placed behind the white curtain. A white paper screen was strategically placed between the official examiners from the shogunate and the death seat, in order to avoid the examiners' being spattered with the blood. This screen was also changed every time. The case of the Akō samurai took place at a relatively early stage in the institutional ritualization of *seppuku*. But at this point, the record shows that the use of a fan was already considered an acceptable and honorable alternative to the earlier custom.

There was no attempt on the part of any of the condemned men to display extraordinary courage or self-inflicted violence. In Lord Mōri's record, only two men's *seppuku* received special annotations of commendation. One man who was thus singled out for praise had calmly thanked the *kaishaku* who was designated to behead him. He greeted the *kaishaku* with these words: "Since I am an old man, naturally I might not perform my duty well. I ask your special care." The shogunate official commended this man for having a good attitude. Another special note was attached to the example of one man who "actually cut" himself deeply. Lord Mōri's own samurai were apparently impressed.[29] The transmutation of the underlying ethos in this description is obvious.

To be sure, not all *seppuku* in the mid-Tokugawa period were ritual decapitations in the guise of suicide, and there are documentable instances of samurai honor being exemplified through displays of violent self-mutilation on the death seat. Overall, however, a trend toward a tamer form of *seppuku* was unmistakable. The former glamorization of violence was clearly fading. The instinctual and glory-seeking manifestations of the warrior spirit in *seppuku* were confined to the official procedures of Tokugawa ritual suicide. In general, Tokugawa disciplinary strategies for the samurai class were not revolutionary. The regime never attempted to replace the samurai tradition with a completely new culture. Not only were the changes implemented gradually, but such changes as there were are better described as partial reformulations of older traditions than as outright abolition.

Guidelines for Samurai *kenka*

Given the cumulative effect of these various measures of changing the style of *seppuku*, it was natural that a different attitude toward samurai violence came into being in Tokugawa society. This was especially apparent in Edo, where the samurai from various daimyo domains lived under the immediate scrutiny of the shogunate. A *kakun,* or set of "house rules," of the house of Lord Sakai Hayato, *Sakaike Kyōrei* (1699), written as a manual of discipline for Sakai vassals serving in the Edo office, is a good example of this reorientation.[30]

This code of conduct acknowledged the symbolic importance of quarrels and honor by stating, "A quarrel and fight is the way to virtuously regain one's dignity when a samurai has been put to shame and is obliged to kill [the man who embarrassed him]."[31] Despite this moral dimension, the code went on to point out that most quarrels actually stem from a short temper. The lord observed that "only a few quarrels really put moral principles into practice. Most quarrels end in meaningless death, because they do not stem from this principle [of honor]." Rather, the lord continued, individuals with hostile personalities or bad temperaments "more often invite stupid quarrels because they more often receive shame, as their bad manners and inappropriate jokes lead to other forms of rudeness and they often ridicule others." It is important to note here that Lord Sakai's set of house rules promoted a bureaucratic type of samurai ethic while carefully avoiding a complete rejection of the older militaristic tradition.

The lord advised that if vassals always conduct themselves politely, and bear insults patiently, "unless the matter definitely brings the way of the samurai into disrepute," the incidence of fights would be lowered. Whereas vassals are obliged to devote their lives to their lord, quarrels are only a private matter. Those who get themselves involved in quarrels, heedless of their public duty, should receive the death penalty according to the great law of *kenka ryōseibai;* although, the lord added, "the circumstances of the quarrel and the man's habitual behavior and manners would be also considered [grounds for leniency]."[32] The Sakai house rules also encouraged the samurai to work toward reconciliation. "If there is a dispute among colleagues that seems likely to erupt into a fight you must encourage the disputants to reconcile and treat the matter so as not to leave any hostile feelings. . . . If peace-making seems difficult, report the situation to a *karō* (elder). If a *karō* himself is involved in the dispute, report the matter to us."[33]

Lord Sakai's manual prescribed even more detailed rules for the treatment of a *kenka* once it actually happened. He made up a list of circumstantial categories that, in his view, affected the precise disposition of the situation: they included when a quarrel (1) broke out within the *Omote zashiki* (an official part of the house); (2) was caused by someone either drunk or insane; (3) happened in the private living quarters of the samurai; (4) involved guests (meaning that the fight involved other daimyo houses), and so on. In particular, guests who started to quarrel with each other posed a delicate problem because mishandling the case could complicate diplomatic relations with another *han* or, even worse, could result in the intervention of the shogunate.

When a quarrel did occur among guests, Lord Sakai's rules prescribed that one witness should immediately run to the executive office to report the incident. Meanwhile, the others should rush to the gates and close all of them (probably to prevent the guests' relatives from running into the house to join the fighting, and also to keep outsiders from knowing about the "shameful" trouble inside). The house rules also warned not to let the guests' servants, waiting in the other room, know of the incident and expand it. If the guests' servants asked a question, the code prescribed, "you should answer that it is a conflict among our men" and conceal the incident from them. If the servants were to witness the incident and attempt to join the fighting to help their masters, Lord Sakai's samurai were instructed to stop them politely by saying, "Your master is fine, and joining the fight is not good for your master." [34]

To regulate the traffic of human interaction, new, more precise social rules were introduced. At various levels of society, conspicuous attempts were made to improve samurai manners and etiquette. Highly differentiated codes of manners, matched to status, reminded a samurai constantly of his position in the new, state-centered hierarchy. The institutionalization of new rules of conduct in every sphere of daily samurai life emerged as another means of suppressing the private use of violence. As the samurai saw his honor code reduced to increasingly meticulous rules of social conduct, the intention of avoiding shame, rather than getting even, became the predominant basis for seeking or measuring honor.

The Ideal and the Reality of the Honor Culture

We are faced, then, with the question: "Were the Tokugawa samurai completely domesticated?" It is difficult to answer this question, because we have to consider regional, temporal, hierarchical, and individual differences in an attempt to formulate an answer. For example, it was generally believed that the samurai of remote regions such as Satsuma han tended to preserve their warrior spirit, whereas those who lived in Edo usually showed more cultural sophistication. In general, however, at least in the late Tokugawa period, it can be said that the direct connection between the concept of samurai honor and the exercise of violence was gradually weakened, and a new ethic of the samurai as law-abiding "organizational men" had clearly emerged. The new dominant sentiment was a safety-oriented attitude replacing, in part, the proud exhibition of personal autonomy through the idiom of violence.

For the majority of the samurai vassals, of modest rankings and stipends, actual life was usually rather dull, uncolored by power and glory. A man at one of these lower levels was tightly enmeshed in a particular section of the hierarchy of the state's organization, and he had few opportunities for upward mobility. From time to time, however, when something touched upon a samurai's sense of honor, he was required to demonstrate that he possessed the qualities of a warrior. Of course, not all samurai managed to live within the confines of this tension by means of moral convictions about the worth of continual self-discipline and noble dignity. Increasingly, a strictly defensive attitude crept into the samurai mentality that combined an orientation toward personal safety with procedural perfectionism.

A contemporary treatise on morality called *Bushi to shitewa (As the Samurai)*, written by a retired samurai who wanted to share his wisdom with others, reflects the Tokugawa samurai's preoccupation with propriety in handling risky conflict situations.[35] One hypothetical situation that the book presents is the following: When you are walking down the street, suddenly another samurai comes up behind you, in hot pursuit of someone, and asks your help by shouting *"Tanomu!* [help me]. . . . Please apprehend and kill [the man being chased]." Among the samurai, it was implicitly understood that once a man was asked for help with the word *tanomu* (a term implying "entrust") he should give that help even at the risk of his life. In this case, even though the second samurai was a total stranger, it was a kind of street etiquette that the samurai appealed to should respond sincerely. Of course, killing the man on the run without knowing the details of the situation was also risky, because the killer could be punished as a murderer by the authorities. The retired author discusses several possible alternative responses, two of the most ingenious of which are to tell the fugitive that you have no intention to harm him, and to encourage him to run swiftly while you also flee the scene. He added, possibly with his own condition in mind, that if you are an old man, it is also wise to pretend that you are hard of hearing and could not hear when you were asked for help. As such a safety-oriented attitude shows, by the mid-Tokugawa period the development of an orderly society supported by a stable regime had already created a different breed of samurai. The defensive mentality of the samurai naturally emerged in this context.

Adding to the changing political environment of the samurai was the development of the urban commercial culture, in which many samurai were submerged. Around the beginning of the eighteenth century, the decadence of the samurai spirit was often whispered about and even openly deplored. By that point in time, people of the period recognized that the fighting spirit of warriors had been on the wane. From the early eighteenth century onward, we often find the samurai nostalgically comparing the "old ways" with the "contemporary ways of the samurai."

In 1717, an essay entitled "Mukashi mukashi monogatari" ("Old-Time Stories"), by a samurai named Niime Masamoto (eighty years old), criticized the lax social attitudes of his contemporaries: "In the old days, at parties, both upper and lower samurai talked only about warfare . . . now, on social occasions, they discuss good food, games, and profit and loss; those with some intelligence are talking about strategies for promotion, games of *go* and *shōgi* [a kind of Japanese chess], tea ceremonies, and [the composition of] *haiku*. The young bloods chatter about *jōruri* [a type of music usually played at puppet theaters], the *shamisen* [a three-stringed instrument], and the reputation of the actors at Sakai, but they never discuss martial arts." [36] In a peaceful society that allowed them the enjoyment of the secure income from their government stipends, many samurai were turning themselves into a new urban leisure class.

Examples of samurai who made the most of the pleasures available to them are numerous and can be culled from every page of Tokugawa literature, arts, and popular culture. The hedonistic lifestyle of Asahi Bunzaemon (1674–1726), a lesser samurai of the Owari han, for instance, is not at all atypical of this period. Bunzaemon was a very ordinary samurai; he was born into a family with a hereditary annual income of 100 *koku* [units of rice]. This amount represented the income of a respectable samurai of lower rank; it was hardly a munificent income. Bunzaemon's highest achievement during his career in the bureaucracy was to serve as a buyer of tatami mats—his official job title was "the tatami magistrate." With the exception of an extraordinarily detailed thirty-seven-volume diary that Bunzaemon left behind him, covering twenty-six years of his life, there was little that was remarkable about this Tokugawa functionary.[37]

Rather than recording the high drama of a soldier's life, Bunzaemon used the security of his hereditary income and the abundant free time at his disposal to join the pleasures of the urban leisure class at a point when the Japanese economy was expanding owing to increased commercialization. He recorded more than a hundred visits to the theater in his diary, and indicated an exceptional interest in good food; as an early modern gourmet, he copied out dinner menus with particular care. In Bunzaemon's undemanding official life, he did what was necessary for a samurai bureaucrat observing all the necessary protocols. He was able to take four official business trips to Kyoto and Osaka over the course of his career. Although the number of these trips might not impress a modern business traveler accustomed to the rapid pace of twentieth-century transportation, Bunzaemon thoroughly enjoyed himself on his junkets. He did not hesitate to make the most of his opportunities to visit the sophisticated prostitutes of Kyoto, sampling the cuisine of urban establishments and taking in performances at the *kabuki* theaters. He recorded for posterity the names of all his sleeping partners as well as all the interesting foods he enjoyed. After all, the tatami merchants of Kyoto and Osaka were eager to entertain this purchasing officer from the Owari han.

When Bunzaemon was at home, he never failed to set down in his journal all "the talk of the town," that is, all the local murders, love suicides, crimes of passion, and other sexual scandals or acts of revenge. Indeed, there were even instances in which Bunzaemon carried out an unofficial investigation of a *cause célèbre* such as a lover's suicide by going to the scene of the incident himself. Although the shogunate officially prohibited games of chance, not only Bunzaemon, but also his mother, enjoyed gambling. He also indulged in social drinking with a circle of boon companions, and he died at the age of forty-five, probably from an illness brought on by his fondness for alcohol.

At the same time, Bunzaemon was still every inch the typical Tokugawa samurai. For example, he conformed outwardly to all the roles and procedures that were required to secure his hereditary status. Although he sometimes confided a straightforward criticism of the administration to his diary, he never made such criticisms public; he regarded his comments as no more than the chatter of a talkative but powerless parrot— as the journal's title, "A Caged Parrot" *(Ōmu rōchu ki)*, suggests. Bunzaemon was not only a conformist bureaucrat in his official capacity; from time to time he liked to reenact the older traditions of samurai valor. Like many samurai in this period, he entered a school of martial arts when he was eighteen. He participated in the sword-testing session, in which samurai tried out new swords during the execution of prisoners sentenced to death, or cut their bodies into smaller pieces afterward. Bunzaemon was excited about cutting into a human body, something he believed that every true samurai should experience.

In sum, if we expect Tokugawa samurai to exemplify stoic self-control and a stern internalized sense of honor, we will find examples of hedonistic and morally inconsistent men such as Asahi Bunzaemon disappointing. And we would not be alone in our disappointment: moralistic contemporaries of the pleasure-loving urban samurai recorded their disapproval of such loose attitudes and conduct. Did these developments indicate that the honor culture of the samurai was on the wane in early modern Japan?

We can perhaps best answer this question on two levels. First, it was certainly true that the intensity of the samurai honor culture diminished as the Tokugawa samurai were confined within the labyrinthine bureaucratic procedures of the Tokugawa state. As the samurai were separated from their original cultural roots in military life, it was hardly surprising that the soldierly dimension of the honor culture went into decline. It is important to note, moreover, that a discrepancy between the ideals of an honor culture and its corresponding behavioral reality is not unique to Japan. In many other honor-based societies, the transformation of the honor culture from its primary to its more "civilized" form often issued in serious discussions as to whether the people were still loyal to their ancestral standard of honor. From this comparative point of view, the critiques of the Tokugawa moralists represent an unavoidable aspect of the process of refocusing the samurai honor culture.

Second, we must note that it is never the case that the people in an honorific culture always behave honorably. The tension between the pursuit of pleasures coupled with unrestricted ambition for glory on the one hand, and the self-controlled ascetic discipline of the military mindset on the other, has always been a problem in samurai culture. But if we confine our attention solely to the tensions, paradoxes, or inconsistencies of Tokugawa culture, we miss some important considerations. We should not impose either a puritanical conception of moral integrity or a modern notion of the unity of inner virtue and rationality on the samurai of premodern Japan. From the perspective of modernity, we are likely to assume that discrepancies between the samurai's ideals and their actual practices represent either self-delusion or the decadence of the honor culture. However, even during the Warring States period, generally regarded as the high point of the samurai's military honor culture, hedonists like Bunzaemon were not unusual.[38] Individual samurai experienced honor as an intense inner sense of self-worth, but their experience does not imply that they developed a strict internal monitor for every aspect of their life on a Puritan model.

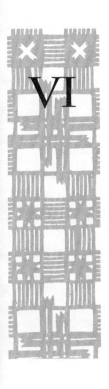

VI

HONOR
POLARIZATION
IN VASSALIC
BUREAUCRACY

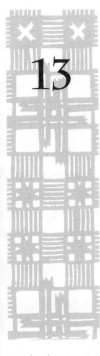

13 State-Centered Honor and Vassalic Bureaucracy

With the institution of hereditary stipends and the circumscription of opportunities to win honor on the battlefield, samurai honor no longer existed, at least officially, outside the Tokugawa system. Although a man could still make a subjective claim to honor on the basis of martial strength, virtue, or an ancestor's military distinction, a samurai dismissed by his lord for any reason was expelled from the official Tokugawa community of honor.

The problem of samurai discipline confronted by the Tokugawa authorities can be seen as a new variation on an old theme, namely, the conflict between the two requirements of long-term exchange relationships, *reliability* and *efficacy*. The *sengoku daimyo* had conducted a long struggle to ensure their vassals' reliability. The more capable a vassal in providing effective armed service *(higher in efficacy)*, the more likely he was to leave the daimyo's employ *(lower in reliability)*. Because of their relative socioeconomic autonomy, and the fact that the daimyo were continually warring with each other, vassals had considerable liberty to change masters. The formation of the Tokugawa state and the resultant stabilization of alliances between the shogunate and the daimyo altered the situation irreversibly. The Tokugawa samurai had little alternative but to remain with the same master. The problem of efficacy remained to plague the system, however, because the samurai were confined in a secure cocoon of "life-long employment."

The authorities introduced objective measurements of honor as a means of constructing a hierarchy of honor rankings, thereby rechanneling the samurai's honor-seeking impulses toward publicly sanctioned rewards and recognition. The new institutional arrangement of state-centered honor emphasized the hierarchical character of honor, specifying not only a relationship between the lord and a particular vassal but also a set of relationships between superiors and inferiors in that hierarchy. The organization of the Tokugawa bureaucracy was distinguishable from this hierarchy of honor but not inseparable from it. The higher offices in the bureaucracy were usually occupied by samurai with higher honor rankings, whereas the lower offices were crowded with men from lower-ranking houses.

The vassals were organized into a status hierarchy defined through a system of propriety *(rei)*. It is important to note that the honor system of the samurai organization was expressed and translated into hierarchical behavior codes. Consequently, politeness and good manners in the Tokugawa samurai community acquired political importance; the samurai's stylized forms of courtesy were by no means simply indicators of good breeding and refinement, but *direct and explicit idioms of power.*

I will call this system of samurai organization under the Tokugawa state "vassalic bureaucracy." The formal organizational structure of the Tokugawa samurai hierarchy sharply reflected the time-honored myth of samurai vassalage; for example, the names of honor titles often derived from the names of military positions. The close conjunction of symbolism and hegemonic politics within the samurai culture restricted the range of options for reinterpretation of the tradition. At the same time, the resulting organizational field that mixed bureaucratic and vassalic characters embraced deep cultural contradictions, which in turn served as the source of intellectual creativity for the Tokugawa samurai. The Tokugawa samurai's social and working situation continuously raised the question of the true meaning of being a samurai—that is, a warrior in seemingly ever-lasting peace under the Tokugawa domination.

The cultural field of honor embraced complex multiple meanings, allowing individual samurai to mobilize an array of honor-related symbolic idioms to reinterpret honor for their own purposes. Many sincere samurai of various ideological camps put forth a variety of intellectual prescriptions in order to make sense of their seemingly contradictory social environment.

In this chapter, I will describe the inner workings of a typical official honor system under what I have termed "vassalic bureaucracy," which provided the most significant institutional field for the reformulation of the samurai's honor culture. The organization of the samurai was significantly different in various daimyo and shogun houses. The following description is admittedly incomplete; however, my intention here is to sketch a sociological description of the important features of Tokugawa samurai organizations.

Three Indices of Samurai Status

The key to an accurate understanding of the Tokugawa honor system is the parallel existence of three major indices of status within the vassal-samurai hierarchy of the Tokugawa samurai communities. These included: honor ranking *(kaku)*; office or position in government *(shoku)*; and income *(hōroku)*. These three indicators were interrelated.[1]

Each governmental position *(shoku)* usually corresponded to an honor ranking *(kaku)* of each samurai house; these *kaku* were more or less hereditary. The higher the honor ranking—that is, the higher the ranking of the house a man was born into—the higher the office a man tended to hold in the government. Throughout the Tokugawa period, the men of samurai status had assigned military duties in times of emergency, since they were still in principle warriors. A vassal was obligated to muster a certain number of soldiers and equipment according to his basic income *(hōroku)* given by the daimyo as measured by a unit of rice output, the *koku*. In an emergency, each vassal was required to contribute the stipulated number of men and amount of supplies to his lord's armed force. But in the perpetual political calm of the *pax Tokugawa,* this military obligation was rarely invoked; as a result, the income *(hōroku)* attached to a samurai's *ie* turned into a hereditary privilege conferred by the state. The sum of a man's hereditary income was consequently regarded as another indicator of his honor. In principle, a samurai's income was not considered a salary earned through his position in the government. Although it was generally true that men with higher *kaku* tended to have higher *hōroku*, there were cases in which a high honor-ranking official had a relatively low income.[2] The correspondence of income to ranking was usually weaker than the correlation between office and honor-ranking.

These three indices were thus usually closely related to one another; their combination signified the relative position of each vassal within the house of his lord. The correspondences among these three indicators were not necessarily always rigidly fixed, and as a result there were some opportunities for low-born samurai to advance to higher rankings. As I will demonstrate, this measure of flexibility within a system of overall rigidity was characteristic of Tokugawa samurai organization; it provided the potential for combining an element of dynamic, achievement-oriented management with a stable, status-oriented hierarchy.

Vassalage as a System of Honor and Proprieties

The most fundamental principle of stratification in the samurai community was honor ranking, or *kaku*. In contrast to the governmental positions *(shoku),* honor ranking had strong ties to the hereditary status of a vassal's family. Although honor ranking, one's income, and one's position in the government were closely interrelated, the fact that *kaku* was the most fundamental determinant of one's relative position in the samurai organization reveals some important characteristics about the structure of the Tokugawa government. Indeed, it clearly indicates that the system of Tokugawa vassalage had become a status honor system in the samurai community.

The honor ranking of each vassal's *ie* was primarily understood as a representation of its historical relationships with the lord's house. In other words, the past contribution of a vassal's ancestor to the rise of his master's house significantly affected his present honor ranking, if the lord's house had originated in the Warring States period. In fact, in many old daimyo houses, the highest honor rankings were often granted only to a limited number of families. The house ranking of a newly employed vassal, arriving from outside the hereditary system, was carefully designated by the lord in such a way as not to upset the precarious balance between the higher rankings of most of the members of the older families.

In many daimyo domains, specific honor titles originally derived from the hierarchy of military organization. Because the Tokugawa state had emerged after intense military competition at the beginning of the Tokugawa period, the governmental administrations of the shogunate and the daimyo houses were originally nothing more than the military organizations themselves. Nonmilitary functions were minimal in this form of government, and they too were chiefly geared to the efficient provision of necessary supplies and infrastructure to the troops of the daimyo house. In this way, each daimyo house was always staffed according to the tables of military organization and emergency disposition for battle, and the titles in these tables directly indicated the status rankings of the individual samurai in the hierarchy of the lord's house.

Although the military titles of the daimyo's domain were originally intended for use in wartime emergencies, they increasingly became employed as honor rankings rather than designations of actual military functions, since crises requiring armed intervention rarely troubled the peaceful surface of Tokugawa society. Taniguchi Sumio has described this situation as it pertains to the Okayama han: "The lord placed each vassal in the military organization according to his degree of closeness to the lord at the time of hiring, the distinction between a newcomer versus a hereditary vassal, individual talents, quality of service for a long term, and so forth. This hierarchy defined each vassal samurai's relationship with his lord and the hierarchy of all the vassals under the lord . . . Honor ranking, the *kaku* system, was the order of status hierarchy based upon the military organization and the core of the structure of vassal organization in the *han* state system." [3]

At Chōshū, in the house of Lord Mōri, for example, more than 5,000 samurai (including foot soldiers) were divided into 70 honor rankings. [4] These 70 rankings included titles of nonmilitary origin, such as *jisha gumi* (temple unit), which was a derivative of the function of administering temples and shrines. The majority of honor rankings, however, were related to military titles. For example, the ranking called *ōgumi*, "the large unit" (the third ranking among the 7 major status categories; attributed to 1378 samurai), had to do with mounted soldier status, the core of this daimyo's fighting force in times of emergency. *Yorigumi*, "the core unit" (the second rank, attributed to 62 samurai), represented the divisional commanders of the *ōgumi* samurai force. Although these *kaku* derived primarily from military functions, the titles became merely honorific rankings in daimyo domains everywhere, describing precisely each samurai's position in the hierarchy of the daimyo's vassal organization. As a result, a discrepancy between the nominal meaning of a specific *kaku* and its holder's actual governmental function was commonly observed; for example, a samurai could be "musket officer status in charge of cooking." [5]

The names of Tokugawa honor rankings were not always necessarily

formed from army titles. Given the long period of domestic peace, the
state borrowed names from officially permitted styles of ceremonial
dress, formal seating arrangements in the daimyo castles, and even administrative positions to express *kaku* in a manner appropriate to a specific position. In particular, the strict order of the vassal hierarchy took
visual form in the seating arrangement in the castle *(rei seki)*. This seating
arrangement determined the precise order of greetings to the lord on
formal ritual occasions, in order to symbolize each individual's closeness
to the ultimate source of honor, the lord. Lesser samurai were usually
not permitted to greet the lord formally. In fact, many daimyo domains
upheld a strict distinction between subordinates who were admitted to
audiences with the lord and those who were not.

The lifestyles of the samurai vassals were meticulously prescribed according to their positions in the *kaku* system. These detailed prescriptions included the manners and etiquette of formal socialization among
the vassals (for example, the conventions of a proper greeting); officially
approved dress codes; correct gift exchanges; and the styles and scales of
wedding ceremonies, residential houses, and so on (see Illustration 8).[6]

The hierarchy of honor ranking was by no means entirely identical
with that of governmental positions. The Tokugawa bureaucratic and
military hierarchies existed as chains of command and responsibility outside the ceremonial honor rankings. Despite this separation, status stratification strictly regulated the patterns of socialization among the samurai, thereby helping to discipline the samurai organization as a whole.
Strict rules of propriety (usually called the system of *rei*) were enforced
in accordance with one's honor ranking in official ceremonial settings;
the *rei* system also pervaded all aspects of a samurai's social life, from
dress codes to conventions of speech and manners. Some features of
these rules of propriety were enforced by official ordinances, whereas
others developed from unwritten codes of customs and rules of politeness. Together, both written and unwritten canons of behavior prescribed a precise, visible differentiation of status for every social occasion.

Thus, the day-to-day existence of an individual samurai vassal of a
lower standing who received a fixed stipend from his lord was usually
quite simple and sober, far removed from settings of worldly power and
glory. His supposed status as a member of the ruling class was only symbolic, and he did not reap many material and political benefits from it.

In daily life, he had to assume a humble demeanor and manners, some-times to the point of servility, in the presence of his "betters."

There were penalties attached to violations of the official *rei* system. For example, there was a case in 1689 in which a samurai of Aizu han was punished because he made an improper ceremonial bow to his lord outside the Edo Castle. The samurai had bowed from a standing posi-tion, slightly bending his knees, but he did not kneel down on the spot.[7]

There were obvious ethical conflicts inherent in this system that could lead to everyday struggles for a proud samurai. When one behaved ac-cording to the rules of *rei*—that is, when one tailored one's manners according to relative social status differences, humbling oneself before seniors—one could easily find oneself in situations involving a stupid or immoral master or senior. Should one defer to such a person out of fidel-ity and humility? Was it possible to practice elegant and modest manners in front of a senior without questioning whether the person's character really entitled him to such treatment? If one could separate one's external behavior from his inner judgment, would this conflict with an internal-ized sense of honor, pride, and dignity? The Tokugawa strategy of or-ganizing the samurai community by externally defined codes of propriety posed a genuine and serious moral question to the samurai population.

Bureaucracy and Honor Rankings

Although in theory all samurai would serve as warriors in times of emer-gency, only some of these samurai were posted to strictly military duties in peacetime. Many of these military duties entailed no more than stand-ing guard. The remainder of the samurai mostly assumed positions in the civil administration. To be sure, this distinction between military and civilian positions was filled with ambiguities; often, men who were for-mally assigned to military posts also held administrative offices, or as-sisted the lord in private capacities.[8] Unfortunately, the administrative posts were largely "window dressing," as Harold Bolitho observes, be-cause "there was not enough business to engage the service of such a vast number of the samurai."[9] Tokugawa society did not have the kinds of public service, such as schools, prisons, and police forces, that require large amounts of manpower. Even those office-holders who did not have actual work to perform still continued to receive hereditary economic and social privileges, because vassalage was constructed upon the basic

assumption that, in a time of emergency, all the vassals would be reacti-
vated as military men supplying the requisite armed force.

Despite these complexities and limitations, by the mid-Tokugawa period the sophisticated samurai bureaucracy had become particularly conspicuous in the Tokugawa shogunate government and the large daimyo
houses. In this bureaucracy, each position usually had clearly articulated
job specifications, a range of responsibilities, and a specific budget allocated for the performance of those duties. All inquiries, decisions, and
orders were carried out through a system of bureaucratic paperwork
with its own properly prescribed vocabulary, phraseology, and calligra-
phy. This paper-shuffling mentality had a significant impact on the rest
of Tokugawa society. Not only were various ordinances sent to outlying
communities in the form of written documents, but the commoner execu-
tives of villages and town wards were also required to submit an inordi-
nate amount of paperwork to the samurai authorities. These documents
ranged from summary statements of agricultural production, various
kinds of petitions, to lists of family registration and crime reports. All of
these had to be composed in the style deemed proper to each category.

The complicated merger of a vassalage-status hierarchy with a governmental bureaucracy clearly resulted in problems related to efficient management of government, since the inflexible nature of the *kaku* (honor)
system prevented the adoption of a meritocratic principle of recruitment.
In order to be eligible for a particular governmental position, one usually
needed to have the proper honor title. Each *kaku* was correlated with a
range of corresponding positions. Returning to the case of Chōshū han,
for example, we see that there were 143 types of governmental positions
that were considered appropriate for the men who held the ōgumi (large-
unit) *kaku* ranking.[10] Theoretically, samurai below the ranking of ōgumi
were ineligible for these positions unless they were promoted to higher
rankings. As a result, whenever the institutionalization of a new administrative position became necessary, the first priority of the Tokugawa authority was the determination of the appropriate honor ranking for
that position.

Because a man's relative honor status in the daimyo government was
primarily determined at birth, the Tokugawa authorities had to contrive
ways to motivate the samurai toward excellence in government service.
The medieval samurai had a powerful drive toward military achievement,
stimulated by their knowledge that superior performance on the battle-

field led directly to glory, honor, and material rewards. Would this older achievement-oriented ethos be completely negated by the introduction of a rigid, status-oriented ranking system?

There was some flexibility incorporated into the management of this seemingly rigid system. Unlike basic incomes and honor rankings, which were primarily attached to samurai houses, bureaucratic offices were not hereditary. Even though a man might be born into a high-ranking house, privileges of birth did not automatically entail his acquisition of a powerful office. Indeed, on occasion a capable young man from a lower honor ranking might be promoted to a higher governmental position because of his proven ability on the job. Such a man might be formally adopted by a family of higher status, an event that would facilitate his promotion. In the later Tokugawa period, the daimyo's mounting financial problems occasionally led to the promotion of a problem-solver, a man of exceptional vision in economic and social policies. In addition, the absolutistic nature of the Tokugawa state often made unconventional promotions possible. Because the daimyo had ultimate authority in their domains, their personal favoritism toward certain samurai resulted from time to time in exceptional promotions outside the conventional boundaries. The unusual pattern of promotion could not be a regular recruitment incentive, however, because it always caused serious political tensions in a samurai community in which preservation of the *status quo* was the basic principle of organization.

In the middle Tokugawa period, the authorities were confronted with the necessity of introducing more meritocratic methods of recruitment and promotion in order to effectively administer increasingly complex government institutions. The shogunate and many daimyo domains introduced a system of temporary additional payments attached to governmental positions as rewards for officials with greater responsibilities. The basic income of the samurai was usually hereditary, and payments were not considered compensation for services rendered in the bureaucracy. This temporary payment system did, however, supplement a samurai's basic house income during the time the man occupied the office.

In the transition to state-centered honor, the samurai's aspirations of rising to higher honor, the legacy of the medieval mind, were by no means rejected. Rather, the new state-centered mechanisms for the conferring and transmission of honor transformed the honor of the individual samurai and of the samurai's *ie* in ways designed to further the purposes of the state. There was an obvious trend in daimyo governments to give "explicit recognition to 'merit' in the appointment of administrators," though "the merit ideal spread much faster than its application in practice."[11] Although each house's *kaku* tended to be hereditary, there were still occasional opportunities to improve one's honor ranking and income by personal effort. A man of ordinary officer status might not rise as high as the position of elder, but he could hope to advance his ranking and income one step beyond his father's. If he did not achieve this measure of advancement, he might still be rewarded with the privilege of wearing a more honorable style of dress on ceremonial occasions, or with some other symbolic compensation above that permitted to his peers in honor ranking.

Samurai usually compared their own promotion, not to the position of someone of much higher honor ranking, but to that of a peer of similar rank. Outwardly trivial adjustments in honor stratification and income within a field of contenders of similar hereditary status constituted the real breeding ground of competition. In this way, the Tokugawa system was still able to stimulate the achievement-oriented ethos of the samurai; the instinctual search for glory on the battlefield through physical strength and endurance had undergone a remarkable transformation into a sober and subdued competition for alterations in one's style of dress or the seating arrangement in the castles.

Cultural Contradictions of Vassalic Bureaucracy

The institutionalization of a status-oriented honor ranking system was the process through which the Tokugawa state gradually monopolized the determination of criteria of honor. The lively samurai culture of honor, deeply rooted in the emotional subjectivity of individual samurai, was cramped within the constraints of the institutional arrangement of state-centered honor. The relation among men had become a relation among objects of honor symbols such as seating, dress, and the amount of *koku* (income in rice units) that displayed a person's attributes of honor to the outside world. The traditional honor of the samurai, based upon their sovereign pride, was losing its spiritual and socioeconomic foundations. Its connection with the samurai's emotional wholeness and dignity was weakened. The objective criteria of honor presented to the samurai as external norms, forcibly imposed, compelled serious samurai to construct new approaches for making internal sense of these conditions of life.

Another aspect of the development of a state-centered conception of honor was that each daimyo state itself became the locus of honor. It was the state that determined and apportioned, in highly visible forms, the individual samurai's standards of honor. Each samurai's honor was always attached to the honor of the *ie* of the lord. If a vassal incurred public shame, his own honor was not the sole issue at stake; he would also be accused of bringing shame on the name of his master.

The cultural paradox of the Tokugawa samurai is only an apparent one. Because of the intimate, inseparable organizational interrelations of the state's bureaucracy and vassalage—two institutions that were otherwise quite different in their respective functional and ideological orientations—these two samurai organizations in the Tokugawa period showed distinctive characteristics that were remarkably different from what is usually considered the intrinsic natures of bureaucracy or vassalage. In short, the inner workings of the bureaucracy of the Tokugawa state were affected by the traditional and personal aspects of the master-follower relationship, building upon the logic that assumed the relative social autonomy of the vassal to the master. In turn, Tokugawa vassalage was inevitably affected by the samurai's daily involvement in a bureaucratic organization that was developing a more impersonal and regulatory culture.

Despite this, theoretically and practically, from the daimyo lord himself down to a lowly sentry guard, all samurai participated in the community of honor because they shared a common standing as warriors. This cultural solidarity was illusory, considering the radically stratified nature of the samurai population, but its symbolic importance was remarkably persistent. In other words, all samurai, regardless of their rank, lived according to the same set of cultural idioms. These in turn not only affected their judgments concerning questions of honor or order but filtered their perceptions of the objective world itself. A mental mirage it might be; nevertheless, the culture of honor still provided individual samurai with a sense of belonging to a samurai brotherhood.

In the following two chapters I will examine some individual samurai's intellectual attempts to reinterpret the cultural identity of the samurai in Tokugawa society.

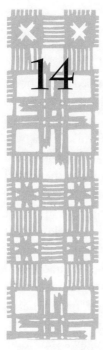

14   Hagakure: The Cult of Death and Honorific Individuality

The Origins of *bushidō*

With the state's increasing restrictions on spontaneous or aggressive individual expressions of the spirit of honor, some samurai began to contemplate more seriously the meaning of being a samurai in peacetime. The famous term *bushidō* ("the ethics of the samurai," or, translated literally, "the way of the samurai") was actually coined only during the early Tokugawa period. The term has typically been regarded by modern Japanese as the symbol of the samurai culture—as if it were a generic term for the samurai class since its first emergence as a historical phenomenon—although the word was never used during the medieval period. The way of the samurai had existed prior to the emergence of the term *bushidō*, but it was rarely expressed consciously as a structured ideology centered around a preoccupation with moral behavior. In medieval Japan, the "action" of a warrior was the most eloquent visible presentation of his internal quality; at the heart of the samurai's sentiments and values was an implicit understanding that decisive acts would be placed above polished words. The invention and popularization of the term *bushidō* symbolize the new cultural climate of the Tokugawa samurai community. Although not all samurai had a serious investment in ideals of moral behavior, there were many samurai who, in the hope of making sense of their everyday world, were searching for the meaning of their lives. In the Tokugawa period, for the first time in Japanese history, the fertile

278

social ground for producing samurai intellectuals was prepared and cultivated.

When many Tokugawa samurai were finding new satisfaction in the life of the urban leisure class, an extraordinary document reflecting the samurai ethic was taking shape in the far southern province of Saga, which was governed by Lord Nabeshima. This book, known as *Hagakure,* is a compilation of narratives told by a retired samurai, Yamamoto Jin'uemon Tsunetomo (1659–1719), to a fellow samurai, Tashiro Matazaemon Tsuramoto, together with Yamamoto's thoughts about these tales. *Hagakure,* the most famous and aggressive evocation of *bushidō,* was a manifesto of protest against the majority of the samurai, who accepted their destiny of domestication. Tsunetomo expresses his ideal of samuraihood not so much through coherent construction of a refined system of norms as through the retelling of stories of actual samurai behavior. In this fashion the author described sentiments that would have been impossible in a more philosophical manner of presentation.

Because of its idiosyncratic expressions and ideas, *Hagakure* was preferred reading for pre–World War II Japanese militarists and right-wing ultra-nationalists, who considered it an unsurpassable behavioral guide for soldiers who wished to exemplify the true spirit of the samurai. In addition, *Hagakure* was a source of inspiration for Mishima Yukio, one of the most renowned postwar fiction writers.[1] Mishima's suicide— death by *seppuku* after he broke into the office of the Ground Self-Defense Force of Japan in an attempt to "reawaken" Japan's army officers to the importance of his nationalist movement—made headlines throughout the world. Consequently, the peace-oriented majority of modern Japanese either largely ignore or openly criticize the book because of its association with emotionally unstable extremists; they regard subscription to its ideas as evidence of an outdated attachment to militarism. In agreement with the general postwar Japanese attitude toward *Hagakure,* Western scholarship tends to consider this fascinating book little more than an extremist presentation of the samurai ethic that does not speak for the majority of "true" samurai, and therefore refuses to investigate it further.

In contrast to these commonplace opinions, I find *Hagakure* a study in complexity, a work that reflects the "ethnomentality" of the Tokugawa samurai in all its diversity. The book represents one of the most acute reflections of the samurai's self-understanding, expressed by a man who internalized and wrestled with the tensions of samurai existence in the early eighteenth century. One cannot fully understand this dimension of *Hagakure* without taking into consideration the paradoxical stresses placed on the samurai by the emergence of the Tokugawa order.

The teaching of *Hagakure* remained largely on the fringes of Tokugawa intellectual circles. Both the radical philosophy of *Hagakure* and Tsunetomo's unsparing criticism of contemporary local politics made this book unquestionably dangerous. Aware of this marginality, the editor, Tsuramoto, left the following note: "This eleven-volume book must be thrown into the fire later." Thus, unlike the more mainstream Confucian-oriented attempts at refocusing, *Hagakure*'s influence was confined to the Saga han. Because of the *han*'s remote location, the extremism of the death cult advocated by Tsunetomo did not blend very well with the mentality of the more sophisticated samurai in Edo and other advanced areas in the mid-eighteenth century. This was not simply due to geographical disadvantage—Saga Province being in the backward southern part of Japan—but also because the author's prescription of an antirational cult of obsession with death was too radical for the majority of the Tokugawa samurai. Even within the Saga han, *Hagakure* was not forbidden reading, but it was not officially recommended either. The book was only privately circulated, and to that extent it remained influential in formulating the cultural climate of the Nabeshima samurai.

The marginal and private nature of this book is an advantage for modern scholars researching the elusive ethnomentality of the Tokugawa samurai. The book is filled with unpolished and unapologetic descriptions and endorsements of samurai behavior that are not available in more formal samurai writings. After 1945, *Hagakure* was not a popular subject of scholarly inquiry in Japan for a number of years. In recent Japanese scholarship, however, *Hagakure* has been heavily cited and analyzed, not because it embodies the code of the Tokugawa samurai, but because a newer generation of academics regards it as a valuable historical source for the native sentiments of the Tokugawa samurai.[2] From this perspective, it is not enough to study *Hagakure*'s ethical prescriptions, such as its emphasis on absolute loyalty and its peculiar fixation on death, as sufficient conceptual answers to these tensions. Rather, we must look at the depth and intensity of the emotional field that generated such an extremist ideological construction. By examining the motivations behind the author's moral prescriptions and the means by which he arrived at them, we can come to understand his sense of personhood and his feelings as he moved about in a world that we have lost. Thus, *Hagakure* serves as a rich resource for the history of ethnomentality.

Hagakure and Death

The unusual power of this book derives from its fundamental tone, which evokes and stimulates the most dangerous part of the samurai ethos: a fusion of class honor and personal self-esteem in the crucible of an obsession with death. At one point in the story, Tsunetomo tells his younger colleague how to discipline himself as a samurai in the course of his daily activities:

> Your day must begin with a meditation upon death as the ultimate event. Every morning, with a calm mind, form a picture in your head of the last moment of your life—such as being slain by bow and arrow, gun, sword, or spears; or being carried away by ocean waves; jumping into a big fire; being struck by lightning in a thunderstorm; swallowed up by a great earthquake; falling down hundreds of feet from a high cliff; death by sickness; or unexpected sudden death. Every morning, be sure to take time to think of yourself as dead.[3]

Self-discipline through a system of directed meditation was not new to samurai culture. Because of the high risk of sudden or violent death, either on the battlefield or at the hands of assassins, some medieval samurai had developed a set of religious practices to handle this high stress level. These practices enabled them to prepare through meditation or chanting for the ultimate crisis of death.[4] For Tsunetomo, however, death was not simply a calculated risk or unforeseen contingency for which a noble samurai should always be prepared; it was the gateway to proper induction as a samurai in the first place. Only through learning how to die honorably could a man attain the mindset of a true samurai, in peacetime as well as during war. Furthermore, one could live as a true samurai only by cultivating a state of mind that dispensed with rational calculation, a mentality that Tsunetomo called *shini gurui*, or "death frenzy." And, since there were virtually no open hostilities in the Tokugawa period, this meant that only by schooling his mind about death could the samurai live as a warrior in peacetime. To live as a samurai was to confront death, if only imaginatively, every day. The message of this behavioral ideal is eccentric but spiritual. The birth of this cult of death was subtly different from the medieval samurai's attitude toward his own death.

It is important to note that *Hagakure* was written in the middle of the Tokugawa period, at the time when virtually no samurai were survivors of actual battles. The book is best understood as its author's reinterpretation of samuraihood in confronting the cultural double bind of Tokugawa "vassalic bureaucracy" in which the Tokugawa samurai were caught. In contrast to the generally rationalistic Confucian reinterpretations of samuraihood, which I will discuss in the next chapter, *Hagakure* presents the opposite extreme: a militant, emotionally charged refocusing of the samurai's culture of honor.

In order to evaluate *Hagakure* adequately by looking beneath its aggressive and eccentric exterior, we should first study this extraordinary book against the historical backdrop in which Tsunetomo wrote.

The Historical Background of *Hagakure*

The manuscript of *Hagakure* is said to have taken shape between the seventh year of Hōei and the first year of Kyōhō (1710–1716), when Tsunetomo was leading a secluded life after his master's death. Tsunetomo was born into a reputable samurai family. His father and grandfather were loyal, powerful vassals of Lord Nabeshima. They had earned renown for their military merits and had performed honorably in several famous battles.[5] Tsunetomo's grandfather, Nakano Jin'uemon Kiyoaki, was a vassal of Lord Nabeshima and a typical samurai of the Warring States period. His father, who was adopted by the Yamamoto family, also took part in the Osaka battles and the Shimabara Rebellion. Tsunetomo's father was seventy when his son was born, and he provided him with a strict military education. Tsunetomo himself never saw actual combat, however, and his career never carried him beyond undistinguished political positions. He served his lord as an immediate attendant, starting as a young page and later becoming a secretary and an officer of document writing.

Despite Tsunetomo's aspirations for a real warrior's life, it was obvious that seeking fame through heroics on the battlefield had become unrealistic. Indeed, after years of service as a close associate of his master, Lord

Nabeshima Mitsushige, he could not even opt for the glorious death of *junshi* (suicide following the master's death), for in the first year of Kanmon (1661), Mitsushige had prohibited *junshi*. Mitsushige's hand was forced by the fact that thirty-six samurai had been planning to commit suicide following his uncle Naohiro's death, something he wanted to prevent. His decision came three years earlier than the shogunate's decree forbidding *junshi*.[6] Instead of dying a hero's death, then, after his master Lord Mitsushige's demise, Tsunetomo shaved his head and entered a secluded life with "a determined mindset of *seppuku*" in order to demonstrate his loyalty to his deceased lord.

Ironically, the superior whom Tsunetomo had served since his childhood, Lord Nabeshima Mitsushige, was famous for introducing many new rational policies that effectively bureaucratized the structure of his government.[7] Mitsushige had assumed the third lordship of the Saga han in the third year of Meireki (1657). Inheriting the legacy of his grandfather, Lord Katsushige, Mitsushige further streamlined the structure of government. He reorganized his vassals into a strict hierarchy, with meticulously defined job specifications for each office. He further strengthened and rigidified the *ka kaku* (house-honor ranking) system. In the Saga han, most vassal samurai continued to receive *chigyō* (fiefs) from the lord; however, Mitsushige attempted to increase the proportion of directly taxed land as much as possible in order to increase the power of his government over and against his vassals. After Mitsushige's retirement in the eighth year of Genroku (1695), the fourth lord, Tsunashige, further institutionalized this bureaucratic style of governing, introducing more refinements in the status hierarchy system.

Hagakure was written when this development of the bureaucracy in the Saga han had reached its apex. The author's intense anger against the political trend of the time was enmeshed with his nostalgia for and admiration of the earlier regimes of Lord Naoshige and the second lord, Katsushige. That was the time, he thought, when samurai still lived according to the spirit of real warriors, and the relationship between lord and vassals was not so distant and impersonal.

In this era of increasing bureaucratization, *Hagakure* was deeply concerned with upholding a tradition of warrior honor. Tsunetomo called the military version of honor *haji* or *chijoku* (both meaning "shame"). Avoiding *haji* was a central moral precept in *Hagakure*. Tsunetomo was indignant about contemporary samurai who never thought of their honor and were satisfied with an undisciplined, pleasure-oriented life. He deplored the fact that such samurai could "unexpectedly incur *haji* but not even recognize it as shameful."[8] *Haji* in *Hagakure* was not simply a matter of reputation among others, external to the recipient, but rather something deeply rooted in the samurai's own existence; it was a matter of inner dignity. Only through continual guarding against *haji* could a samurai retain his dignity and self-esteem.

The Behavioral Philosophy of *kenka*

Hagakure is regarded in modern Japan as a book about "the way of the samurai" that propagates a cult of death and militant stoicism. In fact, most of the pages of *Hagakure*'s eleven volumes are filled with entertaining stories about the exploits of individual samurai rather than abstract philosophical discourses. Many samurai stories in *Hagakure* had been told by Tsunetomo.[9] But Tashiro Tsuramoto, the editor of *Hagakure,* also added a number of stories from contemporary sources that illuminated the *Hagakure* way of the samurai. The individuals who were described with admiration and affection by the author tended to be the kind of people who did not readily accept the values and rules handed down from the authorities. And the most mystical part of this teaching, namely, the cult of death, was inextricably intertwined with the samurai behavioral philosophy exemplified in these vivid stories.

Hagakure includes many narratives about samurai involved in *kenka* (quarrels) or similar unexpected crises in which the samurai's sense of honor and the requirements of law and order conflicted. For example, *Hagakure* admiringly describes the response of a samurai who heard that his colleague was involved in a street fight. Rushing to the scene of the incident, he found that his colleague had already been killed. He issued a challenge on the spot, and forthwith killed his colleague's two opponents. After the fight, the local magistrate accused the samurai of violating the law by assisting his colleague in a dispute. The samurai's reply proudly asserted the superiority of the claims of honor to those of civil law:

> You have accused me of breaking the law, but in reality I did no such thing. Indeed, being alive is important not only for human beings but for all living creatures. I also cherish my life very much. However, when

I was told "Your colleague is involved in a fight," I thought that if I stayed out of it, I would dishonor the way of the military; therefore, I rushed to the spot. If, after seeing that my colleague had been killed, I had not done anything and left the scene, the way of the samurai *(bushidō)* would have been sacrificed even though I would have extended my own life. Thus, I decided to preserve the way of the samurai and give up my life. By having forfeited my life at the scene, I observe the law of the samurai and uphold the rule of the samurai. I have already laid down my life there. Thus, I humbly ask you to order my swift execution.[10]

For this individual, the law of the samurai was superior to the law of the state. The law of the samurai does not mean *dōri,* the principle of reasonableness, here. This particular man simply asserted that he could not act otherwise because he would have received shame. What we clearly identify in this story is a defiant sense of honor not unlike the medieval samurai's passion for honor clothed with dignity. By asserting his devotion to the honorific sentiment, this proud samurai was able to claim an individualistic moral judgment in front of the state official.

The kind of story cited above is a vivid indication of the seriousness of quarrels for the Tokugawa samurai. What prompted Tsunetomo to construct his unique moral philosophy was a pressing contemporary moral dilemma shared by many Tokugawa samurai: how to reconcile the samurai notion of honor with the seemingly uninterrupted peacefulness and bureaucratization of samurai life. For example, one cannot properly understand the following famous passage in *Hagakure* without considering the dilemma forced upon the samurai by the law of *kenka ryōseibai:*

Bushidō, or the way of the samurai, means death. Whenever you confront a choice between two options, simply choose the one that takes you more directly to death. It is not complicated; just advance to meet it with confidence. It is the saying of the superficial *kamigata*[11] way of the military that death without aiming [at the right purpose] is meaningless. It is difficult to make a right decision. We are human beings who prefer to be alive. Our highest preference, that is, self-preservation, will naturally find a rational argument in its favor. If you made a mistake in aiming, and you live to tell about it, you are a coward. This is a very dangerous thought. If you make a mistake, and you die, you might be thought crazy, but it will not bring you shame.[12]

The famous first sentence of this passage, "*Bushidō*, or the way of the samurai, means death," has been used as a slogan by twentieth-century Japanese militarists and ultranationalists because it neatly encapsulates the samurai spirit. During the Second World War, this phrase encouraged Japanese soldiers to throw themselves into desperate battles. But, upon closer examination, this paragraph is not as simple as it first appears.

The above passage clearly indicates that Tsunetomo had the concrete situation of *kenka ryōseibai* in mind. The Tokugawa samurai were continually exposed to the dangerous possibilities of getting embroiled in a quarrel, and thus being liable to the penalties prescribed by *kenka ryōseibai*. The grave conflict between respect for law and order on the one hand, and upholding a sense of samurai honor and self-esteem on the other, is the background explanation of this passage. Whether one survived or died at the scene of the incident, a quarrel would most likely result in the samurai's death. If he chose to fight, regardless of his reasons and circumstances, he would be sentenced to death by the law of *kenka ryōseibai*. Those who took the course of patience and did not retaliate might survive, technically, but they usually sustained lasting public disgrace in the samurai community. When the samurai used their rational minds, Tsunetomo thought, the desire to live would naturally win out, and therefore might result in the most shameful consequences. It was useless in an emergency situation to reason calmly about the better way of the samurai. Undue attachment to his life simply hampered a samurai from showing absolute mastery over his life at the moment of crisis. Thus, it was better to school one's mind resolutely to choose death.

Tsunetomo at one point discusses the tactics of conducting oneself in a quarrel: "The way of making a counterattack [in a quarrel] is simply to rush out and attack [the enemies] and just get killed. In this way, you will never incur shame. If you think about winning, you will lose your timing; if you think about such things as the large number of enemies and spend time thinking, you may end up doing nothing. . . . Winning or losing depends upon the situation. The way to avoid shame is different. Just die there. . . . The really able man will race into the act of 'death frenzy' without giving a thought to winning. In this way, one can be awakened from one's dream."[13] Although Tsunetomo encourages death on the spot, his true aim is obviously winning, achievable only by placing oneself at risk to die. This result would be possible only for those who habitually trained themselves to meditate upon death.

By an extension of this logical progression, Tsunetomo criticizes even the famous Forty-seven Samurai because they took too much time deciding to act: "The night attack of the *rōnin* (masterless samurai) of the late lord Asano was also a mistake; they should have cut their bellies immediately at the Sengakuji Temple [after the attack]. Above all, they took a long time after the enemy had killed their master. What would have happened if Lord Kira had died of sickness in the meantime? The *kamigata* people are intelligent and shrewd when it comes to plotting a strategy to get praise . . . but they are not able to suspend rational judgment—as in the case of the Nagasaki *kenka*."[14] Unlike other critics of the Forty-seven Samurai, Tsunetomo did not find fault with them because they defied the law. He pressed the question of why, if they had decided to avenge their slain master, they did then not act at once, after their master was condemned to die?

Surrendering the instinctive human desire for self-preservation is of course not an easy task. To facilitate that measure of self-control, the recommendation of daily training in the art of death entered Tsunetomo's line of argumentation. He states repeatedly: "Every morning and every evening, rehearse your death again and again. If you already die to yourself, you obtain freedom in a military way, and you will perform your tasks in the house without mistakes throughout your whole life."[15] Being dead was the only way that one could properly and effectively achieve—without becoming overly attached to them—the samurai's two primary goals: the way of the military and service to one's master. *Hagakure* implies that "being dead to one's self" allows a man to live free— free from the constraints of desires ordinarily associated with life, desires that impair sound judgment. The person who thinks about death on a daily basis is able to devote all his energy to the service of his master. Because he will never misjudge a moment of crisis, he can be a true warrior. "If one lives with a mental attitude of 'constant death on the field,' and makes oneself a total corpse, there will be no shame in one's service to the lord and in the martial way."[16]

Tsunetomo's aspirations for the truly honorable samurai were inextricably connected with learning to die rightly. His thinking had its own internal logic and consistency and, in fact, reflected some of the deepest Buddhist teachings. The main difference was that the Buddhist ideal of "giving up the self" was directed more toward the spiritual goal of giving up one's attachment to one's limited (sense of) self—and in that way not so different from the Christian notion of "dying to the world" in order to be "born again." It was no wonder, then, that an appeal to universal mystic tendencies found a willing ear among some of those searching to give a deeper meaning to their everyday activities. Thus, Tsunetomo had constructed a system in which what he called "death frenzy" increased the efficacy of a samurai's service.

Redefining the Master-Follower Relationship

Had *Hagakure* achieved nothing except the encouragement and stimulation of passionate and instinctually violent behavior among the samurai, its impact on post-Tokugawa Japan would have been much smaller than it proved to be. The usefulness of the book to prewar Japanese militarism lay in *Hagakure*'s combination of the cult of death with the ideal of faithful and efficacious devotion to the public good—and in its defining of this combination as the way of the true samurai.

Service as Secret Love

In his reconception of the master-follower relationship, Tsunetomo attempted to bring living personal and emotional ties back into the reality of Tokugawa vassalage. He considered loyalty in the master-follower relationship a highly personal bond predicated on a feeling of absolute unity between the two parties. As we have seen, intense personal and emotional ties of this sort can be found in the medieval form of vassalage prior to the Tokugawa bureaucratization of the samurai's world. But Tsunetomo's ideal master-follower relationship was not a straightforward return to medieval vassalage. What was significantly different was that *Hagakure* rejected the exchange aspect of vassalage—the pattern of *go'on* (debt) and *hōkō* (service). Emphasized in its place was absolute devotion on the part of followers without any expectation of an appropriate reward from the master.

Unlike medieval samurai, who were proud of their socioeconomic independence, Tsunetomo positively acknowledged and even celebrated the utterly subordinate position of Tokugawa vassals by saying that "all the people of the household are the lord's possessions." [17] On the basis of this understanding, a vassal should serve the lord with absolute and unquestioning loyalty—to serve the lord is to be dead to one's self—thereby overcoming his own egocentric nature and instinctive desire for self-preservation. According to Tsunetomo, this self-abnegating state of mind could be achieved only by being in *shini guru,* or "death frenzy." The notion of exchange was rejected as contaminated by an impure motive, in contradistinction to a selflessly strong emotional tie to one's master: "An expanded fief, a gift of gold and silver, should naturally be appreciated. But what we value much more highly [than a material reward] is a word [of commendation] from the master. Only such a word can produce a samurai willing to cut his belly." [18]

Tsunetomo illustrated this observation by recounting an episode from his own relationship with his lord. He was deeply touched on one occasion when his master gave him warm personal words of appreciation, together with some unpretentious gifts—the master's own futon and a nightgown. He was thereby moved to lament the passing of the old ways: "Oh, if only it were the olden days [when *junshi* suicide was not prohibited by law], I would have cut my belly beside this futon, covered my body with this nightgown, and followed my master!" [19]

It is important to state at this point that Tsunetomo's ideal was not simply an ideological by-product of the organizational mentality of the *bakuhan* state. The Tokugawa samurai were structurally incorporated ever more tightly into the bureaucratic hierarchy of the state, and therefore deprived of their ancestral socioeconomic independence. In practice, the state demanded the absolute loyalty of the Tokugawa samurai vassals because of their incorporation into its machinery. Tsunetomo's emphasis on absolute loyalty was not a derivative of this political-organizational reality, however. Rather, his aim was to revive a sense of intense personal bonding between the individual master and his vassals.

Indeed, in order to make his point about the intensity of this sentiment, Tsunetomo used the term *shinobu koi,* or "secret love," as an analogy for the kind of devotion and loyalty that a follower should have for his master. "The ultimate love is a secret love." [20] "Secret love," in Tsunetomo's usage, means loving someone without letting the person know about one's feelings, that is, without expecting any reward or reciprocity. The vassal's mindset should also be "like the mindset of true love. The more it is painful and sad [because he cannot express himself], the more his love will increase. On the rare occasion when he has an opportunity to see his loved one, he will be able to lay down his life. Secret love is the model [for the vassal]. For his entire life, he will not express it, but, deep in his mind, he will be determined to die [for his master]."[21] Therefore, the loyal samurai should not expect any reward, either material or honorific, from his master. The samurai should not even desire that his true loyalty and service be known to the master. Tsunetomo called this "service without recognition," or *kage no hōkō* (literally, "service to the public in the shadow"). The title of the book itself, *Hagakure*, which can be translated as "in the shadow of leaves," may stem from the same concept.

When Tsunetomo was writing about the intense emotional connection between master and vassal, his descriptions of the ideal master-follower relationships sometimes incorporated erotic metaphors. The imagery of secret love reminds us that Tsunetomo lived in a period when male-male love was considered not abnormal or perverse but often the purest form of human bonding based upon mutual trust, honor, and the appreciation of one's partner's inner qualities. The iconography of samurai male love as enunciated in Tokugawa popular literature emphasized loyalty between lover and beloved and valued honorific loyalty to the point that a man might forfeit his life for love. The most famous example of this literary genre is a series of short stories about samurai written by Ihara Saikaku that Tsunetomo duly cites in *Hagakure*.[22] Tsunetomo basically agreed with an opinion that relationships between boys and older lovers should be exclusive and based on mutual trust and fidelity. To be sure, Tsunetomo did not specify the nature of secret love in this particular context.

Tsunetomo openly discusses homosexual liaisons in other passages of *Hagakure*, however. For example, he quotes a saying attributed to the samurai who was regarded as "Nabeshima's first arbiter of *shūdō*, or man-boy love," that losing one's life for the sake of the loved one was the ultimate ideal of this form of love.[23] In this cultural climate, it was predictable that a vassal's devoted service and loyalty to his master would acquire the coloration of homosexual love. In some instances, devoted love in male-male relationships went beyond metaphor. Quite often those samurai who committed *junshi* after the death of the master had sexual liaisons with him. Thus, it was no wonder that the idealized form of the master-vassal relationship, an intensely personal commitment between two men, could resemble the romantic image of perfect male love.

Tsunetomo's reinterpretation of the master-follower relationship in personal and devotional terms, as well as his inclusion of the ideal of a noninstrumental "secret love," was an unrealistic behavioral and attitudinal standard for most Tokugawa samurai. Although homosexual love itself was generally still considered an aspect of normal social life in the samurai community when *Hagakure* was written, it was often considered poor form to make such relationships public because they interfered with the impersonal operations of bureaucracy. Some daimyo domains also attempted to curb homosexual activities involving the seduction or rape of young boys.[24] By the same token, loving personal relationships with their lords became increasingly unrealistic for the majority of the samurai, as they were ever more tightly incorporated into the impersonal Tokugawa vassalic bureaucracy. Yet, however unrealistic it may have been, by combining devoted service with a passionate sense of military honor, *Hagakure* represents a powerful refocusing of samuraihood in Tokugawa Japan.

Although it may impress modern readers as overemphasizing the vassal's one-sided devotion and subordination, *Hagakure*'s notion of the ideal master-follower relationship paradoxically underscored the power of the free will of one who chooses to serve another. The samurai who decided upon the path of such commitment and perseverance was exercising his free choice. Tsunetomo's teaching of *shinobu koi* might have touched the hearts of some proud samurai who were compelled to accept the reality of their subordination in a hierarchical government structure. In exalting the ideal of submission to the absolute authority of a master, Tsunetomo was paradoxically constructing *a moral framework for restoring and reasserting the individualistic and assertive ego* of the samurai, which was a legacy from the medieval tradition of samurai honor. At the same time, by reframing the absolute loyalty that was forced on Tokugawa samurai by the social and political structures of their society as the vassal's free moral decision, the logic of *Hagakure* relegitimated the samurai's obedience to the lord.

Tsunetomo's method of refocusing the samurai culture of honor was not to condemn the assertive, spirited, or prideful aspects of the warrior ethos but to provide a logical reconciliation between the samurai's sentiment of honor and the authority of the lord. Once loyalty and service were redefined as "secret love," a seemingly simple act of obedience became an inner virtue of honor and dignity. Since "secret love" should not expect a reward, whether material or honorary, the external evaluation of one's honor should be subordinated to the inner honor of the samurai. Tsunetomo did not explicitly state it in these terms, but the logical outcome of his thought assumed that the inner virtue of the samurai should be the preeminent source of their pride and honor.

Although Tsunetomo stressed absolute loyalty and fealty, the ideal samurai in *Hagakure* is not a spiritless follower who faithfully performs only his routine assigned tasks. On the contrary, he is a politically active, passionately engaged man who has the energy and courage to assert what he believes to be best for his master. In *Hagakure*, one of the most valuable expressions of samurai loyalty is to disagree with one's master. "It is an act of great loyalty to correct the mindset of one's master, and thus to confirm the foundation of the country."[25] If the master does not listen to the vassal's remonstrance, then the samurai should persevere in his attempts repeatedly. Because *Hagakure* valued the responsible voicing of disagreement, it also held the view that a good samurai should hope to be promoted to the highest position of elder *(karō)*. By having an appropriate promotion of this sort conferred on him, the subordinate is enabled to speak his real mind to his master.[26] Thus, the aspirations of a Tokugawa samurai to rise in the bureaucratic ranking of the official hierarchy were fully accepted by Tsunetomo. It is, however, a poignant affirmation, coming as it does from a man who had only limited success in realizing his own career ambitions.

The high valuation that Tsunetomo placed on the act of remonstration itself is reflected in many other discussions of the samurai ethic during the Tokugawa period. This fact reveals the underlying depth of concern among the Tokugawa samurai to protect a sense of personal political engagement and individual action in an age of ever-increasing bureaucratization. The theme of honorable remonstrance received considerable emphasis in the writings of Confucian samurai intellectuals as well as in the more indigenous *bushidō* literature such as *Hagakure*. Both kinds of writing typically described the action of remonstrance as a virtuous samurai's duty. Remonstrance, however, was also a device that allowed the Tokugawa samurai to restore a sense of active moral autonomy within a culture circumscribed by an overvaluation of duty.

If we compare the Japanese situation with its Chinese counterpart, we note that the Chinese Confucian classics also valued the act of remonstrance in certain situations between superiors and inferiors. The Chinese literature also generally advised the would-be Confucian gentleman to protest to his sovereign according to the dictates of his moral sense. In cases in which the lord rejected his subject's remonstrance, the Chinese writers simply suggested that the man leave that master. This attitude stands in stark contrast to the absolute valuation of *kō*, or the virtue of filial piety as defined by Chinese Confucianism. In a comparable situation involving the parent / child relationship, children were allowed to disagree with their elders three times. If, after the third protest, the parent still rejected the child's position, adherence to the virtue of *kō* required the child to submit to the parent's will. In Japan, the ethic that developed under the Tokugawa bureaucracy resembled the Chinese definition of *kō* in that it did not allow the subject to separate from a problematic master.[27] If remonstrance proved ineffectual, the vassal samurai had no further recourse within the system of the *bakuhan* state. The author of *Hagakure* never advocated revolt against the authority of the lord Nabeshima; rather, he considered *kō* to be a corollary of *chū*, or loyalty to the sovereign.[28] The supremacy and continuity of the house of Nabeshima were the precondition of any admonition coming from a vassal, and any persistency in assertiveness was expressed only within these boundaries.

The Prideful Ego and the Law of the State

Tsunetomo said, "I simply made up my mind [as a youth] that 'I am the lord's only vassal. His true military might resides in me alone'; this determination penetrated to the very marrow of my bones."[29] This belief in individuality and self-esteem was the foundation of *Hagakure*'s samurai sentiments. One of the most beloved and admired samurai characters appearing in *Hagakure* is Saitō Yonosuke, a true *sengoku* samurai, the kind of man whose assertive individuality is evidenced in his actions. Yonosuke was a famous mighty vassal of the lord Nabeshima Naoshige. He was admittedly eccentric. For example, it was said that when Yonosuke was commanded to demonstrate his gun-shooting skill in a public tournament, he shot only at the sky. He claimed that he had never hit a fixed target but had never missed a living one. "Because I did quite well in the field," Yonosuke claimed, "my lord is still alive!"[30]

This samurai's self-assertiveness, combined with a straightforward masculine attitude, was affectionately described in another episode:

One day, because they were poor, Yonosuke's wife was weeping that there would be no rice for the evening meal. Yonosuke told her, "Even though you are a woman, it is disappointing that you, a member of a samurai household, are shedding tears simply because of a lack of rice. There is a lot of rice. Just wait for a while." Then Yonosuke robbed a carriage full of rice paid as tax, by saying, "Take the rice to my place. My name is Saitō Yonosuke. . . . I will give you the receipt." . . . Threatened with a sword, the farmers carried all the rice to Yonosuke's home. Yonosuke proudly said to his wife, "See—here is a lot of rice. Use it as you like."

Yonosuke never attempted to hide what he had done from the authorities, and they consequently sentenced him to death. The report of his condemnation reached Lord Naoshige, who was already retired at that time but had fought many battles with Yonosuke during the Warring States period:

> As soon as Lord Naoshige heard this report, he started to cry and bewail the situation to his wife. "Listen, my dear, Yonosuke is going to be executed. . . . Because of his skill in combat, we [the lord and his wife] are alive at this moment and are living the peaceful life of a lord . . . Yonosuke was my strongest soldier, and his name was honored on several occasions. It is a great crime on my part to have left this man without rice. . . ." The old lord and his wife cried endlessly.[31]

Lord Katsushige, Naoshige's son, who was in charge of the government at that time, pardoned Yonosuke for the sake of his parents. In many ways, this story is a fitting symbolic representation of the world that *Hagakure* valued most—a simple and straightforward soldier who had the courage to act as he thought right; a lord who deeply understood his vassal's worth and was, moreover, wise enough to understand the meaning of Yonosuke's highway robbery; and their deep emotional tie that had been forged in the heat of battle. It was a beautiful lost world, however, for the author of *Hagakure,* who lived in the middle of the Tokugawa period.

Despite these qualities, however, the assertive egocentricity and self-esteem displayed by the *Hagakure* samurai had their limitations. The samurai's spirit of resistance and moral autonomy were confined to the level of personal morality and did not develop into a universal political philosophy. The contradiction between the law of the samurai and the law of the state was resolved only by the samurai's death. Yonosuke acted in the way he believed right as a warrior. But at the same time, he accepted the law of the state by willingly surrendering himself to the authorities. His pardon was made possible only by the tears of the old retired lord and his wife. Recall the case of the unnamed samurai, cited earlier, who came to the assistance of his friend in a quarrel. The man made an impressive argument to the court, claiming the superiority of "the law of the samurai" to the legal code of the state. Yet in spite of his proud and persuasive argument, the man ended his apologia with the statement, "Therefore, I humbly ask you to order my swift execution." The supremacy of the law of the samurai to the law of the state was operative only at the level of the samurai's personal behavior, and it never developed into a transcendent principle that could arguably modify the actual form of governing. The contradiction of the two levels had always to be resolved by the willed death of the samurai in the world of *Hagakure*.

Nabeshima "Nationalism"

The primary underlying tone of *Hagakure*'s philosophy is one of Nabeshima chauvinism. It eventually leads Tsunetomo to a very proud but narrow-minded belief in Nabeshima superiority. Every action of the samurai should be taken for the sake of both master and country, or *o-kuni*, meaning the Saga han polity, or the house of the Nabeshima. "If you are a vassal, you do not need to know about any other locale. If you have mastered the traditional lore of your country *(kokugaku)*,[32] then you may learn ways of other places as your personal amusement."[33] The "lore of the country" means the traditions of the Nabeshima han, or learning the history, labor, and efforts of the Nabeshima founders, undertaken in order to build "the everlasting foundation of the Nabeshima [house]."[34] For the vassals of the Nabeshima, no other knowledge is necessary. "Buddha, Confucius, Kusunoki [a medieval hero famous for his military strategy], and Shingen [a famous warlord] never entered into vassalage with Ryūzōji or Nabeshima"; therefore, Tsunetomo claimed, their teachings are irrelevant to the ways of the house.[35]

Hagakure's Nabeshima chauvinism was related to Tsunetomo's occasional criticisms of his master, Mitsushige. Mitsushige had grown up in Edo, and he did not know his own country until he became the head of the Nabeshima han. His ignorance was the result of a policy of the Tokugawa shogunate, according to which the son of the daimyo who would succeed to the lordship had to stay in Edo. But from Tsunetomo's point of view, all the rational policies Mitsushige introduced appeared to be caused by his ignorance of the tradition of the Nabeshima.

The logic of *Hagakure* implicitly reflects an underlying change in the samurai mentality, a shift of the locus of loyalty from the person of the lord to the organizational *han* polity itself. This observation might sound contradictory, considering Tsunetomo's desperate efforts to recover an "old-fashioned" sense of intimacy and personal bonding within the Tokugawa vassalage system. We must note, however, that when Tsunetomo used a phrase such as "secret love" what he sought was more than an anachronistic reconstruction of a social world, now lost, in which human ties were valued and preserved. He also sought the restoration of social relationships in which an individual samurai could maintain his moral autonomy and personal dignity. For these reasons Tsunetomo's emphases on remonstrance as a moral act and "secret love" as a mental orientation together constituted a picture of the ideal vassal.

When the lord himself was not an ideal master (which was usually the case) and could not appreciate the true value of a loyal samurai's service, however, the vassal's life became a perpetual round of frustration. Of course, it was precisely because of this situation that the mental attitude of "secret love"—that is, loyalty as a moral commitment that would not seek a reward for service—was so strongly emphasized in *Hagakure*. Although Tsunetomo rejected materialistic and worldly honorific rewards as the basis of a samurai's devoted service, however, he was duly appreciative of the power of emotional and personal recognition; as he phrased it, "A word [of commendation from the master] can produce a samurai willing to cut his belly." If the master could not give his followers even a hint of emotional recognition, how could they be faithful in his service? Tsunetomo attempted to solve this problem by introducing a higher value than the lord's person as the object of the samurai's loyalty, namely, his master's house *(o-ie)*. Although the lord as an individual might share the fallibility and impermanence of all things mortal, the order of his house could be regarded as perpetual. As such, the master's house represented permanence and stability for the samurai. It was in this context that Tsunetomo idealized the founder of the Saga han, the lord Nabeshima Naoshige, and his relationship with his loyal and brave vassals. The ideal foundation of his house was an essential part of the moral scenario of *Hagakure*.

Although the shift to organizational loyalty never emerges in *Hagakure* as an explicit part of the argument, there existed by the mid-Tokugawa period a growing sentiment of "*han* chauvinism," a kind of patriotic sentiment centering on the daimyo's regional state. The *o-kuni* (the country) in this sentiment was the focus of a samurai's loyalty and pride. Whereas the daimyo as an individual might not be especially competent or wise, the tradition of the country was still perpetuated through him. This is a particularly important sentiment in *Hagakure;* that within the framework that valued personal and emotional ties to the master and follower there was a correlative sentiment that honored the samurai government of the Nabeshima polity itself rather than the person of the master.

During the late Tokugawa period, this *han* chauvinism developed in many local daimyo states into a kind of regional nationalism.[36] The object of loyalty and collective identification shifted from the personal authority of the daimyo lord to a more abstract organizational concept of the house, *ie,* or *han.* Even in *Hagakure,* a book that elevates the personal tie of the master-follower relationship above the bureaucrat's obligations to the machinery of an organization, we can observe the beginning of this tendency.

We can further conclude that *Hagakure* was the product of a samurai who struggled to make sense of his changing world, not by adapting himself to the new environment, but by seeking to restore what he perceived as the world of a true warrior. *Hagakure*'s project—namely, restoring the lively warrior spirit without challenging the law of the state head-on—was inherently very difficult; *Hagakure* proposed to rescue the moral autonomy of the samurai while simultaneously protecting the absolute authority of the lord. Absolute loyalty to the lord was redefined as the moral choice of the samurai vassal who entered upon the difficult path of devotional service through "secret love" without expecting any reward. In spite of accepting the absolute power of the lord and subjection to the laws of the *bakuhan* state, *Hagakure* rejected the regulatory aspect of the state that reduced the samurai to a mechanical cog in the bureaucratic wheel of the state. When a samurai was forced to make a choice between conflicting contractual requirements, *Hagakure*'s distinctive prescription was for him to suspend rational thought and fling himself instead into the world of the "death frenzy."

In the deepening national crisis of the nineteenth century, the book gained popularity among Nabeshima samurai, and many reading circles were formed around it. Despite this increased readership at the end of the Tokugawa period, however, *Hagakure* was never adopted by the official schools for samurai even in the Saga han.[37] It was obvious to the authorities that the *Hagakure* type of samurai vassal—a self-assertive, "death crazy" fanatic who would resort to violence instinctively—would not fit smoothly into the official world of Tokugawa bureaucracy.

In spite of this limitation and marginality, however, *Hagakure* is a reminder of the cultural climate of the early modern state system, of how deeply the nonrational warrior spirit was embedded in the minds of the bureaucratic Tokugawa samurai. Although few samurai could conduct themselves according to the dictates of *Hagakure,* the book had a power to resonate with a sympathetic echo in the minds of a minority within the samurai community. The book can be considered the desperate effort of a sincere man who wanted to live in the world of the Tokugawa samurai in a way that afforded him a modicum of dignity and pride. The militant ethos of the samurai was increasingly tamed and softened in the peaceful Tokugawa society, but it was never completely eradicated because it was closely connected to the samurai's sense of self-worth and dignity. This violent element of honor culture thus retained the potential to reemerge during a change of social climate. By attempting a profound answer to the question of "honor or order," *Hagakure* created a "time bomb" in Japanese culture.

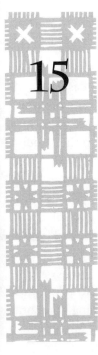

15 Confucian and Post-Confucian Samurai

In contrast to the extremist position articulated in *Hagakure*, Confucian thought in the Tokugawa period provided a number of acceptable idioms for samurai who wished to discuss questions of attitude and behavior in public discourse. Confucian concepts gave thoughtful samurai a set of common conceptual tools and an agenda for ethical debates. In general, the Confucian redirection of samurai standards of morality emphasized the inner moral quality of a person as the basis for measuring honor, while correspondingly deemphasizing old-fashioned military definitions. Since Confucianism tended to support a hierarchical social order, it also promoted the virtues of public and corporate responsibility and loyalty. This aspect of Confucian moral philosophy helped to redirect the inherited samurai culture toward socially accepted goals and responsibility. Furthermore, the concept of meritocracy advocated by the various Confucian schools also helped to reorient a primarily soldierly definition of achievement in the direction of a more intellectual emphasis on scholarship and administration. This latter transition was seriously impeded by the fact that the Tokugawa regime never abandoned the fundamentally status-oriented principles that prevented it from evaluating samurai for promotion to higher positions in the government on the basis of achievement.

Confucianism in this era of Japanese history was by no means a unified school of thought; rather, it was divided into a variety of factions. The rich and diverse offerings of the Tokugawa Confucian schools, along with their effects on the development of samurai cultures, deserve a full account in their own right, but, because of the scope of this project, I cannot fully explore those aspects here. In this chapter I will introduce only a few examples of specific Confucian contributions to the samurai discipline and mark the boundaries of their influence.

Despite these contributions, the influence of Confucian thought on Tokugawa samurai culture is often overemphasized to the point of misleading Western readers. More precisely, the myth that the Tokugawa shogunate deliberately employed the neo-Confucianism of the Hayashi school (derived from the formulae of the Chinese scholar Chu Hsi) as the new philosophy of governance has gained some currency. According to this myth, the first shogun, Tokugawa Ieyasu, used Confucian political philosophy as his ideological tool of choice in strengthening his moral control over Japan. Behind this view of Ieyasu's strategy lies the implicit theoretical assumption that any state's regulation of morals must always be strategic and intentional in order to elicit the kind of moral consensus that will support its domination. Fortunately, recent scholarship on Tokugawa intellectual history has challenged this widespread myth, presenting in its place a more balanced and thoroughly documented picture of the relationship between Tokugawa Confucianism and politics. This has been accomplished through a careful reexamination of the actual intellectual discourse of the period, as well as by an investigation of neo-Confucianism's specific relationships with the Tokugawa power structure.[1]

As described in detail in Herman Ooms's investigation of early Tokugawa political ideology, the Tokugawa shogunate in the initial phases of its development lacked an overarching ideological strategy. The early shogunate did not make a deliberate selection of neo-Confucianism as its official ideology, nor did Confucian thought introduce the rationalized reconstitution of the structure of the Tokugawa government. Ooms states, "All evidence indicates that neo-Confucianism was never perceived by the early-Tokugawa shogunate as a tradition deserving specific support. . . ."[2] He continues, "The shoguns were uninterested in pushing an overall ideology, while the Hayashi were drawn to it belatedly as a weapon in their struggle to secure a place for themselves within the *bakufu*."[3] The belief that Ieyasu had decisively chosen neo-Confucianism as the shogunate's official ideology was so prevalent because the Hayashi school deliberately promoted that myth, and writers of the later Tokugawa period, not to mention modern scholars, came to take it for granted as an accurate account of the facts.

When even the Hayashi school, whose family heads held hereditary positions as Confucian scholars under the Tokugawa regime, had to struggle so hard for recognition, it is not difficult to imagine how problematic it was for other Confucian scholars in this period to combat the view that the "way of sages" was no more than a "foreign" philosophy. In order to establish a higher regard for Confucianism as an acceptable philosophy of life, they also had to battle against the predominantly anti-intellectual cultural climate of the seventeenth-century samurai community. For example, Nakae Tōju, a distinguished early Tokugawa Confucian scholar, described the situation around 1641 as one in which people usually criticized samurai who were devoted to learning as "too soft and good-for-nothing when it comes to military service."[4] Fearful of such criticism, Tōju himself studied Confucian books only at night. It was the cumulative moral leadership of various schools of Confucian scholars that sought the regime's acceptance of "the way" of Chinese sages by "neutralization of those alien elements," as well as through their own refocusing (though not repudiation) of the samurai's honor culture.[5] As both representative government authorities and individual samurai gradually discovered the usefulness of these Chinese imports, Confucian ideology and Confucian thought idioms became influential in Tokugawa Japan.

The discoveries of revisionist scholarship on early Tokugawa Confucianism, which are now largely accepted by both Japanese and Western intellectual historians, correlate well with my findings, presented earlier in this book, regarding samurai *kenka,* or quarrels. The rulers' attitudes toward the samurai's personal recourse to violence for conflict resolution were full of ambivalence in the early period. Had the shogunate implemented an intentional strategy of moral regulation, the Tokugawa policy-makers could have instituted more decisive sanctions against honor-related violence and samurai law-breakers. It is fair to say that the shogun and the daimyo did not have a very clear theoretical foundation for moral reconstruction, at least not in the early period. The shogunate and its subordinate daimyo governments eventually arrived at an ethical consensus on newer definitions of samuraihood only through a process of reaction to various forms of samurai behavior that affected issues of *kōgi no goikō* (literally translated, "the shining authority of the public power").

Confucianism did not initiate the domestication of the samurai class, nor was it the shogunate's preferred ideology from the inception of the regime. In general, Confucian thought gained a perceptible measure of influence and corresponding institutional support only in the late seventeenth century, around the time of the fifth shogun, Tsunayoshi. Around that point, Confucianism replaced Buddhism as the primary force in Tokugawa intellectual discourse with impressive speed. Even so, the rapidity of this intellectual transition did not keep pace with the speed of contemporary political change. In the analysis that follows I will attempt not to repudiate the extent of Confucian influence on the taming of the samurai, but to assess and present a more accurate account of the pattern of cultural development. To understand this development, we must first examine the nature of the cultural-institutional field in which the moral leaders of Japanese Confucian scholarship lived and struggled for recognition.

The Institutional Weakness of Tokugawa Confucianism

The course of Confucianism's influence on Japanese culture cannot be adequately evaluated without reference to Japan's neighbors. From one point of view, the civilizations of China, Japan, and Korea can be grouped together as Confucian East Asia. Given this generalization, some observers have arrived at the hasty conclusion that Japanese standards of moral discipline are a derivative of Confucian tradition, and that the samurai's historical reputation for self-control is likewise a by-product of Confucianism. Upon closer inspection, however, we find that Japan's experience in borrowing Confucian thought and integrating it into its culture was quite different from that of China or Korea.

In China, Confucianism was much more than a philosophy or a religious tradition; it comprehended a number of deeply entrenched social institutions. For example, the elaborate ceremonies of state, kinship practices, and family rituals all played important parts in Chinese Confucian civilization. More significantly, the state civil service examinations, which were based upon Confucian curricula, played a key role as guardians of both the form and the content of Confucian civilization. This institutional aspect of Chinese Confucianism also found a warm reception in Korea. Under the Yi dynasty (1392–1910), the Korean state established a state-administered civil service examination on the Chinese model. In addition, the rulers of the Yi dynasty reconstituted the structure of government and education in order to bring them closer to what they considered Confucian ideals. The Korean family rituals began to resemble more closely Confucian style. The Korean pattern of government differed from the Chinese with regard to the existence of a hereditary ruling class; whereas China, in theory at least, lacked an aristocracy based on birth, Korea under the Yi was ruled by a privileged class of *yan bang*. Nonetheless, in spite of this difference in class structure, the Korean government incorporated a number of institutional changes in order to approximate the ideals of neo-Confucian China.[6]

In contrast with their Chinese and Korean counterparts, however, the rulers of Tokugawa Japan made no use of a Confucian civil service examination system as a formal gate for elite recruitment. Even at the height of Confucianism's influence during the Tokugawa period, the *bakuhan* state did not consider the potential utility of either a formal civil service examination system or a ritual appropriation and embodiment of Confucian thought. Instead, the rulers of Japan simply attempted to utilize the moral idioms of Confucianism in a less formal manner. Moreover, the indigenous customs of the Japanese population never came under significant Confucian influence; there were no widespread changes in family rituals or kinship practices. Thus, although Japan adopted one dimension of the moral teachings of Confucianism, the fact that its institutional aspect was never imported generated recurrent problems for Confucian scholars in Japan. It was as if, by selectively borrowing only those aspects of Confucian thought that served their immediate political ends, the Tokugawa rulers willed that Japan remain a society of (at least in theory still) warriors.

Confucian thought in Japan was a relatively minor intellectual force prior to the Tokugawa period. Although it was seriously discussed in the intellectual circles of the famous Gozan, a group of five Zen Buddhist temples, Japanese Confucianism lacked independent temples or institutional centers of its own, unlike its Buddhist and Shinto rivals. To be sure, some moral idioms of Confucianism had been well known to the Japanese since the ancient period, but its social-institutional influence was neither deep nor systematic. Understandably, Confucianism had little popular influence among members of the samurai class before the Tokugawa period. Its weaker institutional basis was symbolized by the fact that the first Confucian scholars employed by the Tokugawa shogunate or daimyo houses were typically required to assume the tonsure characteristic of Buddhist monks, or to cut their hair in the style of medical doctors, which differed markedly from that of the samurai. In this way, hair style served as a visual indication that Confucian scholars had no guaranteed position within the Tokugawa political hierarchy. Their appearance told onlookers that they were not formal members of the "honor society"—that is, not "real" samurai.

The implications of the regime's attitude toward these men of learning were described by a Tokugawa Confucian scholar, Satō Naokata, as follows: "I deplore this situation, in which Confucian learning is considered no more than a kind of art [on a par with others]: Confucian scholars, medical doctors, Buddhist priests, military theorists, *waka* and *haiku* [forms of short verses] poets, fortunetellers, and *go* masters are all placed on the same level as equivalent types [of experts]."[7] Naokata's lament reflects the striking difference between the Japanese attitude toward Confucian scholarship and its corresponding position in China, a society in which Confucian learning was established as the royal road to elite positions in government.

The most serious obstacle confronting Japanese Confucian scholars was the fact that they were dealing with an elite class defined by their collective identity as fighters rather than as a group of scholars comparable to the Chinese Mandarins. The main ethical tenet of Confucianism was primarily addressed to China's ruling class of scholars, who were taught pride and self-control in order to govern the people. In particular, one form of Chinese Confucianism that had a heavy impact on Tokugawa intellectuals was the neo-Confucianism that originated under the Sung dynasty when the state civil service examinations had been established firmly under the emperor's absolute authority.[8] This Sung version of Confucian thought conflicted with the Tokugawa state's hierarchy of values, since Chinese Confucianism did not accord high value to military matters.

Needless to say, the warrior samurai of Japan, with their hereditary status, and the scholarly Mandarin elites of China, systematically selected by a competitive state-administered civil service examination, lived in very different cultures. In order to survive the stiff competition of the government examination, members of the Chinese elite had to learn classical Confucian texts in a rigorous fashion beginning in childhood. In their society, Confucian scholarship was almost the sole gate to power. Ideally, these leaders of the Chinese people were moral philosopher-statesmen who governed the unlettered classes by dint of their scholarship and correlative moral authority. In contrast, the elites of Tokugawa Japan were samurai whose collective identity was based on military values rather than on scholarship. Until the very end of the Warring States period, a samurai's proudest accomplishment was to meet enemy troops in battle, kill the bravest warrior on the opposing side, and report back to his own general bearing the defeated foe's head in hand. Even after Japan's pacification, at the beginning of the seventeenth century, many early Tokugawa samurai still dreamed of fighting gloriously in the performance of some outstanding deed of valor, and so leaving behind a great name for generations to come. Confucian scholarship and its gentlemanly morals were at odds with this inherited warrior mentality.

As a result, instead of pushing to change Tokugawa social institutions according to Confucian values, most Japanese Confucian scholars struggled to transform the teaching of Confucianism to fit the Japanese ruling warrior class. These scholars tried a number of different modifications, such as conceding that certain Confucian institutions may be "foreign," or very different from Japanese customs, but that nevertheless the moral teachings of the Chinese sages carried universal value as personal creeds for individuals. For example, Japanese neo-Confucians did not openly oppose such entrenched customs as Buddhist funerals (which did not follow Confucian funerals), homosexual liaisons among the samurai, or the practice of adopting male children from outside one's biological kinship line in order to guarantee the continuity of one's *ie*. These Tokugawa men of letters usually acknowledged that these indigenous customs were not consistent with the teaching of the sages, but they extended a certain tolerance to these "minor vices," as Kumazawa Banzan (1619–1691) termed them, in order to expand the influence of Confucianism.[9]

Members of Korean diplomatic missions to the Tokugawa shogunate, who were well-educated Confucian intellectuals, left observations for later historians revealing that the Japanese did not follow an acceptable Confucian lifestyle in their customs and rituals.[10] Shin Yu-han, a highly respected scholar who worked for a Korean mission in 1719, remarked that Japan did not have the cultural and ritual basis of Confucian society.

He also recorded an interesting conversation with a Japanese Confucian scholar regarding male-male love—which was considered unnatural from the viewpoint of neo-Confucian orthodoxy. Observing the popularity of homosexual practices and liaisons, Yu-han criticized Japanese custom as contrary to the Confucian belief in the complementary forces of yin and yang (positive and negative). He said to the Japanese scholar, "If only the positive [male principle] is involved, how can one have pleasure?" The Japanese Confucian scholar replied with a smile, "It's only because you, learned man, have never experienced its pleasure." Yu Han deplored this reply even from such a respectable scholar; in his opinion, it indicated the pervasiveness of this vice in Japan.[11] Japanese Confucians, in contrast, generally regarded the prevalent custom as a minor problem that was not worthy of sustained attention. Preferring to concentrate their energies on spreading the wisdom of the sages, they did not campaign against these particular practices.[12] Inflexible ethical attitudes did not sit well with this society. In discussing ethics and norms, Tokugawa Confucian scholars never rejected indigenous practices *in toto*, even though some of these activities might deviate from strict Confucian principles. They consciously or unconsciously modified the content of Confucianism in order to make it more palatable to the Japanese.

This realism on the part of intellectuals who reformulated Confucian norms to fit the Japanese "reality" was a distinctive characteristic of Tokugawa Confucianism, and it contributed in significant measure to the flexible adaptation of Confucianism to Japan. From this perspective, the development of Tokugawa Confucian thought is best understood as a process of naturalization: that is, of translating foreign modes of thought in terms of Japanese social situations and categories. Confucianism in Japan never became an ultimate religious value transcending the norms of a social group (in this case, the ruling samurai class), but it was received as a philosophy that could be used intelligently to enhance the quality of the existent morality within the group. This relative balance of power between Confucian thought and secular authority in Japan— or, in more general terms, the tendency for Japanese religion to become a means for the achievement of political ends—is one of the most important points to focus on in the course of the samurai's cultural transformation.

The relatively low position of Confucian scholars in the Tokugawa political pyramid was the source of both the weakness and the strength of Tokugawa Confucian thought. To begin with, their inferior social status was connected to the fact that most of these men were recruited from the lower samurai or from groups on the fringes of the samurai class. Examination of a list of well-known Confucian scholars of the Tokugawa period indicates that the majority were drawn from the margins of samurai society—they were either the sons of *rōnin* (masterless samurai), medical doctors (considered marginal to the samurai community), or *rōnin* themselves.[13] As a result, even in the late Tokugawa period, when scholars were employed as teachers in the official samurai schools, there were perennial disciplinary problems that erupted because the sons of noble samurai families found obedient subordination to their lower-class teachers thoroughly distasteful.[14] Thus, Confucian scholars during the Tokugawa period were torn between a sense of their high calling as men of letters and the political reality of living under a regime dominated by hereditary noble samurai families.

The low status of Japanese Confucian scholars did, however, give them a certain measure of intellectual flexibility. Unlike the Mandarin elites of imperial China, the majority of early Tokugawa Confucians looked to their philosophy less as a means of justifying and upholding their present position than as "a means of changing it, or at least resolving some of its ambiguity."[15] To outward appearances, their inferior social position was a drawback, in terms of the influence they could wield within a daimyo's inner power circle; at the same time, this lowly status permitted a flexibility in perspective that differed markedly from the dogmatism that characterized the institutionally fortified version of Confucianism.[16] This paradoxical dimension of the Tokugawa Confucian scholars' social position conferred an advantage on them, in permitting and encouraging the reinterpretation of strict Confucian codes in line with the social and personal needs of the Japanese population.[17] The spread of Confucian moral philosophies to nonsamurai populations and the rise of commoner Confucian scholars were possible only in this context.

In spite of the generally low position of scholars on the social scale, Confucian scholarship could nevertheless serve as a springboard for ambitious men who had no other resources for upward mobility. A man of eminent scholarly reputation could find gainful employment in a daimyo house even though his family background was very humble. For example, a man who was hired as a tutor for a young son of the local daimyo might be able to exercise some influence as a political advisor to the younger lord once he was grown. In addition, even scholars who were not attached to a daimyo house, if they had a sufficient reputation, could open a private academy and support themselves on the tuition they charged their students. After all, this peaceful Tokugawa era with an increasingly commercialized economy constituted the first time in Japanese history that independent scholars could survive financially outside Buddhist monasteries and the official patronage of noble houses.

If we move from the viewpoint of the early shogunate to the perspective of the mid-to-late Tokugawa periods, when the Tokugawa social system assumed its mature form, the dominant moral values of neo-Confucianism—that is, organizational loyalty, hierarchical social ethics, assumption of public responsibility, maintenance of self-discipline, and internalization of virtue—appeared to mesh so well with the state's political apparatus that the interdependence of coercion and consensus looked as if it had been well planned from the beginning. This apparent congruity came to the surface only belatedly, however, as a result of the cumulative efforts of Confucian scholars who attempted to use their intellectual skills as tools for self-promotion and self-fulfillment; and through the authorities' gradual discovery of the utility of neo-Confucian philosophy in the task of governing.

In sum, the limited degree to which Confucianism was imported into Tokugawa Japan had a positive effect on Japanese sociocultural development: it permitted flexible and diverse intellectual activities as well as Japanese adaptation of useful disciplinary idioms of Confucianism. Had Tokugawa Confucianism gained an institutional dominance as the sole "gatekeeper" for elite recruitment, the resulting state regulation in the moral sphere could have been more strict and stifling; it could have had a suffocating effect on nonorthodox intellectual and cultural activities. Although the Hayashi school received support from the shogunate in the form of patronage, other Confucian schools, Buddhist sects, and various intellectual and cultural experiments were generally allowed to grow. This decentralized pattern of religious and intellectual development may have been instrumental to Japan's quick and flexible response to Western science and civilization in the nineteenth century. In this sense, it is rather questionable to label Japan's quick modernization simply as one of the "Confucian success stories" in East Asia.

The Cult of Duties

In the preceding analysis, I described the nature of the institutional fields in which Tokugawa Confucianism came to flourish. It was the social field that was circumscribed by the prior emergence of the distinctive Tokugawa garrison state. From this perspective, the author of *Hagakure* and his Confucian contemporaries shared the set of contradictions and paradoxical tensions created by the institutional field of the Tokugawa state, and they attempted to resolve them, if only in part, by their independent intellectual efforts. This set of tensions included the predicament of the warrior in peacetime, in the case of *Hagakure,* and the necessity of translating Confucian thought for the military mind, in the case of the Tokugawa Confucian scholars. Neither attempt at reformulation of samuraihood, however, rejected the samurai's class privilege, nor did they challenge the sentiment of honor that had been the core of the samurai's collective identity. Thus, Tokugawa Confucian interpretations of samuraihood emerged as interesting interactions between the two traditions, Confucianism and the warrior culture, rather than as the former's complete reconstitution of the latter.

We may consider a specific example of this cultural interaction. One of the Japanese Confucian scholars who clearly demonstrated a tendency to transpose samurai identity into a neo-Confucian key was Yamaga Sokō (1622–1685). Although Sokō was a learned Confucian scholar, he was primarily known to his contemporaries as an outstanding lecturer on military matters *(heigaku);* his lifelong aspiration was to reconstruct existing military scholarship along the lines of what he understood to be the proper Confucian world view.[18] Against this background, redefinition of the meaning of being a samurai became a central theme of Sokō's works.

In his *Yamaga gorui,* a large proportion of the discussion is devoted to "the way of the samurai" *(shi-dō).* Equating the role of the samurai with that of the Mandarin elites of China by comprehending both in the same word, *shi* (gentlemen), Sokō emphasizes the samurai's legitimate social role in governance through moral leadership; that is, the samurai realizes society's ethical ideal through raising the level of popular morality and through competence in political leadership.[19] Yamaga Sokō also exhorted samurai to control their manners with dignity. Every samurai move, every samurai word, should be controlled and disciplined to command the respect of other classes. Sokō did not depict his model samurai only as a sober, scholar-like man of moralistic character and manners, however. For this seventeenth-century scholar, a strong personality, or what he termed "[the] personality of a great strong man" *(daijōbu no kishō),* was the single most important component of his notion of the perfect samurai. This "personality of a great strong man" implied, above all, courageous and self-enhancing conduct in pursuit of the moral ideal.[20] His emphasis on the personality of a great strong man and his high evaluation of individualistic attitudes had a certain element in common with the honorific ethos of *Hagakure.* For Sokō, military valor was an essential part of the way of the sages because it was a necessary tool for molding the moral character of the samurai.

There were also significant differences between Sokō's portrait of the ideal samurai and the corresponding model in *Hagakure.* As a Confucian scholar, Sokō felt little attraction toward the intimate emotional world of master-follower relationships that was of central importance to the writer of *Hagakure.* To give a specific example, Sokō rejected the moral legitimacy of *junshi* (ritual suicide after the death of one's master), considering it to be the questionable result of homosexual liaisons between masters and vassals. The vassal's devotion in the conduct of military duty should be motivated by public values and corporate moral ideals, not by private emotional attachments. Sokō also believed that the warlike competitive passions of an earlier generation should be converted to the task of building up the individual's internal strength of character. In the emotional world of *Hagakure,* the purest form of honorific sentiment was exhibited in the immediacy of action, when one canceled the considerations of the rational mind. In contrast, Yamaga's "great strong man" was a purposeful individual intentionally striving toward the attainment of moral ideals in accord with reason. This ideal warrior would always conduct himself with an internal sense of honor *(shūchi)* and deliberately aim at what he considered proper goals.

The basic premise of Sokō's argument is derived from the theory of the division of social responsibilities, or *shokubun* (*shoku* can be literally translated as "occupation" or "role," *bun* means "division"), which assumed that each social group should be answerable for a particular sector of labor and responsibility in society. According to this theory, the samurai should exhibit a higher standard of morality than members of other classes because their *shokubun* was to govern the common people.

In the context of Sokō's understanding of the larger society, the samurai in particular should be equipped with learning and military skill as well as moral virtue. In Sokō's opinion, a worthy samurai would seek to be a virtuous person.[21] This definition of the samurai as an exemplar of noble moral character was basically shared by Confucian scholars of various schools. From this understanding there emerged a common thread, woven from the themes in Confucian moral teaching that exhorted the samurai to be compassionate in governing the people, and likewise self-controlled.

Yamaga Sokō also insisted that the object of loyalty should be the state *(kokka),* that is, an impersonal organization rather than a human master. His well-known saying, perhaps the most famous line in *Yamaga gorui,* runs as follows: "The human sovereign rules for the benefit of the people; therefore, the sovereign should not privatize the country."[22] In line with this belief, the daimyo's house represented the state *(kokka),* an organizational mechanism that ought to work for the benefit of the people who lived within it and depended upon it. Consequently, samurai who were hereditary vassals of the daimyo's house should regard themselves as servants of the country rather than retainers of the lord's person.

At first glance, Yamaga Sokō's definition of sovereignty may remind one of Western democratic idealism. Indeed, Sokō's idealism, which emphasized the samurai's public responsibility to serve the people, appears to be an approximation of such modern views. But upon closer inspection within its historical context, we find that Sokō's understanding of the nature of government never challenged the foundation of the Tokugawa state, namely, the samurai's privileged hereditary domination over other classes. If anything, it is precisely because of this elitist assumption that Yamaga demanded a higher level of moral character in the samurai.

One of the important areas in which Tokugawa Confucianism contributed to the samurai culture as a whole was its reflections on the nature of the state and social hierarchy. The political doctrine of the Hayashi school emphasized the hierarchical order of society—implicitly equated with the order of the Tokugawa regime itself—as a fundamental cosmic principle. Hayashi Razan (1583–1657), the founder of the Hayashi school of neo-Confucianism, wrote as follows: "The sky is high above, and the earth is low beneath it. In the same manner, there is a distinction between the upper and lower classes of society. In human relationships, a master is more honorable, and a vassal is less so."[23] In this system of thought, the hierarchical order of human society is equated with the order of nature itself. Phrased slightly differently, human hierarchy reflects a universal cosmic order.

Hayashi Razan and his followers also stressed proper behavior, its propriety being determined by one's position in the world. This understanding of one's position should be based upon the *li* (principle), the neo-Confucian definition of the cosmos, the perpetual natural law of the universe. Razan's writing does not carry the tone of intense conviction that characterizes an original thinker, and his moral philosophy was often criticized by others as being more or less the result of self-promotional activities within the shogun's circle of advisors. His group's efforts to connect personal virtue to a larger world view did, however, contribute to Japan's indigenous samurai culture, which before that point had not possessed a systematic and inclusive moral philosophy. The native samurai culture had always expressed itself in the form of sentiments or reactive behavior rather than in an articulated system of normative or reflective philosophy. Although many virtues—such as loyalty—that Tokugawa Confucianism promoted already existed in the idioms of the samurai culture in a somewhat unrefined manner, they still lacked any connection to a larger systematic world view. For example, construction of personal moral norms through discussion and debate over fundamental questions of basic human nature and the structure of the universe was an intellectual innovation of the first order for the samurai community. When the customs and normative practices of Tokugawa society conflicted with the Confucian world view, Razan did not attempt to change the "reality" through Confucian redefinition, nor did he make this conflict into a theoretical point of departure for the development of a dialectical philosophy.

There was an alternative to Razan's compromise. In contrast to the school of Hayashi, which tended to equate the hierarchical social order with the mythical law of the universe, Ogyū Sorai (1666–1728), an influential Confucian scholar of the mid-Tokugawa period, championed a more rational approach to the social order.[24] For example, Sorai criticized the Hayashi school's version of loyalty as the self-immolating devotion of a featureless nonentity: "It is a popular opinion these days to regard the individual as a nonperson, insofar as his life has been subordinated to his master. But this view is not the way of sages."[25] For Sorai, the ethic of loyalty should be based upon a more fundamental human virtue, a sincere and deeply held conviction that "regards the other as if the other is in no way different from oneself."[26]

This compassionate "mirroring" of other persons was for Sorai the foundation of the ideal political position. Loyalty to one's master should be regarded as only one aspect of a general ethical stance, as a master's task is to lead and to govern the people, and the vassal's corresponding obligation is to assist the master in the business of government. From this perspective, a samurai's devotion to public duty should issue from an ethical attitude that is the moral choice of a politically active individual. It is not self-effacing anonymity but rather a forceful individuality that should function as the engine of the samurai's political service. By extension of this line of reasoning, Sorai predictably concluded that relationships between master and vassals, and between samurai colleagues in the hierarchical rankings of the government, should be considered functional divisions of labor within a bureaucracy rather than a reflection of an inherent stratification of human nature.

Throughout samurai history, the virtue of loyalty had always been emphasized by the master class in order to increase the trustworthiness of vassals. Under an integrated polity such as the Tokugawa state, however, the virtue of blind loyalty, expressed only at the level of personal attachment between vassals and their immediate masters, could be dangerous for the emerging social order. Recall the ethos expressed by the radical members of the Forty-seven Samurai and the debates regarding their personal conception of loyalty. The Confucian interpretation of loyalty, a more rational and internal definition combined with a cosmic basis of obedience to the superior ideologically (in the case of the Hayashi school) or with a rational bureaucratic view of government (in the case of Sorai school), reinforced the subordination of the samurai to the order of the Tokugawa state. The fact that even Ogyū Sorai, whose philosophy contained a rational element that has often been considered a precursor of modern political theory by Japanese scholars, did not question the dominance of the samurai class indicates a distinctive characteristic of the Tokugawa consumption of Confucianism at this historical point, the mid-Tokugawa period.[27] In fact, the flexible use of religious or moral teachings for the sake of political ends can be observed throughout Japanese history.

Another important contribution of Tokugawa Confucianism to the domestication of the samurai was its reinforcement of the performance-oriented mindset of the samurai. Confucian thought helped to refocus the samurai's military professionalism in the direction of a meritocratic form of government appropriate to peacetime. The Confucian understanding of the polity previously articulated, as well as the philosophy of division of labor in society that attributed the responsibility of rulership to the samurai, predictably resulted in the assignment of higher value to those human abilities that were useful for government. A correlate of this development was a redefinition of meritocratic standards in terms of scholarship and ability to govern. The native samurai culture, to be sure, had already inculcated a strong drive toward achievement and excellence as measured by the standards of the battlefield. This military version of a performance-oriented ethos gained in legitimacy through its encounter with Tokugawa Confucianism in the new areas of scholarship and political ability.

Symbolic of this renewed competitive ethos was the emerging usage of the term *benkyō* (learning, literally, "to make an endeavor") in late Tokugawa writings. The term *benkyō* originally appeared in a classic text of Confucianism that signifies the great effort involved in learning. In modern Japanese, *benkyō* is most commonly used in reference to studying and learning. However, the two root characters (*ben* and *kyō*) imply that learning is the process of labor (and even suffering) and possible only with concentrated effort and self-discipline. In other words, *benkyō* symbolizes an attitude of learning that was characterized by a hard-working and competitive mentality. The rise of the term *benkyō* in Tokugawa society reflects the fact that "learning" started to be considered a means of social competition, a new battle for honor that could be won only by continuous and concentrated efforts of *benkyō*.[28]

In spite of the newer awareness of the importance of meritocratic attitudes and competition, however, the Tokugawa bureaucracy (at the levels of both daimyo and shogunate government) failed to develop a systematic recruitment and promotional system based solely upon abilities. The status-based principle continued to dominate the social organization of the samurai class, and family bloodlines remained the primary factor in decisions concerning the promotion of individual samurai. As a result, meritocracy tended to remain on the level of an ideal within the day-to-day reality of the status-oriented Tokugawa samurai hierarchy.[29]

Confucianism finally achieved a position of ideological and institutional dominance in Japanese culture during the middle to late Tokugawa period, through the emerging efforts of Confucian scholars who were interested in an aggressive reconstruction of a viable system of ethics and its popularization, with some newly powerful noble patrons. The history of samurai schools in early modern Japan reflects a synthesis of moral entrepreneurial activities and patronage.

Since the publication of Ronald Dore's pioneering work on Tokugawa education, Western readers have acquired a much better understanding of the educational interests of Tokugawa samurai and the presence of various school systems in Japanese society.[30] We have come to recognize that Confucianism and the classical Chinese texts constituted the core curricula in these systems, particularly in the samurai schools. Students who attended these schools learned to read from Confucian materials. Contrary to the widespread notion that the Tokugawa authorities promoted samurai education, however, this development came very late. By the end of the Tokugawa period, there were 215 daimyo domains—out of approximately 260—that had established official samurai schools. This impressive figure is offset by the fact that only 4 of these schools had been established before 1667, and only 10 by 1715.[31] It was only in the late eighteenth century that the remainder of the 215 daimyo domains instituted samurai schools. Until this time, many daimyo domains did not have samurai schools, and samurai children relied primarily on private tutorials for their education.

The basic pedagogical method of Confucian samurai schools for elementary students was largely traditional; teachers had their pupils read the text aloud and later memorize well-known interpretations of the text. Although this technique of instruction was not designed to encourage students to inquire into the deeper meaning of the literature, it served to inculcate high standards of personal discipline. Furthermore, although attendance at samurai schools was not compulsory in all daimyo domains, it was nonetheless strongly encouraged, particularly for oldest sons.

This institutionalization of the samurai's educational systems was at least in part a reaction of the Tokugawa authorities to the deepening social contradictions of the late Tokugawa period. Discontent was most typically represented by the significant increase of peasant rebellions that fundamentally threatened the Tokugawa system of domination, which was dependent on the rice tax. The number and scale of peasant rebellions significantly increased in the late eighteenth and nineteenth century.

In facing this domestic crisis, the Tokugawa authorities gave more attention to improving the morale and governing abilities of the samurai officers.[32]

The Samurai Spirit and the Confucian Mind

The foregoing analysis of the contributions and limitations of Confucianism brings us to a pertinent question: What factors were responsible for generating change within the Tokugawa samurai culture? If samurai culture had been affected by a neo-Confucian ideology that reinforced the devotion of the warrior class to the existing hierarchical order, there would appear to be little room for the development of nonconformist views or political activism. When we accept the conventional modern understanding of Tokugawa culture, a view that overemphasizes neo-Confucian influence on the samurai population in particular, we have no explanation for the demonstrable upsurge in political zealotry and interest in militant ideologies among the samurai at the end of the Tokugawa period.

A partial explanation for this phenomenon of political unrest lies in the nature of Japanese neo-Confucianism itself. The Confucian scholars of the Tokugawa period were by no means a collection of theoretically oriented intellectuals who valued only dispassionate moralism and self-control in thinking and in the social order. When we examine their writings at closer range, we often find that they incorporate a stimulus to passionate action and a fervent sense of individuality under a veil of philosophical moralism. A number of eminent Tokugawa intellectuals combined the logical skills that were part of their Confucian heritage with a remarkably strong sense of personal autonomy, expressed in the idioms of the indigenous samurai culture. The traditional samurai spirit can be described *not* as a coherent system of thought but rather as a sentiment, ethos, or mentality. Consequently, a samurai's subscription to a Confucian world view or moral philosophy did not require him to replace or reject his warrior enculturation, which remained at the deepest level of his personality as the source of his passion and commitment to his autonomy and dignity. As a result, we often discover in the works of these samurai intellectuals a fusion of the warrior spirit and the trained rational capacities of the Confucian scholar.

Arai Hakuseki (1657–1725) was perhaps the most successful Tokugawa Confucian scholar in terms of his degree of influence in the political affairs of the shogunate.[33] A man of encyclopedic knowledge with a firm political philosophy of his own, Hakuseki was an influential advisor to the sixth Tokugawa shogun, Ienobu, and his successor, Ietugu, and played an important role in shogunate politics between 1709 and 1716. In reading Hakuseki's autobiography, *Told Round a Brushwood Fire (Oritaku shiba no ki),* however, one is impressed by the intensity of martial fervor in a man of practiced rationality and cultivated Confucian scholarship.

For example, in recounting an incident that took place in December 1674, when he was eighteen years old, Hakuseki proudly describes his decision to participate in samurai *kenka* (quarrels). Toward the end of that month, a quarrel arose among the samurai, splitting them into two factions. The adherents of one party were all long-standing friends of Hakuseki's father. They assembled at the house of a man named Seki, a good friend of Hakuseki's family, and there they decided to set out to fight their opponents. At this point, Hakuseki was placed under house arrest by order of his lord for having committed some kind of mistake in service. Hakuseki still had to respond properly to his family's involvement in the quarrel in order to avoid shame. He wrote: "I sent a sharp-witted fellow to Seki's house, telling him to bring me back word with all speed when he saw them set out and start fighting. . . . I put on chain armor next to my skin, and dressed in fresh clothes. . . ."

Fortunately, the two factions reached a compromise with the help of intermediaries before Hakuseki had actually left the house to participate in the fight. The next day, one of Seki's sons came to him. Hakuseki recounted the man's reproach and his own response: "'Yesterday I was told that you too had intended to come and help us.' When I [Hakuseki] replied, 'That was my intention,' he then said: 'How did you, when you were then in disgrace and confined to your house, intend to get through the gate of our lord's mansion?'" [Hakuseki's residence was inside the wall of his lord's mansion.]

Hakuseki explained to his visitor that one of the mansion's gates was guarded only by an elderly couple. He had intended to tell them that he was going out to die, and that they need not tell anyone that he had left through the gate they guarded. But he had also made up his mind that, if necessary, he would kill the old people, steal their key, and open the gate himself. Then Seki's son posed a critical question: If Hakuseki had

escaped while he was confined by his lord's order, and even worse, if he
had killed the elderly gatekeepers, would it not have been piling crime
upon crime? His behavior would have violated his lord's command in
two respects. Hakuseki responded as follows:

> Suppose I had not been in disgrace at the time, and, although aware of
> your plans, I had not gone to help. The Kōho [lord] might have said
> nothing, but in his heart he would have thought my conduct was not
> bound hand and foot. Therefore, if I had stayed alone, confined to my
> house, once I had heard from some other source that you were going to
> start a fight, people would have thought I had taken advantage of my
> dilemma to save my life. I might have behaved in a lawless fashion but
> why should I fear my lord's displeasure? Were I of mature years, there
> might have been a more seemly way for me to act. However, I am not
> yet twenty and so my only concern was to avoid dishonor.[34]

Hakuseki concluded his remark to Seki's son with strong words: "I do
not expect thanks," implying that his decision to join the fight was a
matter of his own pride. It may surprise a contemporary reader that a
scholar trained in Confucian thought placed higher value on military
honor and the regard of his peers than on loyalty to his superior. As we
have seen in the analysis of samurai quarrels, the native culture of the
samurai accorded a high place to fellowship within the group; for a
samurai to desert his friends and colleagues when they were attacked by
others was as shameful as disloyalty to one's lord. A man who failed
to help his comrades in a crisis forfeited the right to be considered an
independent honorable samurai. Indeed, Hakuseki did not consider this
emphasis on samurai comradeship a contradiction of the virtue of loyalty. Loyalty, in his opinion, was not constituted by mechanical obedience; it was mediated and expressed by autonomous and competitive
spirits who did not permit themselves displays of weakness. Only when
the vassal possessed such strength of personality could he serve his lord
as he ought to.

The similarity of the ethos expressed in this episode from Hakuseki's
autobiography to the many stories retold in *Hagakure* is also striking.
Indeed, many other samurai stories from Hakuseki's life might easily
have appeared in the pages of *Hagakure*. For example, the martial spirit
that characterized the mind of Hakuseki surfaces elsewhere in his auto-

biography, in a passage in which he discusses swords as the primary symbol of samurai honor. The theme is particularly evident in a story that Hakuseki's father told him. On one occasion when Hakuseki's father was traveling, he encountered an old friend, a warrior who was living in poverty as a *rōnin* (masterless samurai) at the base of a mountain. The father stayed the night at his friend's humble hut, talking over their past and present circumstances while keeping the fire going. Around midnight, the *rōnin* pulled out a set of bamboo tubes, opened the ends, and drew out his samurai swords. Both blades glittered like ice decorated with steel ornaments. The old soldier said to Hakuseki's father, "I do not regret any part of the equipment I possessed in the past, but, while my strength lasts, I intend to keep my set of swords with me."[35] The high polish of the swords reflected the man's internal pride as a samurai. In an anecdote of this kind, the samurai's sense of class honor became the individual's sense of dignity itself. Hakuseki understood the samurai's spirit as a sense of dignity and strong individuality expressed through military honor, and he was proud to share such an ethos in his autobiography.

Hakuseki composed this autobiography in his retirement, after he had been thrown out of the inner circle of shogunal politics. He observed that the projects he had started in the shogunate government were abandoned or reversed one by one under the new leadership. The symbol of the swords in his father's story perhaps represented his own lasting defiance in a situation of personal adversity. Although a warrior's intensely passionate energy might be directed to the search for a moral creed in many a samurai intellectual's thought, it was often the samurai's sense of pride that fundamentally sustained the Confucian moral inquiry.

From time to time, a number of Confucian teachers attempted to rechannel the passions aroused by the samurai's cultivation of a fighting spirit in a more rational and moralistic direction. These attempts were only partially successful, however, because Tokugawa Confucianism could not dismiss the reality of the Tokugawa social order, predicated as it was upon a belief in warrior dominance. Confucian teachers did not and could not fundamentally challenge the emotional dimension of the samurai's honor culture as long as they accepted the political reality of the samurai class domination. Consequently, it was difficult for Confucian intellectuals to completely transform the samurai into a class of moralistic bureaucrats by dint of Confucian teachings alone. The entire

Tokugawa institutional complex, from the structure of the vassalage system to the retention of ritual *seppuku,* continued to send mixed messages to the samurai. On the one hand, the system conveyed the message that one should exhibit the honorific pride of a brave warrior; on the other hand, one was advised to train oneself in the virtues of obedience and compliance to the demands of a bureaucratic order. This set of conflicting messages provides the basic explanation for the failure of the process of the samurai's domestication to replace fully the older ways of thought with a fresh mentality. The voice of the samurai's traditional ethos was muted but never totally silenced.

It is important to recall that the samurai culture of honor began as an emotional force that sustained itself in a society of competitive warriors. Essentially, it persisted even into the Tokugawa period as an ethos rather than as a fully fledged philosophy. By itself it could not develop into an elaborate system of reflective thought. For this reason, the samurai spirit could function to fuel passionate activism across a wide spectrum of political positions and philosophies to serve their own purposes. That is why, given the deepening social crisis combined with the threat of Western imperialism in the nineteenth century, similar sentiments arising from the samurai's competitive warrior culture could be expressed in the terms of a number of different schools of thought, including Confucian ideologies such as the tradition of Wang Yang-ming, a school of Confucianism with a more intuitive tendency that was a stimulus to social action.

To trace the variety of emerging political ideologies in the later Tokugawa period (such as a part of the Native Learning school, Wang Yang-ming school, and Mito school) would be a fascinating subject in the field of intellectual history; however, that lies beyond the purview of this book.[36] In the section that follows, I will offer only one example of the kind of fusion between the samurai ethos and a political ideology in the later Tokugawa period that occurred within the new political situation connected with the fall of the Tokugawa shogunate and the subsequent Meiji restoration.

The Samurai Ethos and National Crisis

There is a consensus among historians that the great social transition involved in the Meiji restoration and modernization largely resulted from initiatives undertaken by members of the samurai class itself. Unlike many other instances of drastic social change in world history, in which a new class of people replaced an older established class, the unrest that eventually led to the Meiji restoration started within a faction of the samurai class, and ultimately caused the samurai to lose their privileged position in Japanese society. There are many excellent studies of the political and economic conditions that finally brought about the collapse of the long-lasting Tokugawa shogunate, a subject I cannot pursue in this book. What we should note in relation to the samurai honor culture is that, during this final stage of the Tokugawa period, a variety of radical calls for social change were published, ideologically diverse but all in various ways deeply imbued with more traditional honorific sentiments, which had mushroomed within the samurai community.

The samurai's honor culture, together with their collective and personal identity, was continuously created and reformulated in response to a changing social environment across the centuries of their lengthy history. At the end of the Tokugawa period, there was a widespread sense of national crisis, triggered by Japan's first encounter with Western imperialism, which stimulated the samurai warrior ethos, long dormant but never completely extinguished. The arrival of large fleets of Western ships, the news of the opium war, and the defeat of China—the empire of Confucianism—created a sense of urgency among the Japanese people and resurrected the samurai's original collective identity as warriors.

Western insistence that the shogunate open the country to outsiders threatened the honor sentiments of many Tokugawa samurai. The authorities were obliged to yield, however reluctantly, to Western demands, and samurai at all levels of the hierarchy attacked the shogunate's conduct as a disgraceful compromise of Japanese independence. The myth of the shogun's authority as the "Great General, Conqueror of Barbarians" (*seii tai shogun,* the shogun's official title) clearly became a moot subject at this point. Although many samurai joined fanatical antiforeign movements, the more reflective men among them soon recognized the folly of pursuing Japan's traditional isolationist policy in the face of the supremacy of Western military technology. Even though these samurai accepted the political reality of international relations, the fact that Japan had had the Western demands forced upon it was considered a shameful blot on national pride.

It is important to emphasize here that during this period of upheaval,

many samurai felt the Western threat to their country's security as a blow
to their personal pride and independence. Their renewed sense of honor
pushed them in the direction of political activism at this point—toward
many ideological experiments and radical social movements that eventually brought about the collapse of the Tokugawa government. It is perhaps no coincidence that a revival of "real" *seppuku*—not *fan seppuku*—appeared at the end of the Tokugawa period, especially among
radical political activists.

In the philosophy of Yoshida Shōin (1830–1859), one of the most radical theorists of the mid-nineteenth century, we can discern the presence
of an internalized notion of samurai honor, which was used to legitimate
pressures for change. Shōin was born in a lesser samurai house in
Chōshū han, historically a center of the antishogunate movement,
and was executed at the early age of twenty-nine.[37] The shogunate imposed the supreme penalty on Shōin because of his radical political views
and action. Although Shōin's life was brief, he proved to be the most
inspiring teacher of his period. Many of the students who gathered in
his humble private school later became famous political activists who
were instrumental in the Meiji restoration. Shōin's writings reflect the
young teacher's idealistic inner voice, a striking warrior-like sense of
honor combined with a pressing awareness of Japan's national crisis.
Shōin was not a primitive radical samurai who emphasized military action for its own sake, however; he was an educated nineteenth-century
intellectual who harvested the rich fruits of Tokugawa philosophical development.

Shōin often said that "shame *(haji)* is the most important word in
a samurai's lexicon. Nothing is more shameful than not understanding
shame."[38] His honor sentiment, however, was never concerned with a
person's superficial reputation in his *seken,* that is, his existing social
order. Shōin's distinctive philosophy of shame is clearly articulated in the
following excerpt:

> On one occasion someone asked me: Which is more serious, crime
> *(tsumi)* or shame *(haji)?* I answered: Crime belongs to the body, but
> shame lies in the soul. Crime is a less serious matter because it has to
> do with the physical dimension of being human, whereas shame is more
> serious because it affects the soul. Now, people at the grass-roots level
> discuss national politics and criticize office-holders. This kind of behav-

ior is a crime because it is not the job *(shoku)* of ordinary people, and it is not their prescribed role *(bun)* in society. However, if you ask about their internal motivation and find that they are worried about the future of the nation, and have tried to ask questions about its legitimacy—their behavior is less culpable.[39]

Shōin's conception of samuraihood reveals a deeply internalized sense of honor. He reformulated honor as the mainspring of human dignity, as pride in one's individuality expressed through political action for the sake of a better social order. Unlike Ruth Benedict, whose famous conceptual distinction stressed the differences between guilt cultures (internally oriented) and shame cultures (externally driven), Shōin defined shame as profoundly internal. From this beginning, he worked out a logic for political activism based upon the idiom of honor. In Shōin's thought, political commitment that forces someone to overstep the boundary of his proper *bun* (role) is not the real problem; failure to act according to one's principles is more shameful, and thus a more serious offense. This development was a remarkable achievement of Tokugawa samurai culture, which cultivated the native tradition of the samurai for purposes of social change. Shōin explained:

Shame *(haji)* lies in one's soul; if you cannot practice the way *(michi, the moral way)* and are only occupying an honored status and wasting a hereditary income, how can you show your face *(menboku)*? If the number of such shameful people increases, and the moral principles of society are lost, then in effect they are larcenous. In general, although a *crime* may be known to outsiders, it is a matter that affects only the individual. But if a samurai harbors shame [of such kinds] in his mind, this will eventually harm both lord and people.[40]

These words clearly indicate that a firmly internalized sense of honor could stimulate political activism. A samurai might be of humble status with an assigned job in society that had nothing to do with politics at the national level. But Shōin encouraged such "grass-root" samurai to speak their minds. Insofar as their actions went against their assigned social responsibilities, it might be considered a crime according to the present social order. But such action would never be morally wrong so long as its motivation was sincere concern for the future of the country. If the samurai would not express their political opinions for fear of breaking the law of the state, they would thereby harbor shame in their souls. How could a man who was contaminated by inner shame face his peers as an independent man in society? By a clever reformulation of the idioms of honor, Shōin was able to break through the traditional equation of status hierarchy with a particular social order. If a man's internal sense of shame and willingness to act according to principle were the most important gauge of honor, then what significance could other status differences within the samurai community possibly have?

As the product of a strict samurai family, Shōin believed in the virtue of loyalty to one's master. By the nineteenth century, neo-Confucian moralization of samuraihood in terms of public responsibility was also a widely accepted notion within public discourse. The question of loyalty remained a difficult one for any samurai thinker who was committed to political activism. The potential for conflict was obvious: When a samurai's political opinion, derived from his acceptance of his public responsibility, differed from the will of his master, how should he act? Shōin's solution to this intellectual problem involved a redefinition of the virtue of loyalty. It is a form of genuine loyalty, Shōin believed, to remonstrate repeatedly against one's master on the basis of one's convictions. Thus, the apparent moral dilemma need not incapacitate a thoughtful samurai. Shōin wrote, "When you serve your master, you might die as the result of your remonstrance. You can also die in prison, or perish from hunger."[41] Loyalty as such was not rejected by Shōin, but he believed that it should not restrict a man's political activism.

Because Shōin's political philosophy could not do without the virtue of loyalty, he had to occupy a new locus in the center of his argument. It was not only in Shōin's case, but in the political thought of many other samurai intellectuals of this period as well, that the emperor entered ideological discussions as the focus of a new loyalty. Although a discussion of the complex intellectual developments concerning Japanese nationhood and the imperial system during this period is beyond the scope of this book, we should observe that the symbol of the emperor provided a new locus of national honor for the samurai class. In this context, Shōin's work was not unusual. By regarding the emperor as the supreme head of the honorable nation of Japan, the samurai could redirect their loyalty.

Shōin was in one sense a dreamer, always thinking of the possibility of making a name for himself in history. "Among his many anxieties,"

H. D. Harootunian once noted, "Yoshida Shōin feared most that his death might go unnoticed."[42] Indeed, when he confronted the possibility of death at the hands of the Tokugawa authorities, Shōin never attempted to escape his tragic fate, though he could have, had he responded differently to the interrogation by the shogunate officers. A Japanese historian wrote that Shōin "did not live in the present. Not calculating the short-term interest, he hoped to live for the long-term, eternal goal of leaving his name in history."[43]

Shōin's heroism reminds us of the warrior of the medieval period who preferred self-willed death in a desperately contested battle in the hope of keeping his honorable name. To be sure, Shōin's writing resonates throughout with an exalted conception of honor. Many samurai, struggling for a sense of meaning at the chaotic end of the Tokugawa regime, participated in Shōin's romanticized vision, insofar as the cultural myths generated by the history of the samurai retained their strong symbolic power. Shōin's students and friends who were inspired equally by his writings and his untimely death eagerly answered calls to political action, and many of them died as a result in the ensuing chaos. Although the actual political developments that led to modern nation-building under the Meiji were led and implemented by realistic samurai political activists who were shrewd enough to survive the dangers of a period of upheaval, there were still a number of samurai who initiated actions for change when the odds against them were quite desperate. The mythological richness of samurai culture, reflecting as it did centuries of social development, once revived in the mind of the young samurai activist Shōin served to inflame the imaginations of many others who sought involvement in the militant political action groups that brought about the Meiji restoration.

VII HONORIFIC INDIVIDUALISM AND HONORIFIC COLLECTIVISM

16 *Themes of Control and Change*

The political and social taming of the samurai during the Tokugawa period had a twofold cultural impact. On the one hand, the process of domestication produced a remarkable achievement of cultural refocusing, namely, the establishment of a mental climate conducive to individuals' harmonizing their sense of personal identity with institutionally prescribed roles and responsibilities. This refocusing of the culture of honor supplied an indigenous moral resource that was subsequently fully utilized for promoting organizational solidarity and efficacy during the later phases of national efforts to industrialize.

On the other hand, however, the process allowed the Tokugawa samurai to retain the most volatile component of their honorific sentiments—their aggressive aspiration toward autonomy, which had originated in the medieval period and was directly connected to their sense of dignity and individuality. Having become deeply embedded in their self-definition, this synthesis of honor and dignity provided a common source of passion for individual samurai in different ideological camps, whose social and political patterns of behavior otherwise varied widely. The tension these two cultural themes created in turn served as a source of cultural and intellectual creativity, during the Tokugawa as well as the Meiji and more modern periods.

An examination of the historical evidence indicates that the samurai culture of honor elaborated two important themes: control and change. By "control," I intend two constituent elements. The first component involves control on the personal level, that is, regulation of one's own short-term desires in order to achieve long-term goals. The second element relates to those corporate aspects of control that harmonize individuals' drives and desires with socially and organizationally defined objectives. The first form of control had clearly been embodied already in the medieval tradition of honor culture, insofar as it was focused upon the warrior's strong desire for an illustrious posthumous reputation. This early ethos, oriented toward control and military achievement, was then redirected toward a more organizationally collaborative and publicly responsible form during the Tokugawa period.

The second major theme, change, became manifest in samurai culture when the presence of a clear sense of resilient individuality emerged in expressions of self-assertiveness combined with dignity and pride. A sense of individuality is deeply connected to capacities for courage and deliberation, which are necessary to initiate change. This is the case because persons who think in individualistic terms can resist social pressures to conform to predictable courses of action. As demonstrated in the case of *Hagakure*, a statement such as "Even though I should forfeit my head, I would not do the thing that I should not do" encapsulates the samurai's ardent sense of personal independence and integrity undergirded by convictions of honor and self-esteem. This kind of intense sense of selfhood could, when properly connected to an appropriate social goal, serve to generate an initiative for social change. The coexistence and combination of the twin themes of control and change in samurai culture are an important key to understanding Japanese cultural tradition.

The two themes are also major elements in Max Weber's conception of the spirit of capitalism. In Weber's view, the Calvinist doctrine of predestination—that the number and identity of the elect are predetermined by God without regard to human actions and intentions—generated two important attitudes congenial to the capitalist mentality. The first is that the purposeful concentration on the last judgment typical of Puritanism encouraged the cultivation of self-control and concentration on long-term goals; this attitude was expressed in the daily lifestyle of Puritans as frugality, self-denial, and devotion to one's occupation based on the assumption that success in one's earthly vocation is an index of one's election to salvation. It is important to note that, in contrast to a concept of discipline oriented toward short-term ends, the theme of control in Puritan culture was directed toward long-term objectives; as such, it was congenial to rational planning at all levels of society and long-term accumulation of capital.

The second attitude included in Weber's argument regards individualism. According to Weber, Protestantism—particularly Calvinism—is characterized by religious individualism stemming from the conviction that a believer does not require spiritual intermediaries between himself and God, and therefore such believers possess a mental landscape marked by emphases on self-reliance and self-direction. The Puritan mentality, connected to an internal understanding of personhood defined through direct conversation with God, was instrumental in producing an ethos that encouraged a behavior intentionally determined only by the individual's conscience. As a result, Weber thought, societies dominated by Puritan forms of Protestantism tend to be populated by risk-taking individuals capable of investing and innovating on their own initiative according to their best judgment.

Out of a completely different cultural matrix, the Japanese samurai also constructed a society that was conducive to self-control and concentration on long-term ends, as well as an individualistic attitude that encouraged risk-taking. To be sure, the internal logic of these themes of control and change is different in Japan, and it must therefore be articulated on its own terms. One should also note that the source of dynamism that created the samurai's characteristic mental outlook cannot be defined through an examination of the internal logic of a specific religion or intellectual school; rather, it should be understood as a *"path-dependent"* phenomenon.

State Formation and Samurai Transformation Revisited

After our journey across centuries of samurai history, the reader may find a summary of the samurai's historical transformations to be a helpful transition to the theoretical material in this section. I have argued that the distinctive trajectory of Japanese state formation, which was closely correlated with the lengthy process of the samurai's transformation as a social class—namely, the reorganization of their internal power structure and their changing relationships with other social classes—is the key to a proper understanding of the samurai's cultural transformation. Although this structural change did not automatically produce a set of linked cultural consequences in a linear cause and effect fashion, it nonetheless provided a basic institutional matrix within which the individual agents of change had to make their various contributions to cultural reformulation.

Over the period of several centuries characterized by the continuing process of samurai transformation, we can discern a series of developmental stages in samurai culture that correlated with the economic and political development of the samurai as a class. The evolution of samurai honor forms an intricate tapestry; the historical and sociological dimensions in which the cultural developments took place are briefly summarized in Table 1. I have listed only one or two primary characteristics of the transformation of the samurai class in each entry of this table, in order to give the reader a bird's-eye view of several centuries of complex social change.

The first stage of the samurai's transformation was characterized by the emergence of a striking and distinctive culture, on which the organizational dynamics of the samurai class exerted the most direct influence. The medieval warrior state, whose structure was semicentralized, derived its power from the coordinated activity and mediation of socially autonomous lords. In this phase, the various distinctive customs of the samurai honor culture reflected the process of the samurai's emergence as a discrete category of social status. The political and economic system of medieval samurai vassalage, the sovereign nature of the samurai house, the military ethos, and the samurai's gaining of hegemony over other classes were all closely related to the creation of the medieval honor culture, which placed a high value on aggressive competitiveness. The samurai's resulting cultural identity as a warrior class, and their concomitant valuation of honorable violence, formed a sharp contrast to the aristocratic culture; this clear social differentiation in turn helped the samurai to gain political hegemony. It was at this stage in Japanese social development that a fiercely competitive, militaristic, and self-aggrandizing culture of honor was institutionalized in the samurai community.

After the disintegration of the samurai hierarchies at the end of the Kamakura period, the second transitional period covers a time of continuous wars extending to the emergence of the centrally organized Tokugawa state. By then, the power of the aristocracy clearly declined, but

Table 1   The Reorganization of the Samurai

	Time Periods		
	Kamakura (1190–1333)	Warring States (late 15–16th century)	Tokugawa (1603–1867)
State formation	First samurai semicentral government	Transitional period of regional state-making by warlords	Pacification and consolidation into "neo-feudal state"
Class relationships	Samurai as military specialists gaining hegemony over the aristocracy ⇒	Aristocracy in total decline; increasing resistance by villagers	Collective victory of the samurai class; nonsamurai demilitarized
Vassalage characteristics	Personal relationship; relative autonomy of vassals	Transition to hierarchical vassalage: "high-exits"	Hierarchical bureaucratic vassalage: "low-exits"
Vassalage economic base	*shōen* (estate) system ⇒	*kandaka* system	Hereditary stipend or fief controlled by daimyo
Ie (house) structure and vassalage	Vassal's *ie* has strong political autonomy; *sōryō* system ⇒	Political autonomy of vassal's *ie* decreased; single-heir system	Daimyo's *ie* rules vassal's *ie*; inheritance needs daimyo's permission
Military characteristics	One-on-one combat of mounted samurai in private armies	Technological and organizational military revolutions	Military function of samurai nominal and symbolic
Honor culture	Honor based on pride in violence and autonomy	Military practice of honor culture glorified	Honor remains critical as class identity, but is "refocused"

(Vertical label spanning the middle columns: Disintegration and Reintegration, with ⇒ marks)

the organized resistance from agrarian communities significantly increased. In this process, the older, medieval version of vassalage, that is, a network of loosely organized and socially autonomous landed elites, was transformed into a strict, hierarchically structured system, and this tighter, more organizational form of vassalage became the foundation of the Tokugawa government. The *sengoku daimyo* not only devised a more hierarchical vassalage system but also streamlined their organization in order to construct a more efficient military machine. I have argued that the change in vassalage was partly a result of the military revolution in the sixteenth century. In comparison with the structure of medieval warfare—one-on-one combat between self-equipped warriors—the *sengoku daimyo* sought tighter control over their vassals in order to plan and execute strategic troop movements.

In my analysis, I have also emphasized the two basic ingredients for the dynamic power shifts in Japanese vassalage: the economic basis of vassalage centered on land tenure, and the internal structure of the samurai *ie*. However, because the continuous civil wars among the warlords provided vassal samurai with opportunities to change their masters relatively easily, by taking an "exit" option—that is, leaving a present master for a new one ("high-exit" situation[1])—the daimyo's attempts to intensify their control over their vassals were subject to obvious limitations. It was only with the achievement of internal pacification and consolidation of the daimyo under the Tokugawa regime that the feudal masters were able to impose tighter controls on their vassals ("low-exit" situation). By streamlining their war machine according to a hierarchical pattern of vassalage, the samurai as a class were victorious in their struggles with other social groups, and effectively reconstituted their feudal mode of domination. The nonsamurai classes were subsequently demilitarized; and the shogun and his associated daimyo constructed a partially decentralized yet hierarchically integrated state structure. This overtly military character of early modern state formation exerted a decisive influence on later Japanese cultural development.

In contrast to medieval Japan, the Tokugawa state presents a much more centralized and integrated picture, although its political and economic foundations were still feudal in nature. The resultant "vassalic bureaucracy" incorporated a set of inherent cultural contradictions that proved confusing, not only to the ordinary samurai as individuals, but also to the shogunate authorities. The study of this third stage of development during the Tokugawa period through the processes of cultural persistence, change, and reformulation indicates that the mechanisms of samurai cultural transformation resulted in a very complex picture. The Tokugawa samurai had inherited a highly institutionalized military version of samurai culture that persisted even though the early modern samurai's day-to-day life had changed significantly. The emerging new order shaped by the formation of the Tokugawa state created a social-institutional field that emphasized the values of order, organization, and conformity. Thus, the samurai culture of honor was considerably "refocused" but still preserved in its essentials because it was the symbolic expression of the status supremacy of the warrior class.

The distinctive trajectory of Japanese state formation and the course of samurai reorganization explain why and how the twin themes of control and change emerged and developed in the samurai culture. In particular, the origin of the Tokugawa version of the cultural complex, consisting of two coexisting modes of aspiration in the Japanese elite for competitive individuality on the one hand and orderly conformity on the other, cannot be properly understood without considering the distinctive nature of Tokugawa state formation.

An accurate assessment of the cultural consequences of state formation requires taking account of any interventions by religious powers in the domain of secular culture. This is especially important in the study of honor cultures because any honor culture is by its very nature liable to serious conflict with a transcendental value system. Honor by definition respects values derived from the public opinions of a social group (the imagined community of honor), whereas universalistic religions inculcate the supremacy of values beyond the boundaries of normative systems of human social groups. Universalist religions did not pose serious challenges to the ethical system of the Japanese samurai, however. Buddhism or Shintoism in Japan did not develop a powerful single institutional center that could represent an independent "public power" strong enough to oppose secular power. Partly because of the relative imbalance of institutional power between organized religions and the state, and partly because of Japan's geographical position coupled with its long period of isolation under the Tokugawa, Japan neither developed indigenous elitist counterideologies nor imported those of Western Europe (such as Christianity or Enlightenment humanitarianism), which might have modified the moral roots of the honor culture. Therefore, the samu-

rai honor culture developed itself as an immanent cultural and ideological resource of a social group intensifying its collective identity and solidarity. The absence of a strong centralized religious authority as an
institutionalized public power in early modern Japan provided favorable
conditions for the preservation of the honor culture.

This does not mean that the content of the samurai culture was completely uninfluenced by religions or other normative systems. Indeed, we
can identify a tendency in which the samurai class drew liberally upon
cultural resources derived from religious teaching for their own ends—
for intensifying their cultural confidence and accommodating to the
changing political economy.

At this point it may be helpful to explore some alternative historical
scenarios that did *not* occur in Japan, but could have, if the history of
early modern state formation had followed a different course. This sociological exercise may help to articulate by means of contrast the distinctive characteristics of Japanese early modern state-making.

For example, we can picture a scenario in which the social autonomy
and feudal prerogatives of the landed elites were preserved and even expanded in the process of early modern state-making, to the point of eventually favoring the formation of a kind of parliamentary institution. This
alternative was not a totally unrealistic scenario in early modern Japan.
Recall that during the late medieval period each samurai's *ie* restructured
itself internally and strengthened its control over its ancestral land. A
new form of coalition arose among the *ie,* namely, the *ikki.* These organizations formed effective alliances by building consensus through the decision of a majority. These *ikki* organizations in the late medieval period
formed powerful, large-scale horizontal alliances embracing independent landed samurai and often involving wealthy farmers who wanted
to protect their mutual interests. If the *ikki* organizations had been able
to empower, structure, or consolidate the powers of their local landed
elites, Japanese early modern state formation would have taken a very
different route. Furthermore, one can readily speculate that in the cultural domain, the honor culture would have continued to prevail, insofar
as the *ikki* were primarily federations of landed elites. However, an
honor culture shaped by a pattern of relatively egalitarian, horizontally
structured political alliances would have been less easily remolded into
a more hierarchically collaborative and state-centered form.

For example, let us consider the hypothetical case in which the various types of local power systems that prospered in late medieval Japan did not coalesce into an alliance on a national scale, but persisted in localized forms into the early modern period. Had the centralized locus of power expanded without interfering with these local power centers, the history of the Tokugawa epoch might have resembled that of Imperial China. In theory, the centralized Chinese state, staffed by Mandarin elites, had always governed the entire country; but in practice, regional clans and warlords provided personal protection at the local level. The functional distance between the central state and the local systems of power (which actually controlled the day-to-day life of the provincial population) was always quite considerable in China; and the arbitrary and unsystematic connections between the center and the local power structures were vulnerable to private monopoly. Had this pattern occurred in Japan, in such a way that the process of Tokugawa state-making had been carried out without integrating lower-level power systems, the honor culture might have assumed the form of localized clan loyalty, with the usual accompaniment of honor-related violence.

In reality, as we have seen, the increase of the power of lower-level samurai in the medieval period had one ironical result: the samurai submitted themselves to stronger regional power-holders (that is, the local daimyo, through entering vassalage with him) in order to secure their own control over land. Thus, it was not the *ikki* type of organization of horizontal alliances but the warlords' vertically structured military machines that ultimately incorporated the local samurai by restricting their social autonomy. The subsequent domestication of the Tokugawa samurai—and of their honor culture—was possible because Japanese state formation in the early modern period took this course of development. The Tokugawa system did not allow the samurai *ie* to continue its earlier tradition of social autonomy based on land tenure. As a result, the honor culture remained the central component of the samurai's collective identity, but its content was reconstituted as a much more hierarchically ordered value. Moreover, the fact that Tokugawa state formation took the form of a vertical integration of the samurai class, rather than a horizontal pattern of consolidation, shaped an environment that was conducive to a hierarchical value system in the society as a whole. The social processes that led to the formation of the Tokugawa state, coupled with the distinctive nature of this samurai regime, had a decisive impact on the reformulation of Tokugawa samurai culture.

The neo-feudal structure of the Tokugawa government also blocked the possible empowerment of the merchant class within the formal political process, even though the commercial economy of early modern Japan was enjoying a vigorous development. Had the warlords of the sixteenth century carried their internecine warfare into the seventeenth century, or had Japan been subject to the vagaries of a less protected geopolitical location that afforded fewer options for isolationism, the relationship between the state's power and that of organized capital might have been very different. The contributions of businessmen to the fiscal growth necessary to sustain large-scale warfare, as well as their potential involvement in international trade, might well have empowered the Japanese merchant class, allowing it to intervene in the political process. However, serious commercialization of the Tokugawa economy did not take place until the military state had firmly established itself. Although the Tokugawa merchants increased their relative influence somewhat through lending money to daimyo whose revenues did not keep pace with their expenses, this improved economic base gave them little political leverage because the daimyo continued to exclude nonsamurai from government positions. This path of development prevented early modern Japan from moving in the direction of a more capitalist economic order in its subsequent social development.

In short, we have seen that the military class in Japan remained the exclusive ruling class—although its social functions underwent significant transformation—until the late nineteenth century, just before the dawn of industrialization. This continuity of political control became a critical condition for preserving the culture of honor in Japan, despite profound changes in the articulation of that culture. As a result, the Tokugawa period represents the decisive phase of Japanese history, in which a competitive yet distinctively cooperative form of honor culture emerged.

Given the country's phenomenal economic growth, comparative sociologists have been aware of the importance of tracing the historical roots of modern Japan. Nonetheless, they rarely go back beyond the discussion of the "Tokugawa roots" of contemporary Japan. Comparative historical sociologists such as Barrington Moore and Perry Anderson, who are interested in Japanese developments for their own scholarly purposes, also focus largely on Tokugawa Japan as the source of their primary explanatory factors. The distinctive social landscape of medieval Japan, and the subsequent fundamental institutional reorganization that preceded the

formation of the Tokugawa state, have rarely been systematically analyzed in the comparative sociological literature. Although I agree that the
Tokugawa period is the critical phase of Japanese history, overconcentra-
tion on the early modern period does not generate sufficient explanatory
power to account for the distinctive trajectories of Japanese social developments. I believe that a comparative assessment of the medieval to the
early modern social transition, together with articulation of the comparative significance of Tokugawa state formation, facilitates a better understanding of the Japanese experience.

An accurate comparative understanding of the transition from the medieval period to the early modern state, and its translation into the organizational structure of the Tokugawa shogunate, is critically important
not only to the study of the samurai culture as I have outlined it in this
book but also to the comprehension of many other aspects of Japan's
discrete social experience. For example, the structure of the "integrated
yet decentralized" Tokugawa state, which reorganized previously autonomous social organizations as agents of social control while allowing
them semiautonomy, has far-reaching implications for the creation of
prototypical organizational patterns in modern Japan. The revised and
refocused samurai culture under the Tokugawa also significantly influenced the culture and institutions of the nonsamurai classes. For example, the revised structure of vassalage and the resulting new ethics of
master-follower relationships under the Tokugawa provided organizational and ideological models for the large-scale Tokugawa merchant
houses that had flourished since the mid-Tokugawa period. The samurai's ethic of obedience to the master's *o-ie* fitted well with the need of
these large merchant houses that typically developed a feudalistic hierarchical organization based upon a long-term employment system. I hope
that my articulation of the path to Japanese early modern state formation will stimulate further discussion among sociologists regarding the
ramifications of Japan's early modern social transformation.

Cultural Change and State Formation

The attribution of significant influence to the historical paths in culture
production does not imply that cultural resources are always the passive
receptors of social change. Once institutionalized, culture exercises a
variety of subtle and not-so-subtle influences both on particular agents'
decisions to act and on the course of action chosen.

My historical investigation indicates that the cultural reconstruction of the samurai under the Tokugawa state was neither an automatic nor a rapid result of the changes in society. The actual refocusing of the Tokugawa samurai culture largely resulted from the cumulative efforts of many individual samurai to make sense of the changing world around them. The older cultural myth, established during the medieval period, demonstrated a remarkable degree of persistence to the extent that it was supported by the very structure of the Tokugawa vassalic bureaucracy. It was also symbolically glorified and popularized through the lens of contemporary popular samurai literature.

Although the social actors of the Tokugawa period struggled as best they could to make sense of the shifting sociopolitical environments caused by Tokugawa hegemony, their responses and cultural adaptations often failed to keep pace with the political changes. The fact that individual samurai could make use of the older cultural idioms, as perceived by them, for their private purposes, either for accommodation or for resistance to the new social environment, complicated the process of cultural transition considerably. In addition, there is an apparent limit to an individual's ability to comprehend the social-institutional matrix in which he or she is situated. Because a full consideration of all the meanings and technicalities of social environments that surround the self is difficult for an individual, a person is consequently not always able to choose the behavioral option that is best suited to his or her interests. It is only with regard to the imperfection of human cognitive possibilities of knowledge that the macro social-structural constraints can be translated into individual actions.[2]

Despite this limitation, the capacity of individual actors for autonomous behavior and the active reinterpretation of their culture is strikingly evident in the case studies of subversive samurai actors who bent the "traditional" samurai idioms to fit their own purposes. We have seen in the analysis of the samurai *kenka* that the ordinary Tokugawa samurai shared the cultural idioms of honorific competitiveness with the state authorities. In this sense, both the practices and the myths of the honor culture were equally important in the process of cultural transformation and (partial) persistence because they affected the individuals' understanding of their own world. The officers of the shogunate achieved their regulatory aims not through the imposition of an overall moral ideology but rather through trial-and-error attempts to control the problematic behavior of the samurai. After all, the authorities themselves had not been emancipated from the spell of the honor culture tradition. The formulation and dissemination of the new style of the samurai honor culture were, as we have seen, less consistent and systematic than has usually been supposed.

The relatively unsystematic process of cultural diffusion did not mean that the Tokugawa state did not play an important role in the cultural sphere, however. The individual actor's decision is not the sole factor to take into account. We should note the strength of the structure of the state as a limiting as well as an empowering factor affecting individual judgments of cultural reinterpretation. *The role of the state in cultural regulation was not limited to defining and orchestrating; it was also extended to the creation of a number of long-term fundamental social and political institutions that directly and indirectly affected subsequent cultural developments.* The most important cultural contribution of Tokugawa state formation was its construction and maintenance of a set of institutions with a cohesive and stable political authority. From the organizational structure of vassalic bureaucracy to various edicts and legal procedures, from the requisite etiquette for formal interactions among the samurai to the visible signs of status differentials, every Japanese institution in the early modern period communicated the implicit assumptions of the neo-feudal state.[3] Although each institution by itself was not necessarily formed with the direct intention of regulating the cultural sphere, taken together they constituted an institutional field that constrained their actors' choices and decisions (structure as "constraint"), thereby restricting the possible courses of future cultural development while providing useful symbolic idioms for their action aimed at change and reformulation (structure as "resource").

When we consider the mechanisms through which the state exerts its power on the cultural sphere, we customarily focus on such relatively recent agencies of direct moral enforcement as police surveillance, bureaucratic regulations, and educational systems, all of which may serve as the institutional implements of the state's moral decisions and regulations. In his insightful classification of the two kinds of "state power," Michael Mann called this social-institutional expression of state power "infrastructural co-ordination power," in contrast to "despotic power," which implies a range of actions imposed from above without any institutional negotiations or mediation through social groups.[4] The Japanese medieval state was weak in both categories of state power. When the

Tokugawa rulers consolidated their power over a unified Japan, around 1600, the central government's "despotic power" was measurably increased. We must note, however, that even during the Tokugawa period the government's implementation of moral regulations was not as sophisticated as has sometimes been presumed. Unlike some European counterparts, the early modern shogunate never developed strong infrastructural agencies of moral regulation, such as a national police force, a national standing army, or a subsidized public school system.

In spite of this relative weakness of the state's infrastructural coordination power for moral regulation, the impact of the Tokugawa neo-feudal state was pervasive and long-lasting in the cultural sphere. I argue that this pervasive influence was possible because Tokugawa state formation took the distinctive course in which the state reorganized the existing, previously highly autonomous, social organizations such as the vassal samurai's house, or *ie*, villages, and other religious, occupational, or status groups. The self-governing abilities of these organizations were generally preserved, but they were restructured to serve the needs of the state. The hierarchical reconstitution of these social organizations exercised a deep influence because they were intimately connected with the daily life and social relations of the people. In comparison to the direct influence of the central government, which tends to affect only the surface of people's lives, the reorganization of these middle-range social organizations in the process of Tokugawa state formation significantly influenced and circumscribed people's autonomous activities of cultural reformulation.

The impact of state formation on the cultural sphere cannot always be clearly defined as the result of a calculated moral regulation and consensus building. Rather, the cultural impact of state formation usually represents the sum of state-regulated and individually generated behaviors. Confining the role of the state to the more easily measurable forms of direct moral regulation by state agents would be to underestimate severely the magnitude of the interrelations between the sociopolitical and the cultural dimensions of state formation.

Control through the Refocusing of the Expressions, Loci, and Sources of Samurai Honor

In my historical analysis of the refocusing of the samurai honor culture under the Tokugawa, I traced three kinds of shifts in the nature of the honor culture related to the expression, the locus, and the source of samurai honor, respectively.

The first transition, *a shift in the expression of honor,* parallels the demilitarization of the concept of samurai honor. During this process, honor was reconceived as *less associated with violence and more with virtuous self-discipline.* The medieval form of honor culture that had been closely allied with the samurai's high standards of military prowess assumed that a man's honor hinged upon his ability to use violence effectively whenever his honor was threatened. This violent notion of honor was no longer taken for granted as acceptable behavior in Tokugawa society. To be sure, this demilitarization of the honor culture remained incomplete because the government's valuation of the military was the single most important instrument of Tokugawa pacification and the shogunate's legitimacy. Despite this critical limitation with regard to taming a violent conception of honor, however, a general trend in the direction of civilizing samurai honor is undeniable.

The second shift in the nature of the honor culture involved a change in *the locus of honor, which moved from personal to organizational.* In the social world of the medieval samurai, the object of a vassal's loyalty was the master himself; warriors and their masters were not only committed to each other by social and material considerations but were also emotionally connected by shared experiences of military combat. The behavioral competition for honor among medieval warriors, however, tended toward a self-centered search for glory and reward, devoid of considerations of solidarity and harmony among the troops to which they belonged.

The beginning of this transition from a personal to an organizational locus of honor can be traced to the advent of a more hierarchical vassalage system under the *sengoku daimyo.* A significant change of the basic conditions of samurai vassalage occurred, however, only with the consolidation of the Tokugawa state. In this newer system, the individual samurai were neatly ranked in a pyramidal power structure. The relationship between a master and his vassal samurai became less personal, and a man's hereditary status in the hierarchy of his master's house government largely determined what he could expect from life. Under these circumstances, the *o-ie,* or organization of the master's house, moved to the center of the vassals' sense of loyalty. In the mind of the Tokugawa samurai, the *o-ie* was not simply the house of the master's family; rather, it embraced all the samurai united to it in a sense of shared destiny and commitment. According to this organizational understanding of the *o-ie*, the head of the *o-ie* was not an absolute despot but a leader who was equally obligated together with his vassals to contribute to the perpetual prosperity of the corporation. I use the term "corporation" advisedly, because the social honor and economic prosperity of each individual samurai and his house depended upon the continuity of his master's *o-ie*.

One of the most typical expressions of loyalty to the *o-ie* organization, exhibited at the expense of personal fealty to the daimyo lord himself, can be observed in the numerous struggles for hegemony that took place within the Tokugawa daimyo houses. Such internal conflicts, related to the succession and political hegemony of the daimyo houses, were called *o-ie sōdō* (literally, "the disturbance of the house"). There were a considerable number of cases during the Tokugawa period in which a clique of major vassals forced their master (the daimyo lord, who was supposedly guilty of misconduct) to resign, and even to submit to a form of house arrest (called *oshikome*, or "confinement"). Unlike some rebellious vassals of the Warring States period, however, these Tokugawa vassals did not attempt to take over the daimyo lordship. They usually turned to someone in the family of the daimyo house who showed promise of being a better ruler for the sake of the *o-ie*, and they often asked the shogunate to support their position.

The distinctively Tokugawa nature of *o-ie sōdō* was that these internal dissensions never took the form of overt rebellion. On both sides of these political struggles, whether on the side concerned to protect the present lord or that of his opponents, the men involved always claimed that their actions were truly undertaken in behalf of the ongoing prosperity of the *o-ie*. Interestingly enough, in quite a few cases, the Tokugawa shogunate sometimes conceded the rightness of such vassals' actions when the upstarts were clearly the recipients of support from the daimyo house itself. This indicates that during the Tokugawa period there was a growing understanding that daimyo houses should be perpetuated through the collective responsibility of those who belonged to their organization.[5]

To be sure, this shift from personal to organizational loyalty was not completed during the Tokugawa period as long as the regime officially used the logic of vassalage as its organizational foundation. The Tokugawa vassalic bureaucracy required a personal representative of its authority, centered around the lord. Thus, even though the samurai's general mindset placed an ever higher value on organizational loyalty, as distinct from an emphasis on personal attachment to the lord, the latter element was never completely replaced by the former. The retention of a sense of personal commitment to one's master was very clearly demonstrated in the case of the radical members of the Forty-seven Samurai, as well as in *Hagakure's* notion of "secret love." Thus, the ideologies of vassalage that competed for dominance under the Tokugawa system included *multiple loci of loyalty,* which were potentially ripe for use in ideological reformulations of various types.

The third shift in the honor culture of the samurai concerns *the changing source of honor from performance to status.* In the period when Japanese society had been subjected to the stresses of successive wars and conflicts, its warrior subculture had valued and honored an individual samurai's military achievement and ability over and above his bloodline. Although a family with a good name was always respected, the reality of a competitive world of warriors did not allow any medieval samurai to rest complacently on the honor of his pedigree. By contrast, the Tokugawa samurai's position became largely hereditary, and there was only a small range of open career possibilities that could be affected by effort and achievement, in order to change one's position in the samurai hierarchy.

A strictly hereditary conception of honor did not completely replace the older performance-based notion, however, owing to the fact that the military tradition of samurai honor could not be officially negated. This military tradition, after all, legitimated the samurai's domination over other classes as the official military guardians of the peace. As such, it prevented the Tokugawa samurai from becoming a purely aristocratic status category. The image of the ideal samurai through its continuation of the medieval tradition of the brave warrior perpetuated a value system connected to human character and performance, in spite of other social realities that bestowed high honor on men from privileged bloodlines. The romanticized image of the heroic samurai of an earlier period never lost its grip on the sympathetic imagination of the Tokugawa samurai.

Bravery was a masculine quality that could not be readily displayed in peacetime; however, an attitude of rigid self-control in daily life came to be considered "the beginning of valor." From this position, it was only a short step toward a redefinition of military performance-oriented values in the direction of an ideology of peacetime meritocracy and self-control without direct relationship to actual physical combat. The neo-Confucian emphasis on scholarly accomplishment and internal discipline provided an intellectual idiom to legitimate the new model of manhood. The concept of honor became more state centered, thereby supplying objective criteria of honor; and the warrior's ethos of aggression was redirected toward competition for titles and other privileges within the samurai hierarchy.

The Emergence of a Multilayered Symbolic Community

One must observe that all three shifts, in the expression, the locus, and the source of the samurai's honor sentiments, were carried out amid critical changes in the structure of the samurai's reference groups. What resulted was *the emergence of multilayered imagined cultural communities,* or *collective symbolic reference groups.* According to a person's primary reference group, his criteria of honor could differ greatly. As we have seen in the example of the Forty-seven Samurai, the samurai in early modern Japan developed a layered set of imagined symbolic spaces, each of which had different loci and criteria of honor. For the ordinary samurai who served a local daimyo, the collective body of the *o-ie* was the most important symbolic reference group. For those who were in service at the master's Edo office, however, reputation within the wider samurai community in Edo also constituted a significant symbolic frame of reference. Through their exposure to experiences and information beyond the outer limits of the local polity, the Tokugawa samurai were also concerned with the emergent new culture that evaluated the honor of the samurai differently from how his hometown measured it.

There was an official honor community within the shogun's castle, in which the honor ranking of each daimyo's house was officially evaluated. Each institutional layer in this system of honor ranking and evaluation had a different locus of honor, with a correspondingly different emphasis and standard of measurement. The debates among the Tokugawa intellectuals over the case of the Forty-seven Samurai reveal, quite dramatically, the actual as well as the potential contradictions elicited by the emergence of a multilayered imagined community of honor. The dynamic dialectical developments that marked Tokugawa ideologies of honor reflected the conflicts, tensions, and coexistence of noncomplementary symbolic frames of reference.

The development of a multilayered symbolic community of honor was directly related to the decentralized yet integrated structure of the Tokugawa state. Each lower unit of social groups was granted semiautonomous power over its members, but it was situated within the wider, integrated framework of the Tokugawa shogunate. In this system of social control, which utilized the indigenous self-governing abilities of middle-range social organizations as much as possible by situating them in appropriate positions within the larger polity, all the various layers composing the symbolic community had some share of legitimacy and cultural authority.

Public and Private Domains

At this point, it is important to remember the idiosyncratic distinction between public (ōyake) and private (watakushi) that pertained in Tokugawa samurai ideology. This particular form of separation between public and private assumed that responsibilities in the public domain were more significant and important than the corresponding obligations in the private sphere. The samurai as a class were defined as men devoted to public concerns. Given this definition, the internal control mechanisms of the Tokugawa samurai encouraged them as individuals to place socially accepted goals and public responsibilities before private, short-term desires.

The complication that disturbed an otherwise orderly distinction between public and private was the fact that the Tokugawa system incorporated *a hierarchy of multiple public spheres*. For example, the daimyo's *o-ie,* or house, was "the" public sphere for those who belonged to it; but, from the perspective of the national polity, the shogunate, the daimyo house belonged to an inferior level of "public" life, and so could be regarded as semiprivate. It was from the shogunate's viewpoint, for example, that the loyalty of the Forty-seven Samurai to their deceased master was labeled as "private" morality, and therefore subject to overrule by the shogun's superior public authority.

In the multilayered power structure that developed under the Tokugawa system, no sphere was considered truly "private," insofar as each level of involvement had its own assigned role and responsibility in the Tokugawa system. At the same time, each layer of authority in the public domain also included private characteristics. For example, the daimyo's local polity was in essence an extension of the house of the daimyo lord, and the basic organization of the government consisted of master-follower relationships. Even at the highest levels of the shogunate, the central government was little more than an extension of the ruling house, and its high officials were basically private vassals to the chief of the Tokugawa house, the shogun. In contrast, from the shogunate to the vassal samurai's *ie* there was no definite "base" within the private domain strong enough to shut out interference from the public authority.

The lower level of the "public" domain was frequently described as *watakushi* (literally, "the private," usually used pejoratively), in contrast to the supposedly higher public sphere. For example, an issue of concern to the daimyo's polity was generally spoken of as "private," in comparison with a problem involving the shogunate. Whereas the daimyo polity represented the "public" to those who belonged to that particular daimyo, the domestic matters of a vassal samurai's *ie* were reduced to "private" concerns. Even the *ie* itself was not completely in the private domain, however. Since the maintenance and continuity of a samurai *ie* were considered the foundation of the hierarchy, insofar as the "houses" were the measuring units of obligations to the daimyo's house, the *ie* would represent the public with respect to issues that concerned particular individuals. For example, domestic matters such as marriage and inheritance could not be totally private because they were issues related to the continuity and maintenance of the vassal samurai's *ie*. In other words, they were connected to the structural foundation of the local daimyo polity, which consisted of a local public domain.

This penetration of the public domain into the domestic life of the Tokugawa samurai is very different from the Chinese Confucian family ethic. The Chinese system accorded the highest moral priority to kinship and house loyalty, rather than to loyalty to masters or sovereigns. The Japanese experience of a system of hierarchical vassalage trained people to sustain long-term relationships of exchange and obligation outside the kinship structure in a very distinctive way. The Japanese have been struggling for centuries to construct institutional (both cultural and sociopolitical) systems of maximizing trust in exchange relationships between parties whose trustworthiness is not immediately apparent. Through successive efforts to coordinate and incorporate fiercely independent actors into more stable forms of social networks, the Japanese have constructed a culture that is more sensitive to the socially embedded aspect of human existence.

In observing this characteristic, we should not assume that the Japanese lack the desire to express their individuality. If one looks no further than the smoothly operating surface of the system of Tokugawa vassalage, to say nothing of the modern practice of long-term employment commitment, one might simply consider that the early modern practice emerged out of the "harmonious" climate of social relations inherent in Japanese society. *Japan's "harmonious culture" is not simply the reflection of an intrinsic social value pattern but the result of a history of active mediation of conflicts.* In this book, I have presented an extended case history in which multiple parties involved in exchange relationships attempted to increase the "predictability of unpredictable human behavior" through instituting various mechanisms of trust. One of these institutions consisted of the culture and ideology of the samurai's honorific loyalty.

This idiosyncratic differentiation between public and private, and the resultant "shrinking" of the private sphere during the Tokugawa period, in turn made the samurai's sentiments of honor a prized cultural resource suitable for generating individualistic action and for expressing individuality. I will now turn to the second aspect of this cultural resource, which I have termed "honorific individualism."

Changes in the Conception of Honorific Individualism

The theme of change in samurai culture emerged from a compound of honor, dignity, and self-reliance. It was this change in honor culture that prevented the samurai's mindset from becoming that of an utterly passive bureaucrat even in the age of Tokugawa hierarchical vassalage. I have termed this aspect of honor culture "honorific individualism" in order to focus attention on the samurai's spirit of self-reliance. This type of samurai individualism, although very different from our conventional understanding of self-definition in modern Western societies, was also the source of innovation and energy at the personal level, which in turn engendered changes in society at large.

The term "individualism," as understood in the West, has largely evolved since the nineteenth century, and our sense of the term's meanings has been framed by this evolution under capitalism in the modern period. The contemporary use of "individualism" contains multiple layers of meaning, starting from religious and economic fields of discourse to political and philosophical notions of individualism. Steven Lukes, in his lucid study of individualism, identifies eleven basic components of the term; he argues that, although each component has its own developmental lineage, they have all become logically and conceptually interconnected.[6] This modern version of individualism has been a dominant force in Western philosophy and social thought, providing an intellectual paradigm for modern Western capitalism.

Honorific Individualism in Comparative Perspectives

I have coined the term "honorific individualism" in order to highlight my view that Japan developed a mode of individualism distinct from what we usually associate with the term in modern Western capitalist societies. Applying the term "individualism" to Japanese society may surprise some readers because outside observers, as well as the Japanese themselves, have conventionally accepted a view that Japan did not develop an indigenous cultural resource for individualism. My first reaction here is to note that the predominant presence of conformist ideologies in Japan does not preclude the simultaneous existence of a countercultural resource that supports individualistic expressions and actions. And indeed, in both past and present Japan, we frequently encounter Japanese individuals who dare to take initiatives for change while taking significant social and personal risks. This observation leads me to a second reaction, namely, to point out a logical flaw in the widespread notion that Japan lacks a pronounced form of individualism, a prejudice that would lead to the following curious paradox if taken to its logical consequences.

First, Japan seems to lack a clear form of individualism of the type that is recognized in the West. Second, we tend to interpret individualism as a major ingredient for triggering changes. These two points together would lead to the conclusion that we do not expect rapid changes to occur in Japanese society. And yet, and this is the paradox, modern Japan has seen several periods of rapid and radical changes. How should we reconcile this flexible ability for swift changes with a perceived lack of individualism to trigger those changes?

It is here that the notion of "honorific individualism" can clarify the Japanese historical developments. Although quite different from the Western modern notion of individualism, to the point of being hardly recognizable as such, honorific individualism does provide a mechanism for change—exactly by giving the individual a tool to go against the prevailing current of society. As we will see below, a similar form of individualism can in fact be observed in European history as well, but at earlier stages, in the form of the sovereign pride of the landed elite.

The prevailing notion that contemporary Japanese society lacks a concept of the individual is to a large extent a matter of definition. If we assume that the modern Western notion of individualism—in particular the commonplace definition of "individual" as a private self, or of "individualism" as the basis of liberal democracy—possesses transcultural and transhistorical validity, we can readily point to a relative lack of "individualism" in indigenous Japanese culture. This "inventory" approach to Japanese society, predicated on the cultural features specific to the nineteenth-century Western model of individualism, would, however, overlook the presence of a cultural tradition that supports and preserves a different pattern of expressing individuality in Japan.

It is important to note here that the Japanese conception of honorific individualism—as we will see in the analysis below—did not elaborate a cohesive political philosophy that defined and celebrated individual independence, comparable to Western systems such as Thomas Hobbes's and John Stuart Mill's. The Western intellectual tradition is distinctive for its tendency to encapsulate its core values within systems that are made as structurally coherent as possible, and reduce them to universally applicable thought forms. This passion for constructing universal philosophies was not part of the Japanese intellectual tradition. Lacking a large-scale theoretical apparatus and framework, the honorific individualism of the samurai class manifested itself primarily in an ethos of behavior. This ethos left a clear stamp on both the collective attitudes and the personal actions of samurai in various ideological camps and positions within the political spectrum. Considering that Western literature does not confine its references to "individualism" to a kind of individualism that has a coherent philosophical substructure, I propose to describe the samurai ethos simply as "honorific individualism," thereby capturing the main distinctive aspect of the Japanese mode of individuality.

By introducing this definition, I do not intend to argue that honorific individualism is a cultural property unique to Japan. Indeed, the prototypical forms of honorific individualism based upon the social autonomy of landed lords are found in many cultures in the form of the honor of precedence; European aristocratic culture fits this pattern, and Southern antebellum white elite culture also matches it. The sociohistorical role played by a conception of honorific individualism among landed elites has been, in my opinion, underestimated in comparison to the frequently analyzed role of the contemporary capitalist version of individualism. We may consider the landed elites of early modern England as a case in point. The enclosure movement, which originated as an extension of landed elites' economic activities in the Tudor period, clearly paved the way for the subsequent great transformation of English society under industrialization. To take another example, the foundation of American economic development in the South before the Civil War was first prepared by landed elites, whose culture resembled those of European honorific landed aristocracies.

I maintain that *Japanese honorific individualism emerged as a form of "possessive individualism," a conviction about the self that grew up among the members of the landed elites, who acquired a firm sense of self-possession paralleling their pride in the ownership of land.* In his famous definition of "possessive individualism" as it arose in seventeenth-century England, C. B. Macpherson associated seventeenth-century political philosophies of individualism with property possession: "The possessive quality [of possessive individualism] is found in its conception of the individual as essentially the proprietor of his own person or capacities, owing nothing to society for them. The individual was seen neither as a moral whole, nor as part of a larger social whole, but as an owner of himself."[7] Macpherson made an important contribution to the literature by pointing out the connection between the mode of property possession and the mode of understanding selfhood. However, he constructed his model of possessive individualism based upon a set of market assumptions of property that he applied to seventeenth-century English thinkers. Could this concept of self-understanding—of an individual as an owner of himself based upon his control of property possession—emerge only with the rise of market assumptions?

In an extension of Macpherson's definition, it is possible to conceive of different kinds of possessive individualism. The possession of property by the landed military elites of feudal Japan differed from the modern private ownership of property in a market economy, which is usually considered the basis of modern liberal individualism. In Japan, as I will argue in the following section, an elitist culture of honor emerged within a class of military lords who regarded themselves as self-sufficient individuals because of their feudal land tenure.

My arguments are in accordance with recent discourse on Western possessive individualism. For example, J. G. A. Pocock recommends a partial revision of Macpherson's argument because the intellectual discourse on property possession in seventeenth-century political thought cannot be interpreted as being based only upon market assumptions. There were arguments among English thinkers "going on as between several modes of property and individuality"; a model of property relationships defined by military tenure was one of them. Consequently, Pocock holds the view that there were "several kinds of possessive individual, and so of possessive individualism."[8] In reevaluating the role of the gentry in the development of British capitalism, Orlando Patterson suggests that there were "not one, but two distinct forms of possessive individualism. . . . One form may be called bourgeois, the other honorific. Both have in common all the elements emphasized by Macpherson. . . ."[9] The samurai's honorific individualism can thus be regarded as a variant of possessive individualism.

The medieval and Tokugawa forms of honorific individualism display their own distinct characteristics, however. In the following section, I will explain what "honorific individualism" meant in the Japanese context by reviewing two stages of its cultural development.

Medieval Forms of Honorific Individualism

The honor of the samurai originally emerged as a sense of warrior pride held by men who wielded their own share of power. Socially and politically, the medieval samurai's honor was based upon the relative social and economic independence of his *ie* (house), his family's sense of sovereignty, or "statehood." Unlike the abstract concept of individuality that a modern intellectual would entertain in his or her quiet study, the samurai's individuality was inseparably connected to his political effectiveness as a landed lord and warrior. In other words, his social and moral autonomy was directly correlated to his ability to subordinate others.

In this type of honor culture, a power-oriented honor sentiment was inevitably connected to an aggressive assertion of individuality. It was not easy for a samurai to protect his own interests in a highly competitive social milieu. In theory, the samurai lord was supposed to defend his turf from invasion by antagonistic peers, and accumulate a reputation for superior might whenever the game of honor was involved. In addition, lords were supposed to subordinate a frequently unruly peasantry and extract revenue from them. Although entering vassalage would help a samurai indirectly to strengthen his control, he nonetheless had to be ever ready to demonstrate his martial abilities to his master in order to prove his worthiness. Therefore, medieval samurai culture always entertained strong aspirations toward independence and self-direction. The honor of the landed military lord was the landmark of his power, to be displayed whenever the occasion demanded. A flamboyant, self-assertive style of honor based upon a spirit of self-reliance was connected to the warlords' drives to defend both their possessions and their reputations. Thus, what I have chosen to label *"honorific individualism"* emerged in this context in medieval samurai society.

The tasks of a landed military lord were not simply confined to the spheres of military and political activity. His business included the complicated management of his property, natural resources, and manpower. More specifically, he had to take measures to improve the agricultural productivity of his lands—for example, by initiating irrigation projects. Nor were a lord's economic activities limited to the agricultural sector. By the late Kamakura period, many samurai lords attempted to obtain revenue from commercial enterprises in their territories, either by lending money at high interest rates to needy borrowers or by collecting taxes from commercial activities carried on within their territorial markets. The competitiveness of the samurai culture was deeply rooted in the warriors' economic life, and in their eagerness to protect and expand their economic interests. Furthermore, these warriors experienced a heartfelt sense of self-worth, an identity constructed around the straightforward expression of military pride in the course of existing, fighting, and surviving in a world that was a fiercely contested terrain. The culture of honor had already evolved to the degree that it could countenance the notion that honor was something for which a man could die.

It is important to note, however, that the samurai's honorific individualism had a limited legal foundation. Although the medieval Japanese vassalage system entailed reciprocal obligations between master and followers, these relationships were not clearly construed as a contractual form of reciprocity. To be sure, medieval samurai governments were entrusted with the critical function of judicial mediation of autonomous samurai conflicts, as exemplified in the concept of *dōri,* or reasonableness, which emerged during the Kamakura period. This conceptual tendency did not evolve into the abstract notion of a contract between the master and followers, however. In contrast, the primary European model of vassalage after the mid-eleventh century was intricately interconnected with the development of feudal law. The new codification redefined previously loose relationships between lords and vassals in a more substantial and precise manner, and with more objective prescriptions of their reciprocal rights.[10] The Japanese system of vassalage failed to develop a clear, legally codified description of vassalic rights and obligations. As a result, the medieval samurai's autonomy in vassalage was primarily grounded in their actual social and economic independence—rather than in the legal system—based upon their direct control over inherited land. It was from this kind of social basis that a possessive individualism emerged in medieval Japan.

The honorific individualism of the samurai military lords could only develop within an existing and effective network of social relationships. The most difficult aspect, politically speaking, of the samurai's task of achieving social autonomy was that he could accomplish it only through the formation of hierarchical political alliances. Entering vassalage with a more powerful man always helped to enhance his sovereign control over his own territory, but the commitment simultaneously limited his independence. However, aspirations toward honorific individualism firmly attached to power could only be realized by organized bands of men. In this sense, the honorific individualism of the medieval samurai was a sentiment with a concomitant social dimension. Even the religious individualism of Puritan origins had an unmistakably social aspect insofar as it embraced the notion of covenant, or the relationship of the religious community as a whole to God. This social dimension of Calvinist doctrine, combined with an introverted form of religious individualism, became the wellspring of passionate involvement in social reform and political activism.[11] In a similar manner, the medieval samurai's honorific individualism became a socially influential value through its connection to a socially accepted goal, honorable vassalage. It is important to note that individualism has the intrinsic capacity to generate considerable structural change whenever it is effectively connected to a social value.

Tokugawa Forms of Honorific Individualism

The medieval form of samurai honor culture was fundamentally threatened by the formation of the Tokugawa state. The social foundation of the individual's sense of sovereign honor was swept away as the result of new institutional constraints stemming from Tokugawa state formation. The *bakuhan* state's formation not only altered the political details of the samurai's life but also defined in fundamental terms a man's anticipation of his life's course, his chances for upward mobility, and, perhaps most important, his opportunities to enjoy stimulating or exciting life experiences. Not only was there no possibility of adventure in a future war, but the newly emerging institutional constraints forced the samurai to recognize that the range of his possibilities was circumscribed already through his status at the time of birth. The criteria of honor were provided in objective form as hierarchical status categories attached to visible symbols in ceremonial distinctions and dress codes.

Despite changing institutional environments that were more conducive to a passive bureaucratic mentality, the honorific ethos remained central to the samurai's identity, its passion hidden under a somber bureaucratic costume. By the beginning of the Tokugawa period, the samurai culture of Japan had already reached its maturity as an established military culture. It was also symbolically glorified and popularized through the lens of contemporary popular samurai literature; and it was embodied in various social institutions, as reflected in the organizational structure of Tokugawa samurai organization. This common vision strongly affected the range of cultural transformations that the Tokugawa samurai could allow without jeopardizing their collective identity as the ruling class.

The increasing tendency toward more objective forms of honor predictably produced a group of psychologically estranged Tokugawa samurai who gave nominal subscription to the official norms of public life while finding personal satisfaction in the private sphere through participation in the burgeoning, sophisticated culture of the larger cities. The existence of these alienated samurai, however, does not mean that the Tokugawa samurai class was cut off entirely from the ontological depth of their honor culture. The grim recognition of the paradoxes resulting from a compartmentalized existence was often converted into an intense inward search for reliable supports for a sense of dignity. The idioms of honor served to express the samurai's resilient personal core, which resisted the total incorporation of their individuality into the structures or purposes of the state.

The key to an understanding of this attitude of inner resistance on the part of the Tokugawa samurai is the usage of the term *ichibun* during the Tokugawa period. The frequent use of *ichibun* (literally, "one part," or the core of a person's pride that cannot be compromised)—implying a sense of "individualistic honor consciousness"—in the literature of the period indicates the presence of an honor sentiment associated with individual dignity and pride in an adversarial situation.[12] Recall the numerous references to *ichibun* in the letters of the Forty-seven Samurai; expressions such as "How can we show our faces? Please uphold the *ichibun* of the vassals" epitomize this sentiment.[13] It was a concept that had its own complexities, but the general consensus was that "receiving an insult or being laughed at was considered a matter of *ichibun*; even when it meant a serious sacrifice, a man attempted to maintain *ichibun* because he considered his own *taimen* [social appearance] important."[14]

The concept of *ichibun* is connected to a person's concern for reputation, but it did not manifest itself only on the level of external concerns; *ichibun* was an entity that was deeply ingrained in the samurai's personal pride and self-esteem. When a samurai discovered that his *ichibun* did not hold up in a moment of personal crisis, he might attempt to challenge the local authority, or to support unconventional ideas even though that decision might entail considerable risks. Even with greater pressures to modify the medieval form of the samurai ethic, such as increasing stress on the more conformist aspects of honor, the self-assertive features of the samurai honor culture did not completely disappear.

The spirit of *ichibun* was observed in various political milieux during the Tokugawa period. It was this sense of honor that provided an ethical impetus for all kinds of early modern ideologies regardless of their behavioral manifestations. If anything, the culture of honor increasingly became a prized moral resource through its provision of idioms for the expression of spiritual and social individuality in the cultural setting of the Tokugawa samurai—a setting in which unconditional loyalty and obedience received an ever stronger emphasis.

The Tokugawa samurai did not develop their individualistic ethos into their dominant system of value, in the way Western bourgeoisie and intellectuals have constructed it; rather, they ranked it below, at least officially, loyalty. Furthermore, the samurai's attachment to what I have labeled "honorific individualism" lacked any connection to transcendental values such as one finds in Christian or Kantian schemes of universal moral principles. The individualism of the samurai was less pronounced as a result, through the absence of an ethical base of support from a transcendental value system beyond the immanent norms of their social group. Moreover, the samurai of this period lacked an independent economic base. Without a political and economic substructure undergirding personal autonomy, the aggressive search for individuality that had been the unquestioned core value of medieval Japanese culture lost its centrality in the Tokugawa period. Thus, in Tokugawa Japan, honorific individualism remained present within the culture as a powerful *sentiment* with a strong ethical thrust; however, given its inchoate form, that is, its lack of a theoretical or systematic framework of articulation, it could not assume the shape of a coherent ideology as did its Western counterpart.

In spite of these differences, we should not underestimate the significance of the individualistic aspirations expressed by the Tokugawa samurai. Even those men who were taught an ethic of absolute obedience learned simultaneously that those who were devoid of a spirit of independence would forfeit the genuine respect of others. The notion that a noble samurai would have *ichibun* or *iji* (pride)—the expression referring to the "bottom self"—was clear in both personal behavior and symbolic representation in Tokugawa samurai culture. Although these individualistic aspirations were comparatively subdued during the Tokugawa period, they remained present in submerged emotional forms in the hearts of the samurai; they persisted as a current of feeling that could easily rise to the surface when social and political conditions stimulated its reemergence.

The cultural themes of control and change in the mind of the samurai could not coexist in harmony and therefore gave rise to serious tensions. Both organizational conformity and individualistic aspirations were considered socially and politically important for the Tokugawa samurai. Usually perceived as a moral dilemma, this inner quandary served as a dynamic source of cultural and intellectual creativity and development. The samurai intellectuals made considerable efforts to relocate their value system so that it would satisfy the two requirements of their honorific code, but such attempts were not fully successful in resolving the tension. Their sincere endeavors to preserve or reconstruct a lively and resilient sense of individuality in a changing sociopolitical environment were nonetheless meaningful. Their various intellectual efforts made individual samurai aware of the socially embedded aspect of human existence as well as the importance of having an independent spirit.

How distinctive, though, is this course of Japanese cultural development? In contrast to the Japanese experience in the early modern period, the development of modern Western capitalism is conventionally interpreted as a hegemonic cultural change resulting from the rise of a new class, the bourgeoisie, which eventually replaced the honor-centered elitist culture of the landed aristocracy. As Charles Taylor notes, "The ethic of glory is confronted here with a fully articulated alternative view, of social order, political stability, and the good [of the bourgeois ethic]."[15] To be sure, this is a highly schematic summary of a transition that required a long period of time to reach fruition, and that was accomplished in different ways in different countries; its timing is also a much-debated subject. When one uses this standard model of Western cultural change as a basis for comparison, however, the distinctive marks of Japanese cultural development become obvious. Japanese medieval honorific individualism shifted directly into its next phase of cultural development by adjusting itself to the new environment of Tokugawa society. Throughout the period in question, the Japanese elitist honor culture did not experience displacement or serious challenge from an articulated alternative class-based elite culture.

Interestingly enough, however, several recent studies of seventeenth- and eighteenth-century England have suggested in various ways that aristocratic dominance played a positive role through its persistent political, economic, and cultural hegemony. In the early phase of England's capitalist development, much of the social and intellectual groundwork that prepared the way for the Industrial Revolution was actually put in place while the landed elites still retained political and cultural hegemony.[16] For example, J. C. D. Clark's detailed study of the seventeenth- and eighteenth-century English nobility claims remarkable persistence for the cultural and political hegemony of old elites, particularly the aristocratic ideal of honor. According to Clark, "Its vitality and power in the eighteenth century is of immense importance."[17] "The very prevalence of the code of honour in such a world, a code carefully tended and explicitly shared by all, meant that such issues were highly sensitive. Where every insult was, or soon became, public, a public vindication of honour was forced on the offended party."[18] Elite culture in Enlightenment England was more than a vestigial survival; it contributed significantly to the development of economic and political theories that in turn brought about the eventual development of industrial capitalism. The example of the

English model seems to suggest that the persistence of Japanese honorific individualism as the landed elite culture in the early modern period itself was not unusual.

The Abolishment of the Samurai Status

Here we must consider the honor culture's loss of its privileged social base following the Meiji government's dissolution of the samurai as a class. After the Meiji restoration (1868), the new government abolished the privileged ruling status of the samurai, including their hereditary stipends and estates *(chigyō)*. The samurai received some partial compensation in the form of government bonds, but the notion of the samurai as the only class entitled to govern all others was abandoned. Former samurai were free to enter any occupation of their choice, and members of other classes could assume public office. In spite of this invitation to vocational exploration, many ex-samurai entered public service anyway under the new Meiji government.

In comparison to the indirect method of Tokugawa social control, which preferred to utilize the disciplinary capacities of middle-range social organizations, the Meiji government determined to rule its citizens directly through the arms of government. It proceeded to introduce Western-style institutions of social control, such as an up-to-date bureaucracy, a national standing army and navy, police, courts, and public schools. With their education and ingrained sense of public duty, the sons of ex-samurai families constituted an invaluable pool of human resources for the initial stage of nation-building. According to Sonoda Hidehiro, "In 1881, the ex-samurai and their families made up 5.3 percent of the total population. This small group occupied 68,556 of a total of 168,594 official posts, or 40.7 percent. Moreover, the higher the official post, the higher the rate of occupation by former samurai . . . In 1885, among 93 high-ranking officials above the bureau heads of the central government, we find 4 members of the peerage, 88 ex-samurai, and one commoner."[19]

In addition, many teaching posts in the newly created elementary schools (the total number of teaching posts was 78,000 in 1881) were occupied by the ex-samurai; without the creation of teaching positions, as the Meiji journalist Yamaji Aizan pointed out, "the ex-samurai's rebellion would have been fiercer" in Meiji Japan.[20] Eventually, the development of public education and the adaptation of meritocratic recruitment systems for the bureaucracy significantly increased the non-former samurai's participation in public life. It must be noted, however, that the first-generation leaders of Japanese modern nation-building were largely former samurai, and it is no wonder that elitist honorific sentiments continued to find conspicuous expression among the members of the early Meiji elite.

Thus, the culture of honor underwent further development and transformation after the Meiji restoration, but without embodiment within an exclusive elitist social group that embraced it as the articulating principle of their dominance. The legacy of the samurai honor culture remained after the dissolution of the class, but in less visible symbolic idioms rather than concrete institutional forms. As a result, modern Japanese can make contact with their samurai legacy only through indirect means and makeshift cultural arrangements. After the Meiji restoration, there were a number of organized and unorganized efforts to reinterpret or manipulate samurai symbolism. Such attempts at the utilization and recreation of tradition can be found in several subsequent historical settings, such as the movement to enhance civic morality and nationalistic solidarity in the late Meiji period; the pre–World War II militaristic education of youth; and the postwar reconstruction of Japanese society through the process of inculcating popular loyalty to business corporations. The scope of this book cannot cover these issues. In the section that follows I will offer only a few primary observations, by way of tracing the diffusion of the resource of samurai symbolism in Japan after the dissolution of the samurai class itself.

Japan gained certain advantages from preserving its culture of honor even into the post-Tokugawa period, because of the timing of its reentry into world politics: the late nineteenth century. Given the coincidence of this reentry with the expansion of Western imperialism, Japan experienced a relatively uncomplicated fusion of honor with nationalism. As the nineteenth century drew to its close, the volatile aspects of the Japanese samurai ethos were stirred up by a spreading sense of national crisis. At the end of the Tokugawa period, when Japan was forced to confront the direct military threat posed by the Western powers, the "sleeping samurai spirit was awakened," fostering a disposition to regard the national crisis as a challenge to one's personal independence and honor.[21] After the Meiji restoration, this resurgent honorific sentiment was again refocused to a transformed locus of honor. This new locus was the nationalistic image of the Japanese state, which, conveniently combined with fresh incentives for individual economic aspirations, could serve as the focal point for visions of glory and honor.

This ideological reformulation under the Meiji rulers as an expression of a vital relationship between the people and their society never assumed a course of straightforward development. It was a complex process, as it had been in the case of the Tokugawa reinterpretation of the samurai culture. Although a discussion of the Meiji restoration falls outside the scope of this book, there is an important consideration I would like to point out within this general historical setting. Although the samurai culture had nurtured a certain regard for competitiveness and meritocracy in Tokugawa society, this meritocratic competitiveness was seriously hampered by their having to work in tandem with a hereditary principle. Thus, to simplify somewhat, the Meiji system paved the way for a pure meritocracy by removing the hereditary element from the previous formulation of the honor culture.

Recall that, during the Tokugawa period, the sons of townsmen and peasants lacked any significant possibility for true upward mobility in the form of gaining entrance to the community of honor. Commoners could accumulate wealth, but their money could not purchase honorable status. Yet it was not only the commoners who were handicapped by the limitations imposed on their station in life; samurai with strong ambitions for upward mobility were likewise frustrated by their fixed position in the status hierarchy. As I discussed earlier, an achievement-oriented ethos and meritocratic values themselves remained as guiding ideals in Tokugawa samurai society, whereas the centrality of honor as a predominant cultural theme raised latent aspirations for higher honor among people at all levels of society. In spite of the high value placed on accomplishment and honor, however, the official Tokugawa system never created direct connections between hard work, economic success, and social honor. Therefore, the Meiji government's abolition of the privileged status of the samurai, and its subsequent introduction of state initiatives for economic growth, released an instantaneous surge of pent-up desires for upward mobility that cut across class lines.

The dissemination of a new, popular ideology, namely, the conviction that even a peasant's son could get *na* (name) in the world through honest toil and economic success, provided an enormous impetus for entrepreneurial activity in this honor-ridden society. The Meiji restoration thus tapped into and aroused the dormant meritocratic and achievement-oriented aspirations of the Japanese people; it then redirected these ambitions toward a renewed passion for success and honor in the market-place.

For example, a Meiji author writing in *A Hundred Stories of Success,* a moral how-to book of the late Meiji period, advised his ambitious contemporaries as follows:

> Success *(seikō)* brings rewards to both individuals and the country. Therefore, the more successful men there are, the wealthier and stronger the country becomes. It is the rule of world history that the country with fewer successful men is always poor and weak. Because of the nature of the situation, the success of an individual not only results in the prosperity of his house but also contributes to the prosperity of the country. Therefore, a human being should motivate himself and strive to succeed in life. Success is a human being's duty. Success not only increases a person's self-interest but promotes the country's interest; therefore, the successful man will be crowned with the laurel of honor.[22]

During this phase of reinterpretation, the ideology of the samurai's *ie,* which had developed under the Tokugawa vassalic bureaucracy, was easily translated into Meiji family law and the ideology of the "family state" headed by the paternal image of the emperor. Just as the samurai understood that the prosperity of their *ie* depended upon the continuation of their master's *o-ie,* Meiji Japanese were persuaded that the prosperity of their *ie* was also linked to the success of their country. For such an eminently acceptable social goal, one could readily justify individual struggles for worldly success. Given Japan's fierce motivation to obtain a position similar to the relatively advanced economies of the Western countries, its newly nationalized culture of honor, attuned to "rising in the world" *(risshin shusse)* and building "a wealthy country and a strong army" *(fukoku kyōhei),* provided the catalyst for an immediate synthesis of nationalism and honor. Energized by a positive "chemical reaction" between "passions and interests," glory-seeking sentiments and capitalism, the Japanese form of honor culture was harnessed for industrial growth.[23]

Any exposition of the cultural themes of conformity and control, as in the case of the Meiji nationalist use of honor shown in the previous section, may hold few surprises for those who are well informed about the best-known organizational characteristics of modern Japanese society. The samurai honor culture was not just used to create a moral consensus in the postsamurai era, however.

After their country was opened to the West, Japanese intellectuals were eager to import Western philosophies. Many progressive intellectuals in the early Meiji period were especially attracted to schools of Western liberal thought that emphasized the value of the individual and a spirit of self-help. The first generation of Meiji intellectuals—including Fukuzawa Yukichi, who was eager to introduce Western philosophies of individualism and civic independence to the Japanese—consisted mostly of former samurai who had grown up within the samurai culture. It was their own indigenous spirit of self-awareness and personal pride that first found Western models of individualism and independence attractive idioms for the expression of their sense of prideful personhood. Having tentatively accepted these Western values, they subsequently had to confront the existence of a moral dilemma between the two kinds of aspirations, connected with traditional Japanese norms and Western imports. It is important to stress here that a similar psychological conflict and sense of moral dilemma between individuality and conformity existed in premodern Japan as well. There was even an ideological tradition of elitist honorific individualism among the samurai that pursued highly personal expressions of selfhood. This indigenous source of cultural expressivity acquired a fresh resource of symbolic idioms from the West during the Meiji cultural transformation. Rather than considering the importation of Western models of individualism as complete innovations or decisive departures from the traditional Japanese mentality, we should look more carefully at the aspect of a continuous cultural development and reformulation.

Tradition as a Source for Change

The identification of an individualistic factor in the cultural complex of samurai honor carries an important sociological implication for our understanding of Japanese social development. Individualism as we understand it always involves an emphasis on innovation, or a drive toward unconventional ideas and action. If all the members of a society followed only its normative prescriptions and dictates, no initiative for change would ever emerge from such stagnation. Thus, the presence of an individualistic drive has been understood to have a number of social and economic implications. The existence of the requisite number of citizens with an individualistic attitude in Japan is evident in the success of the Meiji period of nation-building, in which drastic changes within all sorts of social institutions made themselves manifest, from the reconstitution of the government, laws, and education to that of the family and of business organizations. How could Meiji Japan respond so quickly to the external challenge posed by the West and completely reconstruct its society within a comparatively short period of time?

One might propose the theoretical hypothesis that Japan under the Meiji government was a political late-bloomer, catching up to more advanced countries by copying the requisite institutional models. This hypothesis would argue that the experience of Meiji institution-building was not the construction of social institutions *de novo*, but rather the rapid importation of Western models and their intelligent modification. Some may wish to maintain that, given Japan's status as a late developer combined with a strong state initiative for modernization, the Japanese process of industrialization might have been able to preclude the necessity of individual initiatives in the direction of capitalist development. We must note, however, that it was precisely this importation of Western models that required enormous individual courage and risk-taking. Japan was not simply a passive recipient of Western influence; rather, it was transformed from within by the determination and ambition of a number of individuals in the Meiji period who undertook significant social, psychological, and physical risks. They had to reconstitute indigenous institutions in order to prepare for successful adaptation, to persuade internal opponents, and eventually to set new socially acceptable goals.

Let us consider as an example the case of Ōmura Masujirō, a leader in bringing the Japanese army from its prototypical samurai form into the modern era as an efficient national standing army. Ōmura, as well as many others who attempted to Westernize indigenous Japanese institutions, was the victim of a late-nineteenth-century epidemic of political assassinations. Many Meiji intellectuals went to study abroad, intent upon researching the best models for Japanese social reform. Any agent who promotes changes of such magnitude requires persuasive initiative and determined persistence. These men were people who grew up under or were otherwise heavily influenced by the samurai honor culture. The process of industrialization in any country, Britain perhaps representing the main exception, involved the imitation and adaptation of other countries' experiences. It is impossible to imagine the industrialization of a late-developing society without the presence of individualistic agents of change.

This revised understanding of Meiji Japan leads us to question the conventional image of contemporary Japanese as a suffocating collectivity of faceless nonentities who prize harmony and consensus above all other values. The presence of a Western type of individualism, connected as it is to universalistic patterns of thought, is not a necessary precondition for individualistic initiatives toward industrialization and other aspects of modernization. In my opinion, the indigenous cultural resource of honorific individualism was an important cultural factor in social changes under the Meiji rulers. Honorific individualism need not even hold a dominant ideological position in the culture in order to function as a cultural resource for change, for the following reason: individual agents are not only subjected to the dominant value of the society; from time to time they can, as individual agents, choose to utilize a symbolic resource for their own purposes.[24] An individual actor might use a cultural idiom as a "resource" rather than a fixed "rule" for the aim of his or her specific action. When a person uses cultural resources in this fashion, it is not necessary that the symbolic idiom the person employs be a dominant theme within that particular culture. The agent may regard the idiom as a tool for self-expression, a source of inspiration, or a legitimation of a choice or decision.

The Japanese culture of honor often serves now, as it did then, as a resource for individualistic initiative-taking in a society in which Western-style ideologies of individualism never struck deep roots. As honor and a sense of the dignity of the individual have always been intimately connected in Japanese symbolism, a need to defend the boundaries of individuality against the encroachments of the collective order can also be legitimated in the name of honor. This is often true even in modern Japan, which possesses few alternative indigenous symbolic idioms for expressing the claims of individuality against collectivism. It is through these symbolic idioms that contemporary Japan is connected with its living past. Of course, it would be going too far to argue that there is a samurai living inside the head and heart of every present-day Japanese. In fact, modern Japanese do not usually see themselves as following in the footsteps of ancient samurai. Even so, we can trace some common sentimental threads tying the symbolic idioms held by the modern Japanese to the thoughts and feelings of their warrior ancestors.

I would like to cite here just one example of this symbolic connection between past and present in modern popular culture. In September 1992, when Japan was rocked by a series of political scandals, a middle-aged man suddenly splashed cans of paint one day on the street facade of the public prosecutor's office in Tokyo. He then distributed copies of an explanatory statement to bystanders at the scene. The lone demonstrator was quickly arrested; the large engraved stone tablet on the building was covered by yellow and white paint, however—a graphic image that provided a perfect picture for the mass media. The protester's action was aimed at the public prosecutor's lenient handling of the most controversial political scandal of the year, the case of Kanemaru Shin, a prominent leader of the ruling Liberal Democratic Party.

Sunday Mainichi, a popular weekly magazine, featured an interview with the protester that contained some sensational remarks, such as "Because I was representing Ōishi Kuranosuke Yoshio [the leader of the famous Forty-seven Samurai], I threw the paint on the prosecutor's office!" In the interview, the man explained the motives behind his behavior by appealing to the example of the Forty-seven Samurai. "I know I could be criticized as an exhibitionist spoiling for a fight. . . . But my heart is with the hearts of the masterless samurai of Akō. I know I am speaking too loftily, but . . . Ōishi's action was not simply taking revenge for his master. By his action he protested the unjust decisions of the public authority; that was why the people of that period were so excited about his act of revenge. In the same way, I did what I did in order to raise the consciousness of the prosecutor's office."

This direct reference to samurai culture in legitimation of an act of protest is not necessarily very common in contemporary Japan, nor can we automatically take the demonstrator's word at face value. However, the idiom of the samurai was a remarkably effective device for shaping the man's public image; it enabled the interviewer to present a picture of an ordinary, simple man, with no ideological party affiliation, possessed of a straightforward conscience, willing to raise his voice for what he believed to be right. The interview was written in a warm tone, reflecting the reporter's sympathy for the man.[25]

Modern Japanese society cannot be depicted in a simplistic manner as a collectivity of incompletely individuated people under the spell of a glorified past. When scholars, particularly Western writers, describe the cultural influences on the course of Japanese social development, they often uncritically assume the staying power of the "tradition" as conducive to the outwardly traditional forms and practices of Japanese organizational management—such as long-term employment with promotion based on seniority. A preconceived image of "Japanese tradition" as the chief source of social conformity is a poorly articulated notion. Under the influence of this misconception, some have considered the concept of samurai honor only in terms of self-sacrificial loyalty. The historical examination presented in this book strongly supports a different premise—that the honor culture had multiple layers of meaning, and that these layers contributed to the dynamic usage of the concept of "honor" to fit various individual as well as corporate purposes and goals.

In Japanese studies in the West, the causes that have influenced the introduction of certain characteristics that are by now peculiar to Japanese social institutions and organizations—such as the life-long employment system—have always dominated the interest of sociologists. However, these attempts frequently meet with problems involving questions of historical causal continuity. The question of whether culture plays the determining role in organizational characteristics, or whether this position belongs to social structural variables such as the "late development effect," "the structure of labor markets," and "interference of different organizational models" has always been central to this discussion. For example, Eleanor Westney concluded, after examining the processes of several instances of Meiji modern institution-building (police, postal service, and so on), that the influence of the Tokugawa institutional heritage on the formation of contemporary institutional patterns was comparatively weak. She then maintained that the most important factor in determining the organizational shape of these institutions was the dynamic interference of various foreign organizational models.[26] Her empirical examination of specific case studies is a welcome contribution to a discussion of this complex issue of cultural influence. But what Westney did not mention in her analysis of Tokugawa cultural influence in the Meiji period was the shape that this influence assumed in the minds of the individual Meiji Japanese who initiated these changes: this is the aspect I wish to underscore here. I am not referring only to the identifiable parallels in the patterns of institutions between modern Japan and Tokugawa society. Rather, I am focusing here on the attitudes of those men who carried out these changes, as well as the cultural resources they were able to use for prescribing their own formula for social change.

What we usually perceive as a vaguely defined notion of "Japanese tradition" is actually a double-edged set of concepts, a stock of various cultural idioms that can be put into service either for purposes of individual self-expression or, contrariwise, for inducing people to adopt conformist attitudes and behaviors. From time to time, the citizens of modern Japan will find this rich reserve of symbolic idioms a useful cultural resource, for better or for worse, in the future as they have in the past.

Epilogue: Honor
and Identity

The most impressive theme of honor emerging from the samurai's words and deeds was embodied in their struggle to uphold a profound sense of individuality even in the most adverse situations. The magnetic quality of the samurai culture derived its vitality from the inner depth of this sentiment of honor.

Such an elitist honor culture is sufficiently unusual in the contemporary world that most of us cannot imagine the tight and intricate connections between honor, dignity, and individuality in the warrior society of premodern Japan. In the elitist honor culture of that period there flourished the strong belief that the ultimate responsibility for the different requirements of social honor creating an honorific identity belonged not to the society as a whole but to each member of that society. This conviction formed the vital core of the sentiments that inspired what I call "honorific individualism." This individualism did not imply that a particular samurai would always rebel against the limitations imposed by institutional requirements and designated roles. Rather, "honorific individualism" meant that such a man would always take these boundaries seriously, even though the ultimate decision about whether or not to conform would be his own and no other's. The honorable samurai's behavioral options included generous self-sacrifice, stoic perseverance, and responsible consistency. But he could also choose a course of vigorous verbal confrontation and physical assertiveness involving public fighting, and even open rebellion. When this last course of action was freely chosen (or perceived to be) by a conscious and determined mind it was regarded by the surrounding society as a testimony to the warrior's personal honor. At this deepest level of self-realization, honor and individuality were intimately connected, and the man's dignity and warrior identity were established both socially and personally.

Honor can be experienced as a strong emotion, while simultaneously serving as an ideological device. In Chapter 1, I employed a neglected concept of Thomas Hobbes's as a starting point to observe that the notion of honor is by nature closely related to the problem of trust in its temporal dimension. It is at this point that issues of internal consistency and identity entered the discussion. In order to construct a politically stable hierarchy of vassalage, medieval Japanese society resorted to the political and ideological utilization of honor as a means of enhancing the vassals' predictability; masters would understandably define absolute loyalty as the most meritorious type of action, in order to guarantee the reliability of their subordinate samurai.

We should not, however, overlook the personal and internal operations of sentiments of honor, which were at work alongside its social and ideological functions. At the personal level, the samurai experienced honor as a forceful emotion, but at the same time he drew upon it as an internal resource that helped him to maintain his sense of personal continuity and dignity during periods of strife and adversity. Over the course of his life, he might have had to select from a number of different kinds of social behavioral options. In the competitive warrior society of medieval Japan, every political decision that a samurai would make regarding specific actions related to forming or leaving an alliance would be highly context-dependent; the samurai had to cope with the random variables of political, military, and social situations in constant flux. But he could psychologically legitimate his various decisions as internally meaningful and honorable through the use of the idioms of honor (that is, the man's pride would not allow him to do otherwise). The actual manifestations of the samurai honor culture hinged upon the dynamic interaction of these social and personal uses of honor. It is important to note the fluidity and unpredictability of the human actions that were comprehended within the usage of honor.

The samurai honor culture presents a challenge to our powers of historical imagination. From a modern perspective, we tend to assume that honor is an entity external to the self, connected to archaic hierarchical orders and values, and therefore a comparatively unimportant or barren concept, whereas dignity or individuality is an essential component of the self, related to an *imagined* notion of pure or true selfhood. As a result, it is the latter set of values that is crucial to one's identity. From the viewpoint of modernity, "individuality" is defined as the expression of the "true self." By contrast, a sense of selfhood recurrently emerged in the Japanese honor culture through a process of bringing a socially embedded sense of self (that is, the self considered from an intersubjective viewpoint) and a more subjective sense of self (the self viewed from its own internal perspective) into *proximity*. It is not the separation of these two perspectives but their *proximity* that is taken for granted in Japan.[1] The resulting normative implication following from this latter style of identity perception is that it takes roles and expectations in intersubjective relationships more seriously, not simply as means to achieve various ends, but as an essential component of self-fulfillment.

This process of identity formation through proximity is by no means a monopoly of the Japanese honor culture. The essentials of identity formation are to some extent—and indeed to an important extent—linked to this process of approximation in all societies. The curious part of the contemporary Western myth of the self is that we all know, on a very simple yet profound emotional level, that our true identity cannot be separated from our social relationships. Intuitively, we recognize that we "experience" happiness when we are properly connected to others and valued by them. At the same time, we search—sometimes at great emotional or financial cost—for the grail of the "true self."

The current polarization of honor and individuality is not necessarily a cultural characteristic inherent to the West, but it is in part a significant ideological by-product of the post-medieval era. Speaking of this historical transition, Peter Berger has written, "The age that saw the decline of honor also saw the rise of new moralities and of a new humanism, and most specifically a historically unprecedented concern for the dignity and the rights of the individual."[2] Political liberalism, Enlightenment humanism, bourgeoisie hegemony in Western culture, and the Romantic celebration of private personhood in arts and literature all contributed in various ways to the understanding that self-discovery lies in the process of liberating the genuine self from socially prescribed roles. The concept of honor gradually became associated with an old-fashioned hierarchical order, an empty structural shell that imposed undesirable and artificial institutional roles on captive individuals. Of course, this cultural change took place slowly over time, the process of transition was gradual, and, consequently, its precise course is difficult to pinpoint. Because honor has lost its connection with a personal sense of individuality and dignity, it now seems like a dated and superficial concept in modern society.

A scholar who mistakenly attributes universal validity to the contemporary Western devaluation of honor will be liable to conceptual pitfalls when attempting to decode the Japanese honor culture. Honorific individualism in Japan does not presuppose a self-consciousness isolated from the social relationships that give rise to it. This was quite possibly the fundamental methodological flaw in Ruth Benedict's iconographic description of Japanese society, *The Chrysanthemum and the Sword*. It was this book that first proposed the contrast between a supposedly "shame-based" Japanese culture and a Western culture based on guilt. The book was written during World War II with the explicit intention of understanding "the most alien enemy the United States ever fought."[3] Benedict never visited Japan and never learned its language. In spite of those limitations, however, the book had a powerful impact. The impressive force of this book lies largely in Benedict's considerable literary talent, which intuitively selected and expressed some key observations in a penetrating manner. This classic work might perhaps be better read less as an objective report on Japanese society than as a mirror of the author's underlying definition of "self"—that is, how a scholar born and educated in the West unconsciously projected her culturally constructed notion of self onto the Japanese.

Benedict's picture of a shame-based culture portrayed the Japanese as somewhat passive and obsessed with a sense of obligation, as her preference for the term "shame" rather than "honor" indicates. Unfortunately, this portrait is stiff and one-dimensional. According to Benedict, the Japanese were conditioned by externally enforced obedience to social norms and duties, whereas Westerners were taught to develop an internalized sense of conscience in a culture based on guilt. "True shame cultures rely on external sanctions for good behavior, not as true guilt cultures do, on an internalized conviction of sin."[4] To be sure, Benedict did not entirely miss the point that a shame-based culture has an internal dimension; she seems to recognize that eventually a process of internalization becomes operative within individuals in a shame culture. In addition, she acknowledged that the Japanese also sometimes react to a misdeed with strong feelings of personal guilt. Yet the most pressing concern at the bottom of her inquiries was a need to define the basic difference between the Japanese and "us"; she was concerned with "the us / not-us motif," as Clifford Geertz has labeled it.[5] Benedict's basic strategy was to emphasize the difference between the two societies by using a "shame / external versus guilt / internal" dichotomy.

This approach, which emphasizes cultural dichotomies, is very different from a more recently developed, complex, and dynamic view of honor stemming from the research of specialists in Mediterranean anthropology. In their studies, the interaction between the external and the internal dimensions of honor is the starting point of the argument.[6] When one compares these anthropologists' work with Benedict's, one finds oneself asking how a gifted scholar who was capable of developing some acute and penetrating insights into a society she had never visited could at the same time be so oblivious to the inner dynamics of the Japanese honor culture. That Benedict never had access to Japanese living in their homeland may provide a partial explanation of her limitations.[7] Her unsystematic use of assorted materials—in particular, her appropriation of historical materials such as legends and samurai stories without regard to their historical contexts—prevented her from seeing the manifold aspects of the Japanese honor culture. Her limitations were not confined simply to issues of access and method, however. The basic reason Benedict could not understand the dynamic fusion of individuality and honor lies, in my opinion, in her own unexamined assumptions regarding the constitution of human identity.

Because of this set of assumptions, Benedict automatically considered that her respondents' references to duties and responsibilities concerned matters external to the self. When she was confronted with less passive, formal, or rigidly loyal aspects of the Japanese mentality, she chose to regard them as expressions of a "contradictory character." The Japanese can be described, she wrote, as "the most fantastic series of 'but also's' ever used for any nation of the world."[8] "The Japanese are, to the highest degree, both aggressive and unaggressive, both militaristic and aesthetic. . . ."[9] "Both the sword and the chrysanthemum are a part of the picture."[10] Benedict thought that their shame-based culture made such "contradictions"—note that the validity of this characterization is taken for granted—possible. In the penultimate chapter of her book, which contained the weakest argumentation in the entire monograph, she wrote, "The contradictions in Japanese male behavior which are so conspicuous to Westerners are made possible by the discontinuity of their upbringing. . . . Their early childhood has given them assertiveness . . . The later restraints have been imposed in the name of solidarity with their fellows, and the obligations are reciprocal."[11] The Japanese were destined to be internally contradictory, she concluded, and that was the force of their cultural pattern.

There is a good reason Japanese scholars perceive Benedict's discussion of shame-based cultures as having pejorative implications. These implications emerge when we examine her use of the external / internal dichotomy in the specific context of her "contradictory character" argument. In Benedict's defense, I wish to observe that she was aware of the necessity of a relativistic view of culture, at least in her own terms.[12] As a cultural anthropologist, she attempted to ascribe "a contradictory character" to the Japanese as a nation, on the basis of the intrinsic logic of discrete cultural patterns as distinct from the behavioral pathology of individuals. She did restrain herself from postulating the ethical superiority of guilt-based to shame-based cultures. If I were to summarize the implicit message of *The Chrysanthemum and the Sword* in my own words, it would be as follows: "Yes, the Japanese behave very strangely. But I will tell you that there are good reasons for their actions, and they are not violating the ethical standards or the logic of their own culture."

Ruth Benedict made an admirable attempt to be objective and to distance herself from her own cultural prejudices, given the pressures of wartime propaganda. Regrettably, she managed to step outside her own culture with only one foot, so to speak. Unaware of the fact that she had only partially succeeded in bridging the cultural gap between Japan and the United States, she was understandably puzzled by what she regarded as the internal inconsistencies of the character of Japanese individuals.

The problem that confronted Benedict can be simply and concisely stated. In any culture, people inevitably behave erratically, irrationally, or unpredictably from time to time. Human beings are not robots, ineluctably programmed to follow mathematical laws of logic—far from it. The internal consistency of a given individual cannot be assumed *a priori*, though we might like to believe otherwise. The notion of selfhood is always socially constructed in relation to the particular experiences and circumstances of the individual. Benedict's view of the self greatly differs from the Japanese model she was trying to analyze. The difference revolves around the rational interpretation of commonplace, partly irrational behavior.

Benedict tacitly assumes a distinction between a core self and a comparatively superficial, interactive part of the self. The core self lies at the heart of the person's self-identification, whereas the interactive part of the self is considered to function in a more instrumental fashion, as the changing aspects of personality that we present to others in response to the varying interactions we have with them. There is no direct observational evidence for this distinction between inner self and outer persona. However, because Benedict grew up with this notion, she unconsciously does a form of internal bookkeeping in which every encounter is entered in two separate ledgers. One dimension of the exchange is assigned to the interaction at hand, and another dimension to the core self, the inner essence of the person who somehow functions as a conductor, orchestrating the details of the interaction.

In contrast to Benedict's unstated assumption of a binary self, the Japanese are not conditioned by their culture to feel the necessity of such an (from their perspective) arbitrary split. Rather, the self is seen as one pole of a self-other interaction. Consequently, there is little need to postulate a division within this pole between a relatively unchanging core and a comparatively mutable exterior. Of course, there is a certain degree of consistency and continuity in the pattern of a given individual's behavior, usually termed the "style" or the "personality" of the individual (jibun rashisa), as well as an identity or similarity in the goals that an individual strives after, at least over a certain period of time. The acceptance of a self-other interaction also does not imply that the Japanese were devoid of tensions between the individual and the social dimensions of personhood. Again, the Japanese model is not different from a general description in any culture of an individual as interacting variously in different surroundings. The process of bringing a socially embedded sense of self and a more subjective sense of self into *proximity* is not easy, and often agonizing in any culture. The difference in the Japanese situation has to do with the stronger presence of a cultural resource that helps the Japanese to construct a resilient individuality through an explicit *sensitizing* of a socially embedded sense of self.

Each individual, whatever culture he or she grows up in, is conditioned to develop a sense of selfhood mainly through socializing with others. During this process, the social becomes embedded as a constituent of personal identity through the individuals' interpretations of daily social experiences. In this book I have shown that the samurai culture developed and flourished in parallel to the continuous social and political revisions of their organizations. The individual samurai constructed their self-image while living in these power-dominated organizations and participating in their collective cultural production. In this sense, the dynamics of hegemonic politics and the individual processes of the formation of a self-identity are mutually intertwined. Any attempt to make a clean theoretical separation between the two can only have limited applicability, and is likely to present an oversimplified picture. Indeed, we have to be careful not to fall into the trap of a clinical separation of the individual and the social, especially when we are tempted to assign causal connections between the two.

As a case in point, we cannot conclude that the Japanese style of identity formation is *caused* by the honor culture. However, the cultural theme of honor and shame—which explicitly links the self and society— would tend to sensitize individuals to the context-dependent nature of their human existence. In contrast, if the Western observer of Japanese culture is operating uncritically from a static notion of the "true self" as the firm basis of "individuality," either questioning this conception of identity or observing those who do not share it will usually trigger an anxious compulsion to define the world and the self as stable and predictable. The result of this commonplace, emotionally charged reaction is the Westerner's projection of an image of "inscrutability" on the Japanese by defining their firmness as externally bounded while attributing their spontaneity and individuality to "contradiction."

Our inquiries into the samurai culture of honor have required the careful peeling off of several layers of our modern conceptions of honor and the individual. Our view of honor has become so "civilized" that most of us cannot see how it can coexist with violence. Our view of the samurai has been so strongly shaped by an emphasis on the virtue of loyalty that we often forget the history in which acts of betrayal were often motivated by deep convictions of honor. Our way of seeing honor is so firmly defined by social categories, that is, by a given hierarchy of public evaluation, that we cannot easily understand how it can also be simultaneously rooted in an individual's innermost being. And our notion of individuality has become so privatized that it is difficult to imagine the samurai's sense of individuality as wedded to an equally strong sense of sovereign power. At the very end of this series of explorations, of reconstituting our powers of historical imagination, we have arrived at the question of our own understanding of modern personal identity.

Finally, I propose that we consider the Japanese honor culture's expressions of individuality not simply as the result of cultural patterns of thought that distinguish between *"others"* and *"us,"* but as revealing something of the intrinsic nature of the processes of identity formation that we all share. I have attempted to explore the samurai's cultural legacy to Japan, using "honor" as a telescopic instrument of sociological discovery. But the world of honor is also a spectroscopic device that probes and analyzes our own notion of self and society.

Notes
Index

Notes

Introduction

1. This book has to do with the samurai as political actors, *not* with their role in the historical development of the martial arts. The so-called samurai swordsmanship, developed by some experts in the martial arts primarily from the seventeenth century onward, was an idiosyncratic spiritual and cultural refinement of physical skill, largely independent of the crude realities of the battlefield. This swordsmanship, which absorbed the idioms and spirituality of Zen Buddhism, is an intriguing aspect of samurai culture that has received considerable attention from Western scholars. This book, however, focuses on the honor culture of the samurai as the source of their class identity, emerging from the combination of their two major social characteristics, which can be summed up by the adjective "military" and the noun "landlords." This focus is sufficiently wide in scope to necessitate the exclusion of related topics such as martial arts.

2. Bellah's response to the critique of the Japanese political scientist Maruyama Masao, in the Introduction to the paperback edition of *Tokugawa Religion* (New York: The Free Press, 1985), p. xviii.

1. Honor, State Formation, and Social Theories

1. Jonathan D. Spence, *The Search for Modern China* (New York: Norton, 1990), pp. 40–45.

2. Ki-baik Lee, *A New History of Korea* (Cambridge, Mass.: Harvard University Press, 1984), p. 175; JaHyun Kim Haboush, "The Confucianization of Korean Society," in Gilbert Rozman, ed., *The East Asian Region: Confucian Heri-*

tage and Its Modern Adaptation (Princeton: Princeton University Press, 1991), pp. 84–110.

3. Albert O. Hirschman, *The Passions and the Interests* (Princeton: Princeton University Press, 1977). See also Charles Taylor, *Sources of the Self: The Making of the Modern Identity* (Cambridge, Mass.: Harvard University Press, 1989), p. 214; J. G. A. Pocock, *Virtue, Commerce, and History* (Cambridge: Cambridge University Press, 1985), and *The Machiavellian Moment: Florentine Political Thought and the Atlantic Republican Tradition* (Princeton: Princeton University Press, 1975).

4. Mariko Tamanoi, "Shame, Family, and State in Catalonia and Japan," in D. Gilmore, ed., *Honor and Shame and the Unity of the Mediterranean* (Washington, D.C.: The American Anthropological Association, 1987).

5. Ruth Benedict, *The Chrysanthemum and the Sword* (New York: Meridian, 1974, original edition 1946).

6. Takeo Doi, *The Anatomy of Dependence*, trans. J. Bester (Tokyo: Kōdansha, 1973), p. 48.

7. For example, see the following works of Japanese scholars regarding honor and shame in Japanese culture: Sakuta Keiichi, *Haji no bunka saikō* (Tokyo: Chikuma shobō, 1967); Kaida Yūji, *Nihon jin no ishiki kōzō* (Tokyo: Kōdansha, 1970); Doi, *The Anatomy*; Mori Mikisaburō, *Na to haji no bunka: Chūgokujin to nihonjin* (Tokyo: Kōdansha, 1971); Inoue Tadashi, *Sekentei no kōzō* (Tokyo: Nihon hōsō shuppan kyōkai, 1977); Tamanoi, "Shame, Family"; Sakisaka Hiroshi, *Haji no kōzō* (Tokyo: Kōdansha, 1982). See also a recent review of this topic in English: Millie R. Creighton, "Revisiting Shame and Guilt Cultures: A Forty-Year Pilgrimage," *Ethos* 18 (1990): 279–307.

8. Takie Sugiyama Lebra, *Japanese Patterns of Behavior* (Honolulu: University of Hawaii Press, 1976), p. 80.

9. Thomas Rohlen, *For Harmony and Strength* (Berkeley: University of California Press, 1974); Iwata Ryūshi, *Nihon teki keiei no hensei genri* (Tokyo: Bunshindō, 1977), and *Gendai nihon no keiei fūdo* (Tokyo: Nihon keizai shinbunsha, 1978).

10. Julian Pitt-Rivers, "Honor," in David L. Sills, ed., *International Encyclopedia of the Social Sciences,* vol. 6 (New York: The Macmillan Company and The Free Press, 1968), pp. 42–79. A massive theoretical and ethnographical literature has grown up around the concept of honor since it was reexamined by students of the Mediterranean in the late 1950s. See in particular J. G. Peristiany, ed., *Honour and Shame* (Chicago: University of Chicago Press, 1966); Julio Caro Baroja, "Honour and Shame: A Historical Account of Several Conflicts," trans. R. Johnson, in Peristiany, *Honor and Shame* (Chicago: University of Chicago Press, 1966); J. K. Campbell, *Honour, Family, and Patronage* (Oxford: Oxford University Press, 1964); John Davis, *People of the Mediterranean* (London: Routledge & Kegan Paul, 1977); Jane Schneider and Peter Schneider, *Culture and Political Economy in Western Sicily* (New York: Academic Press, 1976); David D. Gilmore, ed., *Honor and Shame and the Unity of the Mediterranean,*

a special publication of the American Anthropological Association 22 (Washington, D.C.: American Anthropological Association, 1987); Jane Schneider, "Of Vigilance and Virgins," *Ethnology* 10-1 (1971): 1–24; Lila Abu-Lughod, *Veiled Sentiments: Honor and Poetry in a Bedouin Society* (Berkeley: University of California Press, 1986); J. G. Peristiany and Julian Pitt-Rivers, eds., *Honor and Grace in Anthropology* (Cambridge: Cambridge University Press, 1992).

11. Anton Blok, *The Mafia of a Sicilian Village, 1860–1960* (New York: Harper & Row, 1974), p. 211.

12. Pierre Bourdieu, *Algeria 1960* (Cambridge: Cambridge University Press, 1979).

13. Pefkiot is the pseudonym for Herzfeld's fieldwork site, a village in the coastal lowlands of western Rhodes. Michael Herzfeld, "Honour and Shame: Problems in the Comparative Analysis of Moral Systems," *Man* 15 (1980): 348.

14. See also Jacob Black-Michaud, *Cohesive Force: Feud in the Mediterranean and the Middle East* (Oxford: Basil Blackwell, 1975); Bartolomé Bennassar, *The Spanish Character: Attitudes and Mentalities from the Sixteenth to the Nineteenth Century*, trans. Benjamin Keen (Berkeley: University of California Press, 1979).

15. Bertram Wyatt-Brown, *Southern Honor* (New York: Oxford University Press, 1982).

16. Harold J. Berman, *Law and Revolution: The Formation of the Western Legal Tradition* (Cambridge, Mass.: Harvard University Press, 1983), p. 55.

17. Mervyn James, "English Politics and the Concept of Honour, 1485–1642," in *Society, Politics, and Culture: Studies in Early Modern England* (Cambridge: Cambridge University Press, 1978), pp. 308–415.

18. Orlando Patterson, *Slavery and Social Death* (Cambridge, Mass.: Harvard University Press, 1982), p. 79.

19. Davis, *People of the Mediterranean*, p. 98.

20. Pitt-Rivers, "Honor and Social Status," in *Honor and Shame*, p. 39.

21. In this sense, I use *honor* in this book as a technical term for purposes of analysis; as a result, it does not correspond to a particular specific noun in Japanese. The reader should note that the same strategy is also employed by anthropologists who study specific Mediterranean cultures in which various terms are used to express honorific sentiments by people in different regions, classes, genders, and social contexts.

22. See, for example, Peristiany's "Introduction" and Pitt-Rivers's "Honor and Social Status," in *Honor and Shame*; Inoue, *Sekentei no kōzō*; Sakisaka, *Haji no kōzō*. Regarding Aristotle's formulation of honor and dignity, see Stephen A. White, *Sovereign Virtue: Aristotle on the Relationship between Happiness and Prosperity* (Stanford: Stanford University Press, 1992), pp. 247–271.

23. Bernard Williams, *Shame and Necessity* (Berkeley: University of California Press, 1993), p. 95.

24. Thomas Hobbes, *Leviathan* (Oxford: Clarendon Press, 1952), p. 150.

25. Thomas Hobbes, "Philosophical Rudiments concerning Government and

Society," in B. William Molesworth, ed., *The English Works of Thomas Hobbes,*
vol II (London: John Bohon, 1966), p. 160.

26. Hobbes, *Leviathan,* p. 185.

27. Max Weber, *The Agrarian Sociology of Ancient Civilizations* (London:
New Left Books, 1976), p. 276.

28. Max Weber, *Economy and Society* (Berkeley: University of California
Press, 1978), p. 1068.

29. Ibid., p. 1074.

30. Ibid., p. 1069.

31. Ibid., p. 1105.

32. Patterson, *Slavery,* p. 80.

33. Hobbes, *Leviathan,* p. 186. The issue of trust has received considerable
attention in recent years in sociological literature. See in particular Allan Silver,
"'Trust' in Social and Political Theory," in Gerald Suttles and Mayer Zald, eds.,
The Challenge of Social Control: Citizenship and Institution Building in Modern Society (Norwood, N.J.: Ablex, 1985); Niklas Luhmann, *Trust and Power*
(Chichester: Wiley, 1979); Arthur L. Stinchcombe, "Norms of Exchange," in
Stinchcombe, *Stratification and Organization* (Cambridge: Cambridge University Press, 1986), pp. 231–267; Bernard Barber, *The Logic and Limits of Trust*
(New Brunswick: Rutgers University Press, 1983); Lynne G. Zucker, "Production of Trust: Institutional Sources of Economic Structure, 1840–1920," in Barry
M. Staw and L. L. Cummings, eds., *Research in Organizational Behavior* 8
(Greenwich: JAI, 1986): 53–111; James Coleman, "Relations of Trust," in *Foundations of Social Theory* (Cambridge, Mass.: Harvard University Press, 1990),
pp. 91–116.

34. Weber, *Economy and Society,* p. 932.

35. See, for example, Charles Tilly, ed., *The Formation of National States
in Western Europe* (Princeton: Princeton University Press, 1975); Charles Tilly,
Coercion, Capital, and European States, A.D. 990–1990 (Cambridge: Basil
Blackwell, 1990); Michael Mann, "The Autonomous Power of the State: Its Origins, Mechanisms, and Results," *Archives européenes de sociologie* 25 (1984);
Michael Mann, *The Sources of Social Power I* (Cambridge: Cambridge University Press, 1986); Michael Mann, *State, War, and Capitalism* (Oxford: Basil
Blackwell, 1988); Anthony Giddens, *The Nation-State and Violence* (Berkeley:
University of California Press, 1985); Samuel E. Finer, "State- and Nation-Building in Europe: The Role of the Military," in *The Formation of National
States in Western Europe,* pp. 84–163; Gianfranco Poggi, *The Development of
the Modern State: A Sociological Introduction* (Stanford: Stanford University
Press, 1978); Perry Anderson, *Lineages of the Absolutist States* (London: New
Left Books, 1974); Douglass C. North, *Structure and Change in Economic History* (New York: Norton, 1981); Brian M. Downing, *The Military Revolution
and Political Change: Origins of Democracy and Autocracy in Early Modern
Europe* (Princeton: Princeton University Press, 1992).

36. Norbert Elias, *The Civilizing Process,* vol. 1: *The History of Manners,*

trans. Edmund Jephcott (New York: Urizen Books, 1978), and *The Civilizing Process*, vol. 2: *Power and Civility*, trans. Edmund Jephcott (Oxford: Basil Blackwell, 1982), both originally published in 1939; *The Court Society*, trans. Edmund Jephcott (Oxford: Basil Blackwell, 1983), originally published in 1969.

37. See, for example, Philip Corrigan and Derek Sayer, *The Great Arch: English State Formation as Cultural Revolution* (Oxford: Basil Blackwell, 1985).

38. N. Abercrombie, S. Hill, and B. S. Turner, *The Dominant Ideology Thesis* (London: George Allen & Unwin, 1980).

39. Charles Tilly, "War Making and State Making as Organized Crime," in P. Evans, Dietrich Rueschemeyer, and Theda Skocpol, eds., *Bringing the State Back In* (Cambridge: Cambridge University Press, 1985), pp. 69–191.

40. Berman, *Law and Revolution*, pp. 295–315.

41. Otto Hintze, "Wesen und Verbreitung des Feudalismus," *Staat und Verfassung: Gesammelte Abhandlungen zur allgemeinen Verfassungsgeschichte*, ed. Fritz Hartung (Leipzig: Koehler & Amelang, 1941).

42. Thomas Bisson, "The Military Origins of Medieval Representation," *American Historical Review* 71 (1966): 1199–1218. Also, regarding the influence of collegial aspects of medieval social institutions, see Randall Collins, *Conflict Sociology* (New York: Academic Press, 1975), pp. 393–399.

43. Weber, *Economy and Society*, p. 1261.

44. Brian M. Downing, *The Military Revolution and Political Change: Origins of Democracy and Autocracy in Early Modern Europe* (Princeton: Princeton University Press, 1992).

45. Some Japanese legal historians who carried out extensive research of Japanese and Germanic feudal legal and political systems have also presented a viewpoint of appreciative evaluation of the medieval Japanese cultural and ideological tradition of social autonomy. For example, Mizubayashi Takeshi, "Kinsei no hō to kokusei kenkyū josetsu," *Kokka gakkai zasshi*, vols. 90, 91, 92, 94, 95 (1977–1982); and Ishii Shirō, *Nohon jin no kokka seikatsu* (Tokyo: University of Tokyo Press, 1986).

46. Peasant property rights and reciprocity with their feudal lords are often considered the wellspring of medieval European constitutionalism.

47. See, for example, Giddens, *The Nation-State and Violence*; Otto Hintze, "Military Organization and State Organization," in *The Historical Essays of Otto Hintze*, ed. F. Gilbert (New York: Oxford University Press, 1975), pp. 178–215. See also note 35 for relevant works.

48. John Brewer, *The Sinews of Power: War, Money, and the English State, 1688–1783* (New York: Alfred A. Knopf, 1989).

49. Norbert Elias, *The Society of Individuals*, trans. Edmund Jephcott (Oxford: Basil Blackwell, 1991).

50. Anthony Giddens, *Central Problems in Social Theory: Action, Structure, and Contradiction in Social Analysis* (Berkeley: University of California Press, 1979).

51. It is not coincidental that Bourdieu, whose earlier major work was based

upon fieldwork in a highly honor-centered culture in Algeria, eventually developed an influential theory of practice built around the key concept of "habitus."

52. Giddens, *Central Problems,* p. 69.

53. Ibid.

54. Ibid., p. 71.

55. William H. Sewell, Jr., "A Theory of Structure: Duality, Agency, and Transformation," *American Journal of Sociology* 98–1 (July 1992): 1–29.

2. The Coming of the Samurai

1. The term *saburai* was also used for local military men organized under the provincial government offices *(kokuga)* who served governors as the "men of bows and arrows." *Tsuwamono* and *mononofu* were older terms. These terms—*mononofu, tsuwamono, bushi,* and *samurai*—had somewhat different meanings in the early stage of Japanese history, but they eventually converged to describe the same group of people. *Bushi* is now most commonly used in historical literature, whereas *tsuwamono* and *mononofu* are considered classical terms; *bu* means "military" (as opposed to *bun,* which means "literary"), and *shi* indicates the lower and middle nobility. *Bushi* eventually became a general term for military men, but *samurai* was also used interchangeably with it. Considering the popularization of the term *samurai* over *bushi* in the West, I chose the term *samurai* for this book.

2. Satō Shin'ichi, *Nanboku chō no dōran: Nihon no rekishi,* vol. 9 (Tokyo: Chūō kōronsha, 1965), p. 193.

3. See, for example, Takeuchi Rizō, ed., *Kodai tennōsei to shakai kōzō* (Tokyo: Hazekura shobō, 1980), p. 188.

4. Originally, the term *i,* or barbarians, referred to the people of the northern regions of Japan, especially the rebellious *emishi* tribe.

5. Sakurai Shōtarō, *Meiyo to chijoku* (Tokyo: Hōsei University Press, 1971), p. 4.

6. Two such poems written by Ōtomo no Yakamachi are recorded in *Manyōshū.*

7. For a detailed discussion of present scholarly debates on the origins and nature of the early samurai in Japan, see Saki Yukihiko's extensive and enlightening review of Japanese historians' works: *Bushidan Kenkyū no Ayumi,* vols. 1–2 (Tokyo: Shinjinbutsu ōraisha, 1988).

8. To be more precise, *ritsu* as legal or penal codes, *ryō* as administrative codes.

9. *Shiki* is a term "which originally meant 'office' but had come to mean any legally cognizable interest in real estate which was the result of a private transaction . . . All shiki involved specific rights and duties respecting the estate," according to Cornelius Kiley, in "Estate and Property in the Late Heian Period," in John W. Hall and Jeffrey P. Mass, eds., *Medieval Japan* (Stanford: Stanford University Press, 1974), p. 111.

10. Elizabeth Sato, "The Early Development of the Shōen," in *Medieval Japan*, p. 107.

11. Noda Reishi, *Ritsuryō kokka no gunjisei* (Tokyo: Yoshikawa kōbunkan, 1989).

12. William Wayne Farris, *Heavenly Warriors: The Evolution of Japan's Military, 500–1300* (Cambridge, Mass.: Harvard University Press, 1992); Karl F. Friday, *Hired Swords: The Rise of Private Warrior Power in Early Japan* (Stanford: Stanford University Press, 1992).

13. Farris, *Heavenly Warriors*, p. 7.

14. Maurice Keen, *Chivalry* (New Haven: Yale University Press, 1984), p. 1.

15. Ibid., p. 2.

16. Neil McMullin, "On Placating the Gods and Pacifying the Populace: The Case of the Gion Goryo Cult," *History of Religions* 27 (1988): 272–274. The pollution belief was shared by samurai and peasants alike, but it was the court aristocracy of the mid-Heian period that developed the most complicated system of impurity taboos. See Chapter 4 for more details.

17. Sugiyama Haruyasu, *Nihon hōshi gairon* (Tokyo: Seibundo, 1984), p. 124.

18. Yoshie Akio, *Rekishi no akebono kara dentō shakai no seijuku e: Nihon no Tsūshi*, vol. 1 (Tokyo: Yamakawa shuppansha, 1986), p. 176.

19. Takahashi Masaaki, "Bushi no hassei to sono seikaku," *Rekishi kōron* 2–7 (1976). See also Takahashi Masaaki, "Kiba to suigun," in Toda Yoshimi, ed., *Nohon shi chūsei* 1 (Tokyo: Yūhikaku, 1978).

20. Ōishi Naomasa, "Tōgoku, Tōhoku no jiritsu to nihon koku," in *Nihon no shakaishi*, vol. 1: *Rettō naigai no kōtsū to kokka* (Tokyo: Iwanami shoten, 1987), pp. 228–256.

21. Ishii Susumu, *Nihon no Rekishi 12: Chūsei bushidan* (Tokyo: Shōgakukan, 1974), p. 66.

22. Chiba Tokuji, *Tatakai no genzō: Minzoku to shite no bushidō* (Tokyo: Heibonsha, 1991). See also Gomi Fumihiko, *Bushi to bunshi no chūseishi* (Tokyo: University of Tokyo Press, 1992), pp. 3–40; Irumada Nobuo, "Shugo jitōsei to Kamakura bakufu," in *Kōza nihon rekishi: Chūsei 1* (Tokyo: University of Tokyo Press, 1984).

23. This was the predominant view of prominent prewar Japanese scholars. See the review of literature in Torao Toshiya, *Ritsuryō kokka to Ezo* (Tokyo: Hyōron sha, 1975), pp. 26–37.

24. Ibid., pp. 26–37. The Chinese characters for *emishi* are sometimes pronounced *ezo*. *Ezo*, however, is a term that appears only after the mid-Heian period.

25. Takeuchi Rizō, "Yamato Chōtei to Tōgoku no uma," in Takeuchi Rizō, ed., *Kodai tennōsei to shakai kōzō* (Tokyo: Hazekura shobō, 1980), pp. 9–23. Also see Ōishi, *Tōgoku*, pp. 228–256.

26. The eastern technique for iron production was different from that in the western region in that it could use the iron sand that was available locally.

Fukuda Toyohiko, "Kodai nihon no tetsu to shakai," in Tōkyō kōgyō daigaku seitetsushi kenkyūkai, ed., *Kodai nihon no tetsu to shakai* (Tokyo: Heibonsha, 1982); Fukuda Toyohiko, "Nihon kodai tetsu seisan no shoyōso," *Nihonshi ken-kyū* 280 (December 1985): 29–51. Also see Ōishi, *Tōgoku*, pp. 234–236.

27. Muraoka Kaoru, "Hasseiki matsu 'seii' saku no saikentō," in Takeuchi Rizō, ed., *Kodai tennōsei to shakai kōzō* (Tokyo: Hazekura shobō, 1980), pp. 123–144.

28. Yoshie, *Rekishi no*, pp. 175–176.

29. A similar story concerning monkey gods and a brave hunter appeared in other contemporaneous literature—for example, see *Ujishūi monogatari*, vol. 10, no. 6, in *Nihon koten bungaku taikei* 27 (Tokyo: Iwanami shoten, 1960), pp. 288–294. The story has been analyzed by Toda Yoshimi, "Shoki chūsei bushi no shokunō to shoeki," *Nihon no shakaishi 4 futan to zōyo* (Tokyo: Iwanami shoten, 1986), pp. 264–265. Regarding the analysis of the story in *Konjaku monogatari*, see Irumada Nobuo, "Bumin kōhei to zaichi shakai," in *Nihon no shakaishi*, vol. 5: *Saiban to Kihan* (Tokyo: Iwanami shoten, 1986), pp. 167–208.

30. Mabuchi Kazuo, "Kaisetsu," in *Nihon koten bungaku zenshū: Konjaku monogatari shū* 1 (Tokyo: Shōgakukan, 1971), pp. 23–31.

31. A summary translation from the original text of "Hida no kuni sarukami ikenie o todomuru koto," in *Konjaku monogatari*, vol. 26, no. 8, in the edition of *Nihon bungaku zenshū: Konjaku monogatari shū* 3 (Tokyo: Shōgakukan, 1974), pp. 552–568.

32. Irumada, "Bumin kōhei," p. 182.

33. *Konjaku*, vol. 26, no. 7, in *Nihon bungaku zenshū* 3, pp. 545–551.

34. *Konjaku*, vol. 27, no. 18, in *Nihon bungaku zenshū* 4, pp. 71–73.

35. *Shōmonki*, vol 2, ed. Kajiwara Masaaki, Tōyōbunko edition (Tokyo: Heibonsha, 1976), p. 154.

36. From "Owarikoku gunji hyakushō tō ge," a document of the second year of Eien (988), reprinted in *Heian ibun*, vol. 2, no. 339, Takeuchi Rizō, ed. (Tokyo: Tokyōdō, 1964), p. 473.

37. See Toda Yoshimi, "Shoki chūsei bushi no shokunō to shoeki," *Nihon no shakaishi*, vol 4: *Futan to zōyo* (Tokyo: Iwanami shoten, 1986), pp. 269–270.

38. Hotate Michihisa, "Ōbukuro no nazo o toku," in *Chūsei no ai to reizoku* (Tokyo: Heibonsha, 1986).

39. "Obusuma Saburō ekotoba," in *Nihon emakimono zenshū*, vol. 18 (Tokyo: Kadokawa shoten, 1968), p. 47.

40. Umezu Jiro, "Kaisetsu," in *Nihon emakimono zenshū*, p. 5.

41. Sasayama Haruo, *Kodai kokka to guntai* (Tokyo: Chūō kōronsha, 1985), pp. 150–196.

42. "Sandai jitsuroku," in the entry of the Eleventh Month, 16th, the third year of Jōkan, Takeda Yūkichi and Satō Kenzō, eds., *Kundoku Sandai jitsuroku* (Tokyo: Rinsen shobō, 1986), p. 148.

43. Toda Yoshimi, "Chūsei seiritsuki no kokka to nōmin," in *Shoki chūsei shakaishi no kenkyū* (Tokyo: University of Tokyo Press, 1991), pp. 21–36. Also

see Ishii Susumu, *Nihon no Rekishi: Chūsei bushidan* 12 (Tokyo: Shōgakukan, 1974); Kawane Yoshiyasu, *Chūsei hōkensei seiritsuron* (Tokyo: University of Tokyo Press, 1971), pp. 78–93.

44. According to Toda Yoshimi's analysis of an official document *(kanpu)* written in 946. See his analysis "Kokuga gunsei no keisei katei," *Shoki chūsei shakaishi no kenkyū* (Tokyo: University of Tokyo Press), pp. 120–121.

45. Regarding the organization of the armies in the *kokuga,* see Ishii Susumu, *Kamakura bushi no jitsuzō* (Tokyo: Heibonsha, 1987), pp. 2–57; Toda Yoshimi, "Kokugagun no keisei katei: Bushi hasseishi saikentō no ichishiten," in Nihonshi kenkyūkai shiryō kenkyūbukai, ed., *Chūsei no kenryoku to minshū* (Tokyo: Sōgen sha, 1970), pp. 109–150. Regarding the role of *kokuga* and the emergence of the samurai, see also Uwayokote Masataka, *Chūsei seiji kenkyū* (Tokyo: Hanawa shobō, 1970), pp. 39–72.

46. Toda, "Shoki chūsei bushi no shokunō," pp. 248–256.

47. The case of this shōen's history was introduced by Ishii Susumu, *Kamakura bushi no jitsuzō,* pp. 96–115.

48. Ishii Susumu, *Kamakura bakufu* (Tokyo: Chūō kōron sha, 1974), p. 45.

49. Ishii Susumu, *Chūsei bushidan,* pp. 109–112. Regarding sociological meanings of *ie* in general in Japanese history, see Murakami Yasusuke, Kumon Shunpei, and Satō Saizaburō, *Bunmei to shite no ie shakai* (Tokyo: Chūō kōronsha, 1979).

50. "Sanmi nyūdō geitō," in *Genpei seisuiki,* vol. 16 (Tokyo: Kokumin bunko kankōkai, 1911), p. 390.

51. *Konjaku,* vol. 25, no. 3, *Nihon bungaku zenshū,* vol. 3, pp. 442–446.

52. For example, see the story in *Konjaku,* vol. 26, no. 17, *Nihon bungaku zenshū,* vol. 3, pp. 605–614.

53. *Konjaku,* vol. 25, no. 5, *Nihon bungaku zenshū,* vol. 3, pp. 453–466.

54. "The First Man across the Uji River," trans. Helen Craig McCullough, *The Tale of the Heike* (Stanford: Stanford University Press, 1988), p. 287.The original text of *Heike monogatari* may have been compiled around the early thirteenth century and attributed to about a dozen authors in various documents of the period. Among these supposed authors, a retired nobleman, Shinano no zenji Yukinaga, is often considered the most likely candidate, as his name appears in *Tsurezuregusa.* Regarding the nature of *Heike monogatari* as a historical source, see the interesting study by Gomi Fumio, *Heike monogatari: Shi to setsuwa* (Tokyo: Heibonsha, 1987), which discusses the appropriate uses of this literary text for historical inquiries.

3. Vassalage and Honor

1. There has been a large amount of scholarly discussion regarding the nature and role of *tōryō*. An early and influential interpretation is represented by Ishimoda Shō's *Kodai makki seijishi josetsu* (Tokyo: Miraisha, 1966), which stresses the role of the *tōryō* as mediators in the formation of intraclass alliances. See

also Yasuda Motohisa's "Kodai makki ni okeru kantō bushidan no dōkō," in Yasuda, ed., *Nihon hōkensei seiritsu no shozentei* (Tokyo: Yoshikawa kōbunkan, 1960).

2. The date of the establishment of the Kamakura shogunate has provoked scholarly debates among Japanese historians. In 1192, Yoritomo was appointed *Seii tai shogun* (literally, "great general of conquering barbarians") by the imperial court. But prior to this appointment, he had established his offices (governmental and judicial) in Kamakura (1184). As early as 1183, the emperor's court delegated to Yoritomo the supervision of political matters in the eastern provinces. In 1185, the Kyoto court gave Yoritomo permission to appoint an estate steward *(jitō)* and a provincial constable *(shugo)*. Regarding the Kamakura shogunate, see the works of Jeffrey Mass, "The Emergence of the Kamakura *Bakufu*," in John W. Hall and Jeffrey Mass, eds., *Medieval Japan: Essays in Institutional History* (Stanford: Stanford University Press, 1988); *Lordship and Inheritance in Early Medieval Japan: A Study of the Kamakura Sōryō System* (Stanford: Stanford University Press, 1989); *The Kamakura Bakufu: A Study in Documents* (Stanford: Stanford University Press, 1976); and Jeffrey Mass, ed., *Court and Bakufu in Japan: Essays in Kamakura History* (New Haven: Yale University Press, 1982).

3. *Gokenin*, who originated as reclamation landlords, followed a pattern generally set in the eastern region of Japan. For the difference between *gokenin* in the eastern and western regions, see Gomi Fumio, "Shugo jitōsei no tenkai to bushidan," in *Iwanami kōza nihon no rekishi*, vol 5: *Chūsei* (Tokyo: Iwanami shoten, 1975), pp. 101–106.

4. Defined in Article 26 of *Goseibai shikimoku*, or the Kamakura shogunate code of 1232. *Goseibai shikimoku*, in *Nihon shisō taikei* 21: *Chūsei seiji shakai shisō jō* (Tokyo: Iwanami shoten, 1972), p. 23.

5. Recorded in *Azuma kagami*, vol. 1 (Tokyo: Meicho kankōkai, 1967), p. 236. An entry of the Eleventh Month, 21st, the third year of Bunchi (1187).

6. Recorded in *Azuma kagami*, p. 223, in an entry of the Eighth Month, 4th, the third year of Bunchi.

7. Ibid.

8. *Konjaku monogatari*, vol. 25, no. 13, *Nihon koten bungaku zenshū: Konjaku monogatari shū* 3 (Tokyo: Shōgakukan, 1974), p. 498.

9. For example, see *Heike monogatari*, vol. 8: "Hōjōji gassen"; vol. 9: "Kawara gassen" and "Kiso saigo," in *Nihon koten bungaku taikei* 33, *Heike monogatari ge* (Tokyo: Iwanami shoten, 1960).

10. *Azuma kagami*, vol. 1, p. 295, an entry of the Ninth Month, 6th, the fifth year of Bunchi (1189).

11. See Watsuji Tetsurō, *Nihon rinri shisō shi* (Tokyo: Iwanami shoten, 1952), especially chapter 2, "Bandō musha no narai."

12. See Ienaga Saburō, "Shujū dōtoku no ichi kōsatsu," *Shigaku zasshhi* 62–3 (1953): 1–20.

13. Such a distinction was suggested by Satō Shin'ichi. See his "Jidai to jin-

butsu: Chūsei," in Satō Shin'ichi and Ōsumi Kazuo, eds., *Nihon jinbutsushi taikei* (Tokyo: Asakura shoten, 1959). See also Kawai Masaharu, *Chūsei buke shakai no kenkyū* (Tokyo: Yoshikawa kōbunkan, 1978), pp. 81–87.

14. See, for example, Hashita Tokuhiko, "Kosen bōsen o megutte," in Chūsei no mado Dōjin, ed., *Ronshū Chūsei no mado* (Tokyo: Yoshikawa kōbunkan, 1977), pp. 111–141; Ishii Shirō, "Chūsei no hō to kokusei ni kansuru oboe-gaki," in his *Nohon jin no kokka seikatsu* (Tokyo: University of Tokyo Press, 1986), pp. 79–108; and Fujiki Hisashi's work on village armed forces in the late medieval period, *Sengoku no sahō, mura no funsō kaiketsu* (Tokyo: Heibon-sha, 1987).

15. Katsumata Shizuo, *Sengokuhō seiritsushiron* (Tokyo: University of Tokyo Press, 1979), pp. 247–276.

16. For a survey of the judicial systems of the Kamakura shogunate in general, see Ishii Ryōsuke, *Chūsei fudosan soshōhō no kenkyū* (Tokyo: Kōbundo shobō, 1938); Satō Shin'ichi, *Kamakura bakufu soshō seido no kenkyū* (Tokyo: Unebi shobō, 1943). See also Mass, *The Kamakura Bakufu.*

17. *Azuma kagami*, p. 15. It is doubtful that the shogunate was ever able to enforce such a code.

18. Ishii Ryōsuke, *Nihon fudōsan senyū ron* (Tokyo: Sōbunsha, 1952), p. 146.

19. See *Chūsei hōsei shiryō*, vol. 2: *Muromachi bakufu hō*. It includes six examples of such laws.

20. Ishii, *Nohon jin no kokka*, p. 86.

21. Ishii, *Chūsei fudōsan*, p. 65; John Owen Haley, *Authority without Power: Law and the Japanese Paradox* (New York: Oxford University Press, 1991), p. 40.

22. Tsujimoto Hiroaki, "Ryōseibaihō no kigen ni tsuite," *Hōseishi kenkyū* (1968): 108.

23. "Hōjō Yasutoki Shōsoku" ("A Letter of Hōjō Yasutoki"), in *Nihon shisō taikei* 21: *Chūsei shakai shisō jō* (Tokyo: Iwanami shoten, 1972), pp. 40–41, written in the Ninth Month, 11th, the first year of Jōei, or 1232, immediately following the promulgation of the code *Goseibai shikimoku.*

24. *Nihon shisō taikei* 21: *Chūsei shakai shisō jō*, pp. 32–33.

25. Sagara Tōru, "Nihonjin no dōrikan," in Sagara Tōru, Bitō Masahide, and Akiyama Ken, eds., *Kōza: Nihon shisō*, vol. 3: *Chitsujo* (Tokyo: University of Tokyo Press, 1983), p. 157. See also Kawai, *Chūsei buke shakai*, pp. 87–95.

26. "Hōjō Shigetoki kakun," in *Nihon shisō taikei* 21: *Chūsei seiji shakai shisō* (Tokyo: Iwanami shoten, 1972), "Rokuhara dono gokakun," pp. 310–332, "Gokurakuji dono shōsoku," pp. 322–346. Concerning Hōjō Shigetoki and his thoughts, see Momo Hiroyuki, "Hōjō Shigetoki no kakun kaisetsu," *Bukekakun no kenkyū: Momo Hiroyuki chosakushū* 3 (Tokyo: Shibunkaku shuppan, 1988): 101–245; Kakehi Yasuhiko, *Chūsei buke kakun no kenkyū* (Tokyo: Kazama Shobō, 1967); Ishii Susumu, "Gedai," in *Chūsei seiji shakai shisō jō, Nihon shisō taikei* 21 (Tokyo: Iwanami shoten, 1972), pp. 516–520; Ishii Toshio, "Hōjō shigetoki kakunshikō," *Nihon rekishi* 322 (1975): 37–45;

Carl Steenstrup, *Hōjō Shigetoki: 1198–1261,* Scandinavian Institute of Asian Studies Monograph Series (Copenhagen: Curzon Press, 1979).

27. Steenstrup, *Hōjō Shigetoki,* passage no. 1.

28. Ibid., passage no. 7.

29. Ibid., passage no. 14.

30. This passage is my translation in order to illuminate the original usage of *seken.* Passage 3 *in Nihon shisō taikei* 21, p. 311.

31. For an interesting discussion on this important concept, *seken,* see the work of Inoue Tadashi, *'Seken tei 'no kōzō* (Tokyo: Nihon hōsō shuppan kyōkai, 1977).

32. Streenstrup, *Hōjō Shigetoki,* passage no. 12.

33. Ibid., passage no. 9.

34. Ibid., passage no. 16.

4. The Rite of Honorable Death

1. Kōuchi Shōsuke, *Yoritomo no jidai* (Tokyo: Heibonsha, 1990). Accounts of the Hōgen Rebellion (1156) recorded only one aristocrat's "unlucky" death on the battlefield, and accounts of the Heiji Rebellion (1159) recorded only ten casualties on the battlefield.

2. Fujiwara no Kanezane, *Gyokuyō* (Tokyo: Kokusho kankōkai, 1906), his diary in an entry of the Fifth Month, 26th, in the fourth year of Jishō, p. 409.

3. Kōuchi, *Yoritomo no jidai,* p. 28.

4. Takatori Masao and Hashimoto Mineo, *Shūkyō izen* (Tokyo: Nihon shuppan kyōkai, 1968), p. 31.

5. Fujiwara no Teika, *Meigetsuki,* ed. Imagawa Fumio (Tokyo: Kawade shobō shinsa, 1977), pp. 138–139, his diary in an entry of the Eleventh Month, 26th, the first year of Genkyō (1204).

6. Yamaori Tetsuo, *Shi no minzokugaku* (Tokyo: Iwanami shoten, 1990), pp. 183–220.

7. Ishii Shirō, *Nihonjin no kokka seikatsu* (Tokyo: University of Tokyo Press, 1986), pp. 48–69.

8. Yoshitsune is "one of the most illustrious and beloved personalities in Japanese history," according to Ivan Morris, *The Nobility of Failure: Tragic Heroes in the History of Japan* (New York: Holt, Rinehart and Winston, 1975), p. 67.

9. Ishii, *Nihonjin no kokka,* p. 48.

10. *Heike monogatari,* "Kiso no saigo," in *Nihon koten bungaku taikei* 33, *Heike monogatari ge* (Tokyo: Iwanami shoten, 1960), p. 179.

11. Suenaga's scroll is known as "Mōko shūrai ekotoba." The picture and words of the scroll can be found in *Nihon emakimono taisei,* ed. Komatsu Shigemi (Tokyo: Chūō kōronsha, 1978). See also Ishii Susumu, *Kamakura bushi no jitsuzō* (Tokyo: Heibonsha, 1987), pp. 280–300; Ishii Susumu, "Rekishiteki haikei," in *Nihon emakimono zenshū, Heiji monogatari emaki, Mōko shūrai ekotoba* (Tokyo: Kadokawa shoten, 1964), pp. 32–38; Miya Tsuguji, "Mōko shūrai ekotoba ni tsuite," in *Nihon emakimono zenshū,* pp. 56–69.

12. Recorded in *Azuma kagami,* vol. 2, p. 81, in an entry of the Fifth Month, 4th, Kenpo.

13. Gomi Fumihiko, *Bushi to bunshi no chūseishi* (Tokyo: University of Tokyo Press, 1992), pp. 8–10; Chiba Tokuji, *Tatakai no genzō: Minzoku to shite no bushidō* (Tokyo: Heibonsha, 1991), pp. 17–19.

14. *Heiji monogatari,* ed. Nazumi Yasuaki and Shimada Isao, in *Nihon koten bungaku taikei* 31: *Hogen monogatari Heiji monogatari* (Tokyo: Iwanami shoten, 1961), p. 234.

15. See, for example, Fritz Redlich, *De Praeda Militari: Looting and Booty, 1500–1850* (Wiesbaden: Franz Steininer, 1956).

16. *Oan monogatari,* in *Nihon shomin seikatsu shiryō shūsei,* vol. 8 (Tokyo: Sanichi shobō, 1969, originally ca. 1711–1730), p. 373. Translated with the help of Chris Nelson.

17. Ise Teijō, *Teijō zakki,* vol. 1 (Tokyo: Heibonsha, 1986), pp. 16–27.

18. Taira no Kiyomori came from the so-called Ise-Heishi branch of the Taira clan.

19. *Heike monogatari,* vol. 4: "Miya no saigo," in *Nihon koten bungaku taikei* 32, *Heike monogatari jo* (Tokyo: Iwanami shoten, 1959), p. 316.

20. *Heike,* vol. 9: "Kiso no saigo," in *Nihon koten bungaku taikei* 33, *Heike monogatari ge* (Tokyo: Iwanami shoten, 1960), p. 181.

21. Ōkuma Miyoshi, *Seppuku no rekishi* (Tokyo: Yuzan kaku, 1973); Nakayasu Hiromichi, *Seppuku* (Tokyo: Kubo shoten, 1960). Most of the older studies, however, seem not to go beyond the primary literature listed in *Kōbunko* and *Kojiruien.* For the Japanese culture of suicide in general, see Maurice Pinguet, *La mort volontare au Japon* (Paris: Gallimard, 1984). See also the two works on samurai ethnohistory by Chiba Tokuji, *Seppuku no hanashi* (Tokyo: Kōdansha, 1972), and his *Tatakai no genzō,* which reports many cases of *seppuku.*

22. According to Ikemi Sumitaka's computations, in *Chūsei no seishin sekai: Shi to kyūsai* (Kyoto: Jinbun shoin, 1985), p. 146.

23. See Hyōdō Hiromi, "Monogatari to shiten no rekishi," in Akasaka Norio, ed., *Monogatari to iu kairo* (Tokyo: Shinyōsha, 1992), p. 8. Regarding the storytelling of *Taihiki,* see also Gomi, *Bushi to bunshi,* pp. 279–286; Nagazumi Yasuaki, Uwayokote Masataka, and Sakurai Yoshirō, *Taiheiki no sekai* (Tokyo: Nihon shuppan kyōkai, 1987).

24. *Azuma kagami,* vol. 1, p. 454, an entry of the Third Month, 13th, the sixth year of Kenkyū.

25. See, for example, Inoue Mitsusada, "Chūko tendai to Mappō tōmyōki," in *Nihon shisō taikei* 30, *Geppō, Tendai Hongakuron* (Tokyo: Iwanami shoten, 1973), p. 1.

26. Tamura Yoshiro and Minamoto Ryōen, eds., *Nihon ni okeru sei to shi no shisō* (Tokyo: Yuhikaku, 1977), pp. 62–119; Kawai Masaharu, *Chūsei buke shakai no kenkyū* (Tokyo: Yoshikawa Kōbunkan, 1978), pp. 95–118. Although idiosyncratic philosophies of martial artists that developed in the seventeenth century heavily used idioms of Zen, that does not mean that Zen was the single source of religious inspiration for the general population of the samurai. Zen

sects' contribution to the samurai culture appear to be sometimes overemphasized in the existing Western literature.

27. Yanagida Kunio, "Monoimi to shōjin," *Teihon Yanagida Kunio shū,* vol. 10 (Tokyo: Chikuma shobō, 1961), p. 220.

28. To be sure, this did not mean that Buddhism did not have a notion of impurity. Various sects of Japanese Buddhism developed their own theories of pollution and sins.

29. *Taiheiki,* vol. 9: *Nihon koten bungaku taikei* 34 (Tokyo: Iwanami shoten, 1960), p. 310, trans. by the author. Also see an English translation of *Taiheiki,* trans. Helen Craig McCullough (N.Y.: Columbia University Press, 1959).

30. *Taiheiki,* vol. 9, pp. 310–311.

31. Ibid., p. 313.

32. Takahashi Masaaki, "Rakujitsu no ake ni somaru banbajuku," *Nihonshi no butai* (Tokyo: Shūei sha, 1982).

33. Kan Hang, *Kan'yōroku,* trans. Baku Chomyon (Tokyo: Heibonsha, 1984), pp. 176–177.

34. Note that in many societies in history, the emergence of self-equipped soldiers often signified the beginnings of a class of autonomous individuals who were not totally subordinated by higher authorities.

35. Discrimination against members of former outcast groups (now usually termed *burakumin*) is still a serious social problem in modern Japan.

36. See especially the final chapter of Amino Yoshihiko, *Nihon chūsei no hinogyomin to tennō* (Tokyo: Iwanami shoten, 1984), pp. 540–586. The term *shoku-nin* ("job-person") means someone who makes his living working with his hands, hence a craftsman in modern Japanese. During the medieval period, however, *shoku* (the character can also be pronounced *shiki*) signified much broader meanings, including property rights, public offices, inheritable rights, and occupations. Since the term is central to an understanding of the characteristics of medieval Japanese feudalism, Japanese scholars have been debating the meanings of *shoku* for a long time. See, for example, Nakata Kaoru, "Ōchō jidai no shōen ni kansuru kenkyū," in *Hōseishi ronshū* 2 (Tokyo: Iwanami shoten, 1938); Ishimoda Shō, *Kodai makki seiji shi josetsu* (Tokyo: Miraisha, 1964); Nagahara Keiji, "Shōen sei ni okeru shiki no seikaku," in *Nihon chūsei shakai kōzō no kenkyū* (Tokyo: Iwanami shoten, 1973); and Amino Yoshihiko, "Shoku no tokushitsu o megutte," *Shigaku zasshi,* 76–2 (1967). Japanese scholars have also developed a rich historical literature concerning the origins and development of the outcast. To list just a few examples of work in this field: Ōyama Kyōhei, "Chūsei no mibunsei to kokka," *Iwanami kōza, Nihon rekishi* 8: *Chūsei* 4 (Tokyo: Iwanami shoten, 1976), pp. 262–313; Kuroda Toshio, *Nihon chūsei no kokka to shūkyō* (Tokyo: Iwanami shoten, 1975); Yokoi Kiyoshi, *Chūsei minshū no seikatsu bunka* (Tokyo: University of Tokyo Press, 1975); Niunoya Tetsuichi, *Kebiishi: Chūsei no kegare to kenryoku* (Tokyo: Heibonsha, 1986). One good source that is available in English is Nagahara Keiji, "The Medieval Origins of the *eta-hinin,*" *Journal of Japanese Studies* 1 (Summer 1979): 385–403.

37. Ikemi, *Chūsei no seishi*, p. 25.

38. We now know the details of the intricate practices of avoiding pollution among the Heian court aristocrats from the Code of Engi (927) and other diaries and court literature of the period. See Yamamoto Kōji, "Kizoku shakai ni okeru kegare to chitsujo," *Nihonshi kenkyū* 287 (July 1986): 28–54.

39. Kuroda, *Nihon chūsei no shakai to shūkyō*, pp. 127–156; Yamaori Tetsuo, *Nihonjin no reikonkan* (Tokyo: Kwade shobō shinsha, 1976); Neil McMullin, "On Placating the Gods and Pacifying the Populace: The Case of the Gion Goryo Cult," *History of Religions* 27 (1988): 272–274.

40. Many examples of *kegare* (taboos) in the court society are reported by Yamamoto, "Kizoku."

41. See, for example, Niunoya, *Kebuishi*, pp. 20–66.

42. Amino, *Nihon chūsei no hinōgyōmin*, p. 182.

43. Amino Yoshihiko, *Igyō no ōken* (Tokyo: Heibonsha, 1986), pp. 215–241.

44. By the early modern period, the *eta* had become the most powerful outcast group. This group appeared later than the *hinin*, however. The term *eta* first appeared in historical literature around the Kōan era (1278–1286). See Ikemi's survey of the term in *Chūsei no seishi*, pp. 94–98.

45. Mary Douglas, *Purity and Danger* (London: Routledge, 1966), p. 2.

5. Social Reorganization in the Late Medieval Period

1. Takamura Itsue, *Bokeisei no kenkyū* (Tokyo: Rironsha, 1966), p. 627. See also her *Shōseikon no kenkyū* (Tokyo: Rironsha, 1953), and *Nihon kon'inshi* (Tokyo: Shibundō, 1963). The following recent works provide a good overview of the history of Japanese women: Joseishi sōgō kenkyūkai, ed., *Nihon joseishi*, vol. 2: *Chūsei* (Tokyo: University of Tokyo Press, 1982); Joseishi sōgō kenkyūkai, ed., *Nihon josei seikatsushi*, vol. 2: *Chūsei* (Tokyo: University of Tokyo Press, 1990); and Tabata Yasuko, *Nihon no chūsei no josei* (Tokyo: Yoshikawa kōbunkan, 1987).

2. Emori Itsuo, *Nihon no kon'in: Sono rekishi to minzoku* (Tokyo: Kōbundō, 1986), pp. 95–186. Also see Sumi Tōyō, *Zenkindai nihon kazoku no kōzō: Takamura Itsue hihan* (Tokyo: Kōbundō, 1983), pp. 3–222.

3. Sekiguchi Hiroko, *Nihon kodai kon'inshi no kenkyū* (Tokyo: Hanawa shobō, 1993), p. 289.

4. Local commoners maintained varieties of marriage practices.

5. Wakamori Tarō, "Kokushi ni okeru kyōdōtai no kenkyū," *Wakamori Tarō chosakushū*, vol. 1 (Tokyo: Kōbundō, 1980), pp. 130–135.

6. Concerning the elusive historical concept of the *sōryō* system of the Kamakura period in English, see an excellent study by Jeffrey P. Mass, *Lordship and Inheritance in Early Medieval Japan: A Study of the Kamakura Sōryō System* (Stanford: Stanford University Press, 1989), especially pp. 58–93.

7. For example, Toyoda Takeshi reports that an earlier instance of the practice of primogeniture occurred in the mid-thirteenth century, in the Kamata clan. *Bushidan to sonraku* (Tokyo: Yoshikawa kōbunkan, 1963). In contrast, some

larger houses occasionally practiced divided inheritance up through the sixteenth century.

8. To be sure, daughters and widows of the samurai houses continued to inherit some properties throughout the medieval period; it is misleading to draw a simplistic picture of oppressed medieval samurai women. For an overview of this complex picture, see, for example, Tabata Yasuko, "Sengokuki Josei no yakuwari buntan," in *Nihon josei seikatsushi*, pp. 223–257.

9. Regarding medieval *ikki* in English, see David L. Davis, "Ikki in Late Medieval Japan," in John Hall and Jeffrey P. Mass, eds., *Medieval Japan: Essays in Institutional History* (Stanford: Stanford University Press, 1974). There is a large amount of literature regarding *ikki*. The interested reader could begin by looking at five volumes of Aoki Michio et al., *Ikki* (Tokyo: Tokyo University Press, 1981), and Shizuo Katsumata, *Ikki* (Tokyo: Iwanami shoten, 1983).

10. The early kinship-based *ikki* among the samurai lords was usually called *tō*, or band. The best-known examples of *tō* are *Matsura tō* in Hizen Province and *Suda tō* in Kii Province. These *ikki* also included some samurai other than those belonging to the same bloodline.

11. Katsumata, *Ikki,* pp. 21–22.

12. Fujiki Hisashi, *Sengoku no sahō* (Tokyo: Heibonsha, 1987), p. 10.

13. There is a large amount of literature regarding *sō-son* in Japan. See, for example, Ishida Yoshito, "Gōsonsei no keisei," *Iwanami kōza: Nihon rekishi* 8 (Tokyo: Iwanami shoten, 1963), pp. 35–78; Kuroda Hiroko, *Chūsei sō-son shi no kōzō* (Tokyo: Yoshikawa kōbunkan, 1985); Nagahara Keiji, "Chūsei kōki no sonraku kyōdōtai," in *Nihon kodai chūsei se no chihōteki tenkai,* Toyoda Takeshi kyōju kanreki kinenkai, ed. (Tokyo: Yoshikawa kōbunkan, 1973), pp. 321–348. An important recent study in English is Hitomi Tonomura, *Community and Commerce in Late Medieval Japan: The Corporate Villages of Tokuchin-ho* (Stanford: Stanford University Press, 1992).

14. Keiji Nagahara, "Chūsei keizaishi sōron," *Nihon keizaishi taikei* 2 (Tokyo: University of Tokyo Press, 1956).

15. Concerning sō-son and the "public" domain, see Mizumoto Kunihiko, "Mura to sonmin," *Rekishi kōron* 106 (1984); Asao Naohiro, "Sō-son kara machi e," *Nihon no shakaishi*, vol. 6: *Shakai teki shoshūdan* (Tokyo: Iwanami shoten, 1988); and Ishida, "Gōsonsei no keisei." Whereas some emphasize the aspect of small farmers' participation in village government, others stress the hegemony of the wealthier villagers within the village structure. See Nagahara Keiji, *Nihon hōken shakairon* (Tokyo: Tokyo University Press, 1974).

16. *Tabi hikitsuke,* ed. Kunaichō Shoryōbu (Tenri: Tenri jihōsha, 1951). Regarding Hineno and *Tabi hikitsuke* see Katsumata Shizuo, "Sengoku jidaino sonraku," *Shakaishi kenkyū* 6 (1985). See also Shibata Minoru, ed., *Izumisanoshi* (Osaka: Izumisano City, 1960), pp. 113–169; Ishii Susumu, "Masamotokō tabi hikitsuke ni arawareta chūsei sonraku," *Chūsei no mado* 13 (November 1963): 67–90.

17. *Tabi hikitsuke,* p. 117.

18. Ibid., pp. 121–122.

19. According to the account of a priest named Meisei (1491–1560), in "Honpukuji sekisho," *Nihon shisō taikei: Rennyo, Ikkō ikki* (Tokyo: Iwanami shoten, 1972), p. 230.

20. Ibid.

21. In Japanese historical scholarship, *dogō* and *jizamurai*, referring to the results of the increasing stratification of the medieval village, should be distinguished from *kokujin* samurai lords. According to Keiji Nagahara, *kokujin* lords were descended either from the Kamakura land stewards *(jitō)* or from estate supervisors who attempted to increase their exclusive domination during the period of social turmoil following the collapse of the Kamakura shogunate. For more detailed discussion, see Nagahara Keiji, *Nihon chūei shakai kōzō no kenkyū* (Tokyo: Iwanami shoten, 1973).

22. The position of *dogō* was very complicated, owing to the village class structure. On the one hand, the dogō's interests conflicted with those of the samurai lords who extracted tax revenue from them. In that context, they often chose to resist the lord in the name of the entire village community. On the other hand, the *dogō* had control over the smaller independent peasants as well as their own household subordinates. Within this framework of relationships, they might cooperate with the samurai lords by becoming retainers *(hikan)* of the *kokujin*. Later, during the Warring States period, many *dogō* became the direct vassals of the warlord and attempted to acquire full samurai status.

23. Miura Hiroyuki, "Sengokuki no kokumin gikai," *Nihonshi no kenkyū* (Tokyo: Iwanami shoten, 1922), pp. 348–360.

6. A Society Organized for War

1. See John Hall's classic article on the typological evolution of the daimyo: John W. Hall, "Foundations of the Modern Japanese Daimyo," in Hall and Marius Jansen, eds., *Studies in the Institutional History of Early Modern Japan* (Princeton: Princeton University Press, 1968), pp. 65–77. There is a large amount of literature regarding *sengoku daimyo* in Japan. The interested reader can begin by looking at Nagahara Keiji et al., *Sengoku daimyo ronshū*, vols. 1–18 (Tokyo: Yoshikawa kōbunkan, 1983–1985), which presents various perspectives, debates, and findings of postwar Japanese scholarship in this area.

2. Nagahara Keiji with Kozo Yamamura, "The *Sengoku Daimyo* and the *Kandaka* System," in J. W. Hall, Nagahara Keiji, and Kozo Yamamura, eds., *Japan before Tokugawa: Political Consolidation and Economic Growth, 1500–1650* (Princeton: Princeton University Press, 1981), p. 27.

3. The gradual loss of vassal samurai's independence under the *sengoku daimyo* should be viewed as a result of complex interactions of the daimyo, vassal samurai, and village in the context of general economic growth and power struggles among them; however, this is a subject that I cannot discuss in detail here. The development of the *sengoku daimyo's* control over vassals differed

greatly in different domains. See a case study of Hōjō Domain, Michael P. Birt, "Samurai in Passage: The Transformation of the Sixteenth-Century Kanto," *Journal of Japanese Studies* 11–2 (1985): 369–399. In the case of Bizen Province, see John W. Hall's classic work *Government and Local Power in Japan—500–1700* (Princeton: Princeton University Press, 1966). Also regarding the general socioeconomic picture of the sixteenth-century transition, see Kozo Yamamura, "Returns on Reunification: Economic Growth in Japan, 1550–1650," in *Japan before Tokugawa,* and Osamu Wakita, "The Emergence of the State in Sixteenth-Century Japan: From Oda to Tokugawa," *Journal of Japanese Studies* 8–2 (1982): 343–367.

4. This is a conventional view. The origin, production, and use of Japanese versions of muskets have been much debated among Japanese specialists. One possibility is that muskets were introduced into Japan via Southeast Asia, or China. See, for example, Tokoro Shōkichi, *Hinawajū* (Tokyo: Yūzankaku, 1964). Udagawa Takehisa provides a clear literature review of this issue in *Teppō denrai* (Tokyo: Chūō kōronsha, 1990).

5. Udagawa, *Teppō,* pp. 18–95.

6. Geoffrey Parker, *The Military Revolution* (Cambridge: Cambridge University Press, 1988), p. 24. See also G. Parker, "The 'Military Revolution,' 1560–1660—a Myth?" *Journal of Modern History* 48 (1976): 195–214.

7. The major works concerning the law of *kenka ryōseibai* are Miura Hiroyuki, "*Kenka ryōseibai hō,*" in Miura Hiroyuki, *Hōseishi kenkyū ge* (Tokyo: Iwanami shoten, 1944); Takigawa Masajirō, "*Kenka ryōseibai hō,*" in Takigawa Masajirō, ed., *Nihon hōseishi kenkyū* (Tokyo: Yūhikaku, 1941); Hosokawa Kameichi, "*Kenka ryōseibai hō,*" in Hosokawa Kameichi, *Nihon koyūhō no tenkai* (Tokyo: Ganshōdō shoten, 1939); Tsujimoto Hiroaki, "Ryōseibai hō no kigen ni tsuite," in *Hōseishi kenkyū* (Tokyo: Iwanami shoten, 1968), pp. 103–119; Ishii Shirō, *Nihonjin no kokka seikatsu* (Tokyo: University of Tokyo Press, 1986), pp. 79–108; and Katsumata Shizuo, *Sengoku hō seiritsushiron* (Tokyo: University of Tokyo Press, 1979), pp. 247–268.

8. *Chūsei hōsei shiryōshū,* vol. 3., ed. Satō Shin'ichi, Ikeuchi Yoshisuke, and Momose Kesao (Tokyo: Iwanami shoten, 1965), p. 117.

9. *Chūsei hōsei shiryōshū,* vol. 3, p. 197. Shibatsuji Shunroku, "Kōshū hatto no rekishiteki seikaku," in Sugiyama Hiroshi sensei kanreki kinenkai, ed., *Sengoku no heishi to nōmin* (Tokyo: Kadokawa shoten, 1978), provides an excellent account of the historical background of this law.

10. *Chūsei hōsei shiryōshū,* vol. 3, p. 285.

11. Ishii, *Nihonjin no kokka,* p. 81.

12. Katsumata, *Sengoku hō,* p. 254.

13. The same rule was announced during the Sekigahara Battle and the Osaka Summer Battles. *Buke Genseiroku,* ed. Ishii Ryōsuke, *Kinsei hōsei shiryō,* vol. 3 (Tokyo: Sōbunsha, 1959), pp. 12–13.

14. Ibid.

15. Katsumata Shizuo, "The Development of Sengoku Law," trans. Martin

Collcutt, in John W. Hall and Kozo Yamamura, eds., *Japan before Tokugawa* (Princeton: Princeton University Press, 1981), pp. 110–111. The literature on the Sengoku laws includes Katsumata, *Sengoku hō;* Fujiki Hisashi, *Sengoku sha-kaishi ron* (Tokyo: University of Tokyo Press, 1974).

16. Katsumata, "The Development of Sengoku Law," p. 111.

17. In the *Kōyō Gunkan,* cited by Ishii, *Nihonjin no kokka,* pp. 106–107. The *Kōyō Gunkan* was believed to be the record of the Takeda clan during the Warring States period and was a very popular military handbook for the Toku-gawa samurai. The text of the book was probably edited during the early seven-teenth century; therefore, it should not be interpreted as a direct record of the Takeda clan. The book did, however, include some accurate information regard-ing the complex military organizations and operations of the Takeda. See Kobayashi Keiichirō, "'Kōyō Gunkan' no Takeda kashindan hensei hyō ni tsu-ite," in *Sengoku daimyo ronshū* 10, *Takedashi no kenkyū,* Shibatsuji Shunroku, ed. (Tokyo: Yoshikawa kōbunkan, 1984), pp. 236–260. The colorful stories in this book are at least faithful representations of what was believed to be the true story of this legendary military clan at the beginning of the Tokugawa period.

18. Owada Tetsuo, *Sengoku bushō no iki kata shini kata* (Tokyo: Shinjinbutsu ōraisha, 1985), p. 17.

19. A story recorded in "Shōrin yawa," author unknown. *Kaitei zōho shiseki shūran, buke bu,* vol. 17 (Tokyo: Rinsen shoten, 1967), p. 350.

20. Chiba Tokuji, *Tatakai no genzō: Minzoku to shite no bushidō* (Tokyo: Heibonsha, 1991), pp. 153–184.

7. Tokugawa State Formation

1. See the calculations based on the formal *kokudaka* (rice output) measure-ment presented in Conrad Totman, *Politics in the Tokugawa Bakufu, 1600–1843* (Berkeley: University of California Press, 1988), p. 33. Also see the similar calculation based upon *kokudaka* output by John W. Hall, "The Bakuhan Sys-tem," in John W. Hall, ed., *The Cambridge History of Japan* 4: *Early Modern Japan* (Cambridge: Cambridge University Press, 1991), p. 152.

2. For a concise review of the development of the Tokugawa daimyo polities *(han)* in English, see Harold Bolitho, "The *han,*" in *The Cambridge History of Japan* 4, pp. 183–234. Also see Harold Bolitho, *Treasures among Men* (New Haven: Yale University Press, 1974).

3. *Tenka sōbuji rei,* or Realm at Peace Edict, as it has been called by the Japa-nese historian Fujiki Hisashi, was not in actuality a single law, but a group of multiple edicts that embodied Hideyoshi's important policy that the entire coun-try should be *sōbuji* (literally, "all peace") in the name of his public power. These edicts were usually sent directly to the daimyo houses from Hideyoshi's govern-ment on various occasions. For example, an edict was sent to Lord Shimazu, a daimyo of the Kyūshū region, in 1585, ordering the regional daimyo to stop fighting over disputed territories and to leave the matter to Hideyoshi's judg-

ment. The term *sōbuji* clearly appeared in the edict of 1587, which was sent simultaneously to the daimyo of the Kantō and Ōshu regions. An edict prohibiting fighting at the village level *(kenka chōji rei)* has not yet been located in a historical document. But the presence of such an edict is supported by many historical accounts of the period, such as *Tamon'in nikki,* cited below, which refer to an edict that indicated a prohibition of private conflict resolution as being well known to contemporaries. See Fujiki Hisashi, *Toyotomi heiwarei to sengoku shakai* (Tokyo: University of Tokyo Press, 1985). Takagi Shōsaku's series of works concerning the consolidation of power is directly relevant to this subject: "Kōgi: Kenryoku no kakuritsu," in Fukaya Katsumi and Katō Eiichi, eds., *Kōza nihon kinseishi* 1: *Bakuhansei kokka no seiritsu* (Tokyo: Yūhikaku, 1981), pp. 151–210; Takagi Shōsaku, "'Hideyoshi's Peace' and the Transformation of the *Bushi* Class," *Acta Asiatia* 49 (1985): 46–77. Mary Elizabeth Berry's biography of Hideyoshi also describes him as a peacemaker: Mary Elizabeth Berry, *Hideyoshi* (Cambridge, Mass.: Harvard University Press, 1989).

4. *Tamon'in Nikki*, vol. 4, ed. Tsuji Zennosuke (Tokyo: Sankyo shoin, 1938), p. 373. This is a diary of Tamonin Eishun, in an entry of the Tenth Month, 23rd, the twentieth year of Tenshō. Regarding this water dispute, see Nonose Yoshimi, "Toyotomi seikenka no suiron to sonraku," *Historia* 70 (1976): 55–67, and Fujiki Hisashi, *Sengoku no sahō* (Tokyo: Heibonsha, 1987), pp. 151–155.

5. Nonose, "Toyotomi seikenka no," pp. 55–61.

6. Oda Nobunaga's *Kuni okite* (the code of the country), in the Third Month, the third year of Tenshō (1582), cited by Fujiki Hisashi, *Sengoku daimyo no kenryoku kōzō* (Tokyo: Yoshikawa kōbunkan, 1987), p. 81.

7. John W. Hall, "Rule by Status in Tokugawa Japan," *Journal of Japanese Studies* 1–1 (1974): 39–49.

8. Regarding the *koku daka* system, see a detailed study of Iinuma Jirō, *Kokudakasei no kenkyū* (Kyoto: Mineruva shobō, 1974).

9. Totman, *Politics,* p. 43.

10. There were many ways to determine the house ranking of a particular daimyo house other than *koku daka.* Upgrading one's house ranking, which was basically hereditary, was one of the most heated sources of political struggle among the daimyo houses during the Tokugawa period.

11. Katō Takashi, *Bakuhan taiseiki ni okeru daimyo kakakusei no kenkyū* (Tokyo: Kinsei nihon jōkaku kenkyūjo, 1969), pp. 95–235; Shinji Yoshimoto, *Kinsei bukshakai to shohatto* (Tokyo: Gakuyō shobō, 1989), pp. 64–84.

12. It was, however, not always the case that the shogunate supported the local daimyo's government over rebellious peasants. Sometimes, a peasant uprising resulted in punishment of the daimyo or samurai deputies in question, as a penalty for not adequately fulfilling the responsibility of government.

13. Totman, *Politics,* Preface to the paperback edition, p. xiv.

14. Mizubayashi Takeshi, "Kinsei no hō to kokusei kenkyū josetsu," *Kokka gakkai zasshi* 90, 1/2 (1977): 31.

15. Kanai Madoka, *Hansei Seiritsuki no kenkyū* (Tokyo: Yoshikawa kōbunkan, 1975), pp. 11–20.

16. Regarding Tokugawa samurai family laws, see Kamata Hiroshi, *Bakuhan taisei ni okeru bushi kazoku hō* (Tokyo: Seibundō, 1970).

17. The result of the 1721 census was 26,065,000, but this survey excluded some status and age groups. The extent of the exclusions has been a subject of scholarly debate. Eighteen surveys between 1721 and 1846 are now known. The results show a generally stable population trend in the second half of the Tokugawa period. Regarding the shogunate's population surveys, see Sekiyama Naotarō, *Kinsei nihon no jinkō kōzō* (Tokyo: Yoshikawa kōbunkan, 1957), pp. 123–267.

8. An Integrated Yet Decentralized State Structure

1. To conceptualize the Tokugawa organizing principle of social groups as the "system of yaku" is one of the influential viewpoints among contemporary Japanese historians for the interpretation of the structure of Tokugawa society. See Bitō Masahide, "Society and Social Thought in the Tokugawa Period," *Japan Foundation Newsletter* 9 (1981): 4–6; Bitō Masahide, "Tokugawa jidai no shakai to seiji shisō no tokushitsu," in Ōguchi Yūjiro, ed., *Edo towa nanika 2: Tokugawa no seiji to shakai: Gendai no esupuri bessatsu* (Tokyo: Shibundō, 1985), pp. 25–46. See also the works of Takagi Shōsaku, including "Bakuhan taisei to yaku," *Nihon no shakaishi*, vol. 3: *Ken'i to shihai* (Tokyo: Risōsha, 1987), pp. 310–341.

2. Ōishi Shinzaburō, *Edo jidai* (Tokyo: Chūō kōronsha, 1977), p. 115.

3. Ishii Ryōsuke, *Edo jidai manpitsu: Edo no machi bugyō* (Tokyo: Akashi shoten, 1989), p. 25. This is the number given for 1719, including both *yoriki* (mounted officers status) and *dōshin* (foot-soldier status). The number of *yoriki* and *dōshin* increased slightly in later periods, but still amounted to only 326 officers at the end of the Tokugawa period.

4. Ōishi, *Edo jidai*, p. 66.

5. Japanese *bakuhan* authorities attempted to restrict the movement of their subjects in order to secure their revenue from agricultural production. The authorities often attempted to restrict the migration of peasant families to other areas and to prohibit the sale of their land. In practice, however, these restrictions were not effectively enforced. The authorities also found that as long as the village collectively owed the responsibility of paying taxes, and arranged cultivators for the land, it would not do much damage to the daimyo's interest even if there was a turnover of the individuals who composed the labor force. The sale of agricultural land was prohibited by a shogunate decree in 1643, and another decree in 1673 limited the division of farmlands at the time of inheritance. These decrees can be understood as policies of the shogunate intended to protect the small-scale peasants as the unit of production.

6. Regarding the development and structures of early modern Japanese villages, see the excellent works of Mizumoto Kunihiko, including "Kinsei shoki no sonsei to jichi," *Nihonshi kenkyū* 244 (1982): 52–70, and *Kinsei no mura shakai to kokka* (Tokyo: University of Tokyo Press, 1987). See also Harumi

Befu, "Village Autonomy and Articulation with the State," in John W. Hall and Marius Jansen, eds., *Studies in the Institutional History of Early Modern Japan* (Princeton: Princeton University Press, 1968), pp. 301–314.

7. For village codes, see Maeda Masaharu, *Nihon kinsei sonpō no kenkyū: Furoku sonpōshū* (Tokyo: Yuhikaku, 1950).

8. Tsukada Takashi, "Kinsei no mibunsei shakai to shihai," in Rekishigaku kenkyūkai and Nihonoshi kenkyūkai, eds., *Kōza nihon rekishi*, vol. 5: *Kinsei I* (Tokyo: University of Tokyo Press, 1985), pp. 269–273.

9. Tsukada, "Kinsei no mibunsei," pp. 273–284.

10. Hiramatsu Yoshio, *Kinsei keiji soshōhō no kenkyū* (Tokyo: Sobunsha, 1960), pp. 366–401. Decisions handed down by Danzaemon regarding the death penalty were reported to the town magistrate, but lesser penalties were imposed entirely under Danzaemon's authority.

11. See Yamamura Kozo, "Returns on Reunification: Economic Growth in Japan, 1550–1650," in Nagahara Keiji, John W. Hall, and Kozo Yamamura, eds., *Japan before Tokugawa: Political Consolidation and Economic Growth, 1500–1650* (Princeton: Princeton University Press, 1981), pp. 327–372.

12. See Sekiyama Naotarō, *Kinsei nihon no jinkō kōzō* (Tokyo: Yoshikawa kōbunkan, 1957), p. 312.

13. There are various estimates. See, for example, Miyamoto Matarō, "Hitori atari nōgyō sanshutsudaka to seisan shoyōso hiritsu," in Umemura Mataji et al., *Nihon keizai no hatten* (Tokyo: Nihon keizai shinbun, 1976), p. 22.

14. There has been considerable argument as to when the national-scale market economy was established. See Nakai Nobuhiko, *Bakuhan shakai to shōhin ryūtsū* (Tokyo: Hanawa shobō, 1961); Wakita Osamu, *Kinsei hōken shakai no keizai kōzō* (Tokyo: Ochanomizu shobō, 1963). Nakai and many other Japanese scholars stress the importance of the late seventeenth century as the time for the maturity of the national-scale market, whereas Wakita has examined the exchange of rice and stated that the national market was established at the beginning of the century. I shall stress the importance of the "mature" configuration of a national market economy based on the congregation of well-developed, semiindependent *han* economies and the increasing production of various commodities. Regarding the national-scale market, see also the arguments by Sasaki Junnosuke, *Zōho kaiteiban bakuhan kenryoku no kiso* (Tokyo: Ochanomizu shobō, 1985), and Ōno Mizuo, "Bakuhansei teki shijō kōzōron," in Rekishigaku Kenkyūkai and Nihonshi Kenkyūkai, eds., *Kōza nihon rekishi*, vol. 5 (Tokyo: University of Tokyo Press, 1985).

15. Aoki Kōji, *Hyakushō ikki sōgō nenpyō* (Tokyo: University of Tokyo Press, 1971). In postwar Japan, large-scale efforts in excavating local documents have produced remarkable advances in the study of Tokugawa collective actions. Drawing upon these documents, Aoki has catalogued conflicts that took place between 1590 and 1877. In English, see James White, *The Demography of Sociopolitical Conflict in Japan, 1721–1846* (Berkeley: University of California Press, 1992), as an analysis of the types and distribution of the disputes listed

by Aoki. For an overview of Tokugawa rebellions, see Eiko Ikegami and Charles Tilly, "State Formations and Contention in Japan and France," in John M. Merriman, James L. McClain, and Ugawa Kaoru, eds., *Edo and Paris* (Ithaca: Cornell University Press, 1994).

16. For an overview of Japanese premodern agrarian communities in English, see Thomas C. Smith, *The Agrarian Origins of Modern Japan* (Stanford: Stanford University Press, 1959).

17. James White, "State Growth and Popular Protest in Tokugawa Japan," *Journal of Japanese Studies* 14–1 (1988).

9. The Tokugawa Neo-Feudal State

1. Of course, I am aware of the dangers involved in applying labels to Japan that are primarily derived from the European historical experience. When they are used intentionally to designate ideal types derived from European historical experience, however, such labels can be useful tools for comparative identification of the characteristics of Japanese early modern state formation. These concepts offer us an immediate ground for comparison precisely because they are borrowed from European cases. To be sure, it is not my intention to involve myself in the fruitless discussions that some Japanese historians of various Marxist persuasions had at one time generated. In particular, such debates often lead to pitfalls, insofar as they concentrate on the application of Marxist "stage" development theories to various periods in Japanese history, based on the assumption that there is one general theory of historical development applicable to all human history. Although I employ the same terminology in this context, such as "feudalism" and "absolutism," I do not subscribe to the belief that all human societies pass through the same general historical changes. I am indebted to the following Western specialists of Japanese society who have attempted to evaluate Japanese feudalism in world history: Kan'ichi Asakawa, *Land and Society in Medieval Japan* (Tokyo: Japan Society for the Promotion of Science, 1965); John W. Hall, "Feudalism in Japan: A Reassessment," in John W. Hall and Marius B. Jansen, eds., *Studies in the Institutional History of Early Modern Japan* (Princeton: Princeton University Press, 1968); Edwin O. Reischauer, "Japanese Feudalism," in Rushton Coulborn, ed., *Feudalism in History* (Princeton: Princeton University Press, 1956), pp. 26–48; Peter Duus, *Feudalism in Japan* (New York: Alfred Knopf, 1969). Also see an insightful discussion of Japanese feudalism by the European historian Joseph Strayer, "The Tokugawa Period and Japanese Feudalism," in *Studies in the Institutional History of Early Modern Japan*. My analysis as well as the preceding description of Tokugawa state formation has a different orientation from that of historians', however. My analysis primarily addresses the comparative question raised in the field of historical sociology, namely, the impact of the medieval to early modern transition on the subsequent social developments in different countries, which I mentioned in Chapter 1.

2. M. M. Postan, Foreword to Marc Bloch, *Feudal Society*, trans. L. A. Manyon (Chicago: University of Chicago Press, 1961), pp. xii–xiii. Although a quasi-contractual relationship of exchange (*go'on* and *hōkō*) was observed in Japan's system of medieval vassalage, this legal focus does not serve us well for comparative purposes because it is not consciously discussed as an ideal historical type in an abstract form; it is based on a peculiarly Western development in which the judicial function became central to feudal politics.

3. Joseph Strayer, *Feudalism* (New York: Van Nostrand, 1965), pp. 12–13.

4. R. H. Hilton, "A Crisis of Feudalism," in T. H. Aston and R. H. Hilton, eds., *The Brenner Debate* (Cambridge: Cambridge University Press, 1985), p. 124.

5. Bloch, *Feudal Society*, p. 446.

6. Perry Anderson, *Lineages of the Absolutist State* (London: New Left Books, 1974), p. 18.

7. Immanuel Wallerstein, *The Modern World System* (New York: Academic Press, 1974).

8. This has already been proposed by James White as he stresses the absolutist aspect of the Tokugawa state. See his "State Growth and Popular Protest in Tokugawa Japan," *Journal of Japanese Studies* 14–1 (1988): 1–25. See also the discussion of Shōda Ken'ichirō, *Nihon ni okeru kindai shakai no seiritsu* (Tokyo: Mitsumine shobō, 1990), pp. 209–212.

9. Michael Mann, *The Sources of Social Power* I: *A History of Power from the Beginning to A.D. 1760* (Cambridge: Cambridge University Press, 1986), p. 476.

10. Hans Rosenberg, *Bureaucracy, Aristocracy, and Autocracy: The Prussian Experience, 1660–1815* (Cambridge, Mass.: Harvard University Press, 1958), pp. 14–20.

11. John W. Hall, Introduction, in John W. Hall, ed., *The Cambridge History of Japan*, vol. 4 (New York: Cambridge University Press, 1991), p. 18.

12. Eiko Ikegami and Charles Tilly, "State Formations and Contention in Japan and France," in John M. Merriman, James L. McClain, and Ugawa Kaoru, eds., *Edo and Paris* (Ithaca: Cornell University Press, 1994).

13. The fact that Japanese early modern state formation appears to be closer to Anderson's model does not mean that his analysis of Tokugawa Japan is correct. He tends to minimize the degree of political centralization in Tokugawa Japan and uncritically discusses the shogunate as if it were comparable to the typical instance of decentralized European feudalism. He then proceeds to conclude, on the basis of this assumption, that both European and Japanese feudalism paved the way for capitalism.

14. Joseph Strayer, *On the Medieval Origins of the Modern State* (Princeton: Princeton University Press, 1970), p. 22. See also Brian Tierney, *The Crisis of Church and State, 1050–1300* (Englewood Cliffs, N.J.: Prentice-Hall, 1964).

15. Harold J. Berman, *Law and Revolution: The Formation of the Western Legal Tradition* (Cambridge, Mass.: Harvard University Press, 1983), p. 23.

16. Stanley Tambiah, *World Conqueror and World Renouncer* (Cambridge: Cambridge University Press, 1976).

17. See Mann, *Sources of Social Power,* p. 24.

18. For example, see Charles Tilly, *Coercion, Capital, and European States,* A.D. *990–1990* (Cambridge: Basil Blackwell, 1990).

19. Gilbert Rozman, *Urban Networks in Ch'ing China and Tokugawa Japan* (Princeton: Princeton University Press, 1973), pp. 237–238.

20. Miyamoto Matarō, "Hitori atari nōgyō sanshutsudaka to seisan shoyōso hiritsu," in Umemura Mataji et al., *Nihon keizai no hatten* (Tokyo: Nihon keizai shinbun, 1976), p. 22.

21. In confronting their financial difficulties during the mid-Tokugawa period, the shogunate and the daimyo did attempt to impose a higher level of taxation on merchants and also introduced more regulations in these areas of economic activity. But the state's fiscal foundation continued to rely primarily on its agricultural sector. For an overview of the development of Tokugawa commerce and business in English, see Johannes Hirschmeier and Tsunehiko Yui, *The Development of Japanese Business, 1600–1973* (Cambridge, Mass.: Harvard University Press, 1975); S. Crawcour, "The Tokugawa Period and Japan's Preparation for Economic Growth," *Journal of Japanese Studies* 1 (1978): 113–126.

10. Honor or Order

1. The observation of Mori Anzaimon in "Okinagusa," reprinted in *Nihon zuihitsu taikei,* vol. 11 (Tokyo: Yoshikawa kōbunkan, 1973), p. 135.

2. *Konjaku monogatari,* vol. 25, no. 10, *Nihon koten bungakuzenshū: Konjaku monogatarishū,* vol. 3 (Tokyo: Shōgakukan, 1976), pp. 480–483.

3. *Buke giri monogatari,* trans. Caryl Ann Callahan as *Tales of Samurai Honor* (Tokyo: Monumenta Nipponica, 1982), pp. 51–54.

4. See Hirade Kōjirō, *Katakiuchi* (Tokyo: Chūō kōronsha, 1990, originally published in 1909), pp. 147–151.

5. Ruth Horowitz, *Honor and the American Dream* (New Brunswick: Rutgers University Press, 1985), pp. 77–113.

6. Ibid., p. 82.

7. Pierre Bourdieu, *Algeria 1960* (Cambridge: Cambridge University Press, 1979), p. 100.

8. Katsumata Shizuo, *Sengokuhō seiritsushiron* (Tokyo: University of Tokyo Press, 1979), p. 248. See also Hashita Tokuhiko, "Kosen bōsen o megutte," in Chūsei no mado dōjin, ed., *Chūsei no mado* (Tokyo: Yoshikawa kōbunkan, 1977).

9. *Buke shohhato,* the twelfth year of Kan'ei. *Tokugawa kinreikō,* vol. 3 (Tokyo: Sōbunsha, 1959).

10. Regarding the studies of *kabuki* in English, see the works of Donald Shively, such as "Bakufu *versus* Kabuki," *Harvard Journal of Asiatic Studies* 18 (1955): 326–356, and "Sumptuary Regulation and Status in Early Tokugawa Japan," *Harvard Journal of Asiatic Studies* 25 (1964–1965): 123–164. (Shively's works primarily focus on the *kabuki* theaters, not *kabuki mono.*) I am indebted for the analysis of this picture to Moriya Takeshi, *Kabuki no jidai* (Tokyo: Kado-

kawa shoten, 1976); Moritani Katsuhisa, "Toyokunisai rinji sairei to kamo keiba," in Kinsei Fūzokuzu 9 sairei 2 (Tokyo: Shōgakukan, 1982), pp. 86–95; Ujiie Mikito, "Moriyama nikki ni miru 'kabuki' shūen no jidaizō," in Nishiyama Matsunosuke sensei koki kinenkai, ed., Edo no geinō to bunka (Tokyo: Yoshikawa kōbunkan, 1985).

11. Ogata Tsurukichi, Honpō Kyōkaku no Kenkyū (Tokyo: Nishida shoten, 1981), p. 31.

12. According to the record of an ordinance against kabuki mono in 1652, Tokugawa jikki. Kokushi takei, vol. 41 (Tokyo: Kokusho kankōkai, 1930), p. 43.

13. Bitō Masahide, Nihon no rekishi, vol. 19: Genroku jidai (Tokyo: Shōgakukan, 1975), pp. 86–107. Noguchi Takehiko, Edo wakamono kō (Tokyo: Sanseidō, 1986), pp. 63–72.

14. Moriya Takeshi, Kabuki no, p. 124.

15. Recorded in Kaga han shiryō, vol. 2, ed. Kōshaku Maedake henshūbu (Osaka: Shimizudō, 1980), pp. 27–29, an entry of the fifth year of Keichō. This is a fifteen-volume collection of chronologically reprinted primary source materials on the history of Kaga han.

16. Kaga han shiryō, vol. 2, pp. 72–73.

17. See Tokugawa jikki, the Sixth Month, 28th, the seventeenth year of Keichō, Kokushi taikei, vol. 38 (Tokyo: Kokusho kankōkai, 1929), p. 590. Also see the description of this event by another contemporary source, Keichō kenmonshū, vol. 6: "Ōtori Ichibyōe gumi no koto," in Nihon shomin seikatsu shiryō shūsei, vol. 8 (Tokyo: San'ichi shobō, 1969), pp. 561–563.

18. Shinyūki, in Nihon shisō taikei 60, Kinsei shikidōron (Tokyo: Iwanami shoten, 1976), pp. 8–25. See the English translation of Ihara Saikaku's collections of short stories, Nanshoku Ōkagami, as The Great Mirror of Male Love, trans. Paul Gordon Schalow (Stanford: Stanford University Press, 1990); Tales of Samurai Honor, trans. Callahan; and also Hiratsuka Yoshinobu, Nihon ni okeru nanshoku no kenkyū (Tokyo: Ningen no kagakusha, 1983).

19. Ujiie, Edo hantei, pp. 130–160.

20. Kaga han shiryō, vol. 2, pp. 610–613.

21. Regarding early agricultural land policies of Kaga han, in particular kaisaku hō, see the detailed work of Wakabayashi Kisaburō, Kagahan nōseishi no kenkyū (Tokyo: Yoshikawa kōbunkan, 1970).

22. Keibatsu kakinuki, a document of Okayama han, in Naitō Bunko Archives, Tokyo, reprinted in Okayama kenshi 24. I am indebted to Ujiie Mikito for this account, "Nichijō sei no naka no bushi bunka," in Nihon Minzoku taikei 11: Toshi to inaka (Tokyo: Shōgakukan, 1985), and Edo hantei monogatari (Tokyo: Chūō kōronsha, 1988), regarding this incident.

23. Daidoji Yūzan, Bushi Shoshinshū, ed. Furukawa Tetsuji (Tokyo: Iwanami shoten, 1943), p. 33.

24. Aizuhan kasei jikki, ed. Kasei jikki Kanpon hensan iinkai (Tokyo: Yoshikawa kōbunkan, 1975), p. 107.

25. Ibid., p. 109.

26. Ibid., p. 110.

27. Correspondence cited by Nakayasu Hiromichi, *Seppuku* (Tokyo: Kubo shoten, 1960), p. 105.

28. Matsuda Osamu, *Irezumi, sei, shi: Gyakkō no nihon bi* (Tokyo: Heibonsha, 1972), pp. 260–285.

29. Fujino Tamotsu, ed., *Zoku Saga-han no sōgō kenkyū* (Tokyo: Yoshikawa kōbunkan, 1987), p. 97.

30. Ōkuma Miyoshi, *Seppuku no rekishi* (Tokyo: Yūzankaku, 1973), p. 158.

31. Clifford Geertz, "Deep Play: Notes on the Balinese Cockfight," in *The Interpretation of Cultures* (New York: Basic Books, 1973), pp. 412–453.

11. The Vendetta of the Forty-seven Samurai

1. The size of this contemporary literary output is a reflection of the deep emotional response stirred up by the Forty-seven Samurai's retaliation. See Donald Shiverly, "Tokugawa Plays on Forbidden Topics," in James Brandon, ed., *Chūshingura: Studies in Kabuki and the Puppet Theater* (Honolulu: University of Hawaii Press, 1982); *Cūshingura: The Treasury of Loyal Retainers*, trans. Donald Keene (New York: Columbia University Press, 1971).

Even in present-day Japan, fresh treatments of the story appear from time to time in movies, television dramas, and novels. Regarding this revenge story and the nature of its appeal to modern Japanese, see a stimulating argument concerning the modern meaning of this incident: Henry D. Smith, "Rethinking the Story of the Forty-Seven Rōnin: Chūshingura in the 1980s" (a paper presented at the Modern Japan Seminar, Columbia University, 1990); also see Satō Tadao, *Chūshingura: Iji no keifu* (Tokyo: Asahi shinbunsha, 1976).

2. In the memoirs of a *metsuke* (an official in the shogunate government in charge of disciplinary matters regarding samurai and daimyo), Okado Denpachirō. Denpachirō was summoned soon after Asano's attack to investigate the scene. He also filed a complaint with the authorities taking issue with their immediate order of *seppuku* to Asano. "Okado Denpachirō oboegaki," *Akō gijin sansho*, vol. 1 (Tokyo: Kokusho kankōkai, 1900), pp. 306–319.

3. As stated in a report of Kajikawa Yoriteru, who tried to restrain Asano, urging him to hold off. Kajiwara was also one of the officials appointed to receive the imperial delegation on that day. "Kajikawashi hikki," *Akō gijin sansho*, vol. 2, pp. 267–273.

4. Bitō Masahide, *Nihon no rekishi*, vol. 19: *Genroku jidai* (Tokyo: Shōgakukan, 1975), p. 306.

5. This was an interesting reaction, as we have seen that the sentence was in accordance with the original meaning of *kenka ryōseibai*, which was to exclude from punishment those who did not fight back. The effects of *kenka ryōseibai* not only dominated the subsequent Tokugawa era but even now continue to color Japanese society, as can be seen in subtle aspects of practice in legal culture.

For example, underlying the notion of *kenka ryōseibai* was the presumption that both parties involved in a conflict should have some legitimate reasons to quarrel, as well as some faults. The legal scholar Kawashima Takeyoshi, when analyzing some postwar civil court cases concerning traffic accidents, has pointed out that the mentality of *kenka ryōseibai* still affects some of the decisions of modern Japanese judges who are inclined to find both parties to be at fault to some degree. See Kawashima Takeyoshi, *Nihon jin no hō ishiki* (Tokyo: Iwanami shoten, 1967), pp. 143–153. In general, I hold the view that Japanese modern legal practice cannot be explained only by such a traditional cultural legacy, but that social structural causes should be carefully examined as well. In the particular cases studied by Kawashima, however, it is clear that the law of *kenka ryōseibai* still influences the modern Japanese sense of justice.

6. Lord Asano Naganori was childless, and Daigaku had been officially appointed as heir-apparent before the incident.

7. Tahara Tsuguo, *Akō shijūrokushi ron: Bakuhansei no seishin kōzō* (Tokyo: Yoshikawa kōbunkan, 1978), pp. 3–4.

8. "Horibe Taketsune hikki" (a writing of Horibe Taketsune, a radical member of the revenge group), first reprinted in *Akō gijin sansho, hoi.* The same text is also available in *Nihon shisō taikei 27: Kinsei buke shisō* (Tokyo: Iwanami shoten, 1974). I will use *Kinsei buke shisō* in the following citations.

9. For example, Yasui Hikouemon attempted to dissuade the excited radical members by saying, "The deceased lord would be much happier if he could see the recovery of the *o-ie*, rather than the head of Kozuke (Kira). . . ." *Kinsei buke shisō*, p. 194.

10. Ōishi's letter of the Tenth Month, 5th, the fifteenth year of Genroku (1702), recorded in "Horibe Taketsune hikki," p. 210.

11. "Horibe Taketsune hikki," p. 194.

12. Ibid.

13. Ibid., p. 203.

14. Ibid., p. 205.

15. See, for example, the letter of Ōdaka Gengo to his mother, *Akō gijin sansho*, vol. 1, p. 413.

16. "Horibe Taketsune hikki," p. 187.

17. Ibid., p. 188.

18. Letter of Ōdaka Gengo, *Akō gijin sansho*, vol. 1, p. 414.

19. "Horibe Tsuneo hikki," p. 207.

20. Ibid.

21. Ibid., p. 209.

22. This view was repeatedly expressed in several of Ōishi's writings. See, for example, his letter included in "Kōseki kenbunki." This is a record composed by an unknown writer about the development of the case. It is thought that the writer was one of the inner circle of the Asano house with access to special information such as personal letters. *Akō gijin sansho, hoi*, p. 231.

23. Tahara, *Akō*, p. 30.

24. "Hyōjōsho ichiza zonjiyorisho," assumed to be a report issued by the councilors of the state regarding the treatment of the forty-six samurai, dated Twelfth Month 23, the fifth year of Genroku. *Akō gijin sansho, hoi,* pp. 148–149.

25. Ogyū Sorai, "Giritsusho," reprinted in *Akō gijin sansho, hoi,* p. 150. See also his "Shijū shichishi ron," *Kinsei buke shisō,* p. 414.

26. Regarding the distinction between private and public, see Miyake Masahiko, "Bakuhan shujūsei no shisō teki genri: Kō shi bunri no hatten," *Nihonshi kenkyū* 127 (1972): 1–30; Miyake Masahiko, "Kinsei buke dōtoku ni okeru kōshi no mondai," *Nihon shisō taikei geppō* 27, in *Kinsei buke shisō;* Yasunaga Toshinobu, *Nihon ni okeru "kō" to "shi"* (Tokyo: Nihon keizai shinbunsha, 1976). I will return to this question in Chapter 16.

27. "Shijūrokushi ron," in *Nihon shisō taikei: Kinsei buke shisō* (Tokyo: Iwanami shoten, 1974), p. 387.

28. "Fukushūron," *Akō gijin sansho,* vol. 1, pp. 41–42.

29. *Kinsei buke shisō,* pp. 272–370.

30. Ibid., pp. 378–380.

31. Ihara Saikaku, "Hatsumei wa hyotan yori deru," ed. Asō Isoji and Fuji Akio, *Taiyaku Saikaku zenshū,* vol. 8: *Buke giri monogatari* (Tokyo: Meiji shoin, 1951, originally 1688), p. 58.

32. Mizubayashi Takeshi, "Kinsei no hō to kokusei kenkyū josetsu," *Kokka gakkai zasshi,* vol. 91–5 (1978): 373.

12. Proceduralization of Honor

1. See Ise Teijō, "Teijō kakun," *Nihon shisō taikei: Kinsei buke shisō* (Tokyo: Iwanami shoten, 1974), p. 99.

2. See the work of Mizubayashi Takeshi on the transformation of the concept of heaven *(ten)* in Japanese thought: "Kinsei no hō to kokusei kenkyū josetsu," *Kokka gakkai zasshi* 90 (1977): 8–10.

3. Hiramatsu Yoshirō, *Edo no tsumi to batsu* (Tokyo: Heibonsha, 1988), p. 40. See also Hiramatsu Yoshirō, *Kinsei keiji soshōhō no kenkyū* (Tokyo: Sō-bunsha, 1960); Ishii Ryōsuke, *Edo jidai manpitsu* (Tokyo: Inoue shobō, 1959); Hirade Kōjirō, *Katakiuchi* (Tokyo: Chūō kōronsha, 1990, originally published in 1909); and Ōkuma Miyoshi, *Katakiuchi no rekishi* (Tokyo: Yūhikaku, 1972).

4. The daimyo possessed the right to punish their own subjects within their own jurisdiction *(jibun shioki).* The shogunate's banner men and the daimyo's superior vassals who had received relatively autonomous fiefs also held some kind of disciplinary power over the peasant population in their own territories. Their judicial prerogative was conditional, however, upon obedience to the general laws of the shogunate.

5. *Burei-uchi* was duly defined in the shogunate's famous code *Kujikata osadame gaki* (1742), 9 article 71. This influential criminal code, edited by the order of the eighth shogun, Tokugawa Yoshimune, was considered to be a symbol of

(a kind of) judicial "rationalization" and professionalization of the Tokugawa government. The code was, however, kept secret (in principle, not in practice), reserved for the sole use of a limited number of officers of the shogunate engaged in judicial functions. In essence, the code represented a systematization of the collection of established laws and precedents. The customary law of *burei-uchi* must have been established much earlier than the date of *Kujikata osadame gaki*.

6. Hiramatsu, *Kinsei,* p. 573.

7. Katsumata Shizuo, "Chūsei buke mikkaihō no tenkai," *Sengokuhō seirit-sushiron* (Tokyo: University of Tokyo Press, 1979), pp. 3–35.

8. Ishi Susumu, *Nihin no rekishi* 12: *Chūsei bushidan* (Tokyo: Shōgakukan, 1974), pp. 86–100; Sekiguchi Hiroko, *Nihon kodai kon'inshi no kenkyū,* vol. 1 (Tokyo: Hanawa shobō, 1993), pp. 116–288.

9. Katsumata, "Chūsei buke mikkai hō," pp. 12–27.

10. On the subjects of gender and honor, see the following works: J. K. Campbell, *Honour, Family, and Patronage* (Oxford: Oxford University Press, 1964); John Davis, *People of the Mediterranean* (London: Routledge & Kegan Paul, 1977); D. D. Gilmore, ed., *Honor and Shame and the Unity of the Mediterranean* (Washington, D.C.: American Anthropological Association, 1987); M. Herzfeld, *The Poetics of Manhood* (Princeton: Princeton University Press, 1985); S. B. Ortner, "The Virgin and the State," *Feminist Studies* 4 (1978): 19–33; J. G. Peristiany, ed., *Honour and Shame* (Chicago: University of Chicago Press, 1966); J. Schneider, "Of Vigilance and Virgins," *Ethnology* 9 (1971): 1–24.

11. Davis, *People of the Mediterranean,* p. 95.

12. Ōkuma, *Katakiuchi,* p. 158.

13. Hiramatsu, *Kinsei,* p. 581.

14. Hiraide, *Katakiuchi,* pp. 133–141. Also see D. E. Mills, "Katakiuchi: The Practice of Blood Revenge in Pre-modern Japan," *Modern Asian Studies* 10 (1976): 525–545.

15. Early in the Tokugawa period, judicial procedure was simple, arbitrary, and not especially refined. It was during the early eighteenth century—in particular with the reform introduced by the eighth shogun, Tokugawa Yoshimune—that Japanese judicial procedure became more systematic.

16. Hirade, *Katakiuchi,* pp. 34–50.

17. Ibid., pp. 151–156.

18. Ibid., p. 155.

19. Ibid., p. 39.

20. Commoners could also become registered avengers. Through the immediate lord, a commoner could place his or her name on the *katakiuchi* list in the office of the shogunate's magistrate. The authorities often praised commoners who carried out revenge for their elder family members as exemplary models of filial piety *(kō).* For example, *kōgi-roku,* the shogunate's official honor list of morally virtuous commoners, enrolled and rewarded commoners' revenge cases. Commoners' revenge was usually less "official" in nature, however; unlike samu-

rai cases, commoner revenge was not considered a moral and social obligation. To be more specific, the revenge did not affect commoners' inheritance from their *ie*. As a reflection of this difference, commoners' applications for revenge were not always accepted. This difference shows how much more tightly the samurai's *ie* was incorporated into the state system.

21. François Billacois, *The Duel: Its Rise and Fall in Early Modern France*, trans. Trista Selous (New Haven: Yale University Press, 1990); V. G. Kiernan, *The Duel in European History: Honour and the Reign of Aristocracy* (Oxford: Oxford University Press, 1988); Henry Charles Lea, *The Duel and the Oath* (Philadelphia: University of Pennsylvania Press, 1974, originally published in 1866).

22. Miyake Masahiko, "Bakuhan shūjusei no shisō teki genri: Kō shi bunri no hatten," *Nihonshi kenkyū* 127 (1972): 1–30. See also Watanabe Hiroshi, *Kinsei nihon shakai to sōgaku* (Tokyo: University of Tokyo Press, 1985), pp. 140–147.

23. For example, "Sakaike Kyōrei," in *Nihon shisō taikei 27: Kinsei buke shisō* (Tokyo: Iwanami shoten, 1974), p. 59.

24. Hiramatsu, *Kinsei*, p. 1005.

25. Ibid., p. 988.

26. Ibid., pp. 988–992. Naturally, such cases are known only through unofficial testimonies. However, many people at that time believed that the samurai would behave in such a manner, because if the accused man were convicted, his heir might not be allowed to inherit the title and property of the *ie*. Not all incidents of *seppuku* were the result of compliance with an official order. In many cases, a samurai would voluntarily commit *seppuku* in order to clear his name.

27. Ise Teijō, "Kyōrei shiki," cited by Ōkuma Miyoshi, *Seppuku no rekishi* (Tokyo: Yūzan kaku, 1973), pp. 107–108.

28. The record of the house of Mōri is reprinted as "Akō ronin oazukari no ki," *Akō gijin sansho*, vol. 2 (Tokyo: Kokusho kankōkai, 1900), pp. 6–27. Since the shogunate's death sentence conveyed an important symbolic political message to them, these four houses were very careful about making sure that the *seppuku* was carried out according to proper procedure.

29. "Akō ronin oazukari no ki," pp. 23–24.

30. *Sakaike Kyōei*, pp. 44–62. The precept is attributed to Sashi Masanoshin, a military scholar, writing for Lord Sakai. But like any other house precepts *(kakun)* of this period, it was promulgated under the name of Lord Sakai.

31. Ibid., p. 58.

32. Although the lord never explicitly rejected the rule of *kenka ryōseibai*, this consideration of "the situation" is clearly a deviation from the original form of the rule.

33. *Sakaike*, p. 44.

34. Ibid., pp. 44–47.

35. In the archives of Kokuritsu kōbunshokan naikaku bunko. The exact date

of publication is unknown, but it is estimated to be after 1709. The discussion here is based upon the citation from Ujiie Mikito, *Edo hantei monogatari* (Tokyo: Chūō kōronsha, 1988), pp. 18–24.

36. Niime Masatomo, "Mukashi mukashi monogatari" (ca. 1732–1733), in *Nihon shomin seikatsu shiryō shūsei* 8 (Tokyo: S'anichi shobō, 1969), p. 397. The author worked for the shogunate as the chief guard of the treasury. When he was eighty years old, he recorded his reflections of the past seventy years of social change.

37. Asahi Bunzaemon, *Ōmu rōchūki*, reprinted in *Nagoya sōsho*, vols. 9–11 (Nagoya: Nagoyashi kyōiku iinkai, 1965–1969); see detailed studies of this journal, Kaga Kishirō, *Genroku kakyūbushi no seikatsu* (Tokyo: Yūhikaku, 1966) and Kōsaka Jirō, *Genroku otatami bugyō no nikki* (Tokyo: Chūō kōronsha, 1984).

38. Ethnographical studies of other honor-based cultures also support this viewpoint. Wyatt-Brown's study of the honor culture in the American antebellum South is particularly sensitive to this consideration. See Bertram Wyatt-Brown, *Southern Honor* (New York: Oxford University Press, 1982).

13. State-Centered Honor and Vassalic Bureaucracy

1. Kimura Motoi, *Kakyū bushiron* (Tokyo: Hanawa shobō, 1967), pp. 58–59.

2. See, for example, Kanai Madoka, *Hansei seiritsuki no kenkyū* (Tokyo: Yoshikawa kōbunkan, 1975), p. 216, table 26.

3. Taniguchi Sumio, *Okayama hanseishi no kenkyū* (Tokyo: Hanawa shobō, 1964), p. 421. See also John W. Hall, *Government and Local Power in Japan: 500–1700* (Princeton: Princeton University Press, 1966).

4. Kimura, *Kakyū bushiron*, pp. 59–68. Albert Craig provides some further details on the organization of the Chōshū samurai in his article "The Restoration Movement in Chōshū," in John W. Hall and Marius Jansen, eds., *Studies in the Institutional History of Early Modern Japan* (Princeton: Princeton University Press, 1966), pp. 363–374.

5. An example of a title from Chōshū han.

6. For examples of lifestyle regulations in Kishū han see Mizubayashi Takeshi, "Kinsei no hō to kokusei kenkyū josetsu," *Kokka gakkai zasshi*, vol. 92, 11/12 (1979): 783–789.

7. Ujiie, *Edo hantei monogatari* (Tokyo: Chūō kōronsha, 1988), p. 40.

8. Kanai, *Hansei seiritsuki*, p. 216.

9. Harold Bolitho, "The han," in John W. Hall, ed., *The Cambridge History of Japan,* volume 4: *Early Modern Japan* (Cambridge: Cambridge University Press, 1991), p. 220.

10. It was not the case, however, that everyone in the same rank had equal access to these 143 positions. Men in the same *kaku* were differentiated according to their income *(koku)*. Regarding the relationships between *kaku* and corresponding bureaucratic offices, see Kanai, *Hansei seiritsuki*, p. 216, for the

example of Matsumoto han. For the case of Owari han, see Hayashi Kyūichi, *Owarihan kashindan no kenkyū* (Tokyo: Meicho shuppan, 1975), and Niimi Yoshiharu, *Kakyū bushi no kenkyū* (Tokyo: Gakujutsu shinkōkai, 1965). For the case of Kishū han, see Mizubayashi, "Kinsei no hō." For more background on this subject, see Harold Bolitho, "The han," in Hall, ed., *The Cambridge History of Japan*, volume 4: *Early Modern Japan*; Kimura, *Kakyū bushiron*; and Fujino Tamotsu, *Bakuhan taiseishi no kenkyū* (Tokyo: Yoshikawa kōbunkan, 1961).

11. R. P. Dore, *Education in Tokugawa Japan* (Berkeley: University of California Press, 1965), p. 312; Thomas C. Smith, "'Merit' as Ideology," in *Native Sources of Japanese Industrialization, 1750–1920* (Berkeley: University of California Press, 1988), pp. 156–172.

14. Hagakure

1. Yukio Mishima, *The Way of the Samurai: Yukio Mishima on Hagakure in Modern Life*, trans. Kathryn Sparling (New York: Basic Books, 1977). There are several English translations of *Hagakure*, but they are only partial translations and do not include many lively samurai stories. See, for example, Yamamoto Tsunetomo, *Hagakure: The Book of the Samurai*, trans. William Scott Wilson (Tokyo: Kōdansha International, 1979).

2. For example, see the works of Mizubayashi Takeshi, "Kinsei no hō to kokusei kenkyū josetsu," *Kokka gakkai zasshi*, vols. 90, 91, 92, 94, 95 (1977–1982), especially, 364–374; Kasaya Kazuhiko, *Shukun "oshikome" no kōzō: Kinsei daimyo to kashindan* (Tokyo: Heibonsha, 1988).

3. *Hagakure*, ed. Shiroshima Masashiro, Edo shiryō sōsho edition (Tokyo: Jinbutsu ōraisha, 1963), *ge*, pp. 392–393.

4. Yamamoto Tsunetomo also had a close relationship with Zen, which he had learned about from a Zen priest named Tannen. For further information concerning the relationship between Zen and the samurai class in general, see Kawai Masaharu, *Chūsei bukeshakai no kenkyū* (Tokyo: Yoshikawa kōbunkan, 1973); Fuji Naotomo, *Nihon no bushidō* (Osaka: Sōgensha, 1956), and *Bukejidai no shakai to seishin* (Osaka: Sōgensha, 1967).

5. Regarding *Hagakure* and the biographical information concerning Yamamoto Tsunetomo, see Fujino Tamotsu, ed., *Zoku Saga han no sōgō kenkyū* (Tokyo: Yoshikawa kōbunkan, 1987), pp. 89–113; Sagara Tōru, *Bushi no shisō* (Tokyo: Perikan sha, 1984), pp. 166–215; Sagara Tōru, "Hagakure no sekai," *Nihon shisō taikei* 26, *Mikawa monogatari, Hagakure* (Tokyo: Iwanami shoten, 1974).

6. Fujino, *Zoku Saga han*, p. 97.

7. He started to serve Lord Mitsushige at age nine. See *Hagakure, jō*, p. 163.

8. *Hagakure, jō*, p. 60.

9. Not all parts of *Hagakure* are the record of Yamamoto Tsunetomo's discourses. Some samurai stories in *Hagakure* were written by Tashiro Tsuramoto.

Scholars are still undecided as to which parts are actual records of Tsunetomo's conversations (see Fujino, *Zoku Saga han,* pp. 89–92, regarding various opinions on this issue). The samurai stories in *Hagakure* are a symbolic representation of the samurai behavior that the author or editor of *Hagakure* believed worthy of note.

10. *Hagakure, ge,* p. 29.

11. The region including Kyoto, Osaka. The *kamigata* samurai have a traditional reputation for being sophisticated, but deficient in dash and courage.

12. *Hagakure, jō,* p. 27.

13. Ibid., p. 53.

14. Ibid.

15. Ibid., p. 27.

16. Ibid., p. 60.

17. Ibid., p. 114.

18. Ibid., p. 130.

19. Ibid.

20. Ibid., p. 129.

21. Ibid.

22. Ibid., p. 94.

23. Ibid., pp. 94–96.

24. Ujiie Mikito, *Edo no shōnen* (Tokyo: Heibonsha, 1989), pp. 123–140.

25. *Hagakure, ge,* p. 351.

26. Ibid., *jō,* p. 164.

27. Miyake Masahiko, "Bakuhan shujūsei no shisōteki genri: Kō shi bunri no hatten," *Nihonshi kenkyū* 127 (1972): 1–30; Miyake Masahiko, "Kinsei buke dōtoku ni okeru kō shi no mondai," *Nihon shisō taikei* 44: *Kinsei buke shisō, geppō* 27 (1974).

28. *Hagakure, jō,* p. 37.

29. Ibid., p. 129.

30. Ibid., p. 176.

31. Ibid., pp. 174–176.

32. *Kokugaku* here does not mean the famous school of learning associated with Motoori Norinaga and others (also called *kokugaku*) that prevailed in nineteenth-century Japan.

33. *Hagakure, jō,* "Yain no kandan," p. 19.

34. Ibid., p. 19.

35. Ibid. The Saga han has a complex historical origin. The Ryūzōji house first founded the principality. But after the death of Ryūzōji Takafusa and Masaie, the Nabeshima peacefully succeeded to the position of head of state.

36. For example, Albert Craig's *Chōshu in the Meiji Restoration* (Cambridge, Mass.: Harvard University Press, 1961), discusses the "han nationalism" in the case of Chōshū han.

37. Fujino, *Zoku Saga han,* pp. 107–111.

15. Confucian and Post-Confucian Samurai

1. In particular, the reader should consult Herman Ooms, *Tokugawa Ideology* (Princeton: Princeton University Press, 1985). See also his "Neo-Confucianism and the Foundation of Early Tokugawa Ideology: Contours of a Problem," in Peter Nosco, ed., *Confucianism and Tokugawa Culture* (Princeton: Princeton University Press, 1984), pp. 27–61; and Kate Wildman Nakai, "The Naturalization of Confucianism in Tokugawa Japan," *Harvard Journal of Asiatic Studies* 140–1 (1980): 157–199. In Japanese works, see an excellent analysis of Watanabe Hiroshi, *Kinsei nihon shakai to sōgaku* (Tokyo: University of Tokyo Press, 1985), pp. 23–29, and Hino Tatsuo, "Jugaku shisōron," in *Koza nihon kinseishi*, vol. 9, ed. Hongo Takamori and Fukaya Katsumi (Tokyo: Yūhikaku, 1981), pp. 108–151. In contrast, Maruyama Masao's early work *Nihon seiji shisōshi kenkyū*, published in Japanese in 1950, stresses the importance of the Hayashi school as the Tokugawa official ideology from the beginning of the regime. In the Introduction to the English translation, however, the role of the Hayashi school appeared to be deemphasized compared with the Japanese version. See Maruyama Masao, *Studies in the Intellectual History of Tokugawa Japan*, trans. Mikiso Hane (Princeton: Princeton University Press, 1974).

2. Ooms, "Neo-Confucianism," p. 496.

3. Ibid., p. 500.

4. Nakae Tōju, "Okina montō," in *Nihon shisō taikei*, vol. 29, *Nakae Tōju* (Tokyo: Iwanami shoten, 1974), p. 85.

5. Nakai, "The Naturalization," p. 159.

6. Ki-baik Lee, *A New History of Korea*, trans. Edward W. Wagner (Cambridge, Mass.: Harvard University Press, 1984), pp. 172–220. Regarding neo-Confucianism in Korea, see also various collected essays in Wm. Theodore de Bary, ed., *The Rise of Neo-Confucianism in Korea* (New York: Columbia University Press, 1985); Martina Deuchler, *The Confucian Transformation of Korea: A Study of Society and Ideology* (Cambridge: Harvard University Press, 1993); JaHyun Kim Haboush, "The Confucianization of Korean Society," in Gilbert Rozman, ed., *The East Asian Region: Confucian Heritage and Its Modern Adaptation* (Princeton: Princeton University Press, 1991), pp. 84–110. Ping-ti Ho, *The Ladder of Success in Imperial China: Aspects of Social Mobility, 1368–1911* (New York: Columbia University Press, 1962), discusses the "openness" of Chinese civil service examinations. For a comparative overview, see the essays Rozman, *The East Asian Region*.

7. Satō Naokata, "Gakudan zatsuroku," cited in Watanabe, *Kinsei nihon shakai*, p. 23.

8. Watanabe, *Kinsei nihon shakai*, pp. 95–116.

9. Hino, "Jugaku shisōron," pp. 117–120. In comparison, see Deuchler's *The Confucian Transformation of Korea* regarding the pervasive influence of neo-Confucian legislation on Yi Korea's inheritance, marriage, mourning, ancestor worship, and the position of women.

10. Between 1607 and 1811, Korea sent missions to the Tokugawa shogunate twelve times. A mission was usually large-scale, often consisting of about five hundred people. Missions left a rich record of Tokugawa Japan. Regarding Korean missions, see Li Jin-hi, *Edo jidai no chōsen tsūshinshi* (Tokyo: Kōdansha, 1987).

11. Shin Yu-han, *Kaiyūroku* (Tokyo: Heibonsha, 1974), p. 315.

12. Hino, "Jugaku Shisōron," pp. 116–119.

13. Nakai, "The Naturalization," p. 158.

14. For an interesting case study of the management of Kaga Domain's samurai school, see Emori Ichirō, *Benkyō jidai no makuake* (Tokyo: Heibonsha, 1990), pp. 208–277.

15. Nakai, "The Naturalization," p. 157.

16. Here I am referring to the pattern of *institutionalized usage* of Confucianism. I do not imply that Chinese neo-Confucian thinkers were dogmatic compared with their Japanese equivalents.

17. Regarding Confucianism and the Tokugawa merchant class, see Najita Tetsuo, *Visions of Virtue in Tokugawa Japan* (Chicago: University of Chicago Press, 1987).

18. For a detailed discussion of Yamaga's military theory and Confucian world view, consult Noguchi Takehiko, *Edo no heigaku shisō* (Tokyo: Chūō kōronsha, 1991), pp. 65–89. Regarding his reinterpretation of samuraihood, see Tahara Tsuguo, "Kaisetsu: Yamaga Sokō ni okeru shisō no kihonteki kōsei," in *Nihon shisō taikei,* vol. 32: *Yamaga Sokō* (Tokyo: Iwanami shoten, 1970), pp. 453–499.

19. *Yamaga gorui,* 21, "Shidō," in *Nihon shisō taikei,* vol. 32: *Yamaga Sokō,* pp. 30–171.

20. Ibid., pp. 37–40.

21. Ibid., pp. 31–33.

22. *Yamaga gorui,* in Hirose Yataka, ed., *Yamaga Sokō zenshū,* vol. 4 (Tokyo: Iwanami shoten, 1941).

23. *Shunkan shō,* in *Nihon shisō taikei 28: Fujiwara seika, Hayashi Razan* (Tokyo: Iwanami shoten, 1975), p. 131.

24. Sorai's school is usually called *kobunji-gaku* (the study of old phrases and syntax), as he believed that a knowledge of classical terms was an essential precondition for learning the way of the sages.

25. *Sorai sensei Tōmon sho,* in *Ogyū Sorai zenshū,* vol. 6 (Tokyo: Kawade shobō shinsha, 1973), p. 190.

26. Ibid.

27. Maruyama Masao, *Studies in the Intellectual History of Tokugawa Japan,* trans. Mikiso Hane (Princeton: Princeton University Press, 1974), pp. 69–134.

28. We are all familiar with the educational drive of modern Japanese families that has created the infamous syndrome of "entrance examination hell" for Japanese children, and so it sounds almost natural that the institutionalization of a Confucian educational system resulted in the reinstatement of "competitive"

culture symbolized by the term *benkyō*. To be sure, meritocratic competition was part of Chinese Confucian tradition as an institutional aspect in the form of a state-run civil service examination. This congruity of competitiveness and learning was not a natural outcome stemming from the philosophical contents of Confucianism. If one looks at the moral contents of classical Confucian texts as well as the works of neo-Confucian writers such as Chu Hsi himself, one finds that they emphasized the natural development of virtuous character and spiritual freedom of mind. Regarding this point, see Wm. Theodore de Bary, *The Liberal Tradition in China* (New York: Columbia University Press, 1983). They generally stressed the ideal of controlling one's mind in order to develop moral character. For more details of this aspect of intellectual refocusing toward competitive hard-working study in the form of *benkyō*, see Emori Ichirō, *Benkyō jidai no makuake* (Tokyo: Heibonsha, 1990), pp. 66–96.

29. Thomas C. Smith, "'Merit' as Ideology," in *Native Sources of Japanese Industrialization, 1750–1920* (Berkeley: University of California Press, 1988), pp. 156–172.

30. R. P. Dore, *Education in Tokugawa Japan* (Berkeley: University of California Press, 1965).

31. Watanabe, *Kinsei nihon shakai,* p. 16. Ishikawa Shōtaro, *Hankō to terakoya* (Tokyo: Kyōikusha, 1978), pp. 28–29.

32. Robert L. Backus, "The Kansei Prohibition of Heterodoxy and Its Effects on Education," *Harvard Journal of Asiatic Studies* 39–1 (1979): pp. 55–106.

33. Regarding Hakuseki's role in shogunate politics, see Kate Wildman Nakai, *Shogunal Politics: Arai Hakuseki and the Premises of Tokugawa Rule* (Cambridge, Mass.: Harvard University Press, 1988).

34. Arai Hakuseiki, *Told Round a Brushwood Fire,* trans. Joyce Ackrod (Princeton: Princeton University Press, 1979), pp. 64–65.

35. Ibid., p. 52.

36. For example, see H. D. Harootunian, *Toward Restoration: The Growth of Political Consciousness in Tokugawa Japan* (Berkeley: University of California Press, 1970). Regarding the Mito school, see Bob Tadashi Wakabayashi, *Anti-Foreignism and Western Learning in Early Modern Japan* (Cambridge, Mass.: Harvard University Press, 1986); Victor J. Koschmann, *The Mito Ideology: Discourse, Reform, and Insurrection in Late Tokugawa Japan, 1790–1864* (Berkeley: University of California Press, 1987). The thought of Aizawa Seishisai (a Confucian scholar of Mito Domain), for example, discussed and translated in Wakabayashi's work, clearly exemplifies this fusion. See the works of Haga Noboru regarding the National Learning school and popular movements: *Bakumatsu kokugaku no tenkai* (Tokyo: Hanawa shobō, 1963), and *Bakumatsu kokugaku no kenkyū* (Tokyo: Kyōiku shuppan Center, 1980). See also Noguchi Takehiko, *Edo no heigaku shisō* (Tokyo: Chūō kōronsha, 1991), pp. 221–279, and Yasumaru Yoshio, *Nihon nashonarizumu no zenya* (Tokyo: Asahi shinbunsha, 1977).

37. Concerning the special role played by Chōshū han and its people in the

Meiji restoration, see Albert Craig, *Chōshū in the Meiji Restoration* (Cambridge, Mass.: Harvard University Press, 1961).

38. "Kōmō yawa," in *Teihon Yoshida Shōin shū*, vol. 3 (Tokyo: Yamato shobō, 1972), p. 319, his lecture note from prison. Regarding Yoshida Shōin, there are many publications in Japanese. For a review of Japanese scholarship, see a bibliographic survey by Nakajima Chieko, "Yoshida Shōin bunken mokuroku," in Naramoto, Tatsuya, ed., *Yoshida Shōin no subete* (Tokyo: Shin jin butsu ōraisha, 1981), pp. 248–264.

39. Ibid., p. 228.

40. Ibid., p. 229.

41. Ibid., p. 24.

42. Harootunian, *Toward Restoration*, p. 246. Also see Naramoto, "Shōin no shishō kan," in *Yoshida Shōin no subete*, pp. 206–221.

43. Hongō Takamori, "Bakumatsu Shisōron," in Fukaya Katsumi and Hongō Takamori, eds., *Kōza Nihon kinseishi*, vol. 9 (Tokyo: Yūhikaku, 1981). Also see Noguchi, *Edo no heigaku*, pp. 281–317, 391.

16. Themes of Control and Change

1. In the sense of a paradigm presented by Albert O. Hirschman, *Exit, Voice, and Loyalty* (Cambridge, Mass.: Harvard University Press, 1970).

2. See a theoretical argument on this point discussed by Randall Collins, "On the Microfoundation of Macrosociology," *American Journal of Sociology* 86–5 (1981): 984–1015.

3. John M. Meyer and Brian Rowan, "Institutionalized Organizations: Formal Structure as Myth and Ceremony," *American Journal of Sociology* 83 (1977): 340–363.

4. Michael Mann, "The Autonomous Power of the State: Its Origins, Mechanisms, and Results," *Archives européenes de sociologie* 25 (1984): 185–213.

5. Kasaya Kazuhiko, *Shukun oshikome no kōzō* (Tokyo: Heibonsha, 1988).

6. Steven Lukes, *Individualism* (Oxford: Basil Blackwell, 1973), p. 1.

7. C. B. Macpherson, *The Political Theory of Possessive Individualism* (New York: Oxford University Press, 1962), p. 3.

8. J. G. A. Pocock, "Authority and Property: The Question of Liberal Origins," in *Virtue, Commerce, and History* (Cambridge: Cambridge University Press, 1985), p. 59.

9. In his manuscript of the second volume of *Freedom*. Forthcoming from Basic Books.

10. Harold J. Berman, *Law and Revolution: The Formation of the Western Legal Tradition* (Cambridge, Mass.: Harvard University Press, 1983), p. 303.

11. Regarding the inner logic of Puritan doctrine and revolutionary ideology, see Michael Walzer, *The Revolution of the Saints: A Study in the Origins of Radical Politics* (Cambridge, Mass.: Harvard University Press, 1965).

12. Sakurai Shōichirō, *Meiyo to chijoku* (Tokyo: Hōsei University Press, 1971), p. 19.

13. See, for example, "Horibe Taketsune hikki," in *Nihon shisō taikei* 27: *Kinsei buke shisō* (Tokyo: Iwanami shoten, 1974), p. 188.

14. Sakurai, *Meiyo to,* p. 17.

15. Charles Taylor, *Sources of the Self: The Making of the Modern Identity* (Cambridge, Mass.: Harvard University Press, 1989), p. 214.

16. See, for example, J. C. D. Clark, *English Society, 1688–1832* (Cambridge: Cambridge University Press, 1985); Joyce Oldham Appleby, *Economic Thought and Ideology in Seventeenth-Century England* (Princeton: Princeton University Press, 1978); Pocock, "Authority and Property," pp. 51–71; and Mark Girouarad, *The Return to Camelot: Chivalry and the English Gentleman* (New Haven: Yale University Press, 1981).

17. Clark, *English Society,* p. 95.

18. Ibid., p. 109.

19. Hidehiro Sonoda, "The Decline of the Japanese Warrior Class," *Japan Review* 1 (1990): 103.

20. Ibid.

21. Uete Michiari, "Bakumatsu ni okeru taigaikan no tenkai," in Uete Michiari, ed., *Nihon kindai shisō no keisei* (Tokyo: Iwanami shoten, 1974), p. 243.

22. *Seiko Hyakuwa,* cited in Kenda Sōsuke, "Nihonjin no risshin shusse shugi," *Gendai no esupuri* 118 (1971): 51.

23. I realize that these hypothetical arguments regarding the development of the honorific culture after the Meiji restoration require another book-length investigation in their own right. Therefore, my comments here are intended to be suggestive and interpretative rather than definitive. Regarding the moral regulation under the Meiji regime, see especially Carol Gluck, *Japan's Modern Myths* (Princeton: Princeton University Press, 1985), and Irokawa Daikichi, *Meiji no bunka* (Tokyo: Iwanami shoten, 1970).

24. Ann Swidler, "Culture in Action: Symbols and Strategies," *American Sociological Review* 51 (April 1986): 273–286.

25. *Sunday Mainichi,* November 1, 1992, pp. 28–29.

26. Eleanor Westney, *Imitation and Innovation: The Transfer of Western Organizational Patterns to Meiji Japan* (Cambridge, Mass.: Harvard University Press, 1987).

Epilogue

1. A similar discussion of Japanese identity formation under the rubric of "contextualism" is developed by some Japanese scholars. In particular, see the works of Hamaguchi Esyun, *Kanjin shugi no shakai nihon* (Tokyo: Tōyokeizai, 1982); "A Contextual Model of the Japanese," *Journal of Japanese Studies* 2 (1985): 289–321. Although the idea of context-dependent selfhood is very interesting, I do not think that this style of identity formation is uniquely Japanese. One should note that the sociological schools of symbolic interactions and ethnomethodology have developed from similar assumptions regarding human identity and social interactions based upon Western cases. The chief differences

have to do primarily with a cultural-ideological level of articulation and explanation, that is, descriptions of concepts of ideal selfhood. See the collected essays in Nancy Rosenberger, ed., *Japanese Sense of Self* (Cambridge: Cambridge University Press, 1992).

2. Peter Berger, "On the Obsolescence of the Concept of Honor," *Archives Européennes de Sociologie* 11 (1970): 340.

3. As Benedict wrote on the very first page of the text of the book; see *The Chrysanthemum and the Sword* (Boston: Houghton Mifflin Company, 1989, originally published in 1946), p. 1.

4. Benedict, *Chrysanthemum*, p. 223.

5. Clifford Geertz, "Us / Not-Us: Benedict's Travels," in *Works and Lives: The Anthropologist as Author* (Stanford: Stanford University Press, 1988), p. 120.

6. See, for example, Julian Pitt-Rivers, "Honor," in *International Encyclopedia of the Social Sciences,* ed. David L. Sills (New York: The Macmillan Company and the Free Press, 1968).

7. Benedict's direct experience of Japanese culture was limited to her interviews of Japanese-Americans, who were apparently sensitive about their wartime predicament in American society. It is important to note that Benedict interviewed her subjects in the setting of a government-funded research project at a time when Japan was considered an enemy power. Understandably, the respondents answered Benedict's questions in a more formal and moralistic manner than they would have in a less constrained setting. See Ezra Vogel, "Forward" to the 1989 edition of *Chrysanthemum*, pp. ix–xii.

8. Benedict, *The Chrysanthemum*, p. 1.

9. Ibid., p. 2.

10. Ibid.

11. Ibid., p. 292.

12. Millie R. Creighton, "Revisiting Shame and Guilt Cultures: A Forty-Year Pilgrimage," *Ethos* (1990): 279–307, has undertaken to defend Benedict against some Japanese scholars who have criticized her as culturally biased. I agree with Creighton to the extent that Benedict "intended" to be a cultural relativist. However, I am not convinced by Creighton's passionately worded assertions that Benedict is innocent of cultural bias and that her view of Japanese culture can be salvaged. Creighton's decision to ignore Benedict's repeated references to "contradictory characters" is rather curious and requires explanation.

Index